CATHOLICISM BETWEEN
LUTHER AND VOLTAIRE

Catholicism between Luther and Voltaire: a new view of the Counter-Reformation

Jean Delumeau

with an introduction by John Bossy

Burns & Oates · London
Westminster Press . Philadelphia

First published in Great Britain in 1977 by Burns
& Oates Limited, 2–10 Jerdan Place, London
SW6 5PT and in the United States of America
by Westminster Press. Original French text
first published in France in 1971 by Presses
Universitaires de France Copyright © 1971
Presses Universitaires de France. This translation
and introduction copyright © 1977 Search Press
Limited. All rights reserved. No part of this
publication may be reproduced in any form or
by any means for any purpose whatsoever
without the previous written permission of
Search Press Limited, 2–10 Jerdan Place,
London SW6 5PT.

Translated from the French by Jeremy Moiser.

Library of Congress Cataloging in Publication Data

Delumeau, Jean.
  Catholicism between Luther and Voltaire.

  Translation of Le catholicisme entre Luther et Voltaire.
  Bibliography: p.
  Includes index.
    1. Catholic Church—History—Modern period, 1500–
I. Title.
BX1304.D4313 1977 282'.09'03 77-4005
ISBN (USA) 0–664–21341–3

ISBN (UK) 0 86012 043 0
Photoset by The Benham Press,
and printed by A. Wheaton & Co., Exeter
for Burns & Oates Limited

CONTENTS

CHAPTER 2: RELIGIOUS SOCIOLOGY AND COLLECTIVE PSYCHOLOGY: AIMS AND METHODS

CHAPTER 3: THE LEGEND OF THE CHRISTIAN MIDDLE AGES

CHAPTER 4: CHRISTIANIZATION

CHAPTER 5: DECHRISTIANIZATION?

Foreword

Writing a book always involves selection, and sometimes omission, for want of space. To prevent the work exceeding an appropriate length, I omitted a chapter on religious art. This omission should not affect the overall argument of the book.

There was such a thing as the Counter-Reformation. It was not, *NB* however, the most vital part of the transformation of the Catholic Church in the sixteenth and subsequent centuries. In this book I stress the positive and innovatory aspects, the richness and energy, of Tridentine Catholicism, without however any illusions as to its rigidity.

I have opted here for clarity, methodical exposition and a didactic account of questions such as Tridentine theology and the expansion of Catholicism outside Europe, and Jansenism. Eventually, however, I go beyond this more pedagogical framework and propose a thesis which, because it is still unfamiliar to most people, will, I hope, provoke research. As I see it, the 'Christian Middle Ages', as far as the (essentially rural) masses are concerned, is a legend which is being increasingly challenged. And if it is legend, the two Reformations — Luther's and Rome's — constituted, despite mutual excommunication, two complementary aspects of one and the same process of Christianization whose impact and limits have still to be assessed. To adopt this point of view which must be confirmed by a study of collective mentality, is to undertake a complete rereading of modern western history.

JEAN DELUMEAU

INTRODUCTION

This is a book written by a Frenchman for a French audience. English readers may find its form and content surprising, so a word of introduction seems appropriate. It appeared in a series entitled *Nouvelle Clio — Clio* for obvious reasons, and *nouvelle* because it superseded an old series which had attempted to fulfil the same task for an earlier generation of history students. The purpose of the series is not to present a substantive account of some period or problem, but to act as a sort of imaginary (and ideal) tutor, who outlines the state of knowledge, indicates what people who work at it are thinking about and doing at the moment, and provides an extensive bibliography. Hence the two parts of the book: the four chapters of Part I which outline the classic corpus of knowledge; and the five of Part II which represent the tendencies of contemporary research and controversy as they appear to a historian in France.

To use traditional language, this is a book about the Counter-Reformation, and two things are worth noticing about it immediately. *Delumeau* has omitted the question of origins which he and many others have discussed elsewhere, and which occupies a good deal of space in English books on the subject.[1] By contrast he has extended himself more fully on its later phases, and indeed has given us in his final chapters, in place of a simple account of the state of historical questions, an exposition of what a complete history of the Counter-Reformation might look like if it were conducted on the lines of present research.

This change of balance will be welcome in itself, but it is not only a matter of convenience. It reflects what will be for many English readers a novel idea of what religious history — at least the history of Catholicism — is about. If we are finally concerned, as Delumeau puts it [p. 129], with the *Chrétien quelconque* or average soul of another age, then we must try to think on a longer and slower time-scale than the one we are used to. A history of the counter-reformation Church — meaning the ecclesiastical hierarchy, religious orders, saints, theologians, politico-religious conflicts — will have to attend primarily to what was happening from roughly the middle of the sixteenth century to roughly the middle of the seventeenth; a history of counter-reformation Christianity as embodied in the experience of the average man will have to try and grasp a longer movement which was not perhaps very advanced by 1600 and was certainly not over in 1700. This Delumeau has tried to do, and I think it would scarcely have been possible to do it better in the space at his disposal. Such choices are not arbitrary, and this one represents the result of two influences converging in the French academic scene which an English reader may need to have explained. The first is the idea of a quantitative 'religious sociology' as the backbone of religious history: since Delumeau explains what this is about in the second chapter of Part I, there seems no need to go into it here. The second is the notion prevailing in France, chiefly under the influence of the journal *Annales*, of history as a discipline concerned with man in all the dimensions of his activity, akin to a social science in its theoretical interests and its preference for quantitative proof, and hostile to the more Rankean or narrative tradition which retains a good deal of vitality in England.[2]

Seen from inside the French historical world, Delumeau may well appear somewhat detached from this orthodoxy; seen from outside, his work shows a number of its characteristic traits. An exhaustive and invaluable account of the economic and social life of Rome in the second half of the sixteenth century, a book on the alum trade, the direction of a number of research projects on the economy, demography and religious life of Brittany in the early-modern period – these might be thought in England an odd preparation for writing on the Reformation and Counter-Reformation; in France the sequence seems natural enough, indeed to some extent imposed by affinities of documentation and approach. So far, I do not think the *Annales* tradition has proved particularly fertile in religious history: its impatience with traditional pursuits, its tendency to economic or demographic imperialism, have sometimes led to crude reductionism and hasty judgment. Delumeau's book shows none of these deficiencies, and in so far as it is an application of the *Annales* frame of mind to the history of Christianity it seems to me a notable vindication of it.

It contains, densely packed, an extraordinary variety of gifts, and he would be a very dull reader who got no pleasure or excitement from any of them: from the revitalization of a traditional body of material in the chapter on 'Holiness' (Part I, chapter 3), for instance; from the outline of what has been done, in France during this century, to realize the vision of a history of Christianity more attentive to the whole religious experience of the faithful, and what, in the way of documentary, quantitative, geographical and other types of investigation, may be done to realize it more completely (Part II, chapter 2); or from Delumeau's sketch of a fundamental historical revaluation of French Catholicism in the eighteenth century (Part II, chapter 5, *b*). If this is a 'new kind of history', then we may all be grateful for it.

An English historian may offer one or two remarks before leaving the reader to get on with the book himself. Due again, I think, to the exigencies of the series, the history of Catholicism in Europe's off-shore islands does not make an appearance in it, and without wishing to be over-patriotic I feel this is a pity. Restricted in importance as the Anglophone sector of Catholicism may appear during the period with which Delumeau is concerned, to omit it is to leave a measurable weight out of balance. I am not suggesting that to discuss it would necessarily have meant changing his mind about anything he has written: indeed the general drift of the argument conducted in his last three chapters would have been distinctly strengthened by an account of the experience of Catholic Ireland between the sixteenth and the eighteenth centuries.[3]

This is also the only general description of Catholicism in this period with which the particular history of the English Catholic community can readily be reconciled; and, speaking as one who had made an effort to apply some of the recommendations made in chapter 2 of Part II, in a minor way, to the materials of English Catholic history,[4] I can testify that those who wish to do this in future (or indeed to apply them to the history of English religious bodies in general, where there seems plenty of scope for them) will find it *de rigueur* to consult Delumeau first, different as the religious and ecclesiastical traditions of the two countries may be. All the same, this difference is not negligible, and it may have its effect in the interpretation of larger matters. Looking from the viewpoint of a missionary or non-established Catholicism at the range of counter-reformation departures presented in Part I, one might be inclined to put more emphasis on some matters dealt with in chapters 3 (especially section *c*: 'Its Effectiveness') and 4 and less on Tridentine topics discussed in chapters 1 and 2.[5]

The notion of a 'Tridentine Catholicism' may be difficult to apply outside countries where the Catholic Church retained, at least in theory, its identity with the whole body of society. Delumeau remarks very justly that the activity of rural missionaries in seventeenth-century France ought to be placed in a vast geographical and multi-confessional context where Quakers and Methodists would rub shoulders with Jesuits, Capuchins and Oratorians (p. 189); but does this not make one wonder whether 'Tridentine' is the right word for the activity in question? The idea of a missionary Church did not have much attraction for the Fathers at Trent. Since we are on the subject, may I recommend English-speaking readers of Delumeau's final chapter to have a look at the comparable variance of views about eighteenth-century Christianity in England as it may be found, for example, in the writings of Norman Sykes and W. R. Ward?[6] This would, among other things, bring out the contrast of diocesan and missionary notions of the Church with as much clarity as could be desired.

To anyone who has assimilated this argument, one or two reflexions will occur about Delumeau's analysis of the dynamics of early modern Catholicism, and since their occurrence seems an inevitable part of the process of domesticating his book in the English-speaking world I should like, with all possible deference, to raise them here. The simplest of them is about education. In his chapter on seventeenth-century 'Christianization', Delumeau attaches great importance to the advent of catechism and to the relationship between catechism and primary education. This emphasis seems to me wholly justified. I am sure he is right to maintain that we are here at a turning-point in the history of Europe. 'School . . . was it ultimately a factor for or against the faith?' (p. 202) is, as he says, a fascinating question. The reflection, as it might occur to an observer on this side of the Channel, would be this: was not schooling in religion likely to achieve positive or negative results according to whether or not it was part of a more general environment of human growth whose primary *locus* would be the family?

The work of Philippe Ariès on the relationship of Catholicism and the family, drawn on in various contexts in the course of the book (though not in this one), would seem to show that in certain contexts counter-reformation Catholicism was a domestic religion, but I wonder how widely that was so, and have argued elsewhere that a shortage of domestic participation at this point was a cause of long-term failure in the counter-reformation educational programme. The contraceptive revolt of the later eighteenth century is significant in a variety of connexions; I should have thought that a failure of *rapport* between the ecclesiastical hierarchy and the domestic unit was one of them. The failure, I would suggest, was given in the hierarchical character of 'Tridentine' Catholicism as such.[7]

The view may be disputed, but it points to a larger field of problems. In his chapter on Jansenism Delumeau takes issue with the 'vulgar sociologism' (p. 119) of French intellectuals like the late Lucien Goldmann who have sought to interpret the phenomenon within a supposedly Marxist context unhelpful to understanding the religious experience of this, and probably of any, age. One can but cheer. But may it not be that the principal objection to be made to Marxist sociology – that it does not in fact deal with the social as such, with genuine human relations and actual human groups – may also in some degree, Delumeau's intentions notwithstanding, apply to religious sociology as well?

No doubt because of the different character of the English religious past, English historians may have been specially sensitive to the relation between such groups and ecclesiastical structures. During the period Delumeau is concerned with, the relation in the Catholic Church was undergoing a change. Take, for example, the fraternity, or religious association. In using the existence of fraternities as a way of measuring religious vitality in quantitative or geographical terms – within the restrictions of the present studies – he may have underplayed their character as social institutions and the importance of alterations in that character as a sign of qualitative changes in the social constitution of the Church. As an illustration of the point the reader may consult the exceptionally interesting account of the Venetian fraternities or *scuole* given by Brian Pullan in his *Rich and Poor in Renaissance Venice.*[8] Here we find ample evidence of a change they underwent, roughly in the course of the sixteenth century, from artificial kin-groups whose *raison d'être* was mutual aid to professional welfare organizations which were more useful to the general community in precisely the measure that they became less vigorous an embodiment of reciprocal human relations. No doubt it would be risky to take this example as a case of what was happening to fraternities in general between the fifteenth and the seventeenth century, but I should be prepared to interpret in the light of some development of this kind the collapse of the fraternity in eighteenth-century France which Delumeau graphically describes in his last chapter (p. 203). Subtly undermined by renaissance utilitarianism, directly threatened by the Tridentine episcopate and by more authoritarian modes in Church and state, ultimately perhaps a victim to changes in the structure of human relations so deep-seated that a historian can hardly do more than guess at their existence – the fraternities were evacuated of their human substance and the Church lost a dimension of its social reality.

This brings me to a final point. If, as I believe, a different 'sociology' would add a certain shadow to the picture of religious progress drawn in chapter 4 of Part II (without in any way diminishing the importance of the positive changes there described), it might also introduce a touch of brightness into the dark picture of the Christian Middle Ages drawn in the previous chapter. The changes described by Delumeau are as important as he makes out, but I do not know that we are entitled to use the word 'Christianization' to describe them. There is a Christianity of the literate which, as Delumeau rightly says, sixteenth- and seventeenth-century reformers, Protestant and Catholic, were seeking to impose with more or less success (and in forms which were significantly different). But there is also a Christianity of the illiterate, and I doubt if we have exhausted its potentialities when we have drawn attention to the weight of the *folklorique* in the mentality of the rural person in pre-reformation Europe. The work of Keith Thomas, whose *Religion and the Decline of Magic* has done for England on a vast scale what Delumeau's chapter has attempted for Catholic Europe on a small one, can indicate that with all their aberrations the unreformed Church and uninformed Christian of pre-reformation days had some sort of grip on the idea that Christianity meant loving one's neighbour, distasteful as that might be.[9] Without succumbing to the 'legend of the Christian Middle Ages', I think it is possible to believe that the rural Church of mediaeval Europe did, in its own mode, transmit a respectable view of Christianity to the average rustic. The *Ecclesia docens* of the sixteenth and seventeenth centuries took a more strenuous view of things and was, I am sure, the agent of a necessary mutation in the mentality of rural Europe; but I am not equally sure that, in other than a pedagogical sense, it conveyed the essentials of Christianity better than its predecessor. I should add that, on a topic which is of fairly central importance in this field, a different explanation from Delumeau's (and Thomas's) of the rise and decline of witch-phobia has been expounded with great learning and persuasive force in H. R. Trevor-Roper's 'The European Witch-Craze of the Sixteenth and Seventeenth Centuries'.[10]

I make these observations by way of commending a book I greatly admire to a new circle of neighbours and readers, and of launching a conversation which will prove stimulating to all parties. To offer 'a complete re-reading of modern western history' (p. v) is a large claim, even granting that the French modernity stops in 1789. I do not think it is excessive, and I am sure that everyone concerned with the history of early modern Europe should take the opportunity of testing it.

The Queen's University of Belfast, 1976

JOHN BOSSY

PART ONE: WHAT WE KNOW

CHAPTER 1

FROM THE PRE-REFORMATION TO THE COUNCIL OF TRENT

(a) Sporadic attempts at reform

At the end of the sixteenth century and throughout the seventeenth, the Church of Rome went through a period of profound change for which a number of factors had prepared the way: long theological investigations, a great deal of holiness, and many painful gropings. There can be no question today, therefore, of dating this change, this renewal, only from the Council of Trent. The truth is that the two Reformations, which believed themselves — and gladly — to be in opposition, and whose similarities[1] we are only now beginning to appreciate, drew on a common past. This past was certainly one of troubles and 'abuses' of every conceivable kind, but there were not wanting attempts to renew Christian piety by making it more personal for the élite and more alive for the people. The rejuvenation of the Catholic Church and the development of its spirituality therefore saw two distinct periods: the pre-Reformation, and Trent with its aftermath; or in other words, sporadic individual efforts followed by the 'official' activities of the Council which depended on the less conspicuous and sometimes discouraging preparatory work which went on before the 1540s. The converse is equally true: in a Church as centralized as that of Rome, the renewal could not work through to the body of the faithful solely on the strength of initiatives from below and as long as the hierarchy — the pope and the college of bishops — withheld their support.

Towards the close of the fourteenth century — the precise time when 'abuses' (the amassing of benefices, ecclesiastical patronage, the increasing secularity and worldliness of the higher clergy, non-residence, and theological ignorance) were proliferating[2] — the *devotio moderna*[3] emerged under the aegis and inspiration of Jan van Ruysbroeck 'the Admirable', Geert Groote and the Brothers of the Common Life that he founded. The *devotio moderna* laid stress not on liturgy or monastic life, but on personal meditation which was deliberate and methodical (to avoid the dangers of illuminism), and centred essentially on Christ. In different ways Luther and Bérulle, Erasmus and St Ignatius were all heirs to the *devotio moderna*. Admittedly it was of spiritual benefit mainly to the Christian élite, but there was never so much preaching for the people as in the fifteenth century.[4] When Luther, Calvin and the council fathers at Trent insisted that the faithful should be instructed in the word of God, they were fully in line with the great preachers of the Pre-Reformation: Jan Huss, Bernardino of Siena, Savonarola and others.

While Christendom despaired of a general purification of the Church, many religious orders were carrying out partial reforms by a return to stricter discipline: the Dominicans, who formed the so-called Dutch Congregation in the fifteenth century; the Camaldolese, owing mainly to the efforts of Paolo Giustiniani, who considered the practice of absolute solitude to be of paramount importance; and the Franciscans, where the secession of a hero of poverty and commitment, Matteo da Bascio (1526), brought into being a new religious family, the Capuchins. On the other hand one order had always been true to itself — the Carthusians: *Cartusia nunquam reformata quia nunquam deformata*. One of the most widely-read devotional books of the fifteenth and early sixteenth centuries was the *Vita Christi* of Ludolphus the Carthusian, which the caballero Iñigo of Loyola included in his library.

The founder of the Jesuits started his vocation in a country of astonishing religious vitality where the sovereign saw to the residence of the bishop in his diocese and which had accomplished its own reform, by virtue mainly of the work of Cardinal Ximenes de Cisneros (d.1517), at a time when Luther's name was still unknown. Humanism was held in great esteem at the University of Alcala (to the credit of Cisneros), and Salamanca was sometimes called 'little Rome'. Spain's theological strength was soon to become apparent at the Council of Trent. Unlike Cisneros, Cardinal d'Amboise, who was papal legate in France, and Cardinal Wolsey, legate in England, failed to use their authority to reform the Church in their respective countries. The concordats of 1418 in England and 1516 in France, which latter succeeded the *Pragmatique Sanction de Bourges* of 1438,[5] were not designed to assist reform. In the hands of princes, major benefices became the most convenient rewards for political services. But did piety languish in these two countries? In point of fact the pre-Reformation on both sides of the Channel saw the construction or embellishment of a great number of religious buildings. Further, there are many indications to prove that the English people retained their attachment to the Church. In France, where the clergy had increased in numbers from the end of the Hundred Years War (in the diocese of Sées, Normandy, for example, it quadrupled between 1445 and 1514) the country did look for a path towards religious renewal. The Council of Sens (1485), the diocesan synods which followed it at Chartres, Langres, Nantes and Troyes, the work of the great reformer Standonck,[6] the apostolic zeal of bishops like Poncher of Paris, François d'Estaing of Rodez and Briçonnet of Meaux, all show that France did not lose its will to reform. The German Church, too, in the century before Luther's revolt, had its reforming bishops who tried to renew their dioceses 'in head and members': Heinrich von Hewen and Burchard von Randegg at Konstanz, Matthias Ramung at Speyer, Frederik von Zollern at Augsburg, and so on. Therefore the religious situation in Germany at the beginning of the sixteenth century must similarly be reassessed: 'There can be no doubt that more reforming went on in Germany than anywhere else. That things eventually took a very different turn was not due to the fact that the pastoral ministry was more neglected, the clergy worse behaved, or the people more ignorant of their religion, or more indifferent to it, than in other countries. It was due to the fact that the laity, the urban burghers and the intellectuals who were beginning to constitute an estate by themselves, expected more from their priests in their lives. They were determined to make a radical clearance of abuses — real or imaginary ones...'[7]

Renaissance Italy, so pagan in some respects, displayed the first symptoms of religious change even before Luther had made his presence felt, and certainly before the council and pope had taken the Church in hand. Recent historiography has saved from oblivion the names of a man and a confraternity who helped to create this new climate of religious opinion. The man was Battista da Crema (d.1534), 'a priest full of light', a Dominican who preached personal reform, affirmed that it is not God's grace which fails man but man who fails God — the beginnings of Molinism — and encouraged vocations. The confraternity was the Oratory of Divine Love, founded at Genoa in 1497 by a pious Genoese and brought to Rome in about 1514. This initiative on the part of a layman recalls that of the founder of the Brothers of the Common Life. The emphasis was on prayer, personal sanctification and the service of others. Gaetano da Thiene, Gian Pietro Caraffa (the future Paul IV), the humanist Iacopo Sadoleto, Giberti, who later reformed the diocese of

Verona, were all members of this confraternity. The first congregation of clerks regular in history, the Theatines (1524), grew out of it. Such a pattern of communal living was sorely needed at the time, and it was quickly followed by the founding of the Barnabites, the Somaschi and the Jesuits,[8] all before the Council of Trent. These 'reformed priests', living in the midst of the Christian people, set out to give an example of priestly virtue, to teach the catechism, to care for orphans, to give worship decency and solemnity, to bring the faithful to the sacraments. At the same time as these clerks regular were emerging, Angela Merici founded at Brescia (1535) the Institute of Ursulines, who like the Sisters of Charity later founded by St Vincent de Paul were not cloistered; their main concern was the education of girls. As regards the Italian bishops of the first half of the sixteenth century, the list of those who did not neglect their pastoral duties[9] and prepared the way for the Council of Trent is a long one. One of them in particular calls for a word, Gian Matteo Giberti (d.1543), who was Clement VII's datary before becoming bishop of Verona. Living like a monk, he visited his diocese assiduously, restored dignity to worship, encouraged preaching, suspended priests who were no longer capable, imprisoned those who were unworthy, and reformed the monastries. St Charles Borromeo's model at Milan was none other than this 'rude ascetic'.

In the Pre-Reformation period, then, the Church had important reserves of youthfulness and holiness, but its government was corrupt. Since the fourteenth century especially, the hierarchy had assumed an enormous rôle. To the extent that the Roman Church as a whole retained its traditional structures, it could achieve renewal only if the ruling body did. It needed the shock of the Protestant secession to push the Church to that step.

(b) The Council: expectations, disappointments and weaknesses

The Council of Trent created a rupture in the history of the Catholic confession by breaking it into two distinct periods, the second of which lasted right up to Vatican II. Yet it opened in a climate of the greatest scepticism. Only thirty fathers, three-quarters of them Italian, were present at the opening session on 13 December 1545 : a number not very different from that of the bishops, mainly French on that occasion, who took part in the Council of Pisa (1511) convened by Louis XII and Maximilian to discomfit Julius II. However, the conciliar idea was as alive as ever : for almost two centuries it was, in the minds of many Christians, inseparable from that of reform. Not only did the University of Paris

4

adhere to it with some obstinacy, but an advocate of papal absolutism, Cardinal Torquemada (d.1468), regarded a council as the Church's 'last resource in times of great distress'. Ferdinand of Aragon, an ally of Leo X, favoured periodic synods of Christendom. As far as Louis XI, Isabella of Castille and even Savonarola and Luther were concerned, the appeal to a council – or the threat of it – was probably more a means of putting pressure on the pope than an ardent wish on their part, but the fact that this weapon was brandished regularly and in different quarters shows that its wielders could count on a widespread hope that a council would be held.

Such hope had tides and tornadoes to fight. The Council of Basle had been dissolved in 1449. The Council of Pisa had been no more than a political comedy. The Lateran Council of 1512–7 had heard the noble words of Giles of Viterbo and persuaded Leo X to promulgate a grand decree of reform, but the decree proved a dead letter. On the other hand it had confirmed the bull of Pius II (1460) which forbade appeal to a council in defiance of a pope, and with Leo X, declared that the pope had full authority to convene, adjourn and dissolve councils. Despite this, in 1518 the University of Paris, contrary to the concordat of 1516, and Luther, contrary to the citation summoning him to Rome, both appealed to a general council.

If a parliament of Catholic Christendom had met before the condemnation of Luther's theses (1520) and Luther's excommunication (1521), or even just afterwards, it is probable that schism would have been avoided. Rome refused to take the initiative to save the situation; and the familiars of Leo X and Clement VII all stated that no council could revoke a solemn doctrinal condemnation. However, a theological affirmation by an ecumenical assembly could have enlightened the undecided and strengthened the hesitant. The refusal to hold a council enabled Lutheranism to spread, the new worship to be organized, religious frontiers to harden, and the chasm between rival Christian confessions to widen. For too long Rome tried to avoid a council, which a divided and disorientated Germany demanded with such insistence, not only for doctrinal reasons but because, only too conscious of the precedents of Constance and Basle, it feared a defeat for the papacy. Pope for already seven years, Clement VII did not decide to promise the convention of a council, at the urgent request of Charles V, until 1530, and even then only on condition that the Protestants returned beforehand to the Catholic faith. Nothing came of it, of course. Paul III, on the other hand, issued the bull of convocation in 1536, but then put the opening date back half a dozen times. He too gave the impression of wanting to return to Clement VII's stalling tactics, and of simply countering the conciliar idea with the sheer weight of Roman inertia. Yet he is not the only one to blame for the delay. How could a genuinely ecumenical council be convened when France on the one hand, the Empire and Spain on the other were almost constantly at war? These incessant conflicts were one reason why the council was so often delayed. Further, Francis I manoeuvred against the council because he feared it could end the divisions in Germany which were so profitable to France. The emperor pleaded for the council, although he would have limited its brief to disciplinary reforms while searching in other ways − 'reunion talks' at Haguenau, Worms and Ratisbonn (1540–1), and the *Interim* of Augsburg (1548)[10] − for a basis for doctrinal agreement with the German Protestants.

Convened twenty-five years too late, the council lacked the chief objective it should have had: Christian unity. The two sides of the confessional barrier had different views on the ecumenical assembly. The Protestants thought it should be 'free', open to reformed theologians and laymen, above the pope whose authority precisely they contested, and in Germany where the religious differences had arisen. But from the first the pope refused all attempts to weaken his supremacy, and all suggestions that the condemnation of the Lutheran theses should be repealed. He also wanted the council to be held in Italy, a country loyal to Rome and more docile than any other to the prescriptions of his curia. On the other hand, even before the start of the conciliar labours, the breach between Catholics and Protestants had become irreparable at the Ratisbon talks. Even though there was (momentarily) agreement on justification, there was a total theological impasse on the questions of eucharist and penance. The choice of Trent, an Italian city but on imperial soil, and the attendance at the council of a few representatives of German Protestant princes, came too late to modify the situation. The die was cast, the options taken; the point of no return had been reached. Thus it was that in convening the council Paul III no longer had serious hopes of bringing the Protestants back to the Roman Church. He preferred to hope that the assembly would steady the undecided and encourage the Catholics in their faith. If the pope announced the council again in 1541, it was to prevent the holding of a national German council which would certainly have weakened the authority of Rome and would probably have opted for a certain doctrinal tolerance. It was also because he knew that the Lutheran ideas were penetrating Italy itself: in a very short time he was to see the defection of the vicar general of the Capuchins, Ochino. Paul III, therefore, resurrected the conciliar idea as well as organizing the Inquisition (1542), and in the same spirit. This goes some way to explaining the scepticism with which all those who, against the evidence, still believed a reconciliation between Catholics and Protestants to be possible, greeted the Council of Trent. Would this council be capable even of re-establishing discipline in the Church and reforming a permanently reluctant curia? For a century past, so many excellent figures had drawn up plans and projects for reform which had all remained pious wishes: Capranica, Domenichi and Nicholas of Cusa in the fifteenth century, Giustiniani and Querini in 1512–3, and more recently the celebrated and pitiless *Consilium de emendanda Ecclesia* (1537) in which such eminent minds as Contarini, Pole and Sadoleto had collaborated. Could an essentially Italian council remedy a situation which had its origin at Rome, when it was the prelates of Italy more than any others who benefited from the system?

Leibniz, writing to Bossuet in 1693, assured him that the Council of Trent had been 'rather a synod of the Italian nation, to which others had been invited to give a semblance of ecumenicity'.[11] At the opening ceremony on 13 December 1545, there was only one Frenchman out of four archbishops and one Frenchman and one German out of twenty-one bishops. When the assembly sat on 18 January 1562, there were eighty-five Italian fathers, fourteen Spanish, three Portuguese, three Greek, and other nationalities – French, German, English, Dutch and Polish – were represented by a single bishop each. It is true that there were new arrivals in 1562 to increase the council's effectiveness: there were eventually twenty-seven French bishops, for example. But the few fathers who attended the different sessions is striking. While about 300 bishops had contributed to the work of Lateran III and 404 to the work of Lateran IV, there were never more than 237 voters at Trent. Even this figure is deceptive, because the most important doctrinal decisions of the council, in 1546–7 and 1551 – on tradition, original sin, justification, the eucharist and the other sacraments – were taken by assemblies which never numbered more than seventy-two voters.[12] Now in 1545, the number of bishops resident in Europe, apart from England, Scandinavia and the German dioceses which had gone over to the Reformation, was much more than 500. Further, because the regulations governing residence in the diocese were but slackly observed, there were a good many bishops who lived in Rome: in 1556 they numbered 113. There were frequently more bishops at Rome than there were at Trent. It follows that the council was ecumenical in theory but not in fact. It represented mainly southern Europe.

In short, never was there a council so dependent on its historical context as this one, so intelligible only in the religious situation of the time, so fraught with difficulties of every possible kind. In March 1547, fear of the plague moved the fathers to vote for a transfer to Bologna. In

September 1549, Paul III prorogued the council *sine die* because Charles V demanded a return to Trent. The new pope, Julius III, accepted the reopening of the council at Trent in 1551, but the resumption of the Smalkalden war and the advance of Lutheran troops in southern Germany threatened the very city in which the assembly was sitting, and in April 1552, it was decided to suspend deliberations. They did not recommence until 1562, partly because Paul IV (1555–9) opposed the council, and partly because he had thrown in his lot with the French in a war against the Habsburgs. The peace of Le Cateau-Cambrésis and the accession of Pius IV made it possible, in January 1562, to resume a council thought by many to have been long since defunct. Even then a dispute over venues set the Romans at loggerheads with the Franco-Spanish contingent in these last sessions. Peace came late.

How has an ecclesiastical assembly so jostled by events, so thin in most of its sessions, sometimes so hesitant (many of the bishops had no idea what to think about justification by faith and fell back on the opinions of the experts[13]) come to occupy a front seat in history? A few comments are called for here. The first is to modify Leibniz's remark quoted above. It is quite true that the majority of the council fathers were Italian, but at that time Italy was not a political unity. The bishops of the peninsula who were subjects of the crown of Spain did not always react and vote like the bishops from the other Italian states.[14] Again, although the council had few participants at the beginning, in the last sessions there were quite large attendances. On 5 December 1563, 255 fathers, representing all the areas that had remained Catholic, signed doctrinal and disciplinary decisions that had been taken sometimes fifteen or seventeen years previously by other fathers. They therefore took over the work of the entire council period. They did so with all the more conviction in that between 1545–9 and 1562–3 the fathers present had changed because Paul III, Julius III and Paul IV had done all they could to choose better bishops. The religious and political climate in Europe had likewise changed: the age of Charles V had given way to the age of Philip II. Attempts at peace had failed. The era of theological uncertainties was over, it was time to affirm. Yet the anathemas which brought the great doctrinal affirmations to a traditional conclusion, however inflexible they may seem to men of the twentieth century, left more room for theological research than appears at first sight.

The greatness of Trent lies in the fact that it met the religious needs of its time, just as the Protestant Reformation, admittedly with a different doctrine and style, did in the countries which nourished it. We thus return to a scheme developed in our previous volume.[15] At the time of the Pre-Reformation, western Christianity was living through a profound change. It opened itself to personal piety. It hungered for God. Becoming aware of its excessive religious ignorance, it demanded the Word of Life. At the same time, panic-stricken at its sins, it tried to storm the gates of heaven at whatever the cost. In this fertile but unsettling time, the official Church no longer came up to the faithful's expectations, because it merely let theological uncertainty fester. And its structures were cumbersome: from top to bottom of the hierarchy, pastors were demonstrably inadequate, sometimes because of their lack of knowledge, sometimes because of their unwillingness to reside in their dioceses, not infrequently for both these reasons. Christian people needed a limpid and reassuring teaching, a structured theology, which could be imparted only by an invigorated, instructed, disciplined clergy attentive to its pastoral duties. It goes without saying that Trent had no intention of meeting Protestantism half-way. Its chief concern was to counter the Protestant challenge and it retained to the end the mentality of a beleaguered citadel. Having established the fact of a rupture, it gave those who remained faithful to Rome what all western Christians aspired to at the threshold of the modern age: a catechism and pastors.

(c) *Tridentine Theology*

Far from returning to the roots of Christianity, as they affirmed, the Protestants were, in the mind of the fathers at Trent, dangerous innovators. From the beginning, therefore,[16] the council emphasized the continuity of Christian history by defining the 'sources of the faith'. Instead of the 'Bible only' and the 'free examen' of the Reformers, it proclaimed the Bible as clarified by centuries of tradition, or better traditions, by which was meant 'the testimonies of approved holy fathers and councils, the judgment and consensus of the Church'. Contrary to what is often said, there was no prohibition to translate or read the Bible in the vernacular at Trent. The private use of translations was permitted. The only thing was that the Vulgate was to continue exclusively in use in 'public readings, *disputationes*, preaching and doctrinal commentaries'. It was the *Index* of 1559 and 1564 which banned all reading of the Bible in vernacular translation.

1. Original Sin and Justification

Protestant theology started from a highly dramatic concept of original sin.

'Free will after the Fall is nothing but a word', said Luther in 1518. 'Even doing what in him lies, man sins mortally'.[17] Trent, therefore, found itself faced with the need to define the Catholic position on this question, and in substance it expressed it as follows. When God created man, he gave him certain preternatural gifts. Of these the most important was a share in the intimate life of the Trinity. The original sin of Adam resulted not only in suffering, physical death and ignorance for Adam and his descendants, but in 'subjection to the power of the devil'. The Mediator brought about man's reconciliation with God, and it is baptism — either of water or of desire — which applies the merits of Christ to the child or adult. The baptized Christian becomes a co-heir of God again.

Whereas Luther held that, despite baptism, the Christian remains basically a sinner, the council affirmed: 'In those who are reborn, God hates nothing because there is no condemnation for those who are "buried with Christ by baptism into death" (Rom 6,4)'. Concupiscence, of course, remains in the baptized, but, contrary to the Wittenberg theology, only as an inclination to sin that can be successfully overcome, not as real sin. Hence the council's famous interpretation of a Pauline text: 'Concupiscence, which the Apostle sometimes calls "sin" (Rom 6,12ff), this holy Synod states has never been understood to be a sin in the baptized in the sense of true and proper sin; if it is called sin, it is because it is the result of a sin [Adam's] and inclines the baptized to sin in their turn'.

The definitions of the Council of Trent held a steady course between the optimism of the Pelagians and the pessimism of the Lutherans — at least on original sin. Against the former — and Zwingli — the council refused to admit that 'Adam's sin of disobedience transfused to the whole human race "death" and pain "of the body only, and not sin itself which is the death of the soul" '. But against Luther it affirmed that, in Adam, free will was not 'destroyed but merely diminished and inclined to evil'. As a consequence not all actions of the unbaptized are necessarily sinful, which was the Lutheran and Calvinist thesis. The council fathers could therefore be said to have had Erasmian leanings.

As one would expect, debates on justification,[18] the most controverted problem of the sixteenth century, logically followed the debates on original sin. Forty-four particular and sixty-one general assemblies were devoted to examining the question. The final decree that resulted underwent three successive redactions. These long discussions[19] can be explained by the doctinal uncertainty on justification in the pre-reformation period, which was such that in putting forward his own position on the subject, Luther was not at all under the impression of propounding new or heretical theology. At the very outset of the discussions at Trent, Cardinal Cervini – the future Marcellus II – 'showed that according to the report of the general assembly of 21 June 1546 this article on justification was all the more difficult in that it had not been dealt with in previous councils'.[20]

It was important first of all to define justification, and the Council did so in the following terms: justification is 'the grace of God by which an unjust person becomes just', that is, it is 'the transition from the state (of sin) in which man son of the first Adam is born to the state of grace and "the spirit of sonship" (Rom 8,15) of God through the second Adam Jesus Christ our Saviour'.[21] 'It is not only the remission of sins, but also the sanctification and renewal of the inner man by the voluntary acceptance of the grace and gifts whereby the unjust man becomes just, the enemy a friend, "to become heirs in hope of eternal life" (Tit 3,7)'.[22]

It is understandable from this latter definition why, at the invitation of the two Jesuit theologians Lainez and Salmerón, the council did not retain the doctrine of 'double justification' that the so-called Cologne school and Cardinal Contarini had persuaded the Protestants to accept at the Ratisbon talks, and that Seripando, superior general of the Augustinians – Luther's order– defended at Trent.

Luther asserted that justification is merely *imputed,* that is, purely extrinsic: even baptized, man remains a sinner, although God chooses to cloak the sinfulness with his justice. Seripando defended a subtler thesis: the main cause of justification is indeed that God's justice is *imputed* to man; but there is also a place for a justice communicated by the sacraments which *inheres* and which makes up for our imperfections. 'The inherent justice depends on the imputed justice as on its cause, but they are not the same.' Seripando suggested the following analogy: 'My sight is useless without the sun's help, and that help is in the form of rays of light depending on the sun for their origin, existence and conservation . . . For sight I need not the sun only or the light only, but both together'.[23] The sun is *imputed* justice, its light *inherent* justice, the latter dependent on the former. The Council of Trent did not condemn double justification, but it preferred the doctrine of one *inherent* justification. According to this, 'we are not only called just, but we really are just, each person receiving justice according to his capacities, as the Spirit "apportions to each one individually as he wills" (1 Cor 12,11), and according to the individual's disposition and cooperation'.[24]

In keeping with the religious mentality of the time, most of the canons on justification carried a condemnation of the Protestant positions, and first and foremost the opinion which turned man, now deprived of free will, into the passive recipient of the divine action: 'If anyone says that man's free will, moved and stimulated by God, cannot cooperate at all by giving its assent to God when he stimulates and calls him . . . and that he cannot dissent, if he so wills, but like an inanimate creature is utterly inert and passive, let him be anathema (can.4)'.

Man is not manipulated by God, because God would then be responsible for evil as well as for good: 'If anyone says that it is not in man's power to do evil, but that it is God who works evil (through him) as well as good, not only by permitting it but also by willing it directly and formally, in such a way that Judas' betrayal would be just as much his work as Paul's vocation, let him be anathema (can.6)'.

Melanchthon, in fact, with Luther's approval, had written: 'In no matter what creature, everything happens by necessity. It is therefore quite clear that God is responsible for everything that happens, evil as well as good. Just as much as Paul's vocation, David's adultery, Saul's cruelties and Judas' betrayal are all his work'.

God's foreknowledge is therefore not predestination: 'If anyone says that the grace of justification is granted only to those predestined to life, and that the others who are called are called, certainly, but do not receive grace, because they are predestined by God's power to evil, let him be anathema (can.17)'.

Because there is no predestination, only acceptance or refusal of justification, good works and not only faith count for salvation. Also, the commandments of God are not impossible to observe: 'If anyone says that nothing is commanded in the Gospel beyond faith, that everything else, be it commandment or prohibition, is indifferent and up to the individual, and that the ten commandments have nothing to do with Christianity, let him be anathema (can.19)'. 'If anyone says that the justified man's good works are gifts from God to the extent that they are not at the same time his own merits, or that, by the good works he achieves by God's grace and the merit of Christ (of whom he is a living member), he does not genuinely merit an increase in grace and eternal life, as long as he dies in a state of grace . . . let him be anathema (can.32)'.

Faith being a necessary but not sufficient condition for justification, the faithful are not, contrary to Calvin's ideas, beyond all danger of a mortal fall, which, however, would not necessarily result in loss of faith: 'If anyone says that once a man is justified he can no longer sin or lose grace, and that consequently the man who falls or sins was never really justified . . . let him be anathema (can.23)'. 'If anyone says that the only mortal sin is faithlessness, or that no sin except faithlessness, however serious and considerable it is, can lose grace once received, let him be anathema (can.27)'.

2. The sacraments

In such a theological construct, the sacraments[25] hold an important place. Since it had no proper value or objective efficacity, the sacramental rite, for Luther, was merely a preaching of the word in action, a confirmation of salvation. Because of the position taken on justification by faith, the Catholic Church was naturally led to insist on the power and effectiveness of the sacrament. As the die is not cast beforehand, man being able to save or destroy himself depending on his reaction to the offer of God's grace, the channels by which grace comes to him are essential elements in the picture. This explains the council's insistence on the traditional doctrine of 'efficacious sign'. The sacraments 'really contain, as the cause contains the effect, and confer the grace they signify to all those who put no obstacle in their way'.[26] They are not external rites like those of the old Law. Their function is not just to nourish faith (Luther's view), nor are they merely signs of 'Christianness' (Zwingli's view).

Because of their great dignity, not all the sacraments can be administered by all Christians. Baptism, confirmation and holy orders, which confer an indelible character, cannot be repeated. Because of the objective nature of the sacrament, the sacrament's validity does not depend on the grace of the minister (which had been a fairly widespread view in the west since Jan Huss). And finally the council fathers reaffirmed their belief in seven sacraments instituted by Christ — a doctrine that began to emerge clearly in the Church only from the twelfth century.

The Council dealt with marriage only in its penultimate session — a fact to be taken in the context of the mentality of the period. It declared that: 'If anyone says that the conjugal state is to be preferred to the state of virginity or celibacy, and that it is not better or more blessed to remain in virginity or celibacy than to be joined in matrimony (cf Mt 19,11f; 1 Co 7,25ff,38,20), let him be anathema (can. 10)'.

The eucharist, on the other hand, provoked lengthy deliberations, understandably in view of the prominence given to the real presence in the sixteenth century. At the time of Trent, the Catholic Church was faced with a number of quite different Protestant opinions.

Luther maintained a doctrine very similar to Rome's. It is true that he rejected transubstantiation (the fact that the bread and wine are converted into the Body and Blood of Christ), but he did affirm consubstantiation (the fact that Christ is in the bread and wine, like fire in redhot iron, to use his own simile). Article 6 of the *Smalkalden Articles* (1537), drawn up by Luther, reads: 'As regards the sacrament of the altar, our belief is that the bread and wine at the Supper are the true Body and true Blood of Christ, and that not only pious Christians but also the pagans receive them'.[28] For the 'Sacramentarians' on the other hand – Karlstadt, Zwingli, Oecolampadius – the Supper was a memorial rite: this explains Luther's violent hostility. Zwingli explained his teaching as follows: 'When the father of a family leaves for a long journey, he gives his wife a ring with his picture engraved on it, and says: Here I am, this is me, your husband; I'm not leaving you; even while I'm away you can enjoy my company. This father represents our Lord Jesus Christ. When he went away, he left the Church, his spouse, his own image in the sacrament of the Supper'.[29] Thus in the eucharistic rite, the Christian evokes the Saviour and his salvific work. The real presence of God made man, therefore, is to be located not in the elements at the Supper, but in the assembly of the faithful who become the body of Christ. For Calvin, finally, there was a real presence in the elements at the Supper, and he even used the phrase 'substantial presence', but he thought of this presence as 'sublime', as 'so great a mystery which I find myself incapable of comprehending, even in my mind'.[30] What the communicant receives, according to Calvin, if he has faith, is the power, virtue and life of God made man. There is a real but spiritual presence.

In the face of these multiple Protestant doctrines, the Council of Trent simply reaffirmed the Catholic thesis of transsubstantiation: 'If anyone says that in the most holy sacrament of the Eucharist there remains the substance of bread and wine together with the Body and Blood of our Lord Jesus Christ, and denies that marvellous and singular conversion of the whole substance of the bread into the Body and of the whole substance of the wine into the Blood, even though the species of the bread and wine remain, which the Catholic Church most appropriately calls transsubstantiation, let him be anathema (can.2)'.[31]

The Roman Church, consequently, maintained the doctrine of the permanence of the real presence after the consecration even in the hosts which were not used at communion. Contrary to the wishes of several would-be innovators, it refused to countenance the distribution of all the hosts to the assembled faithful. This was a rejection of the Lutheran view, adopted by all Protestants, which held that 'one should not adore Christ in the eucharist, or honour him with feastdays, or parade him in processions, or take him to the sick'.[32] These were decisions of no small consequence; from then on, for several centuries, the popular devotions, manifestations of worship and religious art of the Christian churches were to go their separate ways.

The word 'eucharist', which has retained its currency in Catholic vocabulary, is not, however, the most apt to express the Roman theology of the mass. The latter was defined by Trent not simply as 'an act of thanksgiving', which is what eucharist means, but as a sacrifice. It was this last point that the Protestant Reformation rejected. For Luther and his disciples, it was a blasphemy of the sacrifice of the cross, offered once for all by the only one able to offer it, Jesus, to hold that the priest at mass offered the Son of God once more to God the Father. A minority at the council, including Seripando, believed that the Supper was not a true sacrifice, but the majority followed the opposite view with special insistence on a prophecy of Malachi (1,11): 'From the rising of the sun to its setting my name is great among the nations, and in every place incense is offered to my name, and a pure offering'. One theologian made the following remark, which made a great impression: 'If the mass were not a sacrifice, Christians would have no sacrifice at all, and so would be more unfortunate than the pagans, all of whom have had sacrifice.'[33] The fathers of the Council therefore stated it as their considered opinion[34] that at the mass Jesus is not only given as food, but also mystically immolated; that the mass, which was instituted by the Saviour (the Augsburg confession denied it), applies the salvific power of the sacrifice of the cross for the remission of sins. It benefits both the living and 'those who have died in Christ and are not yet fully purified': hence the practice of 'private' masses.[35] The canon of the mass was stated to be free of errors and deviations. It had, however, to be recited inaudibly, and Latin was to remain the liturgical language: 'If anyone says that the usage of the Roman Church whereby a part of the canon and the words of consecration are said in a low voice (*submissa voce*) is reprehensible; or that the mass should be celebrated only in the vulgar tongue . . . let him be anathema (can.9)'.

(d) Pastoral concerns

The emperor Charles V wanted only disciplinary questions to be broached at Trent, Rome only dogmatic questions. The council took a middle course by studying simultaneously theological points and questions of reform. Reform was vital if the Church were to transmit its message to the Christian people more effectively than hitherto. Now it was unthinkable that 'the sacred treasure of the holy books, given to men by the sovereign generosity of the Holy Spirit, should be neglected'.[36] The Church should no longer suffer the prophet's plaintive reproach: 'The children beg for food, but no one gives to them' (Lm 4,4). So in its fourth session the council issued a decree on preaching, 'the bishops' chief duty' in Christendom. 'Bishops, archbishops, metropolitans and others responsible for the churches', the text of the decree ran, 'will be bound and obliged to preach the Holy Gospel of Jesus Christ themselves. Should they be legitimately prevented from doing so, they shall delegate persons capable of fulfilling this duty of preaching with all competence for the salvation of souls. If anyone neglect his obligations in this regard, he shall be liable to severe penalties.'

The same duty was imposed on the lower clergy: 'Archpriests, too, parish priests and all those who in whatever manner have been placed in charge of parish churches, and those in general who have the charge of souls, will see to the spiritual nourishment of their people, at least on Sundays and major feast-days, either in person or through the delegation of other capable persons if they are legitimately prevented themselves, to the best of their ability and in conformity with the capabilities of their hearers'.

Catholicism and Protestantism shared a common concern here, beyond their differences, that the Christian people's need for the word should be met.

1. The episcopate

Only a renewed pastoral body could effectively proclaim the sacred message to the people: hence a series of decisions on the reform of the clergy, both higher and lower, which often were just revivals of previous constitutions that had fallen into desuetude. In February 1547, anticipating the council, Paul III had decided that henceforward the cardinals could retain only one bishop. Then the council dealt with other forms of accumulation – one of the most damaging plagues of the Church – decreeing notably that: 'No one, of whatever dignity, position or pre-eminence, should be so presumptuous as to receive or conserve simultaneously more than one metropolitan or episcopal church . . . for it is quite as much as he can do if a bishop rule a single church well for the benefit and salvation of the souls in his care'.[37]

If the Church were to be efficiently run, it was important to choose worthy and conscientious bishops, of legitimate birth, good morals and sound doctrine. The council therefore addressed to those who appointed the bishops, and notably the pope, a solemn plea and a reproach for the past: 'Moved by the sight of so many painful obstacles to the Church's work, this Holy Synod cannot but recall that nothing is more necessary to the Church of God than the diligence of the Most Holy Pontiff in his concern for the universal Church, as befits his office, in the careful choice of worthy cardinals, in the appointment of supremely good and competent pastors over the churches, and the more so in that our Lord

Jesus Christ is to reclaim from his hands the blood he shed for the sheep who would perish if the government of the pastors were negligent and apathetic'.[38]

It was not unknown for court prelates, even future popes (Paul III), to wait ten or sometimes twenty years after receiving episcopal jurisdiction before being ordained and consecrated. The council decided that those promoted to a cathedral church must be consecrated bishops within three months under pain of being deprived of all revenues. If they delayed a further three months, they were to forfeit all right to the position.[39]

The residence issue poisoned the last sessions of the council. The fathers were fighting for a principle: was residence of divine or ecclesiastical right? If of divine right, the pope could not dispense from it; this was tantamount to enhancing the episcopacy at the expense of the papacy. The Spanish and French prelates, who cherished the memory of the 'conciliar theory', opted for this interpretation. If, on the other hand, residence was an obligation of ecclesiastical law only, then Rome could repeal it in certain circumstances; in this case the pope stood over the entire episcopal body. The Italian bishops who were not subjects of the king of Spain defended the 'rights of the Holy See'. In the end, because no agreement could be reached, no principle was laid down.

The obligation of residence was forcefully stated at the start of the council against those whose 'sole occupation in life is wandering idly from court to court, or abandoning their flock and neglecting the care of their sheep in the flurry of their worldly affairs'.[40] Seventeen years later the decisions of the sixth session were extended at the twenty-third. To absent himself for more than three months, the bishop would henceforward have to request permission from the pope or metropolitan in writing, except for – and this still offered many bishops a convenient loophole – public service to the state. Authorization of absence granted by the metropolitan – or granted to the metropolitan by the senior suffragan – were to be examined by a provincial council. Should a bishop be absent without lawful excuse, the fruits of his revenue were to be distributed 'for the fabric of the churches or the poor of the district'. Further, short absences during the year must not exceed 'a period of time, either continuous or interrupted, the equivalent of two months, three at the very most'. The bishop should also make suitable arrangements so that his flock did not suffer in his absence. The only exceptions were periods allowed for short absences on the Sundays of Advent and Lent, and the feast-days of Christmas, Easter, Whitsun and Corpus Christi. The bishops' other duties were recalled in the twenty-fourth session: to attend a provincial synod every three years; to hold a diocesan synod every year; to visit their diocese, preach in person, and assure the preaching in all their parishes.

The Council, then, reminded the bishops of their duties. It also tried to safeguard their rights. It is difficult to imagine how impoverished and powerless the bishops were in their own dioceses at that time, and for a long time before. At the end of the fifteenth century, for example, the bishop of Lyons was appointing only twenty-one parish priests out of a total of 392. Since the twelfth century, the archbishops of Bourges appointed to only seven per cent of the parish churches; the bishops of Evreux to only six per cent; the bishops of Sées and Bayeux to only four per cent . . . And then the theoretical powers of the episcopacy — legislative, executive and judicial — had been gradually eroded over the years by the combined action of curia, lay authorities and the bishops' own subjects.⁴¹ The bishop was tied not only by lay and monastic patronage, but also by reservations, vacancies at the court in Rome, apostolic mandates, the right of prevention and the right of inheritance, expected favours etc. Even the small competence left to him was hardly his own because on all sides there were the exemptions of religious, chapters, archpriests, and there was a redoubtable obstacle, the *appel comme d'abus* (this 'appeal against alleged abuse' signified recourse against the abuses of power on the part of the ecclesiastical authority in its relations with the civil authority). The council, then, set out to reestablish the bishop's authority: he was from then on to be 'delegate of the Apostolic See' in his own diocese. In theory at least this should enable him to prevail over exemptions, even monastic exemptions, the best protected of them all. On the other side the excessive power wielded by the curia, legates and nuncios was curbed. The holding of regular provincial councils, finally, was designed mainly to restore due weight and importance to the bishops' decisions, while pastoral visits served the same purpose of reinforcing their authority.

One or two of the measures taken by the council to restore reality and substance to episcopal power are worth mentioning here. A religious, for example, could not preach in a church managed by his order without first obtaining the bishop's 'blessing'; and to speak in any other church he would need the bishop's 'authorization'.⁴² When an abbey or convent was held in benefice and observance of the Rule was slack, the bishop himself was to make the annual canonical visitation. If observance was satisfactory, the bishop was to see to it that the competent superior made the visitation, and if the superior failed to do this he was to make it himself in his capacity as 'delegate of the Apostolic See'.⁴³ He must likewise visit, or arrange for someone else to visit, all the churches of his diocese once a year, even the 'exempt' churches.⁴⁴ It fell to his competence to approve or not the subject 'presented' by the patron of a benefice,[45] to oblige patrons of over-populated parishes to create vicariates or parishes to correspond to the increase or re-distribution of the population, and conversely to fuse in a 'perpetual union' benefices which were too small on their own.[46] In granting minor orders, and even more so major orders, the bishop was to examine the candidates carefully and ordain only those who were 'reliable and capable';[47] he was the sole judge of admissions to the priesthood. In principle ordinations were to be held in the cathedral church. Each candidate was to be ordained by his own bishop, or where this was impossible by another bishop with 'testimonial letters' from the bishop of the candidate's own diocese.[48] No one was to exercise orders once his ordinary had suspended him.[49] In the future Rome would not accept appeals against the bishops' decisions in matters of 'visitation and correction'. In other matters, appeal would not obtain suspension of the bishops' sentence until such time as the latter was reversed by a higher court – if it were.[50] One could no longer cite a bishop to appear in court at Rome or before his metropolitan as long as there was no 'crime' that could involve deposition; in this latter case, the witnesses must be persons of good conduct and repute.[51] Finally, as each prelate was to be master in his own diocese, no bishop was to judge the subject of another bishop without the latter's authorization.[52]

2. The parish clergy

Authority was restored to the episcopate to enable them to take the frequently inadequate clergy in hand. It was to this end that the bishop was enjoined to visit all the parishes of his diocese in the year[53] and to check on the residence of the parish priests. The latter are now forbidden to be absent without the ordinary's permission, which, except for serious reasons, is not to be given for more than two months in any one year. While they are away they must arrange for a replacement approved by the bishop and remunerated by himself.[54] Any clergyman not wearing his clerical dress will be suspended, or even deposed and deprived of his benefice.[55] The hierarchy is to see to the upright behaviour of the clergy: they have to avoid any deviations from accepted standards of conduct, even minor ones, and be 'serious, modest and devout' in dress, attitude, manner, speech and everything else.[56] All this effectively determined the physical and moral image of the priest from the seventeenth to the nineteenth century. A cleric guilty of voluntary homicide, even in private, is held to be barred from all benefice in perpetuity.[57] Priests living in concubinage, 'the disgrace of the clerical corps', are to be 'deprived in perpetuity of all ecclesiastical benefices, portions, offices and pensions and will remain incapable and unworthy of all honours, dignities, benefices and offices' if they do not amend their ways.[58] More generally, the servants of God must 'avoid even the smallest faults, which in them would be considerable, so that their actions inspire in others a sense of reverence'.[59] Bishops are to pay particular attention to the way in which their priests celebrate mass. They must 'forbid and banish everything that greed, which is the worship of idols, or irreverence, which is hardly distinguishable from impiety, or superstition, that false imitation of true piety, have introduced'.[60] Mass is not to be said by a 'vagabond and unknown' priest, or in private houses, or anywhere apart from churches and oratories visited by the ordinary, or at any time outside those permitted. They will see that the Lord's temples are 'houses of prayer'.

One of the scourges of the ecclesiastical society of the time was the enormous number of wandering clerics who were numerous enough to form a class on their own. The council intended to eradicate this abuse by decreeing – rather surprisingly to our modern way of thinking, but understandably enough given the situation of the time and the contemporary mentality – that no one could be admitted to holy orders without having enough to live on. 'It being only too certain that in some places many candidates are admitted to orders almost without any pre-selection and resort to a vast number of dextrous and deceitful subterfuges to give the impression that they have an ecclesiastical benefice or sufficient resources of their own, the Holy Council decrees that no secular cleric, even though from other points of view – morals, learning and age – he might be ideal, may in future be promoted to holy orders unless it is juridically proved beforehand that he is in uncontested possession of a sufficient ecclesiastical benefice to provide him with an honest living'.[61]

The question of promoting clerics to minor and major orders, and particularly the priesthood, was one which preoccupied the fathers of Trent the most. How could they expect to improve the quality of the lower clergy unless they imposed criteria of recruitment and minimal conditions of admission? First of all, bishops are forbidden to accept the least offering or gift, even spontaneous, for the conferring of orders.[62] A knowledge of Latin is required of the candidate before he can be given minor orders. Candidates for the subdiaconate have to be at least twenty-one years of age; for the diaconate, twenty-two.[63] Deacons and subdeacons are asked to communicate on Sundays and feastdays, and this in the churches to which they are attached. There has to be a year's interval at least between the diaconate and the reception of the priesthood. Before being ordained priest, the candidate must undergo a comprehensive examination on both his conduct and religious knowledge. Even then he is not allowed to hear confessions – a particularly delicate duty – without having a benefice involving the cure of souls, or without sitting a special examination, or without at least giving some clear sign of competence as a director of consciences.

The twenty-third session which issued all these directives is especially famous for deciding on the creation of seminaries, 'perpetual nurseries of ministers for the worship of God'. Canon 18 first states the principle that: 'If they are not well educated, young people are all too easily led astray by the pleasures of the world. Thus unless they are formed in piety and religion at the tenderest age, before vicious habits have entirely taken hold of them, it is impossible for them to persevere perfectly in ecclesiastical discipline without the special and powerful protection of almighty God'.[65]

The text does not seem to envisage the possibility of late vocations. The all-important thing is to withdraw the future servant of God from a corrupt world as soon as possible. The next step was to prescribe the setting up of a seminary in each diocese. No candidate will be admitted to these colleges 'who is not at least twelve years old, born of a legitimate marriage, who cannot adequately read and write, and whose natural goodness of disposition and strength of will do not offer the hope that they will undertake the permanent ecclesiastical ministry'.

Poor children will be selected in preference to rich, although the latter, who will, however, have to pay for their board and lodging, are not excluded. From the start they will all wear the tonsure and clerical dress; they will hear mass each day and go to confession once a month. 'They will study holy Scripture, the books of theology, the writings of the saints, in fact everything which will contribute to the wholesome administration of the sacraments, especially confession, and the strict observance of the rules governing all rites and ceremonies'.

In order to establish these seminaries and maintain them, the bishops will avail themselves of certain revenues already put aside for the education of children, and with the help of a bench of advisors will strive to find new resources, even at the expense of abbeys and benefices with a right of patronage.

3. Religious

Six months before ending its deliberations, the council had thus forged the main instrument of Catholic renewal, clearly seeing that unless the secular clergy gained in virtue and theological knowledge, renewal was out of the question. It did not forget, however, to reform the religious orders as well, which it did in a long decree at the twenty-fifth session. Its principal measures are as follows. The regular clergy must practise the strictest observance of their rule ('If in fact the bases and foundations of religious life are not maintained with all possible exactitude, the whole edifice must necessarily crumble to the ground'). They will have no property of their own. They will not establish new houses without the prior authorization of the ordinary. They will not leave the convent without the superior's permission, and those who have to leave for reasons of study must reside in a monastery. 'Under pain of eternal damnation', bishops will re-establish nuns' clausura wherever it has fallen into abeyance, and see that it is rigorously maintained wherever it still holds. Superiors, generals and abbesses will be elected 'without any fraudulence', that is, by secret ballot. Abbesses must be at least forty years of age, and must have spent at least eight years in a convent 'since their profession' and 'with no slur on their reputations'. Monasteries will receive a regular canonical visitation, either from the order's official visitors or from the bishop himself if they should prove negligent. Nuns will go to confession and communion at least once a month, 'so that armed with this salutary safeguard they may boldly overcome all the attacks of the devil'. They will not have reservation of the Blessed Sacrament in the convent. Monks will observe the bishop's censures and the feasts of the diocese. Religious profession must be preceded by at least a year's noviciate and cannot take place before the candidate is at least sixteen years of age. 'Before the profession of a novice, monk or nun, his or her parents, relatives or guardians may not, under any circumstances, donate anything whatever to the monastery during the period of the noviciate beyond what is needed for lodging and clothing. This is to ensure that novices may leave the monastery at will without being under any constraint because the superiors hold the whole or part of their property not readily recoverable'.[65]

If a girl more than twelve years old wishes to take the habit, she must be examined by the ordinary. Those who force a woman to enter religion or prevent her from doing so if she wishes will be anathema. No monk or nun will be able to leave after five years of religious profession on the plea of having entered under force or fear. No monk or nun can be transferred to an order that is less strict. One canon (no.21), finally, deals with benefices. 'In future (monasteries) which fall vacant will be conferred only on regular clergy of an acknowledged virtue and holiness. As regards monasteries which are mother-houses of an order, or abbeys and priories which are their daughter-houses, those who hold them in benefice at this present moment will be obliged, if no regular successor has been provided for, to make their solemn profession within six months in the house's own order, or to relinquish the benefice altogether. Failing this the benefice will be considered automatically vacant'.[66]

Our own age has become aware of the distance that separates us from Trent and Luther alike.[67] Nonetheless, even though critically viewed by Catholic opinion itself today, the work of the Council has dominated three centuries of religious life, as far as Rome is concerned: that, for the historian, is the important point.

CHAPTER 2

THE AFTERMATH

(a) How the council was received

The same remark may be made of the Edict of Nantes and the Council of
Trent: both were fairly widely applied, whereas the pacification edicts
that had preceded the former, and the reform decrees of synods and even
Rome itself that had preceded the latter had remained dead letters. The
Council of Trent came to a close on 4 December 1563; pontifical
approval of its decisions was granted on 26 January of the following
year, and a bull issued in July of that year made them obligatory for the
whole Catholic Church. Two years later the parish catechism was
published – the *Catechismus ex decreto concilii Tridentini ad parochos.*
It had been requested by the council as early as 1546, and Pius IV's
nephew, Charles Borromeo, was largely responsible for it. The breviary
and the Roman missal appeared in 1568 and 1570 respectively.[1] The
council declared the Vulgate 'authentic'. Its revised version, the 'Clemen-
tine Vulgate', was published in 1593. These facts, and others, show that
the papacy had fully appropriated Trent's spirit of reform and renewal.

In an age when political authority was perpetually intervening in
religious matters, the application of Trent's decrees did not depend solely
on Rome's willingness. The Catholic heads of state had to be willing too.
Now there were three distinct areas in the work of the Council of Trent:
dogma; discipine and morals; and ecclesiastical justice and the relations
of bishops with Rome. After 1563, there were no major reservations on
the part of the heads of state in the first two areas. The third was
different. Neither the king of France nor the king of Spain approved of
the title 'bishop of the universal Church' for the pope. They were going to

continue to interpose their *placet* between the Holy See and the Catholics of their respective countries. They had no intention of ceding any of the 'Spanish liberties' or 'Gallican liberties', or of putting an end to the *recursos de fuerza* in Spain and the *appels comme d'abus* in France.[2]

That a large part of French opinion was in agreement is shown by the pamphlets published under Henry IV and Louis XIII against the official acceptance of the council decrees in the country. The council, they said, obliged bishops to judge the printers and authors of scandalous works, clandestine marriages, free unions and adulteries. All tonsured clerics, even married ones, from then on came under the jurisdiction of ecclesiastical courts. Bishops would have sole charge of hospital surveillance and repairs to church buildings. French jurists protested when they saw that the council in practice refused ecclesiastics the right to present *appels comme d'abus* to parliament – bishops having the right to judge certain matters without an appeal – and authorized the Church judges to refuse the official citations of a lay judge. They objected to the fact that any suit involving a bishop should be reserved to the Holy See, since parliament claimed jurisdiction over all royal cases, even when the guilty party was a bishop.

The Italian states, Portugal and Poland made no objection to the official acceptance of the council's decrees signed at Trent by their 'spokesmen'. The solemn acceptance by Philip II took place in July 1564, but with this clause: 'my royal rights being in no way infringed'. Despite the pope, it became customary for royal commissions to attend the provincial councils held, after Trent, in all the dioceses dependent on the crown of Spain. In 1566 the Catholic princes and electors of Germany 'accepted' the council's decrees in all matters of dogma and worship, and contented themselves with requesting a few modifications of detail on the disciplinary matters, especially those touching provincial synods.[3] Ferdinand I, on the other hand, although well disposed to the Catholic Church, forbade the publication in his territorial possessions of all the Tridentine decrees which seemed to him to impugn the prerogatives of the state. Even after the end of the wars of religion, France refused to integrate the decisions of Trent into the constitutional laws of the kingdom. Henry V was afraid of upsetting the Protestants. The government of Maria de' Medici and Louis XIII met opposition from the Gallicanism of the third estate. In the States General (the territories annexed by the United Provinces [= northern part of the Low Countries] after the Union of Utrecht [1579]), the clergy, supported by the nobility, begged the king 'that he be pleased to order the said holy Council of Trent to be received, published and observed by his whole kingdom'. The third estate immediately asked the king, in a declaration prepared by the theologian Edmond Richer, 'to state . . . as a fundamental law of the kingdom . . . that there is no earthly power spiritual or temporal with any right over the king's realm, to the detriment of the sacred persons of our monarchs . . . The contrary opinion is . . . impious . . . (and) contrary to the well-being of the State of France, which depends directly on God alone'.[4] The French ruling house espoused the point of view of the third estate and continued to think that 'the Gallican liberties are truly the common law maintained so powerfully and from such ancient times' in the kingdom.[5] It therefore refused to legalize the Tridentine decrees. The clergy of France solemnly declared that for its part it accepted all the decrees which dealt with matters of faith and pastoral activity.

On 7 July 1615, three cardinals, forty-seven archbishops and bishops, and thirty ecclesiastics stated that: 'The undersigned cardinals, archbishops, prelates and other ecclesiastics representing the general Clergy of France, assembled by permission of the King in the Augustinian convent, Paris, having given the profoundest consideration to the subject of the publication of the Council of Trent, have unanimously acknowledged and declared, do acknowledge and declare, that they are obliged by their duty and in conscience to accept, as in fact they have accepted and do accept, the said council, and promise to observe it as far as they can in their functions and spiritual and pastoral authority, and in order to accept it more amply, more solemnly and more particularly, are of the opinion that provincial councils of all the metropolitan provinces in this Kingdom should be convened and assembled in each province within six months at the very latest'.[6]

This is a quite remarkable declaration of clerical autonomy from the heart of the *Ancien Régime*, and the monarchy made no mistake about it. Louis XIII never sanctioned the 7 July 1615 declaration, nor did his successors. The French episcopate at any rate, who did not altogether lead exemplary lives, thus solemnly affirmed their adherence in heart and mind to the decisions of a council for which France as a whole had long shown but little affection.

(b) Obstacles to the application of the council's decrees

Whereas the dogmatic decisions taken by Trent were subsequently accepted by the various theological schools of the Catholic world, including the Jansenists, with remarkable unanimity, the application of the disciplinary decrees met no small opposition from human habit, routine and frailty. In general the popes who governed the Roman Church from

1565 onwards were animated by a genuine religious spirit, and gave an example of dignity in their conduct. Two of them have been canonized: Pius V (1565–72) and Innocent XI (1676–89), although the most remarkable pontiff of the Catholic Counter-Reformation period was undoubtedly Sixtus V (1585–90). Many of the popes, however, imitating their Renaissance predecessors, paid service to nepotism, thanks to which Rome, Tivoli and Frascati gained magnificent palaces and villas, with names like Aldobrandini, Borghese, Barberini and Pamphili.

Apart from papal nepotism there was the episcopal nepotism of certain bishops from the aristocracy. A typical example of this is the Gondi family who retained the episcopal (from 1622 archiepiscopal) see of Paris for some ninety-three years (1569–1662). Another is the Rohans who were bishops of Strasbourg without a break from 1704 to 1803.[7] The great families almost always included at least one bishop in their ranks. The La Rochefoucaulds, for example, held the sees of Rouen, Beauvais and Saintes when the Revolution broke out. In 1700, three Colberts were prelates: the archbishop of Rouen, the bishop of Auxerre and the bishop of Montpellier.

Contrary to the wishes of the council fathers, the benefice system did not fade out. This was for several reasons. In the first place, it had the approval of the leaders of the curia who resided in Rome because of their positions. Secondly, a state like France, which had not accepted Trent's decrees, felt no obligation to apply them on this point. Henry IV gave two abbeys to Sully, who was a Protestant. Statistics on 1100 French abbeys in the eighteenth century reveal that 850 of them were held in benefice, notably by the almoners, chaplains, preceptors and lectors of the king, queen, princes and princesses.[8] Consequently the accumulation of benefits was not suppressed either, or even eroded. In 1638, Rancé, then only twelve years old but already canon of Paris and abbot of Notre-Dame-du-Val, Saint-Symphorien and Notre-Dame-de-la-Trappe, nominated to forty cures or priory-cures. And residence, particularly of the bishops, left a deal to be desired throughout the West, not least in France.

The Catholic Renaissance, then, found its way obstructed by a variety of factors, principally the inertia of Church dignitaries and the continuing caesaropapism of monarchs. The regular rhythm of provincial synods[9] (every three years) and diocesan synods (every year) laid down by the council, and the regular visitations of parishes (each to be inspected every two years) were disregarded.[10] Further, Hispano-Portuguese colonialism was a redoubtable screen between Rome and many missionary countries. Finally, if the lower clergy were for a long time reluctant to educate themselves, wear clerical dress and teach the catechism, the higher clergy frequently forgot the first chapter of the reform decree of the twenty-fifth session of Trent: cardinals and prelates will live a simple and frugal life. Wealth remained the great weakness in the higher echelons of the Roman Church.

The imposition of artificial periods has deformed the history of the Counter-Reformation and obscured its chronological dimensions. In fact the Catholic religious Renaissance stretched over several centuries. We have shown already that it started with a long preparatory period of concern and effort; then, once the council was over, it was slow to infiltrate customs, institutions and hearts. Although the new Catholic style seemed to carry off a tolerably swift victory in Italy and the Iberian peninsula from the second half of the sixteenth century onwards, it did not really gain a footing in France, Germany, the Low Countries, Bohemia and Poland until the seventeenth. It is true that in France the reign of Louis XIII and the regency of Ann of Austria coincided with a flowering of heroic sanctity – it was the age of St Vincent de Paul and *Polyeucte* (Corneille's tragedy which tells the story of the son-in-law of a third-century Roman governor in Armenia put to death by his father-in-law for embracing Christianity. His martyrdom is followed by the conversion of his wife and her father). But the full effects of the religious revival in the country began to be felt only in the second half of the seventeenth and at the beginning of the eighteenth centuries. This remark is complementary to our previous statements on the inadequate implementation of the council's disciplinary decisions. Two over-simplified judgments must therefore be avoided: on the one hand, that before 1563 the Church of Rome was in a totally parlous state, and on the other, that it was immediately and completely restored after that date. In the diocese of Paris, pastoral visits did not seriously and regularly begin until after the Fronde (a revolt under Condé against Mazarin [1648–52] which spread from Paris to the provinces. Although Mazarin was forced to flee the kingdom temporarily, he eventually triumphed [1653]), and particularly the nomination of Mgr de Péréfixe as archbishop in 1664.[11] One of the first concerns of the new prelate was to convene a synod of all the clergy of his diocese – the first time this had happened in forty-six years![12] And then, despite the establishment throughout the seventeenth century of various specialist organs and institutions for the formation of candidates to the priesthood and young priests (the Saint-Lazare conference for ordinands, the seminaries at Saint-Magloire, Saint-Nicholas-du-Chardonnet, Saint-Sulpice, the *Gueuserie des Bons-Enfants*, the Community of the Holy Family, and the Seminaries of Providence), it was only in 1696 that a diocesan seminary was founded in Paris, at that time a city of some 400,000 inhabitants with 472 parishes in its immediate vicinity.[13] In that year Mgr de Noailles made it compulsory for a candidate for the priesthood in his jurisdiction to attend the seminary course. He also founded the *Séminaire Saint-Louis*, which was the result of an amalgamation of all the Seminaries of Providence that would cater particularly for the less-well-off clerics. Similarly the diocesan seminaries began to function more or less satisfactorily only after 1660 at Rouen,[14] 1671 at Nantes,[15] 1682 at Bordeaux,[16] and 1695 at Angers.[17] The list of reforming bishops at Angers does not begin until Mgr Arnauld (brother of Marie-Angélique Arnauld, the Jansenist abbess of Port-Royal-des-Champs [1591–1661]) who occupied the episcopal see from 1650.[18]

(c) Rome, a renewed religious capital

The foregoing remarks are necessary for a complete understanding of the Catholic Reformation: they must not be taken to underestimate the importance of the religious restoration and revival then at work in the Roman Church.

It is undeniably true that the capital of Catholicism remained an astonishing paradox in that at a time when it esteemed neither poverty nor effort the city claimed the mission of spreading and conserving the message of the carpenter's son who had announced 'Blessed are the poor in spirit'. But at least Rome ceased to be the licentious and pagan city at which Savonarola and Luther had hurled their anathemas. The ascetic and authoritarian Pius V, who wanted to sell off the antique nudities in which the Roman museums then abounded and would have ejected all the prostitutes from the capital, at least tried to transform the moral climate of the Eternal City. His dream was to turn Rome into one vast convent, and naturally enough he did not succeed. Then once this over-exigent pastor had left the scene, and when, with the death of Sixtus V (1590), Rome's heroic period of Catholic reform came to an end, the city began to smile again and live again. From then on, its piety was tempered with humour, its majesty with nonchalence, the pomp of its ceremonies with the gentleness of art. But at least it presented to the public eye a worthy exterior enhancing the nobility of its architectural surroundings. Some fifty-four churches were built or entirely re-built during the sixteenth century. The cupola of St Peter's, finished in 1593, took on symbolic significance: despite recent set-backs, the Catholic confession was holding its head high again. The increase in population – it reached 100,000 in 1600 – the sheer beauty of the religious and civic buildings, the obelisks re-erected by Sixtus V, the thirty new streets built in the sixteenth century, the restoration of three ancient aqueducts between 1565 and 1612, the proliferation of ornamental gardens: all these helped to make Rome at the end of the sixteenth century the leading city of Europe and the artistic capital of the world.[19] Artistic and religious revival went hand in hand. From the middle of the sixteenth century, then, it was a physically impressive and morally respectable city the popes offered to the many pilgrims who came to 'do the seven churches' during the holy years. The Catholic restoration and the re-establishment of pilgrimages to the Eternal City were connected. In 1575 there were at least 400,000 pilgrims, and in 1600 550,000.[20] A confraternity for this purpose lodged 210,000 pilgrims in three days in 1600, 12,866 of them in Holy Week.[21]

The prestige of a city once more conscious of its potential increased the authority of the popes in the Catholic world and thus completed the activities of Trent which, against all expectation, had strengthened the position of the Holy See. It was precisely this, though, that so grieved Fra Paolo Sarpi at the beginning of the seventeenth century: ' . . . the court of Rome,' he wrote, 'which feared and avoided this council as the most likely instrument to modify the excessive and limitless power it had acquired over the years, so hardened its grasp on the party that remained faithful to it that its authority has never been so powerful and so secure. The moral is to surrender everything into God's hands, and not trust in human prudence'.[22]

As part of this same evolutionary movement, and one that contributed to it in no small measure, the government of the Catholic Church was reorganized, from the pontificate of Paul III onwards. The reorganization meant effectively a radical centralization, and this was done by setting up *congregations*, or commissions with the responsibility of preparing the pope's decisions in the various areas of their competence.

There were fifteen congregations under Sixtus V, who had created most of them.[23] Six of them were for examining temporal affairs. The others dealt with: the *Inquisition* (created in 1542), the *Index* (created by Pius V), the *Council* (1564, subsequently reorganized), the *Bishops* (1576), the *Regular Clergy* (created by Sixtus V, as were the following congregations; in 1601 it was amalgamated with the Congregation for the Bishops), the *Signature of favour* (dealing with requests for favours), the *Erection of churches and consistorial provisions, Rites and ceremonies*, and finally the *Vatican Press*. To these must be added a congregation for the *Conversion of the Infidels* (1568) which did not demonstrate its full potential until 1622, when it became the congregation for the *Propagation of the Faith*, and a congregation for the *Construction of St Peter's*, perhaps set up in 1523 but reorganized in 1593.

The members of the congregations were cardinals and experts. At that time the Sacred College as such had lost its importance[24] in comparison with the Pre-Reformation period, despite the growing number of its members (seventy under Sixtus V). Nevertheless the cardinals were now selected more than ever before on genuinely religious grounds, and so although they had less political weight they were far more men of the Church than say in the fifteenth or at the beginning of the sixteenth centuries. Pius V's consistories, in 1568 and 1570, were epoch-making in this respect, and while causing general astonishment created a precedent. A few years later Baronio (d.1607), the friend then successor of St Philip Neri at the Oratory in Rome and author of the famous *Annales ecclesiastici*, and Bellarmine (d.1621), a Jesuit theologian who collaborated in the revision of the Vulgate, were the outstanding models of the new type of devout and erudite cardinal.

(d) Synods, seminaries and pastoral visitations

It is perfectly true that papal authority in the reformed Roman Church was excessive, but it did at least have the advantage of providing an important counter-weight to the caesaropapism of Europe's Catholic monarchs. It also favoured as scrupulous an application as possible of the Council of Trent's decrees. In a revealing gesture on his election, Pius V sent the text of the conciliar decrees to the archbishops and bishops of Goa, Mexico, Guatemala, Honduras and Venezuela.[25] The aim of local synods was from then on to imbue the daily life of Catholicism with the spirit of the council. The synods did not, admittedly, meet as regularly as had been hoped for, but many of them met during the years immediately subsequent to the council, and enabled the spirit of reform to filter down to the clergy and faithful. Charles Borromeo held no less than eleven diocesan and six provincial synods between 1565 and 1581, in an effort to bring the Tridentine revival to bear throughout northern Italy. Over a hundred synods, both provincial and diocesan, took place during the nine years 1564–72, in Europe, Asia (Goa, 1567 and 1570) and America (Mexico, 1565; Lima, 1567).[26]

If the renewal of the hierarchy was to be felt at parish level, dioceses could not be too extensive, and in fact they positively mushroomed in several regions where the Protestant threat was felt to be particularly serious. In 1559 the map of the Low Countries was redrawn at the request of Philip II. Up to then, although well populated and quite prosperous, this region of western Europe numbered only four bishoprics (Cambrai, Arras, Tournai and Utrecht) controlled from two foreign metropolitan sees (Rheims and Cologne). The reorganization decided on by the pope and the king of Spain created three archbishoprics (Cambrai, Malines and Utrecht) with fifteen bishoprics.[27] In France, the bishopric of La Rochelle was established in 1648.[28] In Bohemia, three new dioceses were set up with Litomerice (1655), Hradec Králové (1664) and Budějowice (1785) as centres.[29]

One of Trent's most important reform decisions was undoubtedly that which led to the institution of seminaries, which immediately proliferated in Italy and Spain.

In Italy[30] some twenty seminaries were inaugurated between 1564 and 1584. In Spain, where some seminaries already existed before Trent, namely Granada (1492), Tortosa (1544) and Valencia (1550), twenty-six other establishments for the formation of the parish clergy were opened between 1565 and 1616.[31] In the Low Countries eight conciliar seminaries were created before 1620.

On the present territory of France,[32] seminaries were established at Rheims (1567), Pont-à-Mausson (1579), Avignon (1586), Toulouse (1590), Metz (1608), Rouen (1612), Mâcon (1617), Lyons (1618) and Langres (1619), but at a time when the kingdom was either engaged in civil war or threatening to re-engage in it, these institutions were often on the frail side. In fact France was not well supplied with seminaries until after 1650.

For a long time seminaries in France and Italy were of two distinct types, and the impressive list of seminaries in the Iberian peninsula in the second half of the sixteenth century should not delude the reader: more often than not they were heteroclite agglomerations, under one roof, of all candidates for the priesthood, from twelve to twenty-four years of age, and although the course was long, preparation for strictly priestly duties was short. This explains the mediocrity of the lower Italian clergy in the seventeenth century. It was only in the following century that Italy began to adopt, under the influence of Jansenist ideas, the French-type seminary in which future priests stayed for only about two years but where their genuinely priestly education was considerable.

To facilitate the reconquest by Catholicism of countries that had defected to Protestantism or which were contended by Rome and the Reformation, seminaries were set up 'in exile', anticipating the French model. The *Germanic College* (1552) was set up in Rome, in 1575 receiving 130 candidates for the priesthood from various German dioceses. A *Hungarian College* joined it in 1578. In the same year an *English College* was established in Rome. There were also English Colleges at Douai

(1568, 1593 and 1611), Saint-Omer (1593), Paris (1611), Louvain (1612) and Liège (1626), Irish Colleges in Paris, Louvain, Salamanca and Rome, Scots Colleges at Pont-à-Mausson (subsequently at Douai) and Rome, and a seminary at Louvain for the United Provinces. In 1622 the *Propaganda College* was opened in Rome for priests from all the mission countries of Europe and the world.

In the Empire, diocesan seminaries were for a long time somewhat thin on the ground, although Canisius and the Jesuits fostered 'pontifical' seminaries — creations of the Holy See — in the Empire and Poland: Vienna (1574), Dillingen (1576), Gratz (1578), Olomonc (1578), Braunsberg (1578), Fulda (1584) and Ingolstadt (1600). They later became academies or universities on the pattern of the *Roman College* set up by Ignatius in 1556, which in 1585 became the brilliant *Gregorian University* (so called after Gregory XIII who greatly encouraged its foundation).

Even though not all the objectives of the Council of Trent were attained, even though the rhythm of pastoral visitations and synods had difficult beginnings in some countries, the daily life of the Catholic Church was gradually metamorphosed from 1565. In and around Vienna about the middle of the sixteenth century, over 300 parishes were without clergy.[33] At Cremona there was no resident bishop between 1475 and 1560.[34] Milan was eighty years without a resident archbishop before the arrival of Charles Borromeo. These are some examples from hundreds. Situations like them became increasingly rare. In fact the position improved almost beyond belief. Alain de Solminihac, bishop of Cahors from 1636, carried out nine journeys in his diocese in thirteen years, each one of which took in all 700 of his parishes.[35] In the large, mountainous and wealthy diocese of Besançon, which like Cahors had some 700 parishes, Mgr de Grammont (1665–7) managed four pastoral rounds in three years. The bishops of Auxerre André Colbert (1676–1704) and Caylus (1704–54) both began their visitations from the beginning of their episcopates. Massillon, appointed bishop of Clermont in 1717, made it his business to visit a part of his 750 parishes every year. There are summary but helpful statistics on the average interval between two consecutive visits of a parish in seventeenth-century France: twelve years; in eighteenth-century France: eight. This is a testimony, however insufficient in itself, to the improvement in the bishops' pastoral zeal — a result of the education given by the seminaries. Many of the bishops in France were alumni of Saint-Sulpice seminary founded by Olier in 1641. At the end of the seventeenth century, the bishops from Saint-Sulpice numbered fifty, and in the eighteenth century over 200 Sulpician students became bishops. At the outbreak of the Revolution, the Company of Saint-Sulpice controlled some twenty seminaries over the country; and this was less than the Lazarists (founded by St Vincent de Paul) at the same period. The influence of Saint-Sulpice on the body of the French clergy was enormous, because the seminary received future priests from all the dioceses of France and gave them their own ecclesiastical style compounded of refinement, a spirit of recollection, austerity of manner and a high degree of learning, both theological and profane.

(e) The religious orders

In France, Belgium, the Empire and Poland, priests and bishops imbued with the spirit of Trent did not start to come from the seminaries until 1650, because of the relatively late date of the latter's establishment. In these countries, then, the 'heroic' − chronologically the first − period of the Catholic Renaissance was particularly characterized by the militant action of new or renewed religious orders. In the second half of the seventeenth century, it was the reformed secular clergy who progressively influenced the Christian life. Although they continued to play an important part, the religious orders were to a large extent effaced by the seculars, who began to show a certain impatience of the regular clergy, which can be felt in the Jansenist movement. This general pattern can also be applied, with some modification, to Catholicism as a whole.

Among the new religious orders, the Jesuits were in the front rank. When Ignatius of Loyola died in 1556, the Company totalled 1000 members already, and administered a hundred foundations (houses of residence, noviciates, houses for the professed and colleges). A hundred years later, there were more than 15,000 Jesuits and 550 foundations. Their colleges, in which the organization and teaching was the same all the world over, numbered 150,000 pupils. In 1773, when the Company was suppressed by Clement XIV, there were 23,000 Jesuits in thirty-nine provinces. They had 1600 foundations, including 800 colleges with 15,000 teaching staff.[36]

In France the Company opened its first college in 1556, at Billom, followed in 1561 by the *Collège de Clermont* in Paris. Jean Chastel's attempt on Henry IV's life (1594) had nefarious consequences for the Jesuits for a short while, because Chastel had been their pupil. They were expelled from the territory of several parliaments, including that of Paris. The expulsion order, however, was reversed in 1603, and a Jesuit, Coton, became the king's confessor. The Jesuit *Assistance de France*, comprising the five provinces of Paris, Lyons, Toulouse, Aquitaine and Champagne, was established in 1608. By 1643 the Jesuits had 109 foundations in France. The energy of the Company in France during the first half of the seventeenth century is shown by the fact that in 1710 the Jesuit houses of the *Assistance de France* numbered 149: the growth rate in the personal reign of Louis XIV (1661–1715) had therefore slowed down.[37]

In the Low Countries, the Company reached its apogee in 1625–50. In 1595 there were 420 Jesuits, in 1611 788, and in 1626 1574. In that year France, very much larger, counted only 2156 Jesuits, Germany 2283 and Spain 2962. In 1643, the Jesuits had 5600 pupils in their classes in and Franco-Belgian province alone.[38] To keep contact with their pupils once their formal studies were over, the Jesuits often instituted confraternities. Although these began in the colleges themselves, they soon spread outside thanks to the activities of the alumni. In 1640 the Flemish-Belgian province of the Company managed ninety 'sodalities' with 13,727 members, and the Franco-Belgian province eight with 11,300 confrères. Van Dyck, Rubens and Teniers belonged to Jesuit confraternities.[39]

Confessors of European princes and astronomers of the emperors of China, missioners and remarkable teachers, the Jesuits were the most dynamic element in the Roman Church between 1550 and 1650.

This said, one must restore to their rightful place other religious families of the time, notably the Capuchins. At the start, when they broke away from the Franciscans, the 'Franciscan Hermits' as they were originally called had difficulty in keeping their feet. When they came under fire from the Regular Observance Friars Minor, they were defended before Clement VII by two remarkable women, Caterina Cibo (Duchess of Camerino), and the poetess Vittoria Colonna. Rome, however, forbade them to accept converts from the Regulars (1532) or to spread outside Italy (1537). The defection of their vicar general, Bernardino Ochino, who chose to turn Protestant in 1542, almost precipitated the suppression of the order, but they survived. Towards the end of the sixteenth century, they began to spread outside Italy. In 1643 they held 1379 houses with 21,000 members, and at the beginning of the eighteenth century 1800 houses with 30,000 members spread over thirty-eight provinces.[40] Admittedly when the Capuchins totalled 21,000, in 1643, the Conventuals, from whom they had definitively separated in 1619, totalled 30,000 and the Regulars of the various Franciscan branches no less than 163,000. But it was not the numbers that mattered so much as the vigour of an order which included that extraordinary philologue Laurence of Brindisi (1559–1619), that sometimes very realistic crusader Fr Joseph, the indefatigable adversary of all libertinism Fr Yves de Paris (1590–1678),[41] and a missioner always in the breach, Fr Honoré, who tirelessly travelled France under Louis XIV.[42]

The statistics of the Capuchin foundations in France reveal the importance of their activity, their popularity and then a certain flagging after 1643: 1574–89: thirty-one foundations; 1589–1610: ninety-seven; 1610–24: a hundred and thirty-two; 1624–43: fifty-six; 1643–1715: ninety-five. This is 285 foundations in the fifty-four years 1589–1643, and only ninety-five in the seventy-two following years, or five foundations per year during the first period and only one and a third during the second.[43]

Capuchins and Jesuits were influential in Switzerland, Austria and Bohemia during the 'heroic' period of Catholic reconquest, not without fostering, it is true, a climate of lively intolerance. In Switzerland the Capuchins held fifteen convents by 1604, and they had already established themselves at Feldkirch, Vienna, Gratz, Prague and Brno.[44] The Capuchins and the Jesuits were also particularly active missioners throughout the world.

Dressed in coarse frieze, bare-footed whatever the time of year, accustomed to frequent and rigorous fasts, sleeping on boards, preaching in season and out of season, the Capuchins made a vivid impression on the men of the sixteenth and seventeenth centuries. They cared for the plague-ridden and the incurably sick and buried the dead. Their sermons were enormously popular. During some missions in the Low Countries, Capuchins were to be seen in the churches with an inscription on their backs enumerating their sins.

It is impossible here to describe the rise of all the new religious congregations in the course of the sixteenth and seventeenth centuries. It must be sufficient to mention one or two statistics which will convey some idea of the efforts and results in this direction. In 1631, only two years after its founder's death, the Oratory of Bérulle numbered seventy-one houses, including twenty-one colleges and six seminaries.[45] The Lazarists, whose constitutions were approved by Urban VIII in 1635, had established thirty-three houses when St Vincent de Paul died in 1660. Some fifty more foundations followed in the forty years 1661–1700, both in France and elsewhere (Italy, Poland and distant countries).[46]

The success of some female orders was even more resounding. On the advice of St John of the Cross and anxious on her own account to re-establish her order's primitive rule of austerity, St Theresa of Jesus instituted the first monastery of reformed Carmelites at Avila in 1562. In 1648, there were a hundred convents of strict observance Carmelites in Spain, ninety-two in Italy, fifty-five in France etc.[47] It was Bérulle, under the inspiration of Mme Acarie (who became Mother Mary of the Incarnation), who was instrumental more than any other individual in introducing the discalced Carmelites into France when in 1604 he invited some of the Spanish reformed nuns to Paris. Their convent in the rue Saint-Jacques, where Bossuet preached a famous sermon on the occasion of the *Profession of Mlle de La Vallière* (Duchess of Vaujour) in 1675, became one of the high places of devout Paris.

Unlike the Carmelites, the Ursulines, the Visitation nuns and the Daughters of Charity were all new orders. The Italian Ursulines of the sixteenth century were not cloistered,[48] although most of the Ursuline houses founded in France after the original foundation in Paris in 1610 of Mme de Sainte-Beuve were. At a time when women were slowly but surely gaining in respect, the apostolate of the Ursulines was the education of young girls. It is an important fact in social history that this teaching order held over 300 houses in France in 1715. By then the Ursulines had spread not only in Italy and France, but to Switzerland, Germany and the Danube countries. When St Francis de Sales and St Jane Frances de Chantal started the Order of the Visitation of our Lady at Annecy in 1610,[49] their intention was to create an essentially contemplative congregation, but one which to some extent complemented prayer with visits to the homes of the sick and poor. The archbishop of Lyons refused to recognize any such uncloistered female order, and St Francis de Sales did not insist. As a consequence the Visitation nuns became a 'formal religion' with solemn vows. Visiting the sick was replaced by the education of boarding girls. Be this as it may, the order enjoyed a similar success, and at St Jane's death in 1641 there were eighty-six convents. It also contributed to extending devotion to the Sacred Heart: the apparitions of Jesus to St Margaret Mary Alacoque, a Visitation nun at Paray-le-Monial, in 1673–5, achieved wide fame in the France of Louis XIV.

St Vincent de Paul gave the most important fillip to the female apostolate in the whole Catholic Reformation period. However, the Daughters of Charity, from 1633, under the joint direction of St Vincent himself and Louise de Marillac, at the service of the poor, the sick and children (notably abandoned children), were not strictly speaking nuns in the accepted sense of the word at that time. Bearing St Francis de Sales' failure in mind, St Vincent did no more than establish a confraternity — the 'Confraternity of the Servants of the Poor'.[50]

He decided that the Daughters of Charity should be dressed like women of the people, with a plain, dull grey habit. They would wear no veil. They would take annual vows only. Their founder once remarked, half jokingly half seriously: 'Their monastery will be the houses of the poor and the house of their superior. Their cell, a rented bed-room. Their chapel, the parish church. Their cloister, the streets of the city. Their clausura, obedience. Their grill, the fear of God. Their veil, holy modesty. Their profession, constant trust in Providence, the oblation of all they are'.[51]

The Daughters of Charity, who expended themselves mercilessly during the Fronde, took hospitals over, set up small centres of good works, both urban and rural, and started numberless primary schools. In 1660 they managed over a hundred houses, in 1711 250, and in the middle of the eighteenth century 426 (including fifty-one primary schools in Paris alone).[52]

Statistical details — a quantitative history — is absolutely indispensable if we are to grasp a religious phenomenon like the 'Catholic Renaissance'. Churches and convents sprang up everywhere. During the first half of the seventeenth century, sixteen great churches were begun, continued or completed in Paris. The cities of the west were more than ever the 'ringing towns' evoked by P. Goubert. '135 great bells and dozens of small ones rang out over Beauvais (in the seventeenth century) to mark religious solemnities and public celebrations'.[53] The rate at which religious houses were built at Angers in the seventeenth century enables us to understand a whole age. At the end of that century the town counted ten abbeys, convents and communities founded before 1596, and eighteen others which had originated between 1598 and 1698.[54]

This mushrooming of religious institutions necessarily entailed an extension of ecclesiastical property. We may take the example of Angers again. In 1769 the town had a population of 25,105, with 556 clerics and 227 seminarists. The Church owned sixteen per cent of the houses, and was landlord to a sixth of the urban population.[55]

This amassing of land on the part of the Church was not without causing disquiet. About the middle of the seventeenth century, in the Low Countries,[56] the Church owned three-quarters of the land in Cambraisis, half in Namurois, a third in Hainaut, a quarter in Artois, an eighth in Brabant and a tenth in Flanders. This explains the unease of the civil authorities, who were yet perfectly sympathetic to the Catholic Reformation movement. On the one hand land and goods owned by the Church were not subject to tax, and on the other, in towns where the building fever of the previous century had slowed down, the number of houses still available to private citizens threatened to dwindle to intolerable proportions. In 1628 the municipality of Ghent gave out that with already twenty convents of nuns the city was not willing to accept any more. As statistical researches continue, the figures give an increasingly clearer picture of the economic size of the Catholic Renaissance.[57] In about 1600 Cremona, a city of 40,000 inhabitants, had twelve monasteries with 747 nuns in. Eight of these convents owned more than 120 hectares of farmland each.[58] The Spanish clergy in the middle of the sixteenth century numbered 100,000 and a hundred years later 200,000.[59] An inventory of 1626 for the kingdoms of León and Castille gave the following figures: 6,322,172 laity owned 61,196,166 *medidas* = 9.5 per head, and 141,810 members of the clergy owned 12,204,053 *medidas* = 86 per head.[60]

In Spain more than anywhere else, entry into the clergy was only too often a flight from work, a quest for security in a country that was then poorly farmed and hardly at all industrial, a search for a possible career which, when all was said and done, was enviable despite the sacrifices involved. However, to reduce the Catholic revival to a matter of economics and social history would be to distort a movement which was first and foremost a great spiritual history. The reform, in the sense of return to primitive severity, of the ancient religious orders indicates that many of those who entered religion were not out for easy solutions. Witness Jacqueline Arnauld – *Mère Angélique* – who in 1609, against her father's will, decided to re-establish the clausura at the Cistercian convent of Port-Royal. Witness again Abbot de Rancé at La Trappe, who from 1664 forbade the eating of fish, eggs, butter and spices, introduced perpetual silence, and refused visits and letters to his community.

The extreme case of La Trappe is to be seen in the larger context of the reform and revival of ancient orders.[61] The 'congregation' of Windesheim, prosperous in the fifteenth century, then ruined by the Dutch civil wars of the sixteenth, was re-constituted: it had twenty-seven monasteries in 1600, forty-five in 1650. Cardinal de La Rochefoucauld (1558–1645), bishop of Senlis and titular abbot of Sainte-Geneviève in Paris, undertook the reform of the Augustinian canons of his abbey. The movement soon spread to the whole country, reaching fifty-three houses, and then included the Low Countries, Belgium and Ireland. There was also a revival of Benedictine monasticism which had been started in the fifteenth century when the congregations of Bursfeld and Santa Giustina in Padua were founded. Seeing they could not hope to suppress benefices entirely, the fathers at Trent had at least tried to encourage the federation of several abbeys into congregations with the same rule. Obedience to this instruction was slow and sporadic. Nevertheless federations of Benedictine monasteries were set up at the end of the sixteenth century and during the seventeenth in Switzerland, Austria, Portugal, Spain, Belgium and France, where the congregations of Saint-Vanne (at Verdun) and Saint-Maur (at Saint-Germain-des-Prés) emerged. The reputation of the historical work published by the Saint-Maur Benedictines,[62] under the stimulus notably of Mabillon (d.1705), was considerable. Federations of convents arose in the Cistercians, too, who had carried out their own reform: in Germany (1595), Italy (1605 and 1613), Spain (1616), Ireland (1626) and France, where the reformed congregation (known as the *Feuillants*) was founded in about 1580 and the Trappists were set up at the end of the seventeenth century. In all the religious orders, then, a new spirit was being felt: witness the discalced Carmelites of 1568, the discalced Trinitarians of 1594 and the discalced Servite hermits of the same year, the terminology reflecting a common spirit of self-denial. The Dominicans, the Minims – founded by St Francis of Paola in Calabria in 1436 – and the Carthusians attained their numerical peak at the end of the sixteenth and first half of the seventeenth centuries: respectively, 14,000 friars in 600 convents in 1567–78, 450 convents in about 1620, and 257 convents in 1633. This powerful movement did not die away quickly. In Bavaria, for example, nine convents of monks were founded between 1657 and 1674: Franciscans at Altötting, Benedictines at Michelfeld and Reichenbach, Cistercians at Waldsassen and Walderbach, Premonstratensians at Spenshart, Augustinians at Schönthal, and Capuchins at Burgsthal and Neumarkt.[63]

(f) *New theology. Success of the religious book*

The Roman Church's renewed youth was accompanied by a revival in the domain of theology – which is man's attempt to understand God. In Catholic Europe, owing mainly to the Dominican friar Francisco de Vitoria (d.1549), Salamanca occupied the same theological position during the immediate post-Tridentine period that Paris had occupied in the thirteenth century. No less than sixty-six doctors from Salamanca had in fact attended the council. A golden age of Catholic theology followed Trent, ending only in the first half of the seventeenth century with the successive deaths of Suarez in 1617, Du Perron in 1618, Robert Bellarmine in 1621, Francis de Sales in 1622, Lessius in 1623, Bécan in 1624 and Coton in 1626. However, the passion for theological problems remained alive for the whole of the seventeenth century, as the debate on grace that broke out after the publication of the *Augustinus* in 1640 testifies. Six years later, as a contemporary remarked, 'Never have there been so many theologians'.[64] Despite its 'sombre tenor, too dry and scholastic to be much pleasure to read',[65] the *Augustinus* went quickly through several reprintings. Arnauld's first works, *De la fréquente communion* (On frequent communion), 622 quarto pages, and *Tradition de l'Eglise sur le sujet de la pénitence et de la communion* (The Church's tradition on penance and communion), 420 quarto pages, were best-sellers. His *Apologie de Jansénius* (Apologia for Jansen) was even more successful. As the anti-Jansenist Jesuit Rapin observed, 'It was a treatise on the thorniest and most intricate problems in theology, (but) written so beautifully that courtiers, lords and ladies could read it with pleasure'.[66]

Publication statistics reveal the extraordinary interest shown in matters of religion, at least as far as the reading public were concerned. H. J. Martin's monumental *Livre, pouvoirs et société à Paris au XVIIe siècle* (The book, the authorities and society in seventeenth-century Paris)[67] is the indispensable book of reference here. After a period of stagnation 1540–70, the religious book in France experienced a remarkable resurgence: in 1643–5, forty-eight per cent of works published in Paris were to do with the Christian faith; in 1699–1701, the percentage had risen to forty-nine.[68] There was thus a large public diffusion, in print, of liturgical texts, theological studies, mystical meditations (notably Theresa of Avila and the Franciscans Canfeld and Joseph du Tremblay), apologetical and controversial works, lives of the saints and accounts of miracles. In 1663 a Paris printer contracted to publish 36,000 copies of the account of the *Miracles of Notre-Dame-de-Liesse* in six months.[69] The history of religion and the history of ideas cannot ignore the sheer quantitative facts: never had there been so many books of spirituality – often in pocket editions and in the vernacular – so many praises of the Virgin[70] in printed circulation.

It has been said that at the beginning of the sixteenth century, the western world seemed 'tired of theological minutiae; it (yearned) for the sources of evangelical truth'.[71] The conceptual analysis of revealed truths had been badly abused, to the point where, in the words of Melchior Cano, 'the opinions of the schools were set up as indisputable and indubitable dogmas, and contrary opinions as heresies'. St Francis de Sales, ridiculing the scholastic subtleties some time after Cano, opined that 'there is no very pressing need to know whether the angels have place by their essence or by their operation; or whether they move from one spot to another without passing through intermediate points'. Erasmus hit out at the 'night-flying wasps' and the 'asses' of the theological faculties of his time.

However, there was a remarkable improvement, even in the area of scholasticism, in theology, which is a speculation on revealed data with the aim of defining and clarifying them. Scholasticism was revitalized, and adopted a clearer and more up-to-date form of expression. St Thomas Aquinas became the most honoured theologian – even the Jesuits called themselves Thomists – at the expense of Augustine and Peter Lombard. Above all, the humanist era saw the rise of *positive* theology — the expression appears in about 1509 — which is the study of scripture with the aid of the interpretations of the Fathers and councils. Positive theology seeks not to reason about the truths necessary to salvation, but to strengthen the love of God and faith by contact with the Bible, the writings of the Fathers and Christian history. It rapidly radiated into a number of separate disciplines: exegesis or the study of Scripture, patristics or the study of the common teaching of the Fathers of the Church, patrology or the study of the Fathers as historical persons and writers, the history of dogma and Church history. The New Testament commentaries of the Jesuit Salmerón, the patristic publications of the Benedictines of Saint-Maur, the *Annales ecclesiastici* of Baronio, among many other works, bear witness to this rapid rise of positive theology.

Parallel with this development, *moral* theology too gradually achieved autonomy. Independent minds like Denis the Carthusian (d.1471), Martin Le Maistre (d.1481), Tomás Sanchez (d.1610), St Alphonsus Liguori (d.1787) made steady inroads, in the face of massive conservative opposition, on the impossible Augustinian morality of marriage. They did not, of course, manage to establish a relationship between conjugal and carnal love, but at least they expressed an admiration for pleasure in the relations of marriage, for family planning in the interests of economy, and for the *amplexus reservatus* as a legitimate alternative to contraception.[72] These are mere stammerings, it is true, compared with our own morality, but they made the latter possible. The same moralists were more successful in their fight against the patristic and medieval prohibition of lending money at a rate of interest. By the end of the eighteenth century, the innovating theologians had, on this point, won the day.[73]

There has been excessive ridicule of casuistry, in the wake of Pascal, without sufficient attention to the fact that it corresponded with the growth of a civilization, with the need to answer new problems or problems posed in new terms, with the increasing role of the laity in the Church, with the development of awareness. The discovery of the American continent necessitated a consideration of the salvation of infidels, the natural law and the legitimacy of overseas conquests. It was to the credit of Vitoria, and then of Suarez, that they denied any superiority of the Christian nations, merely insofar as they were Christian, over the barbarian nations, that they unequivocally stated that Christianity should never be imposed by force, and that they gave as their considered opinion that neither the pope nor the emperor could legitimately dispossess unworthy princes. A product of moral theology was thus international law.[74]

Chapter 3

HOLINESS

(a) *Christian heroism*

The decrees of the Council of Trent and the reorganization of the Roman Church provided a framework for a real growth in Christian holiness, and the age of St Ignatius and *Polyeucte* saw the emergence of innumerable Christian heroes.

They all considered themselves to be great sinners. St Ignatius once said, 'I am mere dung, I must ask our Lord that when I am dead my body be thrown on the dungheap to be devoured by the birds and dogs . . . Must this not be my wish in punishment for my sins?'[1] St Teresa called herself a 'wretched inn of the Lord' and an 'ocean of miseries'. She was carried off to hell in a vision and saw with fright the place prepared for her which, she said, 'I had deserved for my sins': 'The entrance, I thought, resembled a very long, narrow passage, like a furnane, very low, dark and closely confined; the ground seemed to be full of water which looked like filthy, evil smelling mud, and in it were many wicked-looking reptiles. At the end there was a hollow place scooped out of a wall, like a cupboard, and it was here that I found myself in close confinement . . . In that pestilential spot, where I was quite powerless to hope for comfort, it was impossible to sit or lie, for there was no room to do so. I had been put in this place which looked like a hole in the wall, and those very walls, so terrible to the sight, bore down upon me and completely stifled me'.[2]

At the end of his life, when he had behind him a whole career of apostolic and charitable work, St Vincent de Paul regarded himself as a great sinner. 'I have been abusing God's grace', he confessed, 'for so many years . . . Alas, my Lord, I have been living for too long because there is no amendment in my life and my sins multiply with my age'.

Because the world is Satan's realm, a Christian must be detached from it: this is a constant theme in the writings of these Christian heroes. St Teresa, for example, wrote that the pleasures of life were like so much dirt, and St John of the Cross that 'the best here on earth, compared with the eternal happiness for which we were created, is ugly and bitter, and although brief in themselves, this ugliness and bitterness will remain for ever in the soul of one who esteems it'.[53] Whereas the Renaissance had attempted to reconcile the earthly with the heavenly city, the Catholic Reformation broke them violently apart. Did not Pascal plead in favour of this divorce when he sadly compared the Church of his time with the Church of the first centuries and seemed to regret the baptism of adults? '. . . Once one had to leave the world to be received into the Church: today one can enter the Church and the world at the same time. Then an essential difference was recognized between the Church and the world. They were considered to be two contraries, two irreconcilable enemies in continual battle . . . Now one can be in both camps together; the moment we are born into the world is the moment we are reborn into the Church. The consequence is that reason makes no distinction between these totally opposite worlds'.[4]

St Vincent de Paul and Tronson, who was superior of the Company of Saint-Sulpice from 1676 to 1700, had the same aversion for the world that St Ignatius, St Teresa and Pascal had. During a retreat Tronson invited the seminarists to meditate on the 'fearful words' of Jesus: *pauci electi*. 'Ah! how startling that is in the mouth of God, in the mouth of Truth himself! what, after the death of the Son of God, and all his blood shed for the salvation of men one drop of which would have been more than sufficient to redeem ten thousand worlds; after so much grace and the institution of the sacraments; after so many powerful, admirable aids — so few men saved! —' And his practical conclusion followed: 'If you want to be heirs of Jesus and paradise, that is, if you want not to be damned everlastingly but to be happy for ever in heaven, then you must renounce the world entirely and bid it an eternal farewell'.[5]

The world or damnation: what a frightful dilemma, to be accounted for, in part, by the sociological context. Fleeing the world meant necessarily breaking family ties. The refusal of 'unworthy tepidity' implies as much. Saints do not walk towards God 'jerking like hens', as Teresa said. She assured her readers that the 'angelic souls' who were assembled round her in the reformed Carmel at Avila 'found their consolation in solitude . . . Visitors, even brothers and sisters, were a trial to them'. St Vincent de Paul, too, has things to say on necessary detachment from one's family which amaze our modern mentality: 'I prayed to God ... so much that at last he took pity on me; he relieved me of my affection for my parents; and although they were and still are living on charity, he granted me the grace of commending them to his providence and of considering them happier than if they had been well off'.[6]

It is not easy to leave one's brothers and sisters; it is less easy still to leave one's children. When St Jane de Chantal left Dijon for Annecy where she was to found the Visitation, her son − the future father of Mme de Sévigné − lay down across the door to stop her. His mother, in tears, hesitated, and then left 'because God was calling her'.[7] Young Celse-Bénigne de Rabutin-Chantal had already started to make his way in the world at fourteen, but Claude Martin was only eleven when his mother, a widow like Jane de Chantal, entered the Ursulines at Tours in 1631. She took the name of Mary of the Incarnation, and later on in Canada she was called 'the Teresa of New France'. Bremond has told the drama of the separation of son and mother; the chapter makes almost unbearable reading: The child, whom the mother avoided kissing in order to prepare him for the great sacrifice, fled from the house when he realized the time was near. Returning to the house, apparently resigned, he accompanied his mother to the convent. 'He did not dare show his sorrow', she said, 'but I could see the tears in his eyes ... I felt as if my very soul were being wrenched from my bosom, but God was dearer to me than all this'.[8] The orphan, who was but moderately loved by his uncle and aunt, tried to see his mother subsequently, despite the convent grill. He used to enter the building unnoticed through doors left open by inadvertence or by workmen. One day his friends took pity on him and said, 'You miss this and that because you haven't got a mother; well, we'll get her back. We'll break the doors down and get her out for you'. And they proceeded to attack the monastery with sticks and stones. For a time Claude left his studies, but overcome by his mother's heroism, he eventually became a Benedictine monk, and an exemplary one, too; but neither mother nor son ever succeeded in convincing themselves entirely that so violent a separation could truly have been God's will.

If the knights of God could accept and triumph over such harrowing sorrow, of what were they not capable? To defeat the flesh, they practised the most frightful mortifications in imitation of the *Poverello* of Assisi. St Ignatius spent whole nights in vigil while he was at Manresa searching for his vocation, went sometimes for three days without eating, flogged himself with barbed chains and beat his breast with a stone. Like St Francis he offered the 'Franciscan kiss' to a wretch whom nobody would look after, putting his lips to one of his wounds and 'sucking the pus to cure the sick man'. St Peter of Alcantara (1499–1562) astonished St Teresa herself. At his death she exclaimed that he was 'so extremely thin he looked like nothing more than a knotted root'. She explained: 'I think it was for forty years that he told me he had slept only for an hour and a half between each night and the next day, and that, when he began, the hardest part of his penance had been the conquering of sleep, for which reason he was always either on his knees or on his feet. What sleep he had he took sitting down, with his head resting against a piece of wood that he had fixed to the wall. Sleep lying down he could not, even if he so wished, for his cell . . . was only four and a half feet long . . . It was a very common thing for him to take food only once in three days'.[9]

Such heroism as this lit up a whole era. When St Charles Borromeo died in 1584 at the age of forty-six and his body was stripped in preparation for burial, the extent and austerity of his penances stood revealed: the shoulders were bruised all over by the discipline, and the body was torn by the hairshirt. St Philip Neri, with his spirit of fantasy, his gaiety and his wit, is more attractive,[10] but this wonder-worker, too – nearly all the Christian heroes of the time were wonder-workers – self-administered the discipline with his companions three times a week. Then there was a poor priest active in Rome towards the end of the sixteenth century nicknamed, perhaps ironically, the *Letterato*. He welcomed abandoned children who were dying of cold and hunger. All this charitable zeal, however, did not liberate him from temptations of the flesh. One day, when he had reached the limits of his endurance, he spied a saucepan of boiling water on a stove and determined to 'overcome the heat of temptation with the heat of boiling water'. These shock therapeutics 'so seriously affected the parts of his body which refused to submit to reason' that he was ill for several months;[11] but the sting of the flesh gave him no more trouble. Dom Claude Martin, too, son of Mary of the Incarnation, went in for heroic remedies in his fight against concupiscence. One night at Angers he decided to follow the example of St Benedict by rolling naked in a gooseberry-bush and then covering his bleeding flesh with stinging-nettles. He was successful in stifling the flames of desire which had tormented him for ten years.[12]

This thirst for mortification, this rejection of the world and nature were essential if the unbelievable tortures to which certain missioners were subjected were to be endured. Here is how the Jesuit Jean de Brébeuf died in New France in 1649: 'Even after they had been stripped naked and beaten with sticks on every part of their bodies, Brébeuf continued to exhort and encourage the Christians who were around him. One of the fathers had his hands cut off, and to both were applied under the armpits and beside the loins hatchets heated in the fire, as well as necklaces of red-hot lance blades round their necks. Their tormentors then proceeded to girdle them with belts of bark steeped in pitch and resin, to which they set fire. At the height of these torments Father Lalemant raised his eyes to heaven and with sighs invoked God's aid, whilst Father Brébeuf set his face like a rock as though insensible to pain. Then, like one recovering consciousness, he preached to his persecutors and to the Christian captives until the savages gagged his mouth, cut off his nose, tore off his lips, and then, in derision of holy baptism, deluged him and his companion martyrs with boiling water. Finally, large pieces of flesh were cut out of the bodies of both the priests and roasted by the Indians, who also tore out their hearts before their death by means of an opening above the breast, feasting on them and on their blood, which they drank while it was still warm'.[13]

(b) The mystical experience

These adventurers into the absolute had probably no desire to beat any records for mortification, but they were of the opinion, as the poet of the *Spiritual Canticle* was, that one may not 'look for Christ without the cross',[14] and that 'suffering is the livery of those who love'.[15] Like Fr Surin, the principal mystic of the Jesuits in France in the seventeenth century, they knew that the man 'who is not an extremist in his love of God will never reach him'.[16] They remembered, too, the teaching of Master Eckhart that the mystic soul must 'lose itself' and 'sink' into the 'desert of the divinity'. This shipwreck on the divine ocean must be preceded by an 'initial denial', a desire for total stripping which makes the 'a priori mystic'.[17] St Teresa of Avila and St John of the Cross were under no illusions. 'The soul that prays', wrote St Teresa, 'will find security in forgetting itself and being satisfied to serve God alone'. A passage from the *Interior Castle* explains more clearly still that, as soon as the soul 'empties itself of all that is created', and if it submits to this trial 'out of love for God', God will 'necessarily fill it with himself'. Prayer is possible only after this fundamental renunciation, because, in the definition of Luis de Granada, 'prayer is rising above oneself and all created things, uniting oneself with God and submerging oneself in this sea of infinite sweetness and love'.[18] Better than any other mystic St John of the Cross has made it clear that to leave the low valleys of the devout life and start on the *Ascent of Mount Carmel*, one must go through the night of the senses, stifling in oneself all appetite for what is not God. The dilemma is a simple one: 'accept this night or renounce the very humblest mystical thought.'[19] For St John of the Cross the mystic must close the window of this prison which is the body. The void that results detaches one's profoundest being, one's deepest intimacy, and opens it up to God. For John of the Cross, then, the only sure way of life is to walk in the darkness cultivating the 'naked love of God'.

The works of St John of the Cross became known very much later than St Teresa's, but the basic *sine qua non* of mysticism, self-dispossession, was well understood in the seventeenth century school of French spirituality. St Francis de Sales wrote: 'Death means that the soul ceases to live in its body or in the enclosure of the body. What is the meaning of the Apostle's phrase: You are dead? He is saying equivalently, You no longer live in yourselves, or in the enclosure of your own natural condition: your soul lives no longer for itself but above itself'.[20] Bérulle, who above all others was responsible for spreading Teresian mysticism in France, is even clearer: 'We must consider our being to be finite and imperfect, like an emptiness that needs to be filled ... like a table waiting to be finished by the carpenter . . .'[21] Fr Lallemant (1587–1635), who started a whole school of mystics among the French Jesuits to which Frs Surin and Rigoleuc belonged, advised his disciples to 'make up their minds' by 'being converted a second time', not to 'barter' with God, to 'decide on the all-out sacrifice', to 'renounce once for all our interests and satisfactions in their entirety, our plans and wishes, to depend henceforward only on God's good pleasure'. Lest his readers should misunderstand the drift of his advice, he asked that prayer should come before action. 'When we have succeeded in possessing God (in contemplation), we can give a freer rein to our zeal'.[22]

Total forgetfulness of self is, therefore, in the mystical experience, the negative aspect and the necessary condition of the desire for God. St John of the Cross wrote:

> This life I live in vital strength
> Is loss of life unless I win You:
> And thus to die I shall continue
> Until in You I live at length ...
> This life I do not want, for I
> Am dying that I do not die.[23]

This poem dates from 1578. Seven years before St Teresa had composed a poem with the same theme and the same refrain: 'I die because I do not die'.

In the 'century of saints' – a century that straddles the sixteenth and seventeenth centuries – there were countless servants of God, men and women, who seemed to have been given the keys to a world to which lesser men had no access. They all had the 'gift of tears'. The doctors forbade St Ignatius to weep during his celebration of mass if he wished to retain his sight. From the moment of his conversion he was favoured with numerous 'visions', consolations and spiritual 'illuminations'. One day at Manresa the Trinity appeared to him in the form of three organ pipes giving out the same note. Several times St Teresa of Avila saw souls flying out of purgatory up to paradise. Some days before he was due to preach at Dijon in Lent 1604, St Francis de Sales was 'carried off in ecstasy, and with the eyes of his mind saw marvellous things, mainly that he would be the founder of an order of nuns; and also saw fantasms or ideas' – the Platonic language is to be noted – 'of the principal persons who would be instrumental in starting the order off.' On 5 March, as he was preaching in the chapel of the Dukes of Bourgogne at Dijon, he recognized in the congregation the person he had seen as the superior of the nuns in his vision. It was the widow of Baron de Rabutin-Chantal. A similar experience occurred to Olier. While he was getting ready to preach a mission in the Auvergne in 1634, he made a preparatory retreat at Saint-Lazare. A nun appeared to him praying for him. He later realized that it was the abbess of the Dominicans at Langeac. Ecstasies were by no means the monopoly of St Ignatius, St Teresa, St John of the Cross: St Francis Xavier, St Charles Borromeo, Mme Acarie (who introduced the Carmelites into France) were all favoured too, and many others. Condren, the second superior of the Oratory and spiritual director of all the saints in Paris between 1630 and 1640, one day experienced 'such a violent palpitation' in a fervour of love for God that several of his ribs moved out 'to give his heart room', and he had a 'protuberance' on his chest until the day he died. Three times, in 1673, 1674 and 1675, a Visitation nun at Paray-le-Monial saw the heart of Jesus consumed with fire. These are a few facts from hundreds. The Catholic Church had certainly not been short of mystics in previous centuries, but in the period covered in this book; the 'contemplatives' proliferated, a 'milky way', said H. Bremond, who with justification spoke of a 'mystical invasion' – from Spain – into the France of Henry IV, Louis XIII and even Louis XIV.

The Jesuits (Lallemant, Surin), the Capuchins (Canfeld, Fr Joseph), the Carmelites, the Visitation nuns, the Ursulines, all held prayer, which surpasses the frontier of human words, in the highest esteem. At the close of the seventeenth century, one of Fénélon's spiritual children, Mme Guyon, rediscovered St John of the Cross and advised 'spiritual' people to tread 'the way of death', of 'annihilation and denudation', by which 'the soul leaves itself and flies to its divine object in permanent ecstasy'.[24] The road which led the mystics to joy does not figure on human maps. They have to blaze it themselves, like adventurers in a jungle. It is by choosing radical insecurity that, after years of groping and cruel suffering, they became totally sure of God. St Teresa counsels those souls who want to follow her to 'risk everything for God' and 'hazard life itself'. The mystical experience entails unutterable torments, mortal anguish, vertigo, unknown to ordinary beings. Satan tries to unhinge the person who, like a moth round a lamp – the simile is St Teresa's – approaches too close to the divine sun. Surin, who exorcised the notorious possessed of Loudun, subsequently declined into a dark melancholy for twenty years, and people thought him mad. He himself thought he was damned. In a letter of uncertain date, he wrote: '. . . plunged into an inky . . . void with all my passions roused' – he was for long tempted by the flesh – 'I surrendered myself in my nakedness to suffering . . . My soul suffered an anguish and an agony from this death, to the point of wanting an immediate end to it all: but its prayer was not granted . . . My wretched soul was in a torment of worry, neither knowing what to do nor being able to do anything except wait for the blows at every passing minute which must destroy it; as the process, however, was maddeningly slow, my soul went into a frenzy'.[25]

Surin wrote a hallucinatory book, *La science expérimentale des choses de l'autre vie* (Experimental knowledge of the things of the next life) retracing the moral tortures he went through.

When joy suddenly floods the mystical soul after all the suffering, the experience is so violent that fear is the predominant emotion. How can human nature not resist the mysterious force snatching it from its native earth? St Teresa has recorded the fear for us. Sometimes, she says, the soul feels itself carried away at frightening speed, and it needs all the courage it can muster, all the faith and confidence, and a total resignation into God's hands.

If the mystic perseveres with boldness and self-surrender, once the time of trial is over the sun bursts through at last. The end of Surin's life was one long ecstasy. He wrote that 'the joy of the Lord came over him like a sea pouring into a small vessel and spilling out again; where the waves of God's anger had as it were submerged him before, he now felt as if he were flooded with divine consolations.'[26] The irruption of the divine in the heart that is thirsting for the infinite is always unexpected. But the soul has to be prepared for it by a long apprenticeship of prayer. With admirable psychological penetration, St Teresa analyzed in her *Autobiography* the four degrees of prayer by which the beginner gradually accedes to the fulness of mystical joy.

She compares the soul to a garden where 'like good gardeners' we must grow flowers 'which will send forth great fragrance to give refreshment to this Lord of ours'.[27] To water these flowers the beginners at prayer have no option but to draw water wearily from a well. In the second state, watering is easier because there is a windlass. In the third state, water flows in abundance; it comes from a river or stream which is very much easier, because the soil is soon saturated and the gardener has much less work. Finally, in the last state, it rains a lot, the Lord himself watering the garden without our having to take any trouble over it.

These images express the soul's ascent towards God. In the first moments of progress, the beginner is happy to stay with the Lord in silence. Despite the lack of fervour, the dryness and the lassitude, he must persevere. At the second stage, the soul enters the realm of the supernatural and rises above its misery. It begins the 'prayer of quiet' where 'everything is yes'. It is granted the experience of some 'heavenly pleasure'. This prayer, she says, is like 'a spark' of God's love which the Lord kindles in the soul, and Teresa thinks — an interesting sidelight on the religious psychology of the time — that many people are capable of reaching this level. The next level is very much more advanced. It is 'an almost total death to everything in the world, in the enjoyment of God', 'a glorious unreason, a heavenly madness, in which one learns true wisdom'. 'I think that at this point one must surrender oneself utterly into the arms of God: if he wishes to take the soul off to heaven, let her go; if to hell, there is no pain for it, on condition that it is there with its Beloved ... may his Majesty do with it what he pleases.' The fourth degree gives access to divine union. Perception ceases, but an enjoyment ensues which is beyond understanding. The soul feels itself almost fainting away in a sort of swoon, its breath coming in gasps, and all its physical strength slipping away, so that it is as much as one can do to move a hand. This prayer of union fills the soul with such immense tenderness that it would like to dissolve into tears of sheer joy. It is not, however, the same as ecstasy, although this fourth degree can effectively culminate in ecstasy. The Lord grasps the soul and takes it right out of itself, and then shows it something of what he has prepared in his kingdom for those that love him. The person who has been granted this great favour is struck with an overpowering fear of ever offending so great a God and a renewed all-enveloping love.

In her writings, the mystic of Avila several times evokes her visions. She saw Christ carrying his cross, and Christ in the Garden of Gethsemane; she also saw him in the splendour of his risen humanity 'with hands so incredibly beautiful I could not describe them'. The sight of glorified bodies was so wonderful that the heavenly splendour of it was enough to send one out of one's mind. The divine presence was accompanied by a light like that of limpid water flowing down over a crystal and reflecting the sun. Several times Teresa experienced the 'transverberation' immortalized by Bernini in his *Ecstasy of St Teresa* (in the Cornaro Chapel of Santa Maria della Vittoria, Rome). As she described it herself in her *Autobiography* (chap. 29), she saw an angel standing at her side, 'very beautiful', holding a great golden spear in his hand, and he plunged its burning tip three times into her heart, leaving her utterly consumed with the love of God. The pain was almost as great as the happiness. As Crashaw wrote in his *Hymn to the Admirable Saint Teresa*:

> Thou art love's victim; and must die
> A death more mystical and high.
> Into love's arms, thou shalt let fall
> A still-surviving funeral.
> His is the dart must make the death
> Whose stroke will taste thy hallow'd breath;
> A dart thrice dipt in that rich flame
> Which writes thy spouse's radiant Name
> Upon the roof of Heav'n; where aye
> It shines, . . .
> O how oft shalt thou complain
> Of a sweet and subtle pain,
> Of intolerable joys;
> Of a death, in which who dies
> Loves his death, and dies again,
> And would for ever be so slain,
> And lives, and dies; and knows not why
> To live, but that he still may die.

In the terminology of the time, Teresa calls these visions 'imaginary', by which she means that they are as images before the eyes of her soul. Similarly St Ignatius saw 'with his inner eyes', at the moment of the elevation one day at mass, white rays coming down from heaven. There is also, apart from the 'imaginary' vision, the 'intellectual' vision, which, although it exceeds the reach of even spiritual sight, lasts much longer and affords mysterious evidence of the divine presence. The soul feels close to Jesus, although it cannot see him, and it feels that God is so near it is encouraged and transformed. This certainty that the Other is present, beyond images and representations, is the essence of the mystical experience. 'Of what use is it', asked St Francis at the beginning of the seventeenth century, 'to imagine the one whose presence one enjoys?'[28] This divine presence revealed to exceptional people seemed to

Bergson to be one of the strongest presumptions in favour of the existence of God – a God of Love.[29] When St Teresa describes the 'spiritual marriage', she hardly mentions visions or even ecstasies: the soul is already a permanent occupant of the Lord's house. At this stage loss of the senses ('ecstasy') and raptures almost disappear. At one time, a sermon or music or a pious picture could provoke an excitement of devotion and the soul would fly into ecstasy. Now, however, either because it has found its peace, or because it has seen so much in this *Interior Castle,* it is no longer surprised at anything, and enjoys divine companionship.

In the *Interior Castle,* an 'imaginary vision' always precedes and announces the spiritual marriage. Even in the marriage, distinct knowledge is not altogether excluded, so that Teresa of Avila, and after her Mme Martin, experienced certain states which 'cannot coincide with a really pure mystical experience'.[30] The true mystical experience, more denuded, more like the pattern set by the Rhenish and Flemish mystics, is also to be found in St John of the Cross. The 'obscure night', as he described it, consists not only in the voluntary refusal of what is sensible and of all affection for external things, but also in the stripping of thought and in the darkness of the mind. The soul that loves God must therefore have the courage to go beyond the natural limits of its external and internal faculties. It is the path of *nada* and again *nada,* which leads to God. God himself, as the Other, the Supernatural, the incomprehensible and the immeasurable, is darkness and night for man.

St John of the Cross echoes the spiritual itinerary counselled by the Pseudo-Denis in his *De theologia mystica*: 'Abandon sensation, renounce intellectual operation, strip yourself totally of non-being and being, and to the extent that you are able, rise to union in ignorance with the One who lies beyond all essence and all knowing. It is in leaving everything, including yourself, perfectly that you will rise in pure ecstasy to the blinding light of the divine Superessence.'

In this night, the soul finally experiences divine union. 'It becomes God in sharing his nature and his attributes.' The delight which it then experiences is 'beyond the power of man to describe'. In the theopathic state reached by St John of the Cross, 'the ecstatic trance and the various forms of psychic obnubilation' seem to hold no place; 'if there is ecstasy, it is an ecstasy of the soul unaffected by any weakness of the body'.[31]

Catholic Europe, especially at the end of the sixteenth century and during the first half of the seventeenth, was filled with mystics and *illuminati.* The path of Teresa and John of the Cross was heroic and consequently accessible only to exceptional persons. Thus the mystical invasion provoked a reaction which the Protestant polemic fomented from without.[32] In France St Vincent de Paul advised the Daughters of Charity to be prudent in matters of prayer and contemplation: 'Let us beware of the all-too-common illusions which make black look like white and white like black.' Effusions of tenderness, sighs of love may be only the proof of feebleness of temperament or of 'a certain disposition of the spleen'. The Jansenists mistrusted mysticism, and Nicole spent thirty years of his life fighting it. His published works on the subject were *Les Visionnaires* (The Visionaries, 1665), *Traité de l'oraison* (Treatise on prayer, 1679) and *Réfutation des principales erreurs des Quiétistes* (Refutations of the principal errors of the Quietists, 1695). He was inspired by Bossuet in the latter's campaign against Fénélon and Mme Guyon.

On their own claim, Molinos (1628–1711), whose *Spiritual Guide* (1675) went through twenty printings and translations in six years, and Mme Guyon were following the tradition of St Teresa and St John of the Cross.[33] They lauded rest in God, the renunciation of desire and fear, self-oblivion in contemplation. Whereas the great mystics had a lively sense of sin, and approached God only after frightful mortifications, Mme Guyon (1648–1717) wrote in her *Moyen court et très facile de faire l'oraison* (A short and very easy method of prayer, 1685) that 'if a person whose will is lost, swallowed up as it were and transported in God were compelled by necessity to do sinful actions, he would do them without sinning'. The notion of salvation disappeared, and this was one of the main reasons why Fénélon's work *Explication des maximes des saints sur la vie intérieure* (Explanation of the maxims of the saints on the interior life, 1697) was condemned. Quietism seemed to carry with it, as consequences of the abandonment into God's hands, the neglect of ordinary religious duties and a sort of apologia for inaction. This explains the condemnations of Molinos' writings in Rome (1687), of the *Moyen court* in France (the *Articles* of Issy, 1695), and of Fénélon's book both at Rome and in France (1699). In fact this avalanche of measures against the 'damnable sloth' corresponded to a lassitude in public opinion, provoked by a rationalist come-back but also by a new conception of holiness. There should be more Marthas and less Marys, or as Fléchier expressed it:

> Passive languours, transports, prayer of ease –
> Not for me refinements such as these . . .
> You contemplatives of heaven born,
> Sharing in the grandeur of God's crown,
> Whom your pure, simple, solemn acts
> Raise above the plain of mortal facts:
> Seek less quiet, look for less excuse

Of Glory, and try to be of use . . .
If the needy world's to have you by,
Get your heads and fancies out the sky;
Thinking, doing things like common folk,
Come down, share the poorer people's yoke.[34]

(c) *Its effectiveness*

The idea of being 'useful' was by no means new to the Roman Church at the beginning of the modern era, but at that time it gained a fresh urgency. The fight against Protestantism, missionary endeavour in Asia, Africa and America, the need to adapt to the mentality and new needs of western man all necessitated a renewal, or better a promotion, of the apostolate, of which St Francis Xavier's brief — ten years — and astonishing missionary career is a significant symbol. He died of exhaustion and fever on the island of Sancian in 1552, when he was getting ready to enter China, but also when his superior, Ignatius of Loyola, was recalling him 'in the name of holy obedience' to entrust him with another mission in Africa. This recall was not in any way a reprimand, although St Francis Xavier's exuberant activity had something of the anarchic about it, but part of a missionary policy. In the Company of Jesus, the only person who, because of his sources of information from the various continents, was in a position to make the best use of the particular skills of the Company's members on the chess-board of the world was the Superior General. And so we find for the first time in Christian history and the history of the apostolate the spirit of organization. Elsewhere[35] we have stressed that this was an enrichment of western man's mental equipment at the start of the modern era. Why did the churches not take full advantage of it? It is true, in an opposite sense, that a person like St Ignatius, with his emphasis on method and organization in the service of the apostolate, must be regarded as one of the chief contributors to the creation of a new mentality.[36] From this point of view one could not insist too strongly on the attention to detail in the *Spiritual Exercises*: the series of examinations of conscience in the first week, the seven double lines on which the penitent is to note his faults point by point, the space given to the procedure of praying with the rhythm of breathing, and so forth. It was a seductive method designed to make its practitioner indifferent to all that is not God, and proved eminently capable of helping still hesitant élite Christians to devote themselves to the active apostolate.[37]

Fortified and confirmed by the *Spiritual Exercises*, the Christian would never, thought Ignatius, abandon his Saviour. Similarly the Jesuit, tested by some fifteen years' formation, would not abandon either his Company or his Church. Ignatius understood much better than most of his contemporaries – and ours – that the Protestant Reformation had been above all the work of churchmen: Luther, Zwingli, Bucer, Oecolampadius, Knox etc. He wanted to form an élite corps that no defection would weaken, and so devised the rule of obedience to the Superior General which has been so often criticized outside the Company, and the special vow of obedience to the pope demanded of the professed. The *Formula instituti*, then, promulgated in a provisional form in 1551, broke with the decentralized and democratic system of the religious orders of the middle ages. Although election was not relinquished entirely, the Company of Jesus was more like a centralized monarchy.

The concern for efficiency, with its corollaries – the desire for method and structure – can be sensed in French Catholicism of the seventeenth century. The Italian Oratories modelled on Philip Neri's Roman Oratory were as many distinct and independent houses as there were groups of priests with the same aims and the same rule. The Bérullian Oratory, on the other hand, was concentrated in the person of its Superior General on whom all the houses of the order depended.

Fifteenth-century Europe witnessed the proliferation of preachers who wandered from one province or country to another exhorting the people to penance. On the one hand they preached mainly in the towns, whereas Europe at that time was basically rural; on the other, because their itinerary was basically the result of successive spot decisions, the missioners rarely kept in touch with the parishes they visited. These mission characteristics had not all, it is true, disappeared in the seventeenth century, but a more rationalized wish to be effective gradually led to a noticeable transformation in missionary policy.[38]

This discipline and method imposed on devotion to a cause was not only to make the service of God more efficient: it was to make the service of man more efficient, too. Admittedly this was not a radical innovation. Art in the fourteenth and fifteenth centuries had exalted the 'works of mercy'. In 1348, at Montpellier, 133 Dominicans out of 140 died of the plague because, if we are to believe the evidence, they had expended themselves in the service of the sick. None the less from the sixteenth century onwards, in Catholic and Protestant countries alike, religious leaders showed more concern than before for man's earthly needs. It was an archbishop, Giovanni della Casa, who in 1558 published a treatise on etiquette – the *Galateo* – which the Jesuits adopted as a manual in their colleges in the following century. All those who were concerned with education, on both sides of the confessional barrier, made it their first concern to form Christians, but they also accorded to education such an importance that Europe had more men of culture from the sixteenth century onwards than any other civilization in the past. When Melanchtron was writing his *Grammar*, the churchmen were turning pedagogue. In the following century, the masters of Port-Royal simultaneously abandoned corporal punishment and wrote some remarkable educational works: a *Logic*, a *General Grammar*, a *Garden of Greek Roots*, and methods for learning Greek, Latin, Italian and Spanish. 1682 is an important date in the history of pedagogy and the rise of primary education, because it was in that year that St John Baptist de la Salle (1651–1719) founded the Institute of the Brothers of the Christian Schools.[39] At first he met with some hostility. Teachers and writers, parish priests, the Châtelet (or the royal Palace of Justice), the Cardinal of Paris Noailles presented a common front against this meek but persistent innovator. Innovator he certainly was, because his idea was to instruct and educate poor children who could not get to any school but a free one. He taught them the rudiments of science and French grammar, and forbade his Brothers to know Latin. He developed in infant schools the class system that had up till then been confined to colleges. For apprentices and adult workers he started 'Sunday schools' where reading, writing, arithmetic and drawing were taught. Finally, he tried to establish 'seminaries for school masters', foreshadowing the *écoles normales*. In 1779 the Institute was teaching 33,000 pupils in 116 different establishments.[40]

Another step forward was that teaching was not confined to boys. In France 1000 schools for girls were opened in the seventeenth century, notably by the different congregations of Ursulines. The Paris congregation, in its constitutions of 1646 and 1705, demanded a fourth vow from its members: that they would devote themselves to the education of girls.[41]

In the period of Tridentine Catholicism, holiness took steps to alleviate physical misery perhaps more than at any time before. This fact of no little importance is to be viewed within the general history of western civilization. St John of God (1495–1550) founded an order of hospitaller brothers, built a hospital at Granada and died a victim of his own selflessness. At Rome, Philip Neri had the novel and gracious idea of setting up a special home for 'the many poor who leave hospital not fully recovered from their illnesses and who need help during their convalescence'.[42] He put them on their feet again and helped them to find work. Still at Rome, at the end of the sixteenth century, a poor priest – the *Letterato* mentioned earlier[43] – took in abandoned boys, and sheltered them in caves. Then, with the healthiest of them, he set himself to sweep the streets in his efforts to earn money, and was finally able to give his boys a roof over their heads. A house similar to the *Letterato*'s but for abandoned girls was opened not long afterwards. In 1600, 370 children in all were being looked after in the two houses.[44]

A colourful but little-known figure must not be allowed to pass unnoticed here when we are considering the changes and new orientations in the apostolate. He was an ex-soldier turned male nurse in Rome, then, at thirty-four, a priest: Camillo de Lellis (1550–1614)[45] – a giant of a man who endured a lot of illness himself and whose familiar companion was physical suffering. Hard on himself, hard on his disciples the 'clerks regular ministers of the infirm', he was gentleness itself with the sick. His usual tool was a broom, because he thought – astonishingly for the age – that hospital wards should be clean.

Concern for hygiene inspired by charity was quite a novelty. One day Camillo forbade a priest of his order to say mass until he had cleaned the glass of one of the patients. Among his recommendations to his nursing brothers we may mention the following: make the beds well, because it is the first comfort a sick person has; change the sheets and body-linen regularly; wash the patients' feet at night-time, their hands before meals, bathe them as often as possible; bring the basin to the bedside so that the patient need not get up, and give him water to rinse his mouth; be there when the doctor calls, to make a note of his prescriptions and tell him something about the patient's condition; keep the different kinds of sick persons separate: those with scabies from those with the plague, those with mental illness from those with fever; organize the turns of duty with punctuality; do not automatically discharge the patients just because they have had no temperature for three days. Like the Ursulines, the Camillians had a fourth vow: that they would devote themselves to the service of the sick and especially the plague-ridden. The nursing brothers had therefore to conserve all their strength for this charitable apostolate. Once, when a young priest took it into his head to sleep on fire-wood for purposes of mortification, Camillo threatened to dismiss him, saying it was of more use to be ready to endure all the labours involved in the care of the sick. The Camillians were to take his message to heart. In 1657, in Naples, ninety-six of them out of a hundred died of the plague; in 1743, at Messina, nineteen out of twenty-five.

Perhaps no less demanding on himself and others, but more relaxed, more balanced, more smiling than Camillo de Lellis, St Vincent de Paul is the perfect prototype of a man born before his time who, with perseverance and intelligence, pioneers new values and methods. More than any of his contemporaries he mastered the art of being charitable with efficiency. The spirit of organization was placed at the service of love. With his first 'charity' at Châtillon-les-Dombes in 1617, he set up a women's confraternity whose members took it in turns, day about, to care for the patients and cook their meals, and he set out a diet for the sick. At Mâcon in 1621, he persuaded a number of well-disposed individuals to guarantee each year a supply of so much wheat, meat, wood and linen for the poor. When later, in Paris, he took in abandoned children who up till then had been but poorly cared for at the '*Couche*' — a crèche run by the chapter of Notre-Dame cathedral — not only did he find money and accommodation, he also worked out an entire rule for the Daughters of Charity who were to be responsible for looking after the children. He provided 'simmered soups' for the infants, and snacks with bread 'and titbits when there are any' for the bigger ones. At five the children would learn to read and write; at twelve they would be found situations as apprentices. When Lorraine was devastated by war in 1635 and after, St Vincent established a central aid committee in Paris, and for seven or eight years this committee organized the transport of food-stuffs, clothing and money into the stricken area. In 1646 the war began to affect Artois, Picardy and Champagne, and St Vincent's efforts were rechannelled into those provinces. One detail reveals the novelty of his ideas on charity: among the items sent to the regions were ploughs and sacks of grain. It was with this enlightened philanthropy in mind that Voltaire wrote in the following century: 'My favourite saint is Vincent de Paul.' St Vincent once told his Daughters of Charity: 'When you leave your prayers for the bedside of a patient, you are leaving God for God. Looking after the sick is praying.'

CHAPTER 4

A WORLD RELIGION

(a) Success

The preceding study on Christian effectiveness and the spirit of method as applied to the apostolate leads us on to the expansion of the Church outside Europe. Was it a success? How far did it reach?

When we ask, Was it a success, the only possible answer must be a resounding Yes. Christianity had never spread so rapidly over such vast areas. Even before the Council of Trent – and this is a point which deserves serious reflexion[1] – Catholic proselytism prepared to conquer the continents that had recently been discovered by western ships and explorers. A religious triumph comparable to the triumph of apostolic times was launched, on the scale not of a Mediterranean empire but of the globe. In the sixteenth and seventeenth centuries, there was a widespread feeling in the Roman Church that the losses due to the Protestant secession were to a large extent compensated by acquisitions beyond the seas. Such feeling was encouraged by the definitive suppression of the Turkish peril in central and eastern Europe. Lepanto (7 October 1571) was the first of the great defeats over the Turks, and the battle of Kahlenberg, just outside Vienna (12 September 1683), marked the beginning of the inevitable Ottoman reflux. Catholics throughout the world glorified the Blessed Virgin who had protected the Christian people, with buildings, paintings, banners and the recitation of the rosary. Instead of being on the defensive against the Turks, the Roman Church took the offensive, spiritually, in the pagan universe that had been brought to light.

1. From Africa to the Philippines

In 1814 Diogo Cão had discovered the mouth of the Zaïre (Congo), and seven years later a Portuguese mission baptized the country's king and queen and their eldest son, who succeeded his father under the name of Don Alfonso and who made every effort to christianize his people. The embassy he sent to Leo X in 1513 has remained famous. His son, Don Henrique, became a priest, and was the first native bishop of black Africa. Towards the middle of the century, the recently arrived Jesuits were baptizing pagans at the rate of 5000 a day. In 1597 Clement VIII created the episcopal see of San Salvador, and his successor ten years later welcomed another Congolese embassy to Rome.

Soon, however, it was Asia even more than Africa that began to attract the Portuguese. Goa was occupied in 1510, and in 1535–7, a vicar general of Goa (which had become a bishopric in 1534) baptized tens of thousands of Indians on the Fishermen's Coast (south-east of the peninsula). This news fired Lisbon with enthusiasm, and encouraged John III to send Francis Xavier. The latter is now emerging from the many pious legends which have for long obscured his real personality.[2] He did not baptize millions of Asians, or even hundreds of thousands, but 30,000 at the most during a harassed apostolate of ten years. He was not gifted language-wise. And the miracles and prophecies attributed to him! Although now demoted from the demigods, Xavier is no less great: his zeal was ardent, his devotion to the cause tireless, and his mind lively: he was able to correct his initial errors and change his method when he left India for Japan. His constant travels over Asia, which his excited letters enabled his European contemporaries, if with some inevitable delay, to follow, astonished the people of his time. When he reached Goa in 1542, he devoted himself in the first place to the Portuguese of the eastern 'little Rome': the sick, the prisoners, merchants and planters. Then, as rapidly as possible, for he had little love for Goa, he left for the Fisheries Coast where the neophytes had been left to their own devices. In 1545 he was at Santo Tomé, near Madras. At the end of that same year, he was at Malacca, from where he embarked for the Maluku Islands. In June 1547 he returned to Malacca, where he met three Japanese whom he took with him to India. The following month he boarded a Chinese junk and sailed to Japan, where he arrived on 15 August and stayed until November 1551. When Ignatius of Loyola appointed him provincial of the Company in India, Xavier returned to Goa via Malacca and Cochin (Kerala). In May 1552 he set off again for Malacca, and then tried to penetrate China, which had always been closed to strangers. He hired a boat to land him secretly on the Chinese coast, but was still waiting two months later to put his plans into operation when he fell ill and died on a deserted island near the Canton river, with only a Chinese cook in attendance (December 1552). He was forty-six years old. This ten-year apostolate aroused admiration – of the orientalist Guillaume Postel, for example – and vocations.

When they settled on the Indian coasts, the Portuguese rediscovered the Christians of St Thomas – about 30,000 families scattered about the villages of the eastern Ghats – whom travellers in previous centuries had sometimes mentioned. This community, who traced their evangelization back to apostolic times, was of Syrian rite. The new hierarchy centred on Goa tried to absorb and Latinize it in the synod of 1599 and by creating the episcopal see of Cranganor: whence the seventeenth-century schism among the 'Syrians' of India. Successes, however, compensated for this near-failure. At Goa 'the Golden', the seat of an archdiocese since 1558, there were some 13,000 indigenous Christians in 1560, and forty years later the Jesuits counted 35,000 faithful on the neighbouring island of Saletta. Provincial councils were held in 1567, 1575, 1585, 1592 and 1606 at Goa, and the Goanese territory, in 1656, comprised eighty-five parishes, twenty-six of them run by Indian clergy.

Outside the Indian territories actually administered by the Portuguese, the missionaries of the sixteenth century succeeded in converting certain castes en bloc – the Paravers from the Fishermen's Coast, the Makuas from southern Kerala – although they were inferior castes. The Italian Jesuit Roberto de' Nobili (1577–1656) tried to convert the Brahmins. He arrived at Madurai, inland from the Fishermen's Coast, in 1606, learnt Sanskrit, lived as a Hindu penitent (*sanyassi*), and argued with his distinguished listeners. In the course of his long career, although contested by some of the Brahmins, and denounced to Rome as a pagan, he gained the support of Gregory XV and all told made some 4,000 converts. As well as these missionaries specialized in an apostolate among the Brahmins (*sanyassi*), there were *pandaras* missionaries, that is, penitents of the class immediately below the Brahmins but able, with precautions, to talk to the inferior castes. The most active of them was the Portuguese Juan de Britto, who arrived at Madurai in 1673 at the age of twenty-six. His apostolate in a region ravaged by the Mahrattas, famine and the plague, was heroic. Welcomed by some of the princes, envied and detested by others, he was arrested several times and eventually died a martyr's death in 1693. In twenty years he effected thousands of conversions. At the close of the seventeenth century, there were about 800,000 Christians in India and Sri Lanka (Ceylon), 100,000 of them St Thomas Christians, 150,000 in Madurai, 100,000 in Ceylon.

Francis Xavier's greatest success was probably introducing

Christianity into Japan, even though the Christian community there did not number more than 1000 faithful when he left. In the following half-century, the number grew rapidly. In 1563, a southern daimyo was baptized, to be followed shortly after by others. Progress was no less rapid in the central provinces, and by 1559 there was a Jesuit at Kyoto where Francis Xavier had been unable to go. Twenty years later the most powerful feudal families of Japan had become favourably disposed to Christianity. A 'great admiral' and a cavalry general became Christians. In 1582 four young noblemen from Kyushu left Nagasaki as Japanese 'ambassadors' to Europe. They were received by Philip II and Gregory XIII, inspiring the liveliest curiosity on their way. In the last decade of the sixteenth century, the archipelago numbered at least 300,000 Christians. The most optimistic went so far as to predict the imminent mass conversion of the Japanese people. The baptized were especially numerous in the north and west of Kyushu, round Hiroshima, in the Osaka-Kyoto region and round Yedo (Tokyo).[3] Several factors favoured this rapid spread of Christianity: the decadence of Buddhism, the slackness and greed of its clergy compared with the disinterest, humility and gentleness of the missionaries; the prestige enjoyed by the first Europeans among a people avid for novelty who admired their boats, their clocks ... and their cannons; the feebleness of the central power which left the daimyos full freedom to be converted; and when the daimyos were baptized, they seem to have affirmed their independence all the more.

In the second half of the sixteenth century, Christianity spread in the Philippines even more quickly than it had done in Japan. The islands were occupied by Admiral Legaspi from Mexico in 1564–5. And from Mexico too came large numbers of religious – Augustinians, then Franciscans, Jesuits and Dominicans – who evangelized the archipelago. The local animism yielded without a struggle to the zeal of the missioners who instituted an 'opulent' Catholicism which with its dances, feasts and processions enraptured the population. In 1585 there were already 400,000 neophytes, in 1591 700,000, and in 1620 no less than two million.[4] Manila, an episcopal see from 1579, became an archbishopric in 1595 with three suffragan dioceses. A Catholic nation had been born in the Far East.

2. China

China, however, confronted Christianity for almost the whole of the sixteenth century with the sheer mass of its population (possibly 75,000,000 in 1575)[5] and the blank wall of its culture. Nevertheless the Portuguese had obtained permission, in 1557, to settle on the Macao peninsula, not far from where Francis Xavier had died, although the Canton mandarins refused to allow them, even temporarily, on the mainland. It was the Italian Matteo Ricci who forced an entry into the Celestial Empire.[6] He learnt Chinese, presented himself as a 'wise man from the west', charmed the people by his modesty and kindness, and astonished them with his knowledge of mathematics and astronomy and his skill in making clocks and maps. He adopted a Chinese name, Chinese dress and a Chinese lifestyle. In 1583 the 'foreign magician' was allowed to settle in the north of Kwangtung, then at Nanking, and finally, in 1601, at Peking itself, where he died nine years later. The ground for his burial was donated by the emperor. Ricci had done his utmost to bridge the gap between the Gospel message and the eclecticism favoured by the Chinese educated classes. His most notable effort in this direction was a Christian catechism preceded by a long philosophical introduction (*A True Disputation about God*) which became one of the classics of Chinese literature. At his death there were some 2500 baptized Christians in the empire, sprinkled along the fluvial Canton–Peking road, members chiefly of the educated classes.

Chinese Christianity in the seventeenth century had a number of difficulties to cope with, quite apart from the exhausting and painful dispute over rites which we shall have occasion to mention more fully later on. The death of Ricci was followed by an anti-Christian reaction set in motion by one of the senior mandarins. Several of the missionaries were driven back to Macao. This first storm died down, but in 1644 the Ming dynasty collapsed under the attacks of the Manchu: Christian evangelization had more often than not benefited from imperial benevolence and the support of the intellectual élite who surrounded the emperor, and the fall of the Mings meant that Chinese Christianity lost a sizeable fraction of its leading laity. This trial, however, was overcome by virtue mainly of the 'Peking Fathers' who managed to gain the favour of the new Ts'ing dynasty. In 1657 freedom of worship was recognized throughout the empire. The premature death of the Manchu emperor Shunti (1661) resulted in a reverse initiated by the regents responsible for the government during the minority of K'ang Hsi. Christians were executed, missionaries transported to Canton (1665) and placed under house arrest. When K'ang Hsi came of age, however, he had the regents tried and recalled the Canton internees from exile (1671). In 1692, as a gesture of gratitude for a cure effected by a French Jesuit (who administered quinine), he authorized the public preaching of the Gospel throughout the empire.

A word more must be said on the extraordinary influence of the Peking Jesuits. In 1622, the German missionary Johann Adam Schall von Bell arrived in the capital. He was a man of a somewhat rigid turn of mind but exceptional scientific ability. The emperor T'ienk'i entrusted him with the management of an observatory and the reform of the calendar. He became technical defence adviser to the Ming emperors at Peking, and the Ts'ing conquerors asked him to stay on and work out the calendar of the new dynasty. He was promoted to mandarin first class. His successor as president of the Board of Astronomers was another Jesuit, the Flem Ferdinand Verbiest, 'a veritable universal genius', who was at once mathematician, engineer and translator of St Thomas Aquinas into Chinese. Verbiest died in 1688, but the year previously five French Jesuits, 'mathematicians of king Louis XIV', had arrived in China. Until its suppression the Company of Jesus retained the management of the imperial observatory. The prestige of the 'Peking Fathers' had enabled Chinese Christianity to gather weight, modestly but substantially. As the seventeenth century drew to its close, there were some 200,000 neophytes in the empire, although – and this was a matter of concern for the future – very few of them were either Manchus or great scholars. They were divided into three dioceses (Macao, Nanking and Peking) and five vicariates under the control of the *Propaganda* congregation. In 1701, 117 missionaries ran 114 houses and 244 churches or oratories, Jesuits being the most prominent with fifty per cent of the missioners, sixty-one per cent of the missions, and eighty-five per cent of the churches and oratories.

3.   Indo-China

In Indo-China Christianity did not really take root until the seventeenth century. After the settlements in Malacca (1511), merchants and a few clandestine missionaries landed on the coasts of the peninsula. In the sixteenth century this resulted only in some isolated conversions. When, however, the persecution hit Japan in 1597 – more will be said on this shortly – European missioners and Japanese Christians fled to Indo-China. The apostolate of the Jesuits began in 1615 in Cochin China, where twelve years later there were 2000 Christians, and in 1626 at Tonking. As in Japan, the missionaries learnt the local language and transcribed its sounds with the help of the Roman alphabet. The Avignonnais Jesuit Alexandre de Rhodes (1591–1660) reached Macao in 1623, and from there was sent to Cochin China and then Tonking; he may be compared with Ricci and Nobili. He had no difficulty in learning the language of the country, and quickly established friendly relations with the educated classes and the monarchy, whom he astounded with his knowledge of astronomy. He was a victim of the intermittent persecutions which ravaged the peninsula for three centuries. Expelled from north and south, he was obliged to mark time for ten years at Macao, but 'China's Father' had got some astonishing results: he had opened a church in Hanoi in 1627, preached before vast crowds, baptized 6700 neophytes in the first three years of his apostolate in Tonking, and most importantly trained catechists who could replace the missioners whenever they had to flee or hide. Did the Christians in Tonking number 300,000 in the middle of the seventeenth century, as Alexandre de Rhodes claimed when he returned to Rome in 1649? The figure would seem to be on the large side, even though reports to the general of the Company of Jesus talked in terms of 100 baptisms a month and 200 churches in the kingdom. For Cochin China the estimate of 60,000 baptized made in 1679 by the vicar apostolic Lambert de La Motte seems probable.

At Rome Alexandre de Rhodes explained that the Christians in Tonking needed at least 300 priests, that it was neither possible nor desirable for the majority of these to be Europeans, and that therefore bishops must be sent to Indo-China to ordain the better catechists. *Propaganda* delegated him to recruit some zealous priests to leave for the Far East as vicars apostolic. He went to Paris where devout circles were active, generous and influential. He came to know one of the numerous pious groups in the capital, the *Bons Amis* (Good Friends), and there made the acquaintance of François Pallu, a young canon of Tours who had, like St Ignatius, offered his life 'for the salvation of souls and the conversion of the pagans'. Pallu agreed to go, and took with him his friend Lambert de La Motte, a former lawyer at the Tax Court in Normandy. The two were nominated vicars apostolic in 1658. Lambert de La Motte sailed in 1660. Pallu stayed behind for two years to establish the Seminary for Foreign Missions, which he did with the help of the Company of the Blessed Sacrament. This was an initiative of great importance, because the seminary was the first society of secular priests to cater exclusively for missions outside Europe. The intention was to train not propagandists for the faith, but 'instructors of native candidates for the priesthood',[7] so that a native clergy and hierarchy could be constituted as soon as possible. The new institution signalled France's great entry into the work of evangelization overseas.

Lambert de La Motte could not proceed immediately to Annam, so went instead to Thailand (Siam) where the king had authorized the setting-up of *camps*, which meant concessions for the various European countries who were trading with Siam. When the famous Siamese embassy came to Louis XIV (1685–6), it was widely believed in France and at Rome that this eastern kingdom was swinging over to Catholicism. It did not. Lambert de La Motte had founded at Ayuthia (Bangkok) the Seminary of St Joseph which offered French priests in Indo-China a base and trained hundreds of native priests from eastern and south-eastern Asia over the centuries, not without troubles.[8] It is unquestionably because of these indigenous cadres that Christianity in Indo-China was able to survive and increase. In 1667 there were already nine Tonkingese priests who held a synod in that year with Lambert de La Motte and three other missioners. Important decisions were taken on the distribution of the clergy among the towns, the duty of the catechists, the choice of some of the faithful in each Christian group to direct the prayers, the distribution of income and alms between the clergy and good works, and the status of women and girls who wanted to consecrate themselves to God. The latter were to take the three usual vows, to live in small communities, to instruct children, to care for the (female) sick, to administer baptisms in urgent cases. These 'Lovers of the Cross' dedicated themselves tirelessly to their work, notably during the persecutions in both Tonking (1696, 1713, 1721, 1735, 1773–5) and Cochin China (beginning of the eighteenth century, 1720–6, 1750). At the end of the eighteenth century, a political crisis broke out and lasted for thirty years, and the inhabitants of Tây Son revolted: nearly half the Christians perished, either by enemy action, or by starvation, or by poverty; others apostasized; convents were broken up, places of worship destroyed. With the victory of Gia-Long, calm returned. He united the country and became emperor in 1806. He owed a great deal to the vicar apostolic in Indo-China, Mgr Pigneau de Béhaine, with whom he had found help and refuge, and so was tolerant of Christianity. Christians in Indo-China were able to recoup their strength . . . only to meet new calvaries.

4. The Americas

(i) The Antilles, Mexico, central America
The results in Asia were limited if encouraging. In America, however, there was a series of grandiose religious conquests, although the beginnings in the Antilles were modest enough. The first mass celebrated in the New World was at Haiti (then called Hispaniola), on the feast of the Epiphany 1494, but evangelization did not really start until the Franciscans sent a mission from Europe in 1500. Round Hispaniola the first Castillian empire in America developed rapidly between 1509 and 1513,

MAP I: Archdioceses and dioceses in North and South America (16th and 17th centuries)

taking in some 300,000 km², including Porto Rico, Cuba, Jamaica, and on the continent the Panama isthmus. Franciscans and Dominicans flourished. An ecclesiastical hierarchy was definitively established in the Antilles in 1511, and a bishop installed at Darien, on the continent, in 1513. It was above all the Spanish penetration into the interior of the American continent, starting with Cortez' expedition of 1519, that inspired the conquistadors with the physical and spiritual energy to carry their evangelization further. Another favourable factor was that the indigenous population of the Antilles dropped catastrophically, to be gradually replaced by blacks, and it was with these more than the Caribbeans themselves, and with the European colonists, that the missionaries dealt particularly. In the seventeenth and eighteenth centuries there was no bishopric in the French Antilles, and there were no companies of priests. The Jesuits, Dominicans and Capuchins were especially active. A report from 1785–6 mentions 170 missioners, but at that time there were 400,000 blacks in San Domingo, 90,000 in Guadeloupe, and 84,000 in Martinique. The missionaries tried to establish contact with the slaves as soon as they were landed, and then catechized them when they had been dispersed to their owners. Although in this way they contacted easily enough those who lived in the family of a master, they found it much more difficult to reach those who worked in the plantations or sugar mills and the quite large class of runaway slaves (maroons). The French Antilles did not have the Christian settlements that Paraguay and the North American Indians had. Even so, the whole of the Caribbean became – officially – Christian between 1500 and 1800.

The most resounding successes for the Catholic Church in the sixteenth century were in Mexico. Evangelization followed hot on the heels of conquest. Cortez wanted methodical Christianization, and he pestered Charles V for missionaires. The Franciscans came first (1523), then the Dominicans (1526) and then the Augustinians (1533). Before the Jesuits arrived in 1572, the evangelization of Mexico depended essentially on these three religious families. The extraordinarily high number of baptisms can be explained by the ardour of these friars, who for the most part belonged to the reformed branches of their respective orders, and the rapid collapse of local civilizations.

A letter from Juan de Zumarrago, the first bishop of Mexico, to the general Franciscan chapter at Toulouse (June 1531) mentions more than a million pagan converts in New Spain (Mexico) since 1524. A similar figure was given by another Franciscan, Martin de Valence, in a letter he wrote to Charles V in 1532. A much more spectacular account is given by Toribio de Benavente, called *Motolinia* (=the poor one) by the Indians; he calculated five million Indians baptized between 1524 and 1536.[9]

These mass conversions explain Paul III's Bull *Sublimis Deus* (1537), in which the pope, standing up for the Indians against the brutal and rapacious colonialists, wrote: 'We consider . . . that they really are men, and not only capable of understanding the Catholic religion but according to our information exceedingly desirous of embracing it'.[10]

According to R. Ricard, the year 1572, the date when the first Jesuits arrived, marks the end of the 'primitive' or 'medieval' evangelization of Mexico. Another style took over. A regular religious life settled in in New Spain during the first century of Christianization. The territory of the viceroyalty included, in 1600, a university (erected in 1553), an archbishopric, both in Mexico, and nine bishoprics controlling the *doctrinas* or Christianized Indian villages. In the villages the pastors, who were usually religious, were frequently in charge of Spanish parishes as well. At the beginning of the seventeenth century, the Franciscans had two hundred convents, the Dominicans ninety, the Augustinians sixty-six. The Jesuits made rapid progress: they had 107 in 1580, 345 in 1603, and by this latter date had already founded six colleges in Mexico.

South of the line Tampico–Zacatecas–Mazatlau, religious life assumed daily rhythm from the end of the sixteenth century, but to the north of it expansion continued, although more slowly than at the time of the great conquest. New governments appeared at New Biscay (1562), New León (1579), New Mexico (1598), Coahuila (1687), Texas (1718), Sinaloa (1734), New Santander (1746) and California (1767). The progress of the missioners which coincided with the new administrative networks was on two axes: a mainly Jesuit one towards the north-west and California, and a mainly Franciscan one towards the north-east. In 1624, in Sinaloa, the Jesuits ministered to more than 80,000 baptized Christians. When they were expelled in 1767, they had twenty-two mission centres as well as thirteen in Sonora and twenty-five in Pimeria. They did not begin their apostolate in California until 1697. The country seemed impenetrable, the Indians were nomadic and at first hostile. The tenacity of the Company was rewarded: between 1697 and 1766 they founded seventeen mission posts of 'reductions' up as far as the thirty-first parallel north. When they were recalled, the Californian basin was handed over to the Dominicans, and the territory north of San Diego to the Franciscans, who recovered their strength in the early part of the sixteenth century. By 1800 they had founded some twenty *doctrinas* (representing 30,000 Christians) in north California.

Ten Franciscans accompanied Oñate on his military expedition to New Mexico (1598). At first the Christianization programme met success: a convent was built in 1622, and there were 80,000 baptisms by 1630. Then the Apaches twice revolted, once in 1680 (when twenty-six missionaries and 16,000 Christians were massacred) and again in 1696. The programme had to start again from scratch. The Apaches were evangelized in the middle of the eighteenth century, and in 1775 the Franciscan missions in New Mexico were joined with the missions in California. In Texas, where missions did not begin until the opening decade of the eighteenth century, accounts from 1787 enumerate twenty-eight central stations and thirty-four *pueblos* or villages: the Franciscans had been as energetic here as elsewhere. Their Florida mission, on the other hand (forty-four stations and 30,000 baptized in 1634), was wiped out in an Apache revolt in 1657, and not restored.

(ii)   South of Panama

When Mexico and its dependencies were scarcely occupied at all, a descent on Peru began from Panama, and a vaster empire than the first was annexed in no time. Conversions were not so swift as in Mexico, the Indians being more varied, more reticent, secretive and unstable, but the sixteenth-century missioners were as active as ever. The Dominicans, who provided the first bishop of Cuzco, were the founders of the Peruvian Church and the University of Lima (1557). In 1544 there were 155 Dominicans on what had formerly been the Inca empire, but they spread south only slowly. The Franciscans, who had arrived shortly after the Dominicans, immediately established three convents at Quito, Cuzco and Lima, and then continued on to La Plata, Potosi, La Paz, Tucuman and Paraguay. The Mercedarians and the Augustinians both had provinces in Peru. The Jesuits, who arrived late in Lima (1568), made progress, creating Jesuit provinces in Peru, at Quito, in New Granada, Paraguay and Chile, and establishing themselves at Santa Cruz, Tucuman and La Plata, trying all the time to set up indigenous parishes.

By about 1575, a regular ecclesiastical organization covered the immense Spanish empire on the South American continent. The metropolitan of Lima was responsible for ten enormous dioceses stretching from Nicaragua to Chile and from Quito to Ascuncion. Cathedral chapters and secular clergy were being organized, and provincial councils were held at Lima in 1552, 1567, 1583 and 1601. Of these the most important was that of 1583, presided over by the saintly bishop Toribio de Mogrovejo[11] – an apostle who learnt Quechua and died during one of his numerous pastoral visits. In 1594 he told Philip II in a letter that he had already confirmed 500,000 people. The council of 1583 decided that there would be one priest for *doctrinas* of 1000 to 2000 inhabitants, and two for *doctrinas* of over 2000; and it issued a catechism graded to three different levels. The first period of evangelization in the

Spanish empire of South America closed with the death of Toribio de Mogrovejo in 1606.

This does not mean that missionary effort and heroism declined. On the northern and southern borders of what had been the Inca empire, Franciscan houses were apparently flourishing until they were swept away in the Indian revolts between the end of the seventeenth century and 1742, and religious were massacred by the score. The rest of the eighteenth century was spent in reconstruction. In Chile too where evangelization began in 1641, there were revolts in 1673 and 1766, and decisive progress was hampered until the last twelve years of the eighteenth century. New Granada, whose dioceses were all set up between 1531 and 1564, and which at the end of the sixteenth century totalled 300 Indian churches, was still in dire need of the apostolate of religious. Mendicant friars and Jesuits carried on rival missions in the seventeenth century. Where the holy Dominican friar Louis Bertrand had laboured, baptizing thousands of Indians in Colombia in 1562–9, St Peter Claver, the Jesuit apostle of Cartago, took over in the following century. Evangelization proceeded in the seventeenth century into Llanos and the Orinoco territories, but the most surprising and successful of the missionary experiences was in the Christian republic of the Guarani Indians, created by the Jesuits on the banks of the Parana. The Guaranis had been scattered to the east of the Andes cordillera, over a territory the size of Europe. Although less civilized than the Aztecs and Incas, they could cultivate the land, spin, weave, make pottery, do wicker-work and use rubber. They were clean, gentle and sociable as well as brave. They offered their god no sacrifice, and had no clergy.[12] To protect the Guaranis from slave-hunting Europeans, to give them the benefits of city life and to facilitate their Christianization, the superior general of the Jesuits, Fr Aquaviva, obtained from Philip III in 1609 the concession of an autonomous territory flanking the Parana. The first community – Loreto – was founded in 1610 with 200 baptized Indian families. These were soon joined by the inhabitants of twenty-three villages in their neighbourhood. Reductions multiplied: thirteen in 1623, thirty-four in 1630 with nearly 100,000 inhabitants in all.

Abundant and savage opposition was not long in coming. Portuguese and Spanish settlers attacked these oases of peace and prosperity from the east from 1628, devastating whole cultures, massacring the recalcitrant and deporting prisoners. Some 12,000 refugees in 1631 and 1638–9 sought shelter to the west near the communities of the Entro-Rios (between Uruguay and Parana) which had been spared. The territory of Guaira, to the north-east, had to be abandoned, although in 1639 Philip IV authorized the Jesuits to buy fire-arms for the Guaranis, and two years later the Indians defeated the Portuguese from São Paulo. In 1649 Madrid recognized the frontiers of the new state, and neither Spanish military nor Spanish functionaries were to be allowed into the territory. Despite this a tribute was to be paid to the Catholic king. From then on the Guarani republic covered territory as large as half the British Isles, and was regrouped into a federation of thirty reductions: eight in what is now Paraguay, seven in what is now Brazil and fifteen in what is now the Argentine. The capital was Yapezu (or Los Reyes). The population fluctuated between 150,000 and 200,000. In the eighteenth century, 15,000 km^2 were won to the north, and three new communities created to help those the Jesuits were then establishing in Bolivia: to the south-east among the Chiquitos (twenty reductions, 90,000 inhabitants), and to the north among the Moxas and the Bauru (sixteen reductions, 60,000 inhabitants).

Two religious with a council of elected elders were in charge of each reduction. The population was grouped into agglomerations of several thousand inhabitants, and the streets were straight, wide and often paved. Round the *plaza mayor* – the square at San Ignacio Mini was 127 m by 108 m – were ranged the church, the cemetery, the school, the hospital, the town-hall etc. Education was compulsory. At school the native language was taught. Great importance was given to sport, feast-days and the theatre. The death penalty was unknown. All the houses were alike. There were no rich and no poor, no wages and no money. Everything was held in common. Accommodation was provided for young married couples, while widows and single women were lodged in a special quarter of the reduction. The orchards were planted with oranges, pine-apples, peaches and pomegranates, while in the fields sugar-cane, cotton, tobacco and especially maté, their main export, were grown. There was textile manufacture and a little iron-work. The Guaranis had become capable clock-makers, and used printing-presses. They had acquired a knowledge of the most sophisticated musical notation of the time, and played the finest French, Italian and German music 'elegantly, artistically and agreeably'. Their churches, wrote a traveller, 'compare favourably with the finest in Spain or Peru, for structural beauty as much as for the richness and good taste of their silverwork and of all the different kinds of ornaments'.[13] Montesquieu, Voltaire, d'Alembert, Lafargue (Marx's son-in-law) and Plekhanov all praised this Christian republic which had perhaps been inspired by the works of Plato and the Renaissance 'Utopias'.[14]

Unlike the Spanish New World, the Portuguese New World was slow 'to establish and delineate itself'.[15] Even at the end of the sixteenth century, it totalled no more than 30,000 whites, 18 or 19,000 Indians and

14,000 blacks.[16] Until 1640 there was a single diocese – Bahia – set up in 1551. The foundation dates of the other dioceses, in the seventeenth and eighteenth centuries, mark the growth of Brazil's sugar and mining industry in which neither France nor Holland had been able to hold their ground: 1676 (Rio de Janeiro), 1677 (Pernambuco and São Luís do Maranhão), 1720 (Belem), 1745 (São Paulo, and Mariana= Minas Geraes). Here again the Jesuits were the mainstay of the missionary effort, and in some sense can be considered the real creators of Brazil.[17] So, for example, we can say that the beginning of Brazilian history coincided with the beginning of its Christian history: the arrival in 1549 of the first Jesuits under Manuel de Nobrega and their foundation five years later of São Paulo, a catechetical centre near the villages in which they had grouped the Indians. The method of evangelizing and protecting the natives owed a great deal to the methods pioneered in Paraguay. Fr Anchieta (d.1597) was the author of a Tupi-Guarani grammar and dictionary. Hymns and catechisms were translated into the local language. The fathers created *aldeas*, which were Indian villages like the reductions, administering their own affairs under the Jesuits' watchful eye. In Brazil, too, they had to arm the natives so that they could defend themselves against slave-hunters, in particular the *bandeirantes*[18] from São Paulo. In the seventeenth century the Jesuit protector of the Indians who impresses us most was Fr Vieira, who had previously been Portuguese ambassador to the courts of England, Holland, France and the Vatican.[19] Between 1652 and 1658 he organized some fifty villages up and down 1500 km of coastline. He signed treatises of friendship with Indians who were still free, and tried to obtain from the colonialists and the king an improvement in the conditions of those who worked on the sugar-plantations. His only reward was to be dragged before the Inquisition, imprisoned and repatriated. However, at seventy-three he set off for Brazil again, and died in Amazonas at eighty-nine (1697). After his death, unable to prevent the continuing slavery the Jesuits in Brazil had to be content to apply the 'politics of the possible'.

(iii) North America
In 1790 there were seven archbishoprics, thirty-six bishoprics, more than 70,000 churches and at least 850 convents in Mexico and South America, while north of the Rio Grande there were only two episcopal sees: Quebec (since 1674) and Baltimore, recently founded (1790). In both New France (=French Canada) and the British colonies in America, the Catholic Church had a modest and difficult start.

The first date is 1603, the year of the first French settlement in Acadia (Nova Scotia and New Brunswick) and Champlain's first voyage to

Canada. In Acadia the reformed Franciscans, the Jesuits and the Capuchins contacted the peaceful Algonquin tribes who showed no hostility to the hundreds of Norman peasant families who were gradually settling on the continent. The Capuchin-run Franco-Indian schools did quite well, the main difficulty being the British who occupied the colony from 1654 to 1670 and then took it over altogether in 1713. Catholicism, which was looked on as part of the French settlements, was viewed with suspicion, indeed persecuted. During the Seven Years' War, there were mass deportations of French settlers to British territories: it was the *Grand dérangement*. However, the Treaty of Paris (1763) and the *Act of Quebec* (1774) gave religious freedom to the Acadians who had stayed or returned to the province, and to the Canadians.

In Canada, where Champlain founded Quebec in 1605, the reformed Franciscans (recollects) arrived in 1615 and the Jesuits ten years later. Both applauded Richelieu's plan of bringing 4000 settlers, all of them Catholic, to Canada (for which purpose he set up the so-called *Compagnie des cent associés,* 1627). For the time the project was somewhat ambitious, especially as the English occupied Quebec from 1629 to 1632. In 1660, the 'New France of America' – Canada and Acadia combined – totalled no more than 2000 settlers. They were faced with 100,000 Algonquins, 10 or 12,000 Huron Indians, and 20,000 Iroquois. The Jesuits, who arrived in force from 1632 onwards (fifty-four of them between 1632 and 1637), tried, under the intelligent leadership of Fr Lejeune, to Christianize and settle the semi-nomad tribes, while the Ursulines (including Mary of the Incarnation)[20] and the Hospitallers undertook the education of the children and the care of the sick and infirm, while the men were away hunting. With the Hurons and several Algonquin tribes they were very successful, but from 1642 to 1665, when the Carignan-Salières Regiment arrived, French and Huron Indians were forced into an exhausting struggle with the British-armed Iroquois. Jesuits died under the most atrocious tortures,[21] Christian villages were burned down, the Hurons were decimated. Montreal was founded in 1642 straight down the St Lawrence to the south-west, in a rather isolated position.

The heroic period came to an end in 1665: the troops managed to keep the Iroquois down from that year, and an administration was set up with a bishop, a governor, an administrator and a sovereign council. The bishop from 1674 (before that he was a vicar apostolic) was Mgr de Montmorency-Laval, a man of somewhat inflexible temperament, who, with support from the Jesuits, was at loggerheads with the Sulpicians supported in their turn by the archbishop of Rouen. He resigned, discouraged, in 1684. His successors were but intermittently resident docile functionaries.

If the Christian population increased, it was less because of conversions among the natives – the number of natives baptized at the end of the eighteenth century was hardly more than 2000 – than by a growth in the number of French Canadians: 16,000 in 1700, 70,000 in 1760: a sturdy population, immune to the 'enlightenment' of the eighteenth century, to whom England, although victorious, was obliged to concede 'free practice of the faith of the Church of Rome' in 1774.

The region of the Great Lakes and the immense prairies between it and the Gulf of Mexico were at first the hinterland of Canada, the departure point of a number of expeditions: Perrot's towards Lake Superior (1672), Du Luth's towards the upper Missouri (1680), Joliet's to the Mississippi which it reached in 1673, and Cavelier de La Salle's which went down the Mississippi and discovered Louisiana in 1682. Missionary endeavour remained extremely desultory in this huge area, partly because the Indians were not very numerous. On the east coast, on the other hand, which was inhabited by the British, Catholic nuclei managed to take root and survive in Protestant territory; in 1785 they numbered 16,000 in Maryland, 7000 in Pennsylvania and 1500 in New York. True, this was only one Catholic for every 115 inhabitants, but in 1789 an ex-Jesuit, John Carroll, was appointed bishop of Baltimore, and with him the Catholic community in the United States, which was then of the most meagre proportions but facing a great future, took its own destiny in hand.

(b) Difficulties and relapses

1. Africa and the Near East

Between 1500 and 1800, fifty-five dioceses and ten archdioceses were established in America (forty-three and seven of each respectively),[22] and Asia (twelve and three),[23] and a score of vicariates apostolic. These figures prove the worldwide spread of Catholicism in that great age of Christianization, the sixteenth and seventeenth centuries. But there were many disillusionments, unfulfilled hopes, and brutal and dramatic relapses in the course of it.

In the Congo, the king Don Alfonso died circa 1545, discouraged by the increasing negro traffic, the mediocrity of the missioners and the inter-Portuguese quarrelling. An embassy to Rome in 1607 from a Congolese prince should not give a false impression. The Jesuits had withdrawn in 1555, and as the poor cousin in the Lusitanian empire, the colony sank into a dangerous economic and political situation; ancestral superstitions regained the upper hand over an ill-assimilated Christianity. In the seventeenth century, São Paulo de Loanda (capital of Angola) took over from San Salvador (in the Congo) as the religious metropolis of Portuguese Africa. At that time Angola was gaining in importance because of the slave-trade. Even here, however, Christianization was superficial. The too few missionaries merely scratched the surface of a vast, poor and impenetrable country; their role was scarcely more than that of chaplains to the Portuguese. In Monomotapa, a country to the south of the Zambesi (its capital today would be Zimbabwe) which was supposed to be rich in gold, a Jesuit apparently made many converts in 1560, before being assassinated. Some Dominicans replaced him in 1577 and some Jesuits returned, but they were able to establish only a small Christian community which vegetated until the nineteenth- and twentieth-century (re-)colonization. The main opposition came from Islam, which was spread by the Arab traders and became the major obstacle to Christian penetration over a large part of Africa. The French attempts at evangelization in Senegal and Madagascar in the seventeenth and eighteenth centuries may also be mentioned in passing. Because of the lack of men and means, the Lazarists were unable to retain their footing in Africa, and were more successful in smaller places like Réunion Island and Maurice Island. It is not therefore an exaggeration to speak of Christian failure in Africa prior to 1800. Would matters have been changed if Ethiopa – the fabulous kingdom of Prester John – had rallied to Rome? In 1545, threatened by Islam, the negus offered to recognize the pope, and via the king of Portugal asked for a patriarch. Ignatius of Loyola set the highest store by this move: he thought of Ethiopia as the reservoir from which rivers of grace would flow down over Africa. But there was delay in the appointment of a patriarch, the negus changed his mind, and the country – already cut off in the middle of the Islamic world – was closed to missionaries.

There was partial failure, too, in the Near East. The capture of Constantinople in 1543 meant the end of the (admittedly precarious) Union concluded by the Latin Church and the Greek emperor at Florence in 1439. The victorious Turks played the card of orthodoxy against Rome. By rights the Byzantine patriarch was the sole representative of the Christians with the sultan. The confiscation of numerous churches, including the most famous of them all Santa Sophia, the loss of Rhodes in 1522, of Cyprus in 1571 – the year of Lepanto – and of Crete in 1669 were so many reverses for Christianity. Still the sultans needed French cooperation in the Mediterranean, and the very Christian king protected the communities at Rome, which succeeded in surviving, in fact growing. The French consuls had an eye not only to trade. François Picquet (1626–85), the son of a banker, was a defender of the Maronites at Aleppo. He became a priest and died on the way to Baghdad where he had been appointed vicar apostolic. As 'consular protégés', the missionaries were free to travel or settle in the empire. The Franciscans remained 'guardians' of the Holy Places. The Carmelites, who had left the east after the crusades, returned at the end of the sixteenth century. The Jesuits established themselves at Istanbul in 1609, at Aleppo in 1625, at Damascus in 1644, at Sidon and Tripoli in 1645, at Ain-Toura in 1657, at Cairo in 1696. On the initiative of Fr Joseph, the Capuchins founded convents at Aleppo, Sidon, Damascus, Mosul and Diarkebir from 1625. The eighteenth century saw the Dominicans settling at Mosul (1750), and the Lazarists taking over from the Jesuits at Aleppo (1783).

The Maronite church enjoyed both consular protection and missionary support. Even without these it had its own dynamism, and in the seventeenth and eighteenth centuries, with all these advantages, it grew. It profited by the autonomy then enjoyed by the Lebanon and Syria under local dynasties, in particular the Chehabs. The patriarchs encouraged the establishment of convents and schools; a seminary was founded in 1789. The Lebanese coasts and mountains welcomed Catholics from the whole of the east. The Lebanese example was a factor in the attraction to Rome felt by certain Melkites[24] at that time from Antioch, Jerusalem and Alexandria. Unionist tendencies came to the fore, and a Catholicizing party emerged at the beginning of the eighteenth century. The only result, however, was a schism in 1724, and the Melkite church split into two branches, the orthodox and the uniate. At the end of the seventeenth century, the Maronites, missionaries and the consul François Picquet succeeded in starting a unionist movement among the monophysite Jacobites in north Syria and Mosul; but because of persecution it had scarcely developed at all by 1790. It did not gather momentum and begin to organize itself until the nineteenth century. The Nestorian[25] churches of Mesopotamia (Iraq) and the Coptic church of Egypt spent the entire period we are studying eyeing Rome distrustfully.

From Egypt we pass to India: and all in all the statistics are of the most modest. Goa, it is true, possessed rich churches, a cathedral, convents, a college, an Inquisition tribunal, but behind the Portuguese establishments (several of which anyway were seized by the Dutch in the seventeenth century) the interior of India was hardly touched. What were 800,000 Christians – an optimistic figure for 1680 – in the human ocean of over 100,000,000 Indians?[26] The Jesuits, who were invited to the court of Akbar at the end of the sixteenth century, were well received and the Grand Mogul showed interest, but they gained not a single convert. Ceylon was another disappointment. From when the Dutch took the island over in 1658, the Catholic community, left without priests, dwindled away.

2. Japan and China

The greatest disappointment of all was Japan. Politically fragmented until 1573, it achieved unification at the end of the sixteenth and beginning of the seventeenth century through the energetic action of three warriors from modest backgrounds, Nobunaga, Hideyoshi and above all Iyeyazu. The latter definitively crushed the dissident daimyos, proclaimed himself shogun and founded the house which subsequently governed Japan for two and a half centuries. Various factors go to explaining the reversal of the missionary situation: the desire of the Japanese people for unity, the growing defiance vis-à-vis the Europeans, the fear of a Spanish conquest the threat of which the Japanese government detected behind the arrival of missioners from the Philippines (1592), and the will of the new leaders of the country to protect the 'land of the shin and of Buddha' against foreign and pernicious doctrines. The Christian daimyos either apostasized to please the shogun dictators, or revolted and were crushed. A first alarm for the Japanese church was in 1587, when Hideyoshi ordered all the Portuguese, both traders and missioners, to leave the country within twenty days. The edict was barely applied. But in 1597 Hideyoshi had six Franciscans and twenty neophytes crucified at Nagasaki out of fear of the Spaniards. The great persecution, however − perhaps the most frightful ever undergone by a Christian community − began only with the edict of 1614 in which Iyeyazu outlawed Christianity and accused the missionaries of 'wanting to change the government of the country and make themselves masters of the soil': there were more than 4000 victims. The Christians of Kyushu revolted in 1637, and were vanquished, some 35 or 37,000 of them being massacred. What remained of Japanese Christianity became a church of silence.

China experienced no such hecatomb, but the already low number of Christians at the end of the seventeenth century (about 200,000) was reduced to 140,000 by the beginning of the nineteenth. The quarrel over rites certainly did a lot of damage to the Catholic Chinese community, but there is a growing body of opinion today that the rites quarrel was not the main cause of the Christian collapse in China in the seventeenth and eighteenth centuries. The fall of the Mings had resulted in the dispersion or disappearance of an intellectual élite who had adhered to Christianity. From then on the only converts, with few exceptions, came from the mass of the people. The educated, who were the real leaders of the empire, obstinately refused the west's religion, morals and ideology. They encouraged the sovereigns in the same direction. The emperors themselves, despite the efforts of the Jesuits to conceal it, saw more and more clearly the tie which bound the Jesuits to the pope. They did not intend their subjects to be under any other authority but their own, even in spiritual matters. In 1722–4, edicts outlawed missioners throughout the empire, but in fact those who could be useful scientifically, notably the Jesuits, were retained. Also local governors tended to turn a blind eye. Nevertheless, by the end of the eighteenth century all the Jesuits had disappeared, and in 1784 most of the missionaries were arrested and all practice of the Christian religion forbidden in the empire.

It has been calculated that in 1800 Asia had a population of between 520 and 600 million.[27] How many Christians were there among them between Beirut and the Philippines? Three or four million perhaps? Even then the Philippines were more American than Asiatic, and so distort the figures.

3.   The Guarani Republic

America, on the other hand, with its 24,600,000 people at the turn of the nineteenth century,[28] was, in principle, largely Christian. The dismemberment of the Jesuit reductions during the 'enlightenment', however, marked a recession of Christianization and civilization. Breaking the promises of his predecessors, Ferdinand VI of Spain ceded the seven reductions in the south-east of Uruguay to Portugal in 1750. It took the combined Iberians six years of murderous and bloody warfare to crush the resistance of the Guaranis. The superior general of the Jesuits, who could see the clouds gathering over the Company's future even in Europe, had preached submission. The reductions excluded from the fighting did not mobilize to assist the victims of the aggression. How could certain Jesuits resist coming to the aid of the attacked Guaranis? So it was that Charles III and his minister d'Aranda accused the fathers of fomenting revolt among the peoples: in 1767 the Company was suppressed in countries dependent on the crown of Spain, and the following year the missionaries were recalled. Between 1767 and 1769, 2337 Jesuits were expelled from Spanish colonies, 150 of them from La Plata and Paraguay, and 200 fathers and brothers of the Company died of ill-treatment in the process. Once the Jesuits had departed, the authorities of Buenos Aires promised the Guaranis access to all services (including priests) and a university. In fact the Christian communist republic was destroyed by people who claimed to be Christians.

(c) Christianization hindered by Christians

1. The weaknesses of the clergy

The death-sentence pronounced over the Guarani republic is an extreme case, but it is only too clear that in general evangelization was constantly being hampered by the Catholics themselves. Was it not to protect the natives from the bad example of the colonizers that the missionaries created villages practically forbidden to Europeans in Mexico, Canada and first and foremost Paraguay? Furthermore, the lack of preparation, more normal than not, for a worldwide campaign of conversion, the rivalries between religious orders, the mediocrity of many missioners, the worse mediocrity of the secular clergy who went abroad, the contradictory ambitions of governments, and the frequent clashes between the governments and Rome were all so many hindrances to the advancement of the faith.

The Roman Church found itself trying to cope with the evangelization of continents before it had set its own house in order. Moreover, in its effort to be everywhere at once, its Heath Robinson politics meant that it was never able to send enough missionaries to distant countries. Africa and the interior of India were untouched by apostles. Of the missioners, most of them roving, many were genuine heroes, but many also were very ordinary men: as Mgr Ingoli, secretary of the *Congregation for the Propagation of the Faith,* underlined in his three reports of 1625, 1628 and 1644. His indictment was categorical: the religious orders sent overseas their most mediocre, lukewarm, troublesome and ambitious members, just to be rid of them. Too many missionaries failed to learn the language(s) of the countries to which they were sent, because they rarely remained more than three years. The mendicant orders offered to repatriate their subjects after six years. Another major weakness of which the Church was not then aware was that only men were admitted for missionary work abroad while nuns were left behind in Europe to cultivate the mystical garden.[29] What a spiritual workforce was thus left out of account! As for the male religious, there is perhaps no need to recall the petty, inglorious wars among them of which the missionary effort reaped the nefarious consequences: Dominicans versus Jesuits in Japan and China, Franciscans versus Capuchins in the Near East, Capuchins versus Jesuits in Pondicherry, and so forth.

The missionaries, however, despite their evident weaknesses, offer a rosier picture than the secular clergy. As the Iberian presence spread through the towns, cathedrals and churches with collegial chapters were increasingly staffed with 'clerical loafers'. In the vast areas of country, in Brazil as in Mexico, the parish priests became — indulgent — chaplains to wealthy landowners. Both seculars and religious, however, suffered the same evolution, slipped into the same easy-going ways. In India as in America they tended to concentrate in the towns. In the archdiocese of Goa in 1722, it is calculated that there was one priest for every ninety Christians. At Quito the clerical population equalled the lay population as early as the seventeenth century. On the other hand rural Christian communities in the immense American continent were isolated, in fact abandoned, religiously speaking. And then both seculars and religious were tempted by wealth. In the eighteenth century, the archbishop of Lima had an annual income of 813,480 real, and the bishop of Cuzco 450,000. In the first half of the seventeenth century, Ingoli castigated the trading fever that had gripped too many missionaries: they were out to get rich quick and then return to Europe to live on their gains.

Individual cases need not be mentioned here; a word may be said on the orders as such. It is quite certain that after 1580 they yielded to temptation. The Franciscans, it is true, did not become landowners, but they accepted alms. The Dominicans had no such scruple, nor the Augustinians, nor, above all, the Jesuits, who, 'starting from nothing', in no time at all owned in Mexico 'the largest flocks of sheep, the finest sugar *ingenios,* the best kept estates'.[30] With this wealth they established new missions and colleges and built sanctuaries which were often not far from sumptuous. But it blocked the spiritual dynamism, encouraged too many priests to opt for an idle existence and concealed behind the dazzling and reassuring façade of a religion that was if nothing else urbane the essentially rural reality of an appallingly impoverished and badly Christianized world.

2. Patronage

(i) A screen between Rome and the missions

There was another obex to evangelization, and no mean one either: the constant interference of lay authorities in religious affairs, at all levels. It was the consequence of the theory and practice of patronage. By papal Bulls from 1493 to 1508, Rome divided the colonial world into two: the sovereigns of Portugal and Spain were entrusted with the evangelization of the non-Christian world, one to the east, the other to the west, of the 'Tordesillas line'. They were made vicars of the Church and responsible for the proclamation of the faith outside Europe. They thereby undertook to send to their respective zones enough missionaries to create an ecclesiastical organization and give the churches adequate resources. This also meant, however, that the missionaries had to obtain their authorization to leave for lands overseas from the chancelleries of Spain and Portugal, that the kings of the two countries would nominate bishops, canons and abbots, and that they would determine or modify the boundaries of the dioceses. As America and Asia were devoid of the various local rights and customs which in Europe somewhat limited the royal authority and had done for a long time, the kings were given free rein abroad. The papal Bulls had the force of law in Goa and Macao, Mexico and Lima only when they had been re-transmitted by the governments of Lisbon and Madrid to the interested parties.

In the seventeenth century, the disadvantages of the system began to alarm the papacy: witness Ingoli's deposition of 1644. He deplored the intolerable interferences of viceroys and governors in the ecclesiastical courts and chapter elections, the nominations, particularly in the east, of unworthy subjects to important bishoprics and benefices, the vexations suffered by prelates and priests who were over-zealous in their fight against the abuses, and the scandal of the royal *placet* interposed between Rome and the colonial churches while the civil authority legislated without scruple in religious matters. There was a further complaint of an even more serious nature: patronage meant the neglect of evangelization, because episcopal sees were staying vacant for long periods; bishops were refusing to ordain native priests; the slaves were being left without religious instruction while forced labour decimated entire populations. Two years before this report, the Holy See had condemned and placed on the Index the work of a Madrid canonist, Solorzano, *De Indiarum jure* (On the rights of the Indians), in which he made an undisguised apologia for patronage.

(ii) Rome's counter-offensive: '*Propaganda*'

Rome, however, was rather slow in coming to realize the importance of its new missionary duties and the screen thrown up by patronage between itself and the churches overseas. The Council of Trent had hardly dealt with evangelization at all, and when Sixtus V had reorganized the curia, he had created no *Congregation for the Propagation of the Faith*. This was left to Gregory XV in 1622. Even then the Congregation considered its primary task to be the conversion of heretics and the struggle against Protestantism.

Once established, however, it attempted to tackle the Church's missionary work under the energetic leadership of Mgr Francesco Ingoli. It assured financial resources for itself, published catechisms in many languages on its own printing-press, educated its missioners in a Roman college, and claimed to control other missioners through the religious orders. In a quarter of a century (1622–1649: Ingoli died in 1649), it founded forty-six new missions entrusted to some 300 religious. From 1663 it relied on priests from the Foreign Missions seminary established that year in Paris in an effort to weaken the pretensions of the Portuguese *padroado* in the east. It was to counter Portuguese inertia and patronage that in 1637 *Propaganda* resorted to the subterfuge of vicariates and vicars apostolic.[31] No new dioceses which in Asia, for example, would not have come under the authority of the metropolitan of Goa were erected, but a clergy with quasi-episcopal status was called in to govern the church of a mission territory in the name of the pope. Vicariates were set up notably in India, Indo-China and later China.

Naturally a long tussle ensued between Rome and Lisbon. When a Brahmin, Matthew de Castro, who had been consecrated bishop secretly, was appointed vicar of the Idalcan in India, the Portuguese made his life impossible (he was, it is true, impulsive and maladroit). *Propaganda*, nothing deterred, proceeded to appoint two of his nephews as vicars apostolic. Then the archbishop of Goa and the Jesuits of Macao – the latter having joined forces in favour of the *padroado* – tried to obstruct the withdrawal of the more obstreperous Jesuits from Tonking, and took the important step of demanding from missionaries in the contested regions an oath of obedience to the vicars apostolic. The French, too, however, objected to any such oath as being contrary to the Gallican liberties. (By then there was a system of *French* patronage, as well.) *Propaganda* had therefore frequently to come to terms with the formidable independent spirit of the Jesuits as well as with the caesaropapism of the monarchs. In 1629 and 1646 it accepted that the Company of Jesus send, replace or recall its subjects without consulting the Congregation. In 1689 it allowed the Portuguese Jesuits back into Tonking, and in 1690 retracted the oath. In the following decade Rome created two dioceses in China – Peking and Nanking – and placed them under the *padroado*. At the same time this did not prevent it from setting up five vicariates in the Celestial Empire, and from excluding from the jurisdiction of Goa, Malacca and Macao Siam, Cochin China, Cambodia and adjacent countries. These compromises were a half-victory for Rome, but only where European domination did not extend: wherever Spanish, Portuguese or French governors laid down the law, the spiritual remained under the thumb of the temporal, the Church of the state, and Rome of patronage.

3. Lay slave-owning

While the papacy was fighting governments for the primacy of religion over politics, the more perceptive of the missionaries were discovering in the field the frequently savage slave-owning of their compatriots.

There are abundant witnesses to the cruel procedures used by the colonizers of the sixteenth century in their acquisition of slaves. It is not – would that it were – a 'negro fairy-tale'. We may recall here the facts quoted by B. de Las Casas in 1547.[32] 'If there were, for example, 200 men in a village, (the Spaniards) told the cacique of the village to send 300 men loaded with maize on such a day for such and such work. When the cacique, alarmed at being unable to fulfil the assignment, delayed a day or two, wondering how he was going to satisfy the settlers, the Spaniards promptly claimed he was a rebel and instigated a war against him. They would find the poor man working, kill those they wanted to, carry off the others as booty in a "just war", and then make them slaves'.

How come 'just war'? The jurist Enciso, who in 1509 took part in an expedition to the coastal regions of what is now Columbia, explains: 'The king has every right to send his men to the Indies to demand their territory from these idolators because he had received it from the pope.[33] If the Indians refuse, he may quite legally fight them, kill them and enslave them, just as Joshua enslaved the inhabitants of the country of Canaan'.[34] It was again the authority of the pope and the Bull of 1493 that were invoked in 1509–13 to justify the procedure called *requerimiento*: the Indians, who more often than not had no understanding of what was going on, were faced with a text proposing adherence to the Christian faith; if they refused to subscribe, war was declared.

The practice of *encomienda* was another one that was given a Christian disguise. The Spanish administration had very quickly adopted the custom of handing natives and their lands over for life to settlers who could use the Indians as labourers. The Burgos laws of 1512 laid down certain duties to be observed by the *encomenderos*: to see to the Christian instruction of the Indians and to the building of churches in their villages. In actual fact the *encomenderos* took no trouble to offer the natives the Gospel; they were cruel and grasping. The system of *encomienda* provoked the eloquent protest of B. de Las Casas: 'The plague which has devastated these countries and will continue to do so if a remedy is not found, the iniquity of iniquities beyond the powers of reason to visualize, is the *encomienda* of the Indians'.[35]

It is to the lasting credit of the Dominicans that in the sixteenth century they solemnly fought the inhumanity and lack of Christian spirit in colonization as it was being practised. As early as 1511 Fr Antonio de Montesinos preached two revolutionary sermons before the astonished colonialists at Hispaniola: 'By what right have you engaged in an atrocious war against these peoples who were living peacefully in their lands? . . . Why do you squeeze them dry . . .? It is you who kill them by wanting more and more gold. And what steps are you taking to instruct them in our religion?'[36] Montesinos' protest persuaded the crown of Spain not to abolish the *encomienda* — in fact it was given juridical foundation — but at least to regulate and humanize it (by the Burgos laws of 1512 and the Valladolid laws of 1513).

The 'collector of Indian tears', the hero of 'the fight for justice'[37] was B. de Las Casas (174–1566),[38] an active and intelligent priest — the first priest to be ordained in the New World (1512) — on whom life and fortune smiled and who was himself an *encomendero*. His 'first conversion' dates from 1514. He was then at Cuba, and began to preach in the same vein as Montesinos. Following his own advice, he gave up his *encomienda*, sailed for Spain and persuaded the regent, the austere Franciscan Ximenes de Cisneros, to send a commission of inquiry to the Antilles . . . but it achieved nothing. Las Casas failed, too, in the peaceful planting of Castillian 'workers' on the coast of Cumana (present-day Venezuela). 'They were inspired only by greed and the desire for riches'. He entered the Dominicans in 1522, and from a reformist became a radical: it was his 'second conversion'. From then on he preached unflaggingly that wolves cannot evangelize sheep, that pagan princes should not be dispossessed, that America should not enrich Spain and that 'it would profit the king more to lose all his temporal possessions in the Indies . . . than to let all these Spaniards persevere in evil . . . casting ignominy on God and his Christian religion'.[39] Sent by his order to the American continent in 1537, with other Dominicans he organized the peaceful occupation of a part of Guatemala known as a dangerous 'land of war' which for several years became the land of 'true peace'. Returning temporarily to Spain, he obtained from Charles V the famous 'New Laws' of 1542, which declared all natives 'free vassals of the king'. In 1543 he was appointed bishop of Chiapa (a post dependent on the audience of Guatemala). He encountered the hostility of the settlers, and in 1547 he again, this time for good, left the New World. His fight, however, was not finished. He was a liberal polemicist, and did not tire in his struggle against the lawyers, both clerical and lay, of the conquistadors. The author of the famous *Abbreviated account of the destruction of the Indies* (1542) was still, at the age of ninety-one, appealing to Philip II, and at his death he left an unfinished letter to Pius V.

The activity of Las Casas must be seen in the context of a Thomist theology which gave Renaissance humanism its true nobility. Cajetan, the master general of the Dominicans, affirmed in 1517: 'No king or emperor, not even the Roman Church, has the right to make war on the pagans'.[40] This theory was taken up by Francisco de Vitoria (1492–1549), who taught at the University of Salamanca for twenty years (1526–46). His *Readings on the Indians and the right to wage war* (1538–9) called the whole Spanish conquest into question[41] and refuted Aristotle, for whom the barbarians were predestined by nature to be slaves. Las Casas was a commited polemicist who had lived in America and who remembered the crimes and misdeeds he had witnessed there. Vitoria was the theoretician teaching from the rarified atmosphere of his university chair. Although less discussed and less widely known in his own time than Las Casas, he was in fact even more radical. His fundamental thesis, which was taken up by Grotius and only recently revived, was that there is a natural world community whose members are both states and individuals. The former are protected by public law, the latter by private law. It is forbidden deliberately to infringe either of these laws, even if the Indians are barbarians, even if they refuse to become Christians: 'In my estimation it is not absolutely clear that the Christian faith has up to now been proclaimed and presented to the barbarians in such a way that they are held to believe under pain of committing a new sin ... on the contrary, I have heard of countless scandals, criminal cruelties and impious treatment ...   But even if the faith had been proclaimed to the barbarians in an acceptable and adequate manner, it is not lawful, if they do not wish to receive it, to wage war and seize their goods'.[42]

Montesinos, 'a voice crying in the wilderness', had already preached on this theme. In his Bull *Sublimis Deus* of 1537, Paul III addressed a solemn appeal to the conquistadors: 'We declare that the Indians, like all other peoples ... may not be deprived in any way of their freedom or property (even though they do not belong to the religion of Jesus Christ), and can, must enjoy them in freedom and legitimately'.[43] Charles V issued the 'New Laws' in 1542–3: 'Henceforward, under no pretext whatever, even of war, rebellion or ransom, may an Indian be reduced to slavery' . . . The Indians 'who had been held as slaves in defiance of all reason and law' must be emancipated immediately. They were to be exempt from porterage, except in cases of absolute necessity, and in this case they were to be employed 'in a way that endangers neither their lives nor their health'. 'No *encomienda* will henceforward be granted to anyone, and on the death of the present *encomenderos* their Indians will revert to the crown'.[44]

The 'New Laws' sparked off a revolt of the colonialists in central America and an upsurge in the civil wars among the Spaniards in Peru. These were not unconnected with Las Casas' return to Europe because of increasing hostility from the whites in his diocese of Chiapa. Charles V was obliged to modify his legislation and retain the *encomiendas*, even though he managed to limit their number. Eventually the institution died its own death: at the beginning of the eighteenth century it had disappeared. Did the lot of the Indians improve subsequently? The establishment of vast properties at the expense of the native communities,[45] the employment of the coloured population as agricultural labour, the forced labour in the silver and mercury mines on the exhausting *mita* system resulted in keeping the native populations in a condition that was in fact slavery. At the beginning of the eighteenth century, the Jesuits were expelled from Chile and Tuccuman because they opposed the exploitation of the Indians. The settlers were so hostile to the reductions because the Company protected the Guaranis from the slave hunters. And then many religious eventually compounded with the system of man's exploitation of man; in practice all of them accepted the enslavement of the blacks to prevent the enslavement of the Indians.

In 1502 Las Casas had recommended the introduction of blacks to Hispaniola, but later bitterly regretted his own advice.[46] The Africans, sons of Ham, were regarded as apostates to be enslaved in 'just' wars. And then the progress of America seemed impossible without importing the hardy blacks for labour at a time when the Indian populations were shrinking so disastrously. The attitude of Fr Vieira, S.J., expelled from Maranhão in 1661 because he wanted to create a reduction like the reductions in Paraguay, is revealing. When he returned to Europe he advocated importing black slaves into Maranhão: not to put too fine a point on it, he was advocating negroes for the settlers, Indians for the Jesuits.[47] It is true that towards the end of his life, addressing a confraternity of blacks, he questioned the astonishing 'transmigration' of people from Africa to America brought by the traders:[48] 'In other countries of the world, it is what men produce by working the soil and women by spinning and weaving that is traded; there (in Angola) it is living beings who are bought and sold ... Aren't those men sons of the same Adam and Eve? Weren't their souls redeemed by the blood of the same Christ? Aren't their bodies born and don't they die like ours? ... What evil star is it, then, that dogs their foosteps?' Vieira went on to state that at least the slave's soul could never be captive; but when all is said and done, he did not reject black slavery, and he considered that fugitives from slavery were *ipso facto* excommunicated and guilty of grave sin. Before God and nature men are equal, but Providence has permitted the slavery of the blacks, to lead them to salvation.

It is a sign of the ambiguity of history and that events can cut both ways that with the European slave-trade coming on top of the epidemics which ravaged the harrowed peoples, the rate at which the Indian population dwindled gave rise to great anxiety: it meant all the fewer Christians! Conversely, the trade landed millions of blacks on the shores of Christianity. The contradictions in the attitude of the missionaries and the difference in their treatment of Indians and negroes show how ill-prepared the Church was when faced with such an immense conversion problem. It is hardly surprising that it hesitated over the methods to be used, or that bitter conflict broke out.

4. How was evangelization to be achieved?

(i) Break with the past

First of all the missioners gave a quantitative answer to the problem of the salvation of pagans. In general they underestimated the difficulty of adapting Christianity to a human context other than Europe, and as with many of their contemporaries it was their overriding belief that the end of the world was near: the last great harvest before the Judgment was beginning, and time was short. This explains the mass conversions on the Fisheries Coast, in the Congo, and on an even grander scale in Mexico. Such conversions were, it goes without saying, of the most superficial. It is worth mentioning here the self-imposed aim of the famous expert in the Nahuatl (Aztec) language, the Franciscan Bernardino de Sahagun (d.1590), in his *History of New Spain*.[49] He wanted to show the missioners that paganism was rampant in Mexico under cover of a Christian facade, and that there was a real danger of syncretism. If, as we shall show later on,[50] magic rites and mentalities remained alive in the western country areas during the classical age of Europe itself, after more than a millennium of Christianization, it is easier to understand how difficult the

Indians in Mexico and Peru and the immigrant blacks found it to detach themselves from such things. The Councils of Lima at the end of the sixteenth century noted that idolatrous rites were continuing under cover of Christian ceremonies, and that nearly everywhere pagan sanctuaries, suspect objects and superstitious customs persisted. The blacks of the Antilles transported from Dahomey in the seventeenth and eighteenth centuries remained secretly faithful to the cult of voodoo and prisoners of its attractions.

On discovering this persistence of ancestral polytheism, and suspecting a merely skin-deep assimilation of Christianity on the part of the new converts, the evangelizers more often than not refused the natives frequent communion and access to a priest. The college of Santiago de Tlatelolco, founded by Zumarraga the first bishop of Mexico and in which he hoped to train an Indian clergy, was abandoned by his successors. In Peru the ecclesiastical hierarchy and royal decrees opposed the ordination of natives. In the Jesuit reductions there were no Guarani nuns and no Guarani priests. In Chile, where Christianization began in about 1640, the first three non-European priests were ordained only in 1794. At the beginning of the eighteenth century, in Manila, Philip V refused to authorize a regional seminary.

However, these refusals can be explained on motives other than religious. All over America European conquerors were arriving, convinced of the enormous superiority of the west. They systematically practised the politics of the 'tabula rasa', and closed their minds to the richness of local cultures, which they dismissed en bloc as pagan and savage. In the subject populations, they attempted to bring about a complete break with a millennial past: they succeeded only in stupefying the people.

(ii) Respect the local cultures

However, another model of Christianization came from the Far East, elaborated first by Francis Xavier in Japan and then by his Jesuit disciples in China, India and Indo-China. In the first half-century of conquest in India, where they could, the Portuguese destroyed pagodas, forced the scholars to hide their religious manuscripts, neglected or tried to quash religious customs, and attempted to assimilate the new converts. On the Fisheries Coast Francis Xavier followed the same line, but when in Japan he discovered the wealth of their civilization, he stopped to think, and altered his policy. He dropped his poverty-stricken garb, impressed the daimyos with his presents, respected local trades, and tried less to encourage mass conversions than get himself accepted by the country's political and religious élite. This 'adaptation' method of

Christianization harked back to the primitive policies in the Graeco-Roman world. From the end of the sixteenth century, it became clear to the more perspicacious of the apostles of the faith that the style of evangelization had to vary depending on which people were being converted. The *De procuranda Indorum salute* (On achieving the Indians' salvation, 1588) of Fr José de Acosta, a Jesuit in Peru, reveals this viewpoint. At the bottom of the ethnographic ladder he placed the 'barbarians', for whom the 'tabula rasa' technique – and sometimes the iron hand – was the most appropriate. Next came the peoples of the ancient American empires, to whom the previous methods could not be applied without modification. Lastly, at the top of the ladder, de Acosta placed the Chinese, Japanese and Indians, peoples with the skill of writing and a rich cultural heritage: the most suitable approach here was to act like the first messengers of the Gospel among the Jews, Greeks and Romans. This respect for a culture radically different from the western lay behind the directives of Fr Valignano, who was visitor of the Company of Jesus in the Far East from 1592 to 1606, and it also explains the style of apostolate pursued by Ricci in China, Nobili in India and Alexandre de Rhodes in Annam and Tonking: the missionary must forget that he was a westerner in order the better to present a message valid for all peoples and all ages. *Propaganda* seemed to adopt this point of view. In 1659 it issued an instruction of strikingly modern tenor: 'Make no effort, advance no argument, to persuade these peoples to change their rites or customs unless they are patently contrary to religion and morals. What could be more absurd than to transport to China France, Spain or Italy or some other European country? Offer the people not our countries, but the faith'.[51]

Such an attitude led logically to encouraging the rise of a native clergy. This was in fact one of the aims of *Propaganda* in both America and the Far East. In America, patronage was impervious to the directives from *Propaganda*. Elsewhere, however, there were Goanese, Chinese and Indo-Chinese priests, although they were never very numerous: this was partly because they came from small Christian communities, partly because the Roman tradition persisted: candidates to the priesthood had to learn Latin[52] and accept celibacy – two demands which in these cases excluded any significant recruitment.

(iii) The 'Rites Quarrel'
What Rome appeared to give the Asians with one hand it took away with the other at the end of the memorable quarrel over the Chinese and Malabar rites. In this long struggle (1645–1744), where the distance between Italy and the Far East was an added complication, two

philosophies of evangelization, equally esteemed at the time, came into collision. Most of the Jesuits wanted to deoccidentalize Christianity and admit in the civilizations of Asia everything that was not incompatible with the Gospel. They were also aware that it was only the goodwill of the emperor of China that permitted the spread of the Christian message in the Celestial Empire. In a fundamentally optimistic approach they believed in the collaboration of God and man and in the effectiveness of 'secondary causes', and they were not far from thinking, as the Renaissance humanists had thought, that each people had received a part of divine revelation. Against them, the Dominicans, Franciscans and vicars apostolic from the Foreign Missions seminary exalted, like St Augustine, the power of grace, refused to accommodate the message to local culture and demanded total conversion, however rare it might be. The quarrel blew up just when Jesuits and Augustinians were already at loggerheads in Europe, and it did nothing to alleviate the situation. It has not, however, been sufficiently emphasized that at the same time the Christians were fighting 'superstitions' − that is to say, the stubborn relics of paganism − in the west itself. Could Bossuet severely modify the rituals associated with the 'fires of St John'[53] in his own diocese and yet accept at the other end of the world honouring the tablets in which the Chinese perhaps located the souls of their dead? In actual fact the Jesuits and their opponents were not arguing on the same level. The former, especially the Peking Jesuits, lived among the educated for whom Confucius was hardly more than a philosopher to whose thought certain social and family ceremonies were attached. The latter dreamed of a mass conversion of the Chinese people. Now for the 'common man' of the Celestial Empire, Confucianism had become a veritable religion. Both sides therefore were right, but not from the same point of view.

In the dispute which set the missionaries of Africa at each other's throats, the question was one of both language and rite. Ricci had rejected as inadequate the Sinicization of the Christian religious vocabulary, and he had advised the adoption of terms from the literary Chinese language to name God. Further, he dressed like a mandarin, adapted the observance of Sundays and fasts to the local calendar, omitted some details in the administration of baptism, did not give extreme unction (anointing of the sick) to women, and accepted ceremonies of homage to Confucius, city heroes and the dead as being in no way idolatrous. His successors followed him in this. In Madurai (and not on the coast, as the phrase 'Malabar rites' might suggest), Nobili and his disciples adopted a similar approach: they respected the caste system, imposed ashes from sacred cows, and omitted the insufflation and the application of saliva from the baptismal ceremony.

The drama started when, in 1631, a Dominican and a Franciscan arrived in China from the Philippines, where the 'tabula rasa' technique had been boldly applied. They discovered, to their horror, that the same character *Tsi* designated both the mass and the ceremonies in honour of the dead, that the words *T'ien* (the sky) and *Chang T'i* (Lord above) which Ricci had used to refer to God, were also used to refer to the emperor, that Christians 'adored' the tablets engraved with the names of ancestors and burnt gold and silver paper before them which became in the burning money for the use of the dead. The Dominican, Morales, submitted his doubts to the pope who replied in 1645 by condemning the pastoral and liturgical modernism of the Jesuits as it was presented to him. Naturally the Jesuits appealed to a by now better informed pope, and in 1654 gave him a fuller account which the Holy Office endorsed two years later. In fact Rome was guilty here neither of self-contradiction nor of deception. It said simply that if matters stood as the Dominican asserted, Chinese Christians must be forbidden to practise superstitious rites and use equivocal terms; if on the contrary they were as the Jesuit report stated, there was no need to intervene. During the persecution of 1665,[54] nineteen Jesuits, three Dominicans and a Franciscan, all in enforced residence in Canton, used their involuntary retreat to thrash the matter out. They finally decided, in a common declaration, to abide by the Inquisition decree of 1656 as being 'founded on a very probable opinion'. The Jesuit method had carried the day (1668).

Not for long, however. The Company's visitor in China took it upon himself to modify two articles of the Canton declaration. A Dominican who had taken part in the talks, Fr Navarrete, promptly considered himself freed from the obligations of his signature. On his return to Europe he published a book which opened the rites quarrel to a wide public, *A historical, political, moral and religious treatise on the kingdom of China* (two volumes, 1676–9), which was at bottom hostile to evangelization of the Jesuit type. The clouds thickened and with the entry into the lists of the French Augustinians the quarrel escalated. On his way to Europe, Navarrete had met in Madagascar and converted to his point of view the vicar apostolic at Fou-Kien, Pallu (d. 1684). The latter, with his friend and successor Maigrot, immediately took up cudgels against the Jesuit missioners. They were the more persuaded in that the Jesuits, taking refuge behind Portuguese patronage, refused to obey *Propaganda's missi dominici*. In 1693 a pastoral letter from Maigrot categorically rejected all accommodation to Chinese rites and Confucianism. In the tense atmosphere, further poisoned by the resurgence of Jansenism, positions hardened and intrigues multiplied. A French Jesuit, Fr Lecomte, outdoing the moderate – 'probabiliorist' –

views of most of his confrères, went so far as to suggest, in his *Nouveaux mémoires sur l'état présent de la Chine* (New theses on the present state of China, 1696) that the Chinese people 'had conserved for nearly two thousand years a knowledge of the true God, and honoured him in a way that could serve as an example and an instruction even to Christians'. In 1699 Maigrot persuaded an *ad hoc* cardinals' commission to examine the question of rites, and at the Sorbonne in the following year, on the advice of Bossuet and Noailles, the commission condemned the Jesuits' missionary laxity. The Jesuits looked around for support, and it was the emperor K'ang Hsi who gave them the guarantees they were after when, at their request, he stated that the ceremonies of Confucianism were only social and domestic. Finally, however, Rome decided (1704) against the practice of accommodation, and despatched a messenger, Mgr de Tournon, to the Far East to relay its decision to the religious of whose good faith it was not in doubt.

Sick, authoritarian, quite ignorant of things Asian, encountering Portuguese patronage everywhere, Tournon failed in his mission. In India the first thing he did was to condemn the Malabar rites, but then he had to accept that the Jesuits in Madurai appealed to Rome against his condemnations. In China he offended the emperor and was imprisoned at Macao, where he died (1710). K'ang Hsi withdrew his protection from Christianity, and obliged missionaries to take an oath (*p'iao*) to follow the line laid down by Ricci. The pope simply replied, in 1715, by imposing a contrary oath in order to 'exclude all pretexts and excuses for avoiding the application of the decrees'. Maigrot, who had also clashed with K'ang Hsi, had been expelled from China. Back in Rome and a wiser man for the drama he had lived through, he suggested granting Christians in China 'eight permissions' in an effort to attenuate the breach with ancestral practices. A new legate, Mgr Mezzabarba, was sent to China in 1720, both to make sure the Holy Office decrees were enforced and if this failed to grant the necessary 'permissions'. His mission, too, miscarried, and Chinese Christianity split into two groups, one utilizing, the other rejecting, the 'permissions', which Benedict XIV – a pope hostile to the Jesuits – quite simply retracted by a Bull in 1742. Rome then subsided into intransigence on the question of the Chinese rites, right up until 1939. Benedict XIV brought the quarrel over the Malabar rites to a similar end with a Bull in 1744.

Voltaire ridiculed a quarrel which ended in a Roman condemnation of the emperor of China. Before him, Bayle had mocked the split in the missionaries: 'The whole of Europe is ringing with their missions; they accuse each other at Rome; congregations of cardinals, the Sorbonne, princes, authors are all of a flutter, and have worked themselves up into quite a frenzy over them'.[55] It was a mean and laconic judgment. But it is true that Catholicism was at that time overwhelmed by the breadth of the new problems it was having to solve outside Europe; and true also that the Jansenist affair, which was contemporary, prevented the Church from judging such a complex and extensive debate with all the desirable serenity.

PART TWO: HISTORIANS' DISPUTES
AND DIRECTIONS OF RESEARCH

CHAPTER 1

JANSENISM

For some thirty years now the historiography of Jansenism has been
overwhelmed with a great mass of hitherto unpublished sources and
erudite works added to a dossier that was already enormous: a
bibliography drawn up in 1950 included over 15,000 titles.[1] Jean Orcibal
has dealt with Duvergier de Hauranne (commonly known in French as
'Saint-Cyran', from the monastery of which he was abbot), his letters
and his spiritual writings, restoring him, against H. Bremond, to a proper
perspective.[2] He has also drawn attention to the 'second Angélique':
Mother Angélique de Saint-Jean Arnauld d'Andilly, the heroine of
Montherlant's *Port-Royal*, with her harsh exterior, intense vigour of sentiment and proud assurance (which was not without its Achilles' heel).[3]
Since L. Willaert, who studied the origins of Jansenism in the Catholic
Low Countries,[4] L. Ceyssens, with the patience of Job, has published, in
some 3000 pages, documents concerning the first Bull against Jansen
and the years 1644–72.[5] J. A. Tans has given us the hitherto unpublished
letters of Quesnel: here again the Low Countries figure prominently.[6] A
philosopher, L. Goldmann, has drawn attention to the correspondence of
Barcos, nephew of Duvergier whom he succeeded as abbot of Saint-
Cyran.[7] An 'extremist' recently rescued from oblivion is Guillaume Le
Roy, abbot of Hautefontaine.[8] There have also been published the letters
of Pontchâteau, that 'tireless traveller, well-informed novelettist, formidable polemicist' and one of the best ambassadors for Jansenism at
Rome,[9] while a Parisian team has on its programme the study of the
themes of the *Nouvelles ecclésiastiques* (Ecclesiastical News).[10] So
archives and libraries in Belgium, Holland, France, Germany, Italy and
elsewhere have recently yielded and continue to yield many works un-

known to previous Jansenist historians like Gazier, Pastor, Préclin and Bremond.

(a) What is Jansenism?

1. A theology

(i) The issues raised by Jansenism

Like the Protestant Reformation, and this can never be stressed enough, Jansenism started off as a theological debate. The seed was sown in the decrees and silences of Trent. On the one hand the fathers affirmed, in 1547,[11] both free will and the need for grace, but without defining the connexion between the two. On the other, the existence of authentic free will is irreconcilable with the more Augustinian of Augustine's theses: those, for example, included in his anti-Pelagian writings: 'We know that grace is not given to all men; and that it is not given . . . because they deserve it by their good will, let alone because their deeds deserve it . . . it is out of God's gratuitous mercy that it is given to those to whom it is given . . . it is by God's just judgment that it is not given to those whom it is not given to'.[12]

According to St Augustine, grace is *efficacious*: seizing the will, it constrains it to do good. Nevertheless the bishop of Hippo maintained freedom but confused it with the will. Now in the sixteenth and seventeenth centuries, Augustine enjoyed enormous credit, in Protestantism as in Catholicism. Many regarded him as infallible. How were the Augustinian formulae, however, to be reconciled with the definitions of an ecumenical council which contradicted them? This problem was the drama of the Roman Church between Luther and Voltaire. It was impossible to sidestep the issues raised by Jansenism and equally impossible to impose silence on those for and against real human freedom. Rome's prohibition, issued in 1611 and periodically renewed, to publish anything on grace without the approval of the Holy Office, and Louis XIV's prohibition, dating from 1668 (the 'Peace of the Church'), to 'use the words heretic, Jansenist and semi-Pelagian, and to write on these matters', were not, or at least not for long, observed. Can one prevent men from asking whether they act or are acted on?

A preliminary skirmish on efficacious grace was engaged immediately after the concluding sessions of Trent. Baius (1513–89), a theologian at Louvain who claimed to have read all of St Augustine nine times and his writings against the Pelagians seventy times, adopted his mentor's

100

pessimism and demonstrated that human nature has been so badly damaged by the original sin that without grace the sons of Adam can love and do only what is evil. Rome took him for a crypto-Protestant and censured his works. Baius explained himself and submitted. At Louvain, however, his message had not gone unheeded.

In 1586 the theology faculty of the university, and shortly afterwards the theological faculty of Douai as well, severely criticized the anti-Baianist theses of a professor at the Jesuit scholasticate in Louvain, Lessius (1554–1623). He was accused of magnifying human freedom and devaluing grace. But for the intervention of Sixtus V, the bishops of the Low Countries, assembled in council, would probably have condemned Lessius too, but another Jesuit, Molina, adopted and reinforced Lessius' humanism in a work that was destined to enjoy immediate fame, *De concordia liberi arbitrii cum divinae gratiae donis* (On the harmony of free will and the gifts of divine grace, Lisbon 1588).

Molina did not deny original sin, but held that it had deprived man only of his supernatural gifts. *Sufficient* grace returns these gifts to him, because it confers the divine assistance necessary for good-doing in all circumstances. If it is not always so, it is because man sometimes accepts and sometimes refuses it. Molina borrowed from his confrères Lessius and Fonseca the theory of predestination *because of foreseen merits*: God does not force man to do good or evil, but he knows in advance what each individual will do with the divine grace accorded him.

Molinism was born and the heavens opened. The Spanish Dominicans saw St Thomas threatened and took up the challenge, to be soon followed by the majority of bishops and universities in the peninsula. Clement VIII decided to judge the matter at Rome, and in 1597 he appointed a congregation *de Auxiliis divinae gratiae* to clarify the difficult problem; it sat for nine years. Clement VIII himself tended towards Augustine, and he admitted as much in 1602 to the congregation. If he had not died in 1605, he would probably have condemned Molinism. His successor Paul V was of the same opinion, and he had a Bull prepared censuring some forty propositions from the *De concordia*. However, he did not publish it, probably because he was afraid of weakening the Company of Jesus who as a whole had gone over to Molinism. His only measure was to impose silence on the protagonists: nothing was to be published on grace without the express permission of the Holy Office. This did not prevent the publication of the *Augustinus* in 1640.

(ii) The *Augustinus*
In 1623, after a meeting with his friend Duvergier at Péronne, the Dutchman Cornelis Jansen, professor of Holy Scripture at Louvain,

resumed a project he had been thinking about for some years: writing a summa of Augustine's thought. The work was almost completed when Jansen was consecrated bishop of Ypres (1636), but his ministry was hardly begun when he died prematurely of the plague in 1638. Some friends of his took over the work of publication, despite the attempts of the Jesuits at Louvain to prevent them. These attempts were fruitless because the theology faculty at Louvain had never been notified of the Roman decrees.

In his large folio volume of 1300 double-column pages, Jansen expounded a doctrine which may be résuméd as follows. Before his fault, Adam's will inclined to good. Even so he needed *sufficient* grace, because however healthy the eye it still needs the light to see by. Since the original sin, man is like a diseased eye and the grace which was formerly sufficient is no longer so. He now needs *efficient* grace, which both heals and gives the strength to prefer heavenly to earthly pleasure. Such a grace cannot exist without faith, and it follows that, for Jansen as for Luther and Calvin, the 'good works' of unbelievers are so many mortal sins.

No commandment of God is beyond man's powers to observe, now that efficient grace is offered to man, because that grace is all-powerful. It is not, however, always given, even to the person who prays for it. In his triple denial of Jesus, St Peter has shown of what goodwill is capable without grace. Grace being a free gift, God chooses those whom he saves and abandons others. Before the original fault he wanted to save all men by a will 'preceding goodness'. Since sin, his 'consequent' will has become a will for 'justice', which punishes, excepting from punishment only the predestined. Jesus did not die 'efficaciously' for all humanity. But then is it just to punish beings who, without the irruption of grace in them, can do only evil? Are they free and responsible? Yes, replied Jansen, who identified 'free' with 'voluntary'. Freedom consists in the absence of external constraint. If the will without grace is capable only of evil, this is because of the nature of sin, and the acts that result are real sins even though the will, by its nature, cannot avoid them. If the sinner desired good but could not do good, he would be excusable: but this is not the case. In the soul attracted by the pleasure of earthly things it is less the power than the will to do good which is lacking.

The further ramifications of Jansenism and the more or less heterogeneous elements which gradually accrued must not obscure this doctrinal core. It is this core which the Jesuits of Louvain attacked with virulence in 1641 and the Bull *In eminenti* (March 1642, published 1643) condemned in the following year. It is this core which Antoine Arnauld (1612–94) defended vigorously when he entered the lists at the instigation of his spiritual director Duvergier with two successive *Apologies pour Jansénius* (Apologias for Jansen, 1644 and 1645). And it is this core again which Nicolas Cornet, rector of the Sorbonne, and the ninety-three bishops of France who, at the prompting of Vincent de Paul, asked Rome in 1651 to examine five propositions from the *Augustinus*, attacked in their turn. The subsequent condemnation (Bull *Cum occasione*, 1653) which Rome renewed three years later, the expulsion of Arnauld from the Sorbonne in 1656 because he too maintained that grace is sometimes not given to the just man to fulfil the commandments of God, Pascal's *Lettres Provinciales* (1656–7) insofar as they make ironic reference to 'power which is not quite power' and 'sufficient grace which is not enough', the obligation on priests and religious and even laity to sign a formula of obedience[13] to the Roman decisions condemning the Five Propositions – all these are proofs that the affair was at first enacted at the theological level.

(iii) The distinction between right and fact

This doctrinal dimension is again only too apparent in the wearying quarrel over the distinction between right and fact (although the problems of grace were not the only ones involved: there was also, as we shall see later, disagreement on the powers of the pope). Debating with Annat in 1654, Arnauld, a small, modest man, no mean scholar and something of a wrangler, tried to demonstrate that if the Five Propositions were heretical it was because they had been taken in a sense which was not that of Jansen, and that moreover the bishop of Ypres had remained faithful to St Augustine on all points.[14] The following year the indefatigable Arnauld developed the argument in his *Lettre à une personne de condition* (Letter to a nobleman) and his *Seconde lettre à un duc et pair* (Second letter to a duke and peer): he accepted the condemnation of the Five Propositions, but on their attribution to Jansen said he would maintain a respectful silence because he had failed to find them in the *Augustinus*. Why was the formula enforced so relentlessly? Why did four bishops (Henri Arnauld at Angers,[15] Pavillon at Alet, Caulet at Panniers and Buzenval at Beauvais) resist, promulgating the Roman Bulls in their dioceses only with covering instructions distinguishing right and fact (1665)? Why did the two Port-Royals – the Port-Royal in the St James suburb of Paris and the Port-Royal-des-Champs – refuse to sign (1664) when their nuns had not even read the *Augustinus*? The new archbishop of Paris – the 'bonhomme Péréfixe' – at first unctuous, then threatening, did not shake the nuns. Two hundred bowmen proceeded to arrest the more turbulent of the Paris Port-Royal nuns and these were then dispersed into hostile convents. However, the recalcitrant nuns were merely disturbers of the peace in the convents to which they had been sent, so all the rebels were reassembled at Port-Royal-des-Champs (1665), which became a fortress of excommunicated Cistercians.

There is a logical explanation for this obstinacy on both sides. On the one hand, doubt was being cast on the sincerity of Arnauld's *distinguo*: it was suspected that he adhered, covertly but tenaciously, to a theology that cut at the roots of free will. On the other, not only was no trace found of the propositions in the *Augustinus* (they were not in fact there, at least not word for word), but it was feared that by signing, the signatories would condemn the St Augustine of efficacious grace, to whom they were attached as to no one else.

In these conditions the 'Peace of the Church' (1668–9), provoked in part by weariness, could only be by way of truce. If the new pope (tacitly) admitted the justice of the distinction between right and fact, it was because at bottom signing meant, for him, the rejection of the doctrines anathematized by Rome. For Pavillon, however, and Caulet and the nuns of Port-Royal, the attack on the Five Propositions did not affect Augustine's theology of grace. Because Rome had condemned Jansen without at the same time condemning St Augustine's doctrine on irresistible grace, the *massa damnata* and the eternal punishment of children who die without baptism, an equivocation persisted which was heavy with future conflict.

This became clear thirty years later when the Jansenist dispute flared up again. In 1696 an intransigent disciple of Baius and Jansen, the Benedictine Gerberon who had fled to Holland, thought fit to publish the *Exposition de la foi catholique touchant la grâce et la prédestination* (Exposition of the Catholic faith on grace and predestination) which another 'extremist', Barcos, had previously drawn up for Pavillon. Bossuet and Noailles, who had recently been made bishop of Paris, stigmatized the work as the product of the very worst kind of Jansenism. They did so, however, in terms eulogizing St Augustine, and at bottom they both favoured a pessimistic theology. They had both approved the *Nouveau Testament en français avec des réflexions morales sur chaque verset* (New Testament in French with moral reflexions on each verse) published in 1671 by the Oratorian Quesnel and gradually enlarged until the monumental new edition of 1695. Noailles, then still bishop of Châlons, had recommended his clergy to read it: '. . . it will take the place of a whole library in your presbyteries; it will fill you with excellent knowledge of Jesus Christ'. Quesnel, it is true, had signed the formula (and several times at that), but in 1676 he had quitted his congregation and then chosen to live in Belgium where from 1685 he shared lodgings with Arnauld, who had likewise fled to Belgium. It is also true that

Quesnel took little notice of the *Augustinus,* opted for Thomism and cultivated a Bérullian-type piety; but he insisted on the small number of the elect and did not admit that the redemption was universal in its scope. In this context the insidious question put to Noailles in 1698 (probably by a tactless Jansenist) becomes understandable: 'Whom is one to believe, Mgr Louis-Antoine de Noailles, bishop of Châlons (recommending the *Moral Reflexions*) in 1695, or Mgr Louis-Antoine de Noailles, archbishop of Paris (condemning Barcos) in 1696?' This riddle exposed the nub of the problem.

Be that as it may, the publication of the *Exposition of the Faith* proved that some Jansenists at least had 'a pretty flexible notion of what is meant by respectful silence'.[17] One could therefore be excused for thinking that as the seventeenth century came to its close, the 'Peace of the Church' had been of especial profit to the enemies of Molinism, despite the interdict forbidding novices at Port-Royal (1679) and the death of Arnauld (1694). Bossuet himself, who was sympathetic to Augustinism, expressed his alarm in 1700 at the danger 'of a multitude of Latin writings from the Low Countries requesting a revision of the Jansen affair and of the constitutions which condemned the Five Propositions'.[18]

(iv) From the *Case of Conscience* to the Bull *Unigenitus*

The publication of the *Cas de Conscience* in 1702 revealed an unavowed but unyielding wish to see the Roman decisions reversed. In 1701 a curé from Clermont in the Auvergne put to the Sorbonne doctors the following question: 'May a confessor in conscience absolve an ecclesiastic' – Pascal's nephew – 'who states that he condemns the Five Propositions in all the senses in which the Church has condemned them, but who, on the matter of whether or not they are to be attributed to Jansen, believes it is sufficient for submission to the decisions of the Church to maintain a respectful silence?' Forty theologians replied in the affirmative, whereas Bossuet objected and Noailles hesitated. By a (probably calculated) indiscretion, the *Case of Conscience* was published in July 1702. The polemic on respectful silence began more acidly than before.

The publication set off a chain reaction. It was rapidly condemned by Rome, then by Noailles, who had been obliged to come to a decision; the forty doctors retracted; Quesnel was arrested in Brussels by order of Philip V of Spain (Louis XIV's grandson); finally, at the request of Louis XIV, Clement XI issued the Bull *Vineam Domini* (1705) which settled the matter: respectful silence is not submission. The seventeen nuns who eventually died at Port-Royal-des-Champs refused to accept the Bull or sign the text unless they could add 'without derogating from the benefits accorded them by the Peace of the Church'. They held out for three years, and were then (1709) dispersed into other convents. The following year the monastery was emptied, then demolished, and the neighbouring cemetry razed: the 'passion of Port-Royal' was over. Quesnel managed to escape from prison and reach Amsterdam, although his correspondence was seized. In this way the network of which he was the nerve centre came to light and he was shown up for a party leader who had to be liquidated. The most appropriate means was a solemn condemnation of his book. On what pretext, however, could one anathematize a work that had been circulating for more than thirty years to the eulogies of numerous lay people, priests, religious and bishops? Again theological argument won the day, and among those who exploited it was Fénelon, who remembered that the Augustinists had been his enemies during the Quietist troubles. By attacking the *Moral Reflexions* he embarrassed his opponent Noailles who had approved it. Fénelon and Le Tellier, the king's confessor, were responsible for the instruction against Quesnel which the bishops of Luçon and La Rochelle drew up in 1710 and which was placarded all over Paris and even nailed to the door of the archbishop's residence itself. However, beyond the Oratorian it was the whole Jansenist theology, still resurgent, that Fénelon and Le Tellier aimed at, and against which Louis XIV again asked Rome for a solemn statement. The all too famous Bull *Unigenitus* (1713) in fact reproached Quesnel with having 'renewed various heresies, and principally those which were contained in the famous propositions of Jansen accepted in the sense in which they were condemned'. Of 101 formulae taken – this time verbatim, to avoid the errors of 1653! – from the *Moral Reflexions*, forty-three dealt with predestination, irresistible grace and man's essential perversion since the original sin ('without the Liberator's grace the sinner is free only to commit evil': proposition 38): an undeniable continuation of theological Jansenism.

2. A rigorist ideology

(i) Against attrition

Jansenism was also a rigorist ideology. This judgment is certainly a simplification and a partly arbitrary one, because the Christianity of Ignatius of Loyola, Teresa of Avila or Vincent de Paul was no less demanding than that of Port-Royal. It is not, however, totally gratuitous, for Jansenism could not fail to be rigorist. Its theology gave rise to a piety and a morality. Attention then moved from lofty doctrinal speculation to the daily problems of Christian living: pastors and Christians-in-the-street became involved.

Against the Scotists Luther had argued that attrition – sorrow for sin from fear of hell – renders the sinner even more blameworthy. The Council of Trent had rejected this position, but did not prevent discussions among Catholic theologians on contrition and attrition. At the trial of Duvergier (who had been arrested in 1638 by order of Richelieu before the *Augustinus* was published), the interrogation of the accused concerned mainly the necessity of contrition. After two years of hesitating, the prisoner signed an attritionist declaration; but he continued to hold that simple attrition was insufficient, it was 'a human invention' and 'the ultimate relaxation of the sacrament of penance'.[18] For his part Jansen taught that to be good, actions must be inspired by the love of God, and that even with the sacrament of penance attrition cannot lead to salvation. Finally, Pascal, in his tenth *Provincial Letter,* ridiculed attrition: by attrition, he said, one can 'be saved without ever having loved God in one's life'. Thus contritionism became one of the key ideas in the Jansenist current of thought, and the Bull *Unigenitus* included a condemnation of this proposition from Quesnel (no.58): 'There can be neither God nor religion where there is no charity'. Rome therefore refused the all-or-nothing alternative, and continued to absolve penitents without demanding perfect contrition.

(ii) Against frequent communion

The rigorist attitude based itself not only on the irreplaceable value of love, but also on a great respect for the sacraments. In the course of his trial Duvergier was accused of turning the nuns and hermits of Port-Royal from absolution and communion. In reality his theory of 'renewals' had been calumniated. For him holy souls should be in a fit state to receive the Saviour every day, although the effort towards holiness was constantly obstructed by concupiscence. Therefore one must sometimes deprive oneself of what one desires most to avoid routine and to break automatic reactions. The time of trial in which the Christian aspires to pardon from the priest and to receive the sacred host will be like a noviciate in which he is purified and renewed.

In a masterly work which Arnauld took care to publish *after* Richelieu's death (1642), he gave the same counsels of piety as his master Duvergier, but supporting them with the Church's highest authorities and oldest devotional practices.

His treatise *De la fréquente communion* (On frequent communion, 1643) took to task those 'seducers of souls' – by which he meant the Jesuits – who allowed their penitents to attend a dance on the same day that they have gone to communion, and deflected them from 'the narrow way of the Gospel'. He intended to restore to its honourable place 'the custom of the Church', recalling that in the fourth and fifth centuries Christians prepared themselves for communion by several days of penances, and that those who had committed grave sins were sometimes excluded from it altogether for years on end. Trent authorized the confessor to 'test' the penitent before admitting him again to communion, and Charles Borromeo tried to reintroduce the ancient discipline in his diocese of Milan.

Because it retained a certain moderation, Arnauld's rigorism coincided with the religious ideal of many devout people. Five archbishops, twenty-two bishops and twenty-four doctors approved the *On frequent communion*. Despite its 622 quarto pages, the well-written work enjoyed extraordinary success. It was in vain that attempts were made to have it censured by Rome. Nouet, a Jesuit, who had attacked it from the pulpit, was made to kneel and read a retraction of his sermons before the united French bishops. And it was in the wake of Arnauld's book that the assembly of clergy in 1657 had St Charles Borromeo's very rigid *Instructions pour les confesseurs* (Instructions to confessors) reprinted and distributed in all the dioceses of the kingdom. People who persecuted Port-Royal praised Arnaldian piety. Péréfixe confessed 'that he had read *On frequent communion* five or six times and not once without being the better for it'. His successor Harlay, who did not impose a very hard regime on himself, bound 'all the missionaries and confessors of his diocese' by St Charles' rules. The Jansenists therefore were not the only ones to insist on the respect due to the sacraments and to advocate 'delaying absolution for habitual grave sins', but because sacramental rigorism was most energetically defended by those who also defended Jansen, confusion crept in over the difference between the two sides.

(iii) Against 'lax morality'

More generally Jansenism had the good fortune (if such it was) to channel the hostility of numerous devout people, clergy as well as laity, towards laxism – to its own advantage. Taking as his targets Bauny's *Somme des péchés* (Summa of sins), which had been put on the Index in 1640, and Escobar's *Liber theologiae moralis* (Book of moral theology, 1644) in which the author had compiled the maxims of twenty-four Jesuit casuists, Pascal gained the sympathy of the mockers and the virtuous.

In the 'moral' *Provincial Letters* (excluding the fourth to the seventeenth), Pascal reproached the laxists with offering 'heaven at low cost and life without constraints' by justifying the worst actions with the method of 'probable opinions' and with the 'direction of intention'. With quotations in his support, the author of the *Letters* demonstrated that the casuists allowed a priest to take several stipends for a mass, a religious to disobey his superiors, servants to be accomplices of their masters' debauches, children to desire their parents' death, creditors to practise usury, debtors to escape by fraudulent bankruptcies.

These anonymously and clandestinely printed 'Little Letters' unloosed polemic, created a sense of shock in public opinion and, very importantly, awakened a widespread echo among the clergy of several dioceses, in particular Paris and Rouen. They verified the texts quoted by 'the secretary of Port-Royal', found them to be exact and alerted the hierarchy. The assembly of clergy of 1657 could not do otherwise than condemn the laxist morality. Thereupon a Jesuit thought it appropriate to publish an *Apologie des casuistes* (Apologia for the casuists, 1657) which to one non-Jansenist bishop seemed to be 'a most monstrous abomination'. The bishop replied with a *Factum pour les curés de Paris* (Pamphlet for the parish priests of Paris, 1658), in the redaction of which Pascal had collaborated, and which denounced 'the scandal' and 'the unbelievable temerity' of Jesuit morality. The *Apologia* was successively condemned by the Paris Faculty of Theology and the Holy Office. Strict Christian morality carried the day. In 1679 Innocent XI censured sixty-five 'corrupt and horrifying' propositions contained in Jesuit teaching, and in 1700 the assembly of clergy in France issued a warning on 123 laxist formulae. It is true that to keep the balance it also condemned a pamphlet by Arnauld called *Le phantôme du Jansénisme* (The phantom of Jansenism), which had appeared in 1686, but for half a century past public opinion had become used to equating Jansenism and rigorism.

3. An ecclesiology

(i) Episcopalism

By moving the battle-field to piety and morality, the friends of Port-Royal had succeeded in creating, among both the clergy and the laity, a movement of opinion that the *Augustinus* on its own would not have been able to rouse. This movement gained in momentum when it became clear that Jansenism was also an ecclesiology. In their concern to restore the Church to its pristine purity, Jansen and Saint-Cyran mistrusted religious orders as purely human institutions, and wanted to rehabilitate the powers and dignity of the episcopate. They sounded the praises of its sacred grandeur. The bishop of Ypres detested equally the Jesuits and the Dominicans; the canonization of Ignatius of Loyola and Francis Xavier scandalized him. Duvergier, under the pseudonym of Petrus Aurelius, carried on a polemic against the English Jesuits (militant antiepiscopists) from 1632 to 1635. As the friend and defender of Bérulle, Duvergier could not but espouse the distrust of the founder of the Oratory for the Company which had tried to obstruct the rise of the new congregation. Jansen and Duvergier were part of a powerful tendency of the Catholic Reformation, notably in France. Bérulle by creating the Oratory, Olier by organizing Saint-Sulpice seminary, Vincent de Paul by establishing the Mission and placing himself at the service of ordinands and priests with his Tuesday conferences, all desired to assist the hierarchy, obey it, and not go over its head as the regulars tended to do by claiming to depend directly on Rome. In the seventeenth and eighteenth centuries the representatives of Jansenist opinion were not by any means the only people to express misgivings over the religious orders and to want to safeguard the independence of the episcopacy from the pope and king, but they were the most bellicose.

This is clear from a reading of the religious history of the classical period. When the four recalcitrant bishops refused to sign the formula of 1657 unless they could add the distinction between right and fact, what point did they intend to make? They certainly wanted to express their convinced Augustinism, but they also wanted to defend the episcopacy against the interference of the state and the encroachments of Rome. As they could not find the Five Propositions in the *Augustinus,* they – and many others – doubted the pope's infallibility in deciding on a question of fact. The attitude of these four rebels was all the more embarrassing for Louis XIV and the pope in that they were exemplary reforming bishops and might well persuade other prelates, in their own anxiety over Rome's ambitions, to follow suit. Nineteen French bishops did in fact write to Clement IX on 1 December 1667 that 'it is a new and unheard of dogma . . . to establish the infallibility of the Church in human matters not revealed by God'. The papacy preferred to step down. The 'Peace of the Church' was achieved.

(ii) Gallicanism
By subsequently opposing Louis XIV in the episode of the *régale* (the king's right of seizure of a bishop's temporal powers during the vacancy of a see. In 1673 Louis XIV tried to extend it from temporal to universal power), Caulet bishop of Pamiers and Pavillon bishop of Alet were being logical with themselves and their doctrine, although paradoxically here they were supported by Rome. Again they wanted to defend the dignity of the episcopate. 'As the Father has sent me, even so I send you'. Innocent XI heartily approved of the noble inflexibility of the two rebellious

prelates, and he said of Caulet: 'He is the model of a faithful priest, as solid as a rock.'

The episode of the *régale* did credit to no one. Two temperaments came into conflict: the Sun King and the pious Innocent XI ('more obstinate than enlightened'); and two political schemes: while the pope wanted a crusade of Christian Europe against the Turks, Louis XIV preferred war against the Dutch and the Spaniards. In most of the French kingdom, during the vacancy of an episcopal see, the king administered the revenues of the diocese (*régale temporelle*) and conferred the benefices for which the bishopric was responsible (*régale spirituelle*). In 1673 Louis XIV decided to generalize the *régale* rights. Caulet and Pavillon were the only ones to protest in France, although Innocent XI fought strenuously against what he regarded as a usurpation on the part of the state. Caulet and Pavillon had both died when, to put pressure on the pope, the king summoned an extraordinary assembly of the French clergy (1681–2) which voted approval of the celebrated *Déclaration des Quatre Articles* (Declaration of the Four Articles). The first article affirmed the independence of the sovereigns in temporal matters. The other three, which, truth to tell, are somwhat awkward in their formulation – Bossuet had played a moderating role in the deliberations – proclaimed the superiority of ecumenical councils over the pope and that 'the rules, customs and constitutions accepted in the kingdom' must be observed. The parliaments registered the declaration and Louis XIV ordered it to be taught in seminaries and theological faculties. Innocent XI replied by refusing the canonical investiture of the new bishops appointed by the king; and by 1689 thirty-five dioceses were without pastors.

The death of Innocent XI in 1689 and Louis XIV's difficulties with the League of Augsburg brought about peace (1693) between France and Rome: the papacy turned a blind eye to the extension of the *régale*; the king no longer imposed the teaching of the *Four Articles*, while each member of the 1682 assembly sent the pope an apology. Disavowals and retractions do nothing to detract from the historical importance of the *Declaration of the Four Articles*, which Napoleon resurrected. During the first half of the seventeenth century, ultramontanism gained ground in France in the clergy and devout circles. The dispute over grace and the attitude of Louis XIV during the 1673–93 crisis resulted in a resurgence of Gallican sentiment – episcopalism and Gallicanism went hand in hand. Gallicanism, which had begun in the fifteenth and sixteenth centuries, was expressed notably in a tome in which the parliamentarian Pierre Pithou had enunciated eighty-three principles, bases and liberties of the Church of France[20]. After 1693 the monarchy became almost ultramontanist in its fight against Jansenism, but Gallicanism was adopted as a policy by several bishops, a fraction of the lower clergy, parliaments and an important section of public opinion. The recurrence of the Jansenist quarrel on the occasion of Quesnel's book permitted the revival of hostilities, and the 'Peace of the Church' faded into the background. The 'second age of Jansenism' had arrived in the form of a Gallicanism with rigorist features which, under pretence of defending Augustinism, although in fact it was concerned less and less with grace, gave rise to a veritable party of opposition against Rome and the king. It was an enemy, and Legion its name, which for some fifty years caused the utmost concern to them both.

In 1705 the Bull *Vineam Domini* condemned the respectful silence. It was a condemnation without leave of appeal, or so it seemed. But not at all, said Noailles, explaining that if the meaning of Jansen's book was heretical (a position certainly some way behind Arnauld's) the pope did not and could not say whether the bishop of Ypres consciously espoused these errors: on that point a respectful silence was called for. The French bishops in council made it clear that the pontifical constitutions 'impose obedience on the whole Church once they have been accepted by the body of pastors'.

This reticence, heavy with defiance of Rome, was again expressed on the occasion of the Bull *Unigenitus* (1713). Even the bishops who accepted the Bull — and most of them did — published it in their dioceses with instructions of their own, by which they intended to demonstrate that the episcopal sanction was the indispensable complement of the Roman decisions. Small wonder that the pope was not amused. Over and above these noiseless gestures of resistance, the Bull loosed a bitter crisis. With the encouragement of the chancellor, d'Aguesseau, the parliament of Paris refused to pass measures ordered by the king. While 112 bishops finally yielded, fifteen, headed by Noailles, persisted in their refusal. The polemic raged — more than 180 book and pamphlet titles in 1714 — and Louis XIV was shocked at the 'spirit of giddiness and disorder' manifested by the episcopate. Shortly before his death he decided on the advice of Fénelon and Le Tellier his confessor that a national council should sit in judgment on the mutinous bishops. The regent, who was at first favourable to the Jansenist cause, abandoned the plan, but this did not calm the troubled waters. In January 1716 a score of prelates wrote to him asking whether he would appeal to the pope for clarifications on the Bull. The following year four bishops lodged an appeal at the Sorbonne for a general council, and they were followed by twelve other bishops and 3000 (out of about 100,000) members of the clergy. In 1718–9 the confusion was at its very worst, and the regent's patience exhausted.

The united efforts of the papacy and the French government, notably under Fleury, gradually reduced the dissidence in the clergy. In 1718 the Inquisition condemned the appeal and Clement XI excommunicated the appellants. In 1722 the regent re-imposed the signing of the formula, which had fallen into disuse. Five years later a provincial council at Embrum judged and condemned Soanen bishop of Senez, who had been the principal author of the appeal and who had just distinguished himself by a particularly aggressive pastoral instruction. Finally, in 1730, a royal declaration gave the Bull *Unigenitus* force of state law and rendered void the benefices of titulars who refused to sign the formula. Noailles, however, had died in 1729 having accepted the Bull – and perhaps retracted. The last appellant French prelate, Caylus bishop of Auxerre, died in 1754. The conversions, 'miracles' and convulsions at the tomb of the deacon Pâris – an appelant of admirable austerity and charity – in the cemetery of Sainte Médard (1730–2) could not check the defeat of the Jansenist party.

Nevertheless there remained amongst the public and in the parliaments a widespread feeling of opposition to Rome and the government which was always ready to give voice. This explains how the *Nouvelles ecclésiastiques*, an intelligent and peevish newspaper, could appear with the utmost regularity from 1728 to 1803, despite its hush-hush publication. It also explains the weakening of the royal power over the affair of the confession notes[21] and the suppression of the Jesuits in the kingdom in 1761–4. And finally neither the *Constitution civile du clergé* (12 July 1790. It reorganized the Church to fit in with the civil administration of the country, making the Church subordinate to the state in the election of bishops, the deployment of clergy, and so on. It was condemned by the pope in 1791 [10 March] and repealed with the concordat of 1801) nor the *Articles organiques* (subsidiary to the 1801 concordat, these [Gallican] articles provided for certain state interventions in religious matters. They were never accepted by Rome) can be explained without this persistent opposition.

(iii) Presbyterianism

A far from negligible part of 'second (Quesnel's) Jansenism' was the presbyterian tendency. The way had been cleared by Saint-Cyran with his anxious, constant reference back to the primitive Jerusalem community and the 'golden centuries' of the early Church. He opposed precipitate ordinations to the priesthood, seeing in priests 'genuine prelates, but in miniature' whom the bishops should treat as sons and not as servants. Then, at the time of the *Provincial Letters* an instinctive sympathy emerged spontaneously between the lower clergy and the opponents of laxist morality. The ground being thus prepared, the championship of presbyterianism by the theologians and second-generation Jansenism was a logical development. In 1676, the Reverend Jacques Boileau, brother of the more famous writer-poet Nicolas, celebrated the rights of the parish clergy in his *De antiquo jure presbyterorum* (On the ancient rights of priests). Three years later, the Reverend Duguet, a friend of Arnauld and Quesnel, recalled in his conferences that in times past priests and people had elected the bishops, and that the former theoretically retained the right to attend plenary councils. It was above all Quesnel, in the course of enlarged re-editions of his *Moral Reflexions*, who accentuated the Richerian tendencies of his ecclesiology.

Edmond Richer (1559–1631), a former member of Henri de Guise's anti-Calvinist League (1576–90), had become rector of the theological faculty of the University of Paris, but after the publication of his *De ecclesiastica et politica potestate libellus* (Pamphlet on ecclesiastical and political power, 1611), which connected presbyterianism and Gallicanism, he was obliged to relinquish his post. As an opponent of the Jesuit Bellarmine and heir to the conciliarist theories of the fifteenth century, he conceived the Church as a democracy in which authority had been conferred by Jesus on the mass of the faithful, who in their turn committed the sacerdotal power to the pastors and sovereign jurisdiction to the bishops. Richer gave councils supreme ecclesiastical authority and denied the divine origin of pontifical power. According to him, the monarch had the right to decide whether the organization of the Church conformed with canonical regulations. The *Libellus* was banned by the provincial synods and by Rome, but 'this little treatise of thirty pages dominated the Church in France up to the *Constitution civile du clergé*'. From the publication of the *De antiquo jure presbyterorum* and the *Moral Reflexions*, Jansenism and Richerism joined forces.

(iv) Holy Scripture for all

The ecclesiology on which this collaboration was possible went so far as almost to reach Protestantism. Quesnel affirmed that the deposit of faith resided in the entire body of the Church, which implied that 'the reading of Holy Scripture is for everyone', that the Bible was 'the Christian's milk', and that it is therefore 'dangerous to wish to sever him from it'. The Port-Royal group, where the concern for instruction and education was so acute – we have only to think of the infant schools – shared these sentiments. It was due to members of this group, Sacy,[22] Nicole and Arnauld, that the *New Testament of Mons*,[23] a fresh and accurate translation, appeared in 1667; and due to Sacy that the *Great Bible in French*, begun in 1672, was published in 1696. These bold efforts, in the line of Erasmus' and the humanists' work for Christian instruction, met repeated condemnation. One after the other the archbishop of Paris, the King's Council and Rome proscribed the *New Testament of Mons*, and similar treatment was meted out to Fr Joseph de Voisin's translation of the *Roman Missal* (1660) and Le Tourneaux's translation of the *Breviary* (1688), in which the canticles were reproduced in a version by Racine. Arnauld, in the breach as ever, refuted the official thesis according to which all the translations of scripture and the Fathers were 'abominations', by publishing in 1680 a work *Sur la lecture de l'Ecriture Sainte* (On the reading of Holy Scripture), and in 1688 a *Défense des Versions de l'Ecriture Sainte et des offices de l'Eglise en langue vulgaire* (Defence of the translations of Holy Scripture and of the offices of the Church into the vulgar tongue). Nonetheless the Bull *Unigenitus* solemnly condemned the following statement of Quesnel (no. 80): 'The reading of Holy Scripture is for all'. This desire that the faithful should be given total access to the Bible was part of Jansenist piety, which, while not rejecting the veneration of our Lady and the saints, expressed concern over the upsurge in 'private devotions', and abhorred superstition, ostentation and bombast.

(b) *Jansenism as an opposition mentality*

1. Theology and state politics

The author of the *Augustinus* had stated in advance that he would abide by Rome's judgment on his book. Duvergier signed an 'attritionist' declaration in prison at Vincennes. The dying Pascal gave the curé of Saint-Étienne-du-Mont the impression of being 'as simple and docile as a child'. Arnauld encouraged the Peace of the Church. However, he was in the Jansenist mould: ready, like Antigone, to contest and refuse. Small wonder that the authorities were exasperated. Richelieu clapped Duvergier in prison. Louis XIV's only effective, in fact his ultimate, resource against Port-Royal was to destroy it. Arnauld and Quesnel were forced into exile. For over 150 years, the state authorities, in France especially, were challenged by the representatives of the Jansenist current of thought in a variety of changing situations.

By launching France into the Thirty Years War, Richelieu repudiated the policies of the devout party who would have united the Catholic states against the Reformation princes. In an immediately famous pamphlet, *Mars Gallicus* (1635), Jansen accused the cardinal of betraying the Roman Church; and from the latter's point of view he was right. Saint-Cyran was a friend of Jansen's. He was also the confidant of Bérulle who disapproved of the Protestant alliances. On the death of Bérulle (1629), he became the oracle for the pious circles of Paris. Richelieu tried to 'mollify' him by offering him a see, but the 'holy abbot' refused and was constrained to 'marry a prison'. In the words of Godefroi Hermant,[24] Richelieu 'had no scruple in using all his authority to destroy those he had not been able to win over to his own interests'.[25] To his credit, Jean Orcibal has uncovered this political side of Saint-Cyran's arrest.[26]

Contrary to what is often thought, many friends of Port-Royal were on the king's side during the Fronde. The Jansenists and their allies never constituted a homogeneous group — we shall have occasion to return to this later — and this is true for the period of the Fronde. Nonetheless several of them did support the rebels. The Duke of Luynes, who in 1651–2 gave military protection to Port-Royal-des-Champs, was the son of the Duchess of Chevreuse, and like her, at the beginning of the Fronde, had joined the rebels. The curé of Saint-Merry, who had prayers said for the imprisoned Retz and a Te Deum sung on his escape, was a militant Jansenist.[27] The president of the Paris parliament (and later French ambassador to England) Pomponne de Bellièvre, who represented the exiled cardinal's interests in Paris, was a friend of the Augustinists.[28]

'The opinion which maintained that the Jansenist ideology was a natural ally of the Fronde is therefore neither inconsistent nor totally arbitrary. As Godefroi Hermant noted,[29] "Cardinal Retz was considered to be the leader of the Jansenists". Mazarin believed that the two movements were connected, if not in their separate developments in practice, at least in their basic inspirations'.[30]

Beyond the vicissitudes of any political kinship, Jansenist theology and state politics were fundamentally opposed. Duvergier preached retreat and flight from the world. 'To love this mortal life', he wrote, 'one must be ill in one's mind and possessed by some malignant spirit'.[31] The world is evil. 'Scripture does not speak of it except as of a desert, a prison, a hospital and an image of hell. Woe to those who love it and who do not try in this present life of die to all things'.[32] 'Since in creating the world God took into account the consequences of the sin man would commit . . . he created it only so that it might serve man as a source of virtue by his flight from it, his detestation of it, his ruination of it to the largest extent possible'.[33] It is not difficult to imagine the disquiet of the leaders of the state when faced with such a negative pessimism. Richelieu apparently decided to take action against Saint-Cyran when the brilliant lawyer Antoine Le Maître, one of Saint-Cyran's disciples, wrote to the chancellor expressing his desire to quit the bar and go to live as a hermit at Port-Royal-des-Champs. What if many more of the élite should follow his example? Was this voluntary solitude not the choice of non-conformist consciences, of individualists electing to live on the margin of a French society which Richelieu and others were striving to focus exclusively on an absolute king? Moreover, the heroic rejection of the world implied disdain for the moderate virtues without which the life of society was impossible. This was brought out by de Marandé, a king's counsellor, in a treatise on the *Inconvénients d'Estats procédans du Jansénisme* (Disadvantages to the state from Jansenism, 1654): if our powers of reason and our virtues of moderation are corrupt and spurious and produce only fruits of concupiscence, if the Christian life requires rejection and retreat, what good purpose is served by society or the state? A Christianity of excess must surely lead to anarchy, they argued, because élites are creamed off and social virtues condemned.

Radical pessimism with regard to sinful man necessarily results in moral relativism, criticism of the law and the contestation of authority. Pascal drew the same conclusion in his *Pensées*, even though he was sufficiently perspicacious and prudent to advocate, in practice, obedience to the law and justice of the country, since established order holds chaos at bay. Pascal's logic is of tightrope finesse. Since the original fault, 'corrupted reason has corrupted everything' (294,60): there is 'nothing just or unjust which does not change its quality by changing its climate' (ibid.). Justice, therefore, is not just, but merely necessary. The law 'is law and nothing more' (ibid.); 'force is queen of the world' (303,554). 'Not being able to fortify justice, force has been justified' (299,81). But 'nothing is so offensive as these laws which put the faults to rights' (294,60). How can one affirm the divine character of royalty? Does the sovereign appear to be above humanity? Usually one sees 'kings accompanied by guards, drums, officers, and all the paraphernalia designed to induce respect and fear' (308,25). If the chancellor is 'grave', it is because he is dressed in finery and wields power. Kings and ministers are merely 'ornaments of the establishment' (310,797). The Christian must therefore reject activity, retire from the world where there is no sure value, and take up an attitude of passive and disillusioned obedience. 'True Christians obey the whims of their rulers: they do not respect them, but they respect the order laid down by God who, to punish man, has enslaved him to these whims' (338,14).

Without necessarily sharing such tragic – and antisocial – ideas, the Jansenists became increasingly an opposition force against the absolute monarchy. This was firstly because they claimed to be defenders of autonomous conscience and free examen (that is, man's right to believe whatever his own conscience tells him, without any obligation to accept the dictates of a higher authority, particularly in matters of religion and politics); and secondly, because whether at the time of the *Provincial Letters* or at the time of *Unigenitus*, their constant tactics were to rely on public opinion to exert pressure on the royal power. Because of this, Jansenism, which had begun as a theological school, gradually became a movement, then a party, 'infiltrating the whole of society in successive layers'.[34] The *Provincial Letters* had alerted the parish clergy. Quesnellianism encouraged the rise of democratic awareness among the lower clergy and certain of the faithful. Finally, the *Nouvelles ecclésiastiques* diffused the Jansenist mentality throughout the population. As Jansenism spread in society, it moved imperceptibly and logically from religious contestation to political contestation, and thereby opened up one of the roads that was to lead ultimately to the French Revolution. One proof of this (amongst many) would be the disquieting parallelism which the Richerian Besoigne established in his *Catéchisme sur l'Eglise pour les temps de trouble* (Catechism on the Church in times of trouble, 1737) and which R. Taveneaux summarizes as follows: 'Just as dogmatic authority resides in the body of the faithful, so legislative authority is based on the national community'.[35] It is understable why Fleury, who was a Gallican but also minister under Louis XV, had little sympathy with the appellants.

2. The Jansenist ideology and class attitudes

The notion of opposition must be clarified. Marxist methodology has accustomed us to looking for the connexions between an ideology and its socio-economic context. It was both inevitable and desirable that it should be applied to Jansenism: Henry Lefebvre[36] and Lucien Goldmann[37] have made capable analyses in this direction. Goldmann, whose problematic is chronologically tighter that Lefebvre's, sees in first Jansenism's (1637–1669) rejection of the world ('with or without modification') the ideological reaction of jurists to state centralization. This reaction was expressed at the cultural level as the resentment of 'officials' increasingly deprived of real power by the rising 'commissioners'.[38] On this view Jansenism and the Fronde were two different manifestations of the same spirit of discontent, because it was equally opposition to the monarchy to opt for systematic abstention as to revolt. Drawing on the work of Roland Mousnier[39] (although the latter did not follow the Marxizing philosopher in his conclusions), L. Goldmann has stressed in support of his thesis that the price of offices had begun to drop in 1637 or thereabouts; that the rise of Jansenism had coincided with the centralizing governments of Richelieu and Mazarin and the failure of the Fronde; and that the ideology of Jansen and Saint-Cyran spread largely among parliamentarians and the members of the sovereign courts. Furthermore, it is significant that the four rebel bishops of 1660–9 were all members of parliamentary families, and that Pascal's father was (for a time) president of the Tax Court at Montferrand in the Auvergne.

L. Goldmann's argumentation has not fully convinced either certain Marxists, who accuse him of a 'vulgar and untidy sociologism',[40] or non-Marxist historians. In the first place it ignores the fact that first Jansenism was essentially a religious phenomenon of interest chiefly to theologians, priests and bishops, and therefore a matter that concerned not the purists at all but ecclesiastical circles. This is a point of basic importance which can be applied equally in the study of the causes of the Reformation[41] and in research into the origins of Jansenism. In the second place, it rests on incomplete historical and sociological data.[42] Jansenist theology was born and matured before the Fronde, that is, before one may legitimately speak of a decline of 'officials' to the advantage of 'commissioners'. On the contrary, the middle of the seventeenth century was 'a time of hope and ambitious projects for officials, and this optimism was expounded with complaisance in the theories of the Fronde'.[43] Furthermore, many parliamentarians numbered Jesuits among their friends. There were men of Jansenist sympathies in the service of the crown. This is not surprising given that the monarchical bureaucracy recruited its personnel from the legal classes. Pascal's father had presided at the Montferrand Tax Court, it is true, but then he later accepted a post as assistant to the administrator of Normandy with the title of 'deputy commissioner for the levy and collection of tallage'. In short, it is difficult to find too close a tie between the theology of the *Augustinus* and the world of the jurists. Finally, L. Goldmann's thesis does not adduce the 'enumerations and studies of filiations, intellectual, family and social relationships, without which the entire structure borders on the tautologous'.[44]

Although at the same time we have to acknowledge, with Sainte-Beuve, that there was a connexion between the Jansenism of the middle of the seventeenth century and 'the upper middle class, the parliamentary class, who under the League were more or less on the side of the politicians', this connexion is surely better explained on cultural grounds. In the French society of the time, this essentially rentier class had both more leisure and education than other classes, and it was perfectly natural that they should take a livelier interest in the movement of ideas and in intellectual innovations. Descartes, whose message was at the opposite pole to Jansen's, was also from a parliamentary background.

H. Lefebvre has stressed this opposition between the *Augustinus* and the *Discourse on Method*. In his view it marks 'a sharply-defined phase in the conflict between ascendant capitalism with its emerging progressionist ideologies of materialism and rationalism (Descartes) and previous ideologies'.[45] Jansen 'gave the impression of being subversive, whereas in fact he was just an archreactionary'.[46] According to H. Lefebvre, 'the unease of traditional Catholics in a world that became daily less familiar suffices to explain the influence of the Jansenist doctrine'.[47] The latter was the sublimated expression of a two-fold opposition: a) on the economic level, to mercantilism, to the increasing power of money and usury; b) on the political level, to the authority which was intent on modernizing the state by imposing a centralized structure. 'In law the Jansenists joined the Gallicans in defending the doctrine of the divine right of kings, but in fact they supported particularisms, the privileges of the old-established corps, the liberties of local and parochial communities'.[48]

The voluntarism and 'generosity' advocated by Descartes were at the antipodes of Augustinist pessimism; and a hermit like Sacy retained his attachment to the Aristotelean philosophy. However, when the *Discourse on Method* and the *Philosophical Meditations* appeared in 1637 and 1641 respectively, 'Descartes' first supporters were continually praising this "conformity of the teachings of St Augustine with the opinions of M. Descartes".[49] In the seventeenth century a whole current of thought placed Cartesianism in the slipstream of Augustinism. Arnauld wrote that reading Descartes one found in St Augustine 'a man of exceptional power of mind and unique doctrine, not only in theology but also in human philosophy'. The Oratorian Malebranche tried to work out a Christian philosophy for the new age by drawing simultaneously on St Augustine and Descartes.[50] A fundamental idea shared by both of them is that the notion of God's existence is innate. Daudin, a Marxist, criticizes Lefebvre's ideas in the following terms: 'Has Henri Lefebvre rightly judged the relationship between Descartes and the Jansenists? He seems to take as proven a polarity which is at least disputable in the opinion of some specialists. Relying overconfidently on sweeping ideological themes, he has overlooked the anxiety with which Arnauld wrote to Descartes and the burlesque decree by which the Jansenist Racine and Boileau the sympathizer spared Cartesianism a parliamentary condemnation'.[51]

In fact H. Lefebvre was very conscious of the complexity of the history and that an ideology is not always adhered to in its entirety by those who profess it: 'The Jesuits', he wrote, 'were defenders of economic and even intellectual progress only so that they could fix it in originally feudal frameworks: the ecclesiastical state, the monarchical state . . . At this period they alone seemed "modern", but it was only to kill the modern spirit. The bourgeoisie, which later wanted to be – and to appear – "progressive", resorted to a "reactionary" discontent and concealed it under an antiquated ideology'.[52]

An understanding of these contradictions, which are the stuff of life, leads the historian to reject a priori constructions which offer serene and comprehensive analyses. At the religious level, and viewed from the twentieth century, Jansenism was both old-fashioned and new-fangled. Contemporary Catholicism rejected its pessimism, its individualism and its theology of grace, but gradually assimilated its reservations with regard to pontifical centralism, its presbyterianism, its sober worship, its concern to give the Bible to the faithful, and its rejection of superstition. At the political level, the royal authority, in fighting against the consequences of feudalism, was probably 'progressive', but the absolute powers of the king 'nurtured the germs of an unbridled reaction' and it 'increasingly turned into a protection of the nobility'.[53] The Jansenists – or 'republicans' as Louis XIV called them – with their distrust of absolutism and their spirit of free examen encouraged the rise of the modern spirit.

(c) *The diversity within Jansenism*

1. Saint-Cyran

A preliminary point, already made by Sainte-Beuve, must be mentioned: Port-Royal and Jansenism were not co-terminous. The Cistercian convent, reformed by Mère Angélique in 1609, was a high place of the Catholic Reformation in France long before Duvergier became its spiritual director (1635). For years the Salesian influence preponderated. The bishop of Geneva came to the monastery, was received by Mother Agnes (sister to Mère Angélique) and called the monastery 'his delight'. Another remark is called for, banal though it is: when Port-Royal turned Jansenist, it radiated piety and charity no less; Racine has recorded the veneration in which the peasants of the district held Mère Angélique. And on a visit to the famous convent in January 1674, Mme de Sévigné could not conceal her admiration: 'It is a paradise; a desert to which the devout of Christendom have retired; a holiness effused over the surrounding countryside'.

Port-Royal slipped into Jansenism under the influence of Duvergier. At first Duvergier, of whom we know so much more since the remarkable researches of J. Orcibal, was overridingly a disciple of Bérulle with whom he held daily conversations for many months. He collaborated in the *Grandeurs de Jésus*, the masterpiece of the founder of the Oratory, introduced it to a wide public and had it translated into Latin by his nephew Barcos. After Bérulle and in his wake, he became the director of devout people in Paris: this was one reason why Richelieu distrusted him. Duvergier was also a friend of Jansen's: they had worked together from 1611 to 1616 near Bayonne, on a property belonging to the Duvergier de Hauranne family. Later they corresponded (in code) until 1635, when war broke out and made communications between Paris and the Low Countries difficult. However, Duvergier did not receive a copy of the *Augustinus* until he was in prison at Vincennes (1641), when his sight had deteriorated badly. He found it lacked 'unction', but instructed young Arnauld to defend it against the attacks that were being launched. The bishop of Ypres and the 'oracle of Notre-Dame cloister' (Duvergier lived there immediately prior to his imprisonment) were both Augustinists, but from different stances. The former was a theoretician; the latter emphasized piety and the practice of Christianity, and as a genuine Bérullian insisted on adoration, the mystical body, the kenosis of the incarnate Word. J. Orcibal has therefore done much to replace Duvergier in the broad current of the French Catholic Reformation, whereas Bremond had done violence to his true stature by attaching him too closely to Jansenism. He has also clarified his psychology. Without denying his quirks of character in which 'fire and water mingled', his verbal violence, his fits of melancholy, he has refused to qualify him as a 'neurotic' or as a wild schemer. He has brought out his prodigious erudition, his lively imagination, his courage in times of trial, his 'slow rise to a more and more complete Christianity, despite the manifold lapses occasioned by a rebellious nature'.[55] We are now in a better position to appreciate his influence and his power as a 'spiritual magnet'.

2. Extremists and moderates

Coming after J. Orcibal and to some extent complementing his work,

L. Goldmann and L. Namer have shown that Jansenism was never 'a monolithic system with its own doctrine and flock on the edge of the Church'. In the light of recent researches it seems that not only are Lovanism, Cyranism and Quesnellianism not interchangeable, but that with regard to the formula three distinct attitudes were discernable in the little world of the friends of Port-Royal, reflecting divergent doctrinal positions. Arnauld and Nicole were in the centre, moderates who tried to avoid a break with Rome by resorting to the distinction between right and fact. Later on Nicole taught that a general grace was given to all men, and Arnauld turned back to Thomism and a conception of freedom as the possibility of choice between contraries. Another moderate was the Oratorian Duguet, a friend of Arnauld's and Quesnel's, who in 1699–1700 published his much admired *Institution d'un prince* in which he maintained, despite original sin, the existence and value of a natural law and therefore the possibility of 'Christian politics'.

The extreme wings of the Jansenist party were represented by two different attitudes, one passive, the other active. Barcos, Singlin[56] and Mère Angélique believed that the truth might not and could not be defended by human means, and that an intrinsically perverted world should be left strictly alone. Barcos recommended both to accept the condemnation of Jansen and not to sign the formula. L. Goldmann has offered convincing proof[57] that this paradoxical attitude was also Pascal's: Pascal broke with Nicole and Arnauld in 1661, drew up an *Écrit sur la signature* (A paper on signing the formula) advising refusal, and in the following year, on the eve of his death, stated that he accepted the pope's condemnation. The other extremist position, highlighted by G. Namer,[58] was proposed by Guillaume Le Roy, abbot of Hautefontaine, who after 1665 was the most determined opponent of the formula. It was he above all who persuaded Jacqueline Pascal and Mother Agnes to refuse their signature. This militant Jansenism was shared by Pavillon, Caulet and a certain number of clergy in Paris and the Paris environs.

According to Goldmann, it is only the doctrinal pessimism underlying the two extremist attitudes that can explain the *Pensées* of Pascal and the more outstanding of Racine's dramas. At the end of his life Pascal abandoned[59] the Arnaldian centrism of the seventeenth *Provincial Letter* for a pitiless analysis of the human condition and the total rejection of a radically evil world. For him not only was the world sinful and man perverted, but the first fault was so grave that God was beyond man's reach in this life. He was the Hidden God of scripture, always both present and absent: 'The continual presence of the Divinity prevents men from sleeping, and the perpetual absence of the Divinity turns this vigil into an agony'. The situation is truly tragic: laying bets for a God who hides and rejecting a world one can see. Is this rejection, which was the experience and choice of the hermits prior to 1669, not the key to the more sombre of Racine's works – *Andromaque, Britannicus, Bérénice*?[60] In these tragedies – and they really are tragedies – heroes and heroines become aware that they cannot hope to live up to the divine demands in this life. Under the watchful eye of the invisible God, they opt for an all-or-nothing morality and rejection.

3. Towards a comprehensive geography of Jansenism

The subtle and penetrating inquiry of present day historiography therefore reveals the variety within Jansenism itself at a time when both the Church and the state believed they were dealing with a homogeneous block. One must insist even more strongly on the variations in content – in terms both of time and space – of the Jansenist ideology. After the death of Barcos in 1678, Jansenism, although still a pessimist's philosophy of life, no longer rejected the world out-and-out, and it became definitively Arnaldian. It increasingly combined rigorism, Gallicanism, presbyterianism and distrust of absolute power. In the eighteenth century Jansenism in France coincided less than ever with any one social class. It was simply a refuge for all malcontents across the entire spectrum of the nation.

This is to say that it extended well beyond the limits of its initial adherents, and that a geography of Jansenism is possible[61] with the French capital as its influxive centre. Its proximity to Paris explains, for example, the large number of appellant parish clergy in the diocese of Rouen, and more particularly the vicariate of Pontoise.[62] It also explains the Jansenist penetration of the diocese of Vannes when a collaborator of Noailles, Mgr Lefebvre de Caumartin, son of a provincial administrator and godson of Cardinal Retz, was appointed to the see.[63] In the Lorraine of the end of the seventeenth century and the eighteenth century, studied by R. Taveneaux,[64] Jansenism spread from the two Cistercian abbeys of Hautefontaine and Orval, and the monasteries of the congregation of Saint-Vanne. Of these communities, the two former were hand in glove with Port-Royal, the latter with Saint-Germain-des-Prés. At the same time Lorraine in the eighteenth century also underwent the influence of Utrecht: in 1723 a French appellant, the bishop *in partibus* Varlet, consecrated at Utrecht an archbishop not recognized by Rome, and the small schismatical Church of Holland which resulted spread its timid presbyterianism and its rigorous Augustinism.[65]

A modification must be added here. It was not really second

Jansenism (Jansenism revised and corrected by Quesnel) which spread throughout the kingdom and beyond: it was much more a para-Jansenism. E. Appolis has demonstrated convincingly that between the Jansenists and the Constitutionists a 'third party' emerged, represented by such men as Malvin de Montazet (archbishop of Lyons), Bazins de Bezons (bishop of Carcassonne) and Beauteville (bishop of Alès).[66] Although they did not take part in the game of reiterated appeals, they fought against Molinism, condemned moral laxity and probabilism, and inclined to Gallicanism.

From France the works of friends and admirers of Port-Royal spread to Europe, as they had spread from Paris to France. The *Provincial Letters* were printed in England with the imprimatur of the official Church.[67] The *Pensées* were translated into English in 1688 and 1704, and this second version went through a large number of editions. John Wesley prescribed the *Pensées* for future Methodist ministers and had extracts from Saint-Cyran's *Lettres chrétiennes et spirituelles* translated into English.[68] Jansenism thus contributed to the modest beginnings of an ecumenical mentality. From 1783 onwards, more and more Jansenist works were printed in Italy, mainly as part of the collection *Opuscoli interessanti la religione* (Little works concerning religion) launched by Scipione de' Ricci.[69] This collection consisted almost entirely of works by Arnauld, Quesnel and French ecclesiastics faithful to the memory of Port-Royal.[70]

In 1938 E. Préclin suggested a work-plan for the study of 'the influence of French Jansenism abroad'.[71] The recent researches especially of M. Vaussard and E. Appolis [72] have clarified this influence, established its extent (for example in the Risorgimento), as well as noting its limits and its nuances. As in France, it was a para-Jansenism or 'degraded Jansenism' as Chaunu called it, rather than an explicit and structured Jansenism proper, which in the eighteenth century affected certain ecclesiastical and lay circles in various countries. An outstanding figure of this tendency was the bishop of Barcelona José Climent, more Thomist than Augustinist, open to the Enlightenment, hostile to laxism, to the Jesuits and to affective devotions, and anxious to introduce a simplified liturgy. Of a similar turn of mind we may mention Enrique Florez in Spain, Eusebius Amort in Germany, the French bishops of the 'third party' and several cardinals close to Benedict XIV.[73]

To understand Jansenism, therefore, one must go beyond it, and this wider problematic leads to the study of such questions as the relationship of Jansenism to Josephism, to Free Masonry and so on. Pre-Jansenism (the conditions which explain why the *Augustinus* was so successful) and anti-Jansenism must be studied likewise. Nicolò Contarini in Venice[74] in the early seventeenth century, when the city was regarded by Rome as 'another Geneva' and Juan de Palafox bishop of Osma in Mexico in the 1640s[75] are the representatives of pre-Jansenist mentality. Wary of the regular clergy, they defended the rights of the ordinary as well as opting for a rigorous religion and sober worship. As far as anti-Jansenism is concerned, there is a tendency today to note that at least in the Low Countries it pre-existed Jansenism itself, as it were,[76] and that particularly in the seventeenth century it was not by any means the monopoly of the Jesuits: the Franciscans contributed in no small measure to the attack on the bishop of Ypres' disciples.[77]

4. New light on Jansenism

Such could come only from a clarification of the Jansenist phenomenon in the light of the psychology of the collective mentality and from religious sociology. Why was there, at the time of the Protestant and Catholic Reformations, on both sides of the confessional abyss, that hyperacute awareness of sin, that obsession with hell, that emphatic and almost morbid delight in the original fault? Why was man so disparaged? Why was there that atmosphere of fear? A society which is afraid needs reassurance. The doctrinal clarifications produced in abundance during the sixteenth and seventeenth centuries by theologians, councils, synods of all denominations, Confessions, Articles and catechisms in which orthodoxy was everywhere condensed seem, from our twentieth century standpoint, to have performed this function of offering security. In such a context one can appreciate the seriousness with which the crime of heresy was invested, and more generally the magisterium's suspicion of all intellectual novelties. These were feared as obstacles on the road that leads to the narrow gate. More than any other centuries, the sixteenth and seventeenth saw a multiplicity of condemnations and warnings: anathemas and repudiations which give some measure of the enormous fear of Satan in the mentality of the west at that time. The chief snare set by the Evil One was the desire for free examen. If, despite the clear affirmations of scripture, Copernicus and Galileo declared that the earth went round the sun, there was no other possibility: they must be wrong.

The works of Copernicus were put on the Index in 1616, and Galileo was obliged to retract in 1633. The Roman Church rehabilitated him only in 1822. Descartes, who was a sincere believer, started from the *cogito* to demonstrate the existence of God and confirm revelation by 'natural philosophy'; but, said the anxious authorities, what if methodic doubt turned against dogma (Bossuet expressed just such anxiety to the bishop of Avranches)? Moreover, Descartes asserted not only the independence of reason but the justice of the experimental method as well. In 1663 his works were placed on the Index *donec corrigantur*. The same thing happened to the Oratorian Richard Simon (1638–1712) who was the originator of biblical criticism. A philologue with an excellent knowledge of the ancient east and a firm attachment to Rome, Richard Simon showed the Reformers who invoked scripture incessantly that there was not one original manuscript of the Bible extant, and that the exact meaning of many of the ancient Hebrew words escaped us. Nevertheless his *Histoire critique du Vieux Testament* (Critical History of the Old Testament, 1678) and *Histoire critique du texte du Nouveau Testament* (Critical history of the text of the New Testament, 1693) unleashed the protests of Bossuet and the censure of the apologists: 'Where should we be if, for example, the Pentateuch were not by Moses ... or if circumcision preceded Abraham?'[78] It is in this context of authoritarianism and dogmatism that the condemnations of Jansenism – and the Jansenist invective against the 'modernism' of the Jesuits – are to be viewed.

When one is considering the Jansenists, and taking into account Rome's attitude towards them, one naturally asks in what way they resembled the Protestants, and by a natural movement our study has moved from collective mentality to retrospective religious sociology. When Mazarin called Jansenism 'reheated Calvinism' he was both right and wrong. Right because the Jansenists and Protestants had, as near as makes very little difference, the same conception of grace and freedom and the same preferences for sober liturgy accessible to the faithful. Wrong because the radical Augustinists of Catholicism maintained the sacraments and the Roman dogmas, devotion to our Lady and the saints, the primacy of the bishop of Rome; and since they counselled retreat from the world, they did not, like the Reformers, exalt vocation in the world. In a pioneer article, P. Chaunu has described a particular form of Jansenism – in the countries on the edge of the Catholic world: the Low Countries, the United Provinces and Lorraine – as a 'compensatory Augustinism'.[79] This fruitful idea is also capable of wider application if it is remembered that a part of the Arnauld family was Protestant, and that in the eighteenth century a good number of 'the newly converted' supported the appellants. However, as P. Chaunu emphasizes, in the regions near the Protestant countries the Augustinism was as much and more so a constituent of Counter-Reformation proselytism. Action against the neighbouring heretics was possible only 'at the price of a convergent march in the direction of Christian radicalism'.

If this hypothesis is exact, it challenges in part a commonly admitted equation which can be expressed as: extensive Jansenist influence = ultimately a falling off of religious practice and a collective loss of faith. The equation is true for the whole archdiocese of Sens, a part of the dioceses of Meaux, Châlons-sur-Marne, Rheims and Beauvais, and the Pays d'Auge in Normandy.[80] But for P. Chaunu, the really atrophying Jansenism was the 'purely negative', 'political, presbyterian and captious brand . . . of the sheltered countries far from the frontiers of Catholicity, far from contact with the integral Reformed Churches'. On the other hand, the primitive Augustinist Jansenisms on the borders of Catholicity were 'particularly edifying', and among these one must also include the Pays de Caux in Normandy which was 'at once strongly practising, strongly biased to Protestantism and of a long Jansenist tradition'.[81]

The field of research into Jansenism is thus greatly enlarged by retrospective sociology, which is the subject of the next chapters.

Chapter 2

RELIGIOUS SOCIOLOGY AND COLLECTIVE
PSYCHOLOGY: AIMS AND METHODS

(a) *Aim: to know the 'average Christian' of the past*

1. From Auguste Comte to Gabriel Le Bras

For a long time religious history concentrated on the high spots. It favoured the study of popes, saints and illustrious figures in the Church; it presented the debate between Bossuet and Fénélon with impressive documentation; it was inexhaustible on theological quarrels and the ecclesiastical politics of sovereigns. If it dealt with devotion – and H. Bremond for example did to excellent effect – it was only to consider its 'literary' expression. In these past few years there has been an intellectual conversion of researchers, in that now they aim to rediscover the 'average' Christian of past ages and to know how and to what extent he practised his religion and lived his faith. We are invited to study the most basic levels of Christianity,[1] the religion of particular groups: from now on every religious history is necessarily sociological[2] and as far as possible serial and quantitative.

Two different but convergent paths have led to this. One started with the work of Comte and Durkheim, the founder of the periodical *L'Année sociologique* (1897), who studied the necessary relations between mores and social types and then examined the elementary forms of religious life.[3] The other began with Gabriel Le Bras who from 1931 to his death

129

invited men of the Church and historians to look for the proximate and remote causes of present-day 'dechristianization'. The main article of his which pioneered this type of research was entitled 'Religious statistics and religious history. Towards a detailed examination and historical explanation of the state of Catholicism in the different regions of France'.[4] This article and all Gabriel Le Bras' articles on this theme up to 1954 have been published in a two-volume work called *Studies in religious sociology*,[5] which is now the indispensable propaedeutic for all research into the present and past religious practice of the Christian people; it impresses us with its deep sense of faith, its courage and its humour. At first Garbiel Le Bras' invitation of 1931 met with suspicion, but the startling revelations of *France, Mission Country* (published 1943)[6] and the works of Canon F. Boulard[7] impressed on the Church the urgency with which it should adopt the methods of sociological investigation. From that time researches have multiplied, both in France and elsewhere, on the behaviour of the faithful today and the collective reasons for the drop in religious practice. Parallel with this, and especially in France, an increasing number of historians are utilizing the retrospective method initiated by Marc Bloch to go back as far as possible into the country's religious past and examine the Christian attitudes of the time with the maximum of statistics available. Here we shall be dealing only with this part of the sociological investigation applied to the Catholicism of the sixteenth to eighteenth centuries, but bearing in mind the twofold direction in research which has made it possible.

2. Religious sociology

The sacred and the profane are interdependent. 'If they create no gods, profane societies offer every religion a cradle and nourishment'.[8] 'Religions, whose proper scope is the beyond, have their roots on earth. They lead the faithful to the lasting and the infinite, but they live in space and time'.[9] 'As a rule man adores, implores and sacrifices with, in and through his group'.[10] The ambitions of religious sociology are therefore immense, because 'they embrace all times, all countries, all man's dreams of the eternal and infinite',[11] all the forms of prayer and all the structures of a particular confession. In short, sociology deals with the totality of religion insofar as it relates to human groupings and is constituent of their destiny.

The various areas of religious sociology need to be clarified further. Adopting the classic division of Hubert and Mauss,[12] we may say that it is the study of a religion's conceptualizations, systems, organizations and practices.

(i) *Conceptualizations.* One may not exclude from the proper domain of sociology the conceptualizations of invisible worlds, pantheons and mythologies, hells and heavens. All of them have a partly social origin, and conversely the ideas conceived over the ages have in their turn influenced social life. Also, the conceptualizations of the beyond are translated into artistic images. Since 'every artist lives in the milieu which produces, supports and judges him',[13] while authority can consciously impose rules on him society unconsciously imposes its language. There is therefore such a thing as the sociology of sacred art, because every artistic venture has a social character.

(ii) *Systems.* All systematized religion elaborates a dogmatic corpus, a theological system. Dogma, like conceptualization, is concretized in variable language. It is therefore hardly surprising that there is a 'history of dogma'. The Divine is a fixed star, but the eyes and instruments with which different periods and places have viewed it vary.

(iii) *Organizations.* Even more patient of sociological scrutiny are religious institutions, living organisms to which may appropriately be applied the rules of social psychology. A religion involves modes of aggregation, exclusion and reintegration which are determined in space and time: there is therefore a need to consider the sociological history of baptism, confirmation, excommunication, penance and absolution. Within a confession such as Catholicism, there are a good many differentiations, notably between clergy and faithful, but also among the faithful. In the hierarchical body, the relations between papacy and episcopate, higher and lower clergy, seculars and regulars have varied over the centuries with the general organization of society. Among the faithful, confraternities, and more recently movements of Catholic Action, have emerged in the past. They are to be seen in relation to certain other phenomena of partial secession within the Church such as eremitism and monachism. The study of religious structures also includes an analysis of the dialectical relationships between a confession and its rivals, between a confession and the world.

(iv) *Practices.* Finally, sociology must tabulate religious practices, 'itemize and classify the visible manifestations' of belief, catalogue and describe the attitudes of prayer. How could a science whose object is collective living afford to ignore the ceremonial — gestures and formulae — with which faith has expressed itself in space and time? How could it neglect its varieties and variations?

Drawing continually on history and geography,[14] sociology — and especially religious sociology — merges into collective psychology. 'Sociology and psychology, far from excluding each other, represent two secant circles which overlap for an essential part of their surfaces'

(G. Gurvitch). As soon as inquiry into a group, be it parish, suburb, town, province or country, succeeds in defining the components of a mentality, the frontiers between the two disciplines blur. Sociologists and mental clinicians share the same object in joint sovereignty. The pluralism of science vanishes behind the unity of the scientists.[15] As an indication of the attempt to reconstruct the sensibilities of the past, we may mention the remarkable and very recent work of A. Dupront in his thesis on *Le mythe de croisade* (The myth of the crusades), and R. Mandrou, both in his *Introduction to modern France* and in his *Judges and sorcerers in seventeenth century France*.[16] If the manifestations and suppression of sorcery are matters of direct interest to religious history, the latter must necessarily benefit from researches into the most varied aspects of collective mentality: games and amusements, escapisms and imaginary worlds, culinary practices, and the use or non-use of excitants and stupefacients. It must pay even closer attention to researches into the development of the attitude to infancy in a civilization[17] and the attitude of various social groups to madness,[18] poverty,[19] miracles and so on. However, we must repeat that these studies into group mentality do not dispense from using the methods of sociological investigation. Conversely the best works of religious sociology in recent years by historians of the *Ancien Régime* – J. Toussaert on *Religion in Flanders at the end of the middle ages*,[20] L. Pérouas on *The diocese of La Rochelle 1648–1724*,[21] and J. Ferté on *Religious life in the Parisian countryside 1622–1695*[22] – necessarily evoke the psychology of the faithful and pastors, and recreate the atmosphere in which they lived.

3. Faith and figures

One cannot talk about science without including measurements. The only sociology is quantitative. Drawing up as complete an inventory as possible of the religious practice of a given group means penetrating the vicissitudes of belief with the dry but necessary instrument of statistics. Figures are drawn up on Sunday attendance at mass, confessions and communions at Easter and throughout the year, confraternities, schools, vocations, concubinary priests, residence and non-residence, indigenous origin of the clergy in a diocese etc. The churches and chapels constructed, reconstructed or embellished in a given period are totted up and entered on a map. Paintings, reredorses and statues of the saints are catalogued. Nor is that all. Establishing the religious index of a parish also means inquiring into the past of this human community, defining its geographical context, identifying its social cleavages.

Religious statistics are to be handled with care when the past is relatively distant. T. Toussaert's book was the first essay in measuring the Christian adherence of a society – in this case a parish in Bruges – in the late fifteenth and early sixteenth century with the help of statistical information. The author broke new ground, not without risk but at least with courage.[23]

He attempted to give a quantitative assessment of the mass attendance and communions at St James's Church, Bruges, between 1445 and 1522, drawing on four series of documents which give: (i) the *Appoort* or amount taken in collections; (ii) the cost of the ablution wine; (iii) the offerings of the faithful to cover the cost of the ablution wine; and (iv) the invoices for the hosts. A specialist in statistics, R. Mols, subjected these documents and J. Toussaert's figures to a ruthless critique.[24] On the Appoort he asks how one is to assess the number of poor people in the congregation who contributed nothing to the collection, or the number of children. How can one judge 'to what extent those who took up the collection really reached the majority of the congregation'? By 'ablution wine' is meant the wine usually offered to the faithful after communion. The registers at St James's in Bruges give the amounts spent and the quantities (in *stopen* $= 2^{1}/_{2}$ litres) bought. However, can one correctly calculate the number of mouthfuls of wine to a litre? 'The sip of an old soldier is not at all the same as the sip of a devout old lady trembling with emotion'. Fr Mols holds that Fr Toussaert is too parsimonious in his estimation of the average mouthful taken by the Brugeois in the fifteenth century, and that he therefore overcalculates the number of communicants, the number of parishioners in St James's and the number of inhabitants in Bruges, which latter, according to Toussaert, was 40,000 in about 1450 and 68,000 in about 1510. As regards the hosts, it is sometimes stipulated that they are 'large' or 'small'; but elsewhere 'hosts' are mentioned without further qualification. For other periods the accounts specify the cost, but not the number, of hosts. J. Toussaert must therefore have decided that all the non-specified hosts were large ones, and on the other hand he converts the amount of money spent into an overall figure of 340 hosts per denier. In this artificial fashion J. Toussaert reaches totals which are much above those for periods for which the number of hosts bought is specified.

These criticisms are irrefutable, but they call for two observations. Firstly, J. Toussaert himself offers the results of his calculations with the greatest reservation. Secondly, R. Mols does not deny his statistics all value. They give figures of little worth in the absolute, but of considerable interest when compared with each other. It transpires, for example, that in 1515 as in 1445, the four main feasts of the year at Bruges were, in order of importance, Good Friday, Easter Sunday, Christmas Day and Whitsunday. However, whereas the popularity of Good Friday appeared to diminish, that of the other three feasts grew, and attendance at the services became more regular. Among the less important feasts, All Saints, Candlemas and the Assumption clearly gained in popularity, supplanting the feast of the patron saint of the parish, St James, and out-shining Corpus Christi. On the other hand, there were more faithful at the services in Bruges during the first decades of the sixteenth century than in the middle of the fifteenth, either because of the increase in population, or because the people were more devout, or for both these reasons at once.

The use of statistics in religious history raises a number of serious problems, some psychological, others philosophical. Psychologically, it would be absurd to identify faith and practice: we shall have occasion to return to this question when we come to study the 'dechristianization' in the eighteenth century – a period in which practice remained relatively stable and regular. Conversely, registering a drop in the number of prac-tising Christians in the twentieth century does not prove that there are proportionally less really religious people or people of inferior religious practice than in the past. Philosophically, the effort to measure the vitality of Christianity does not imply a calculation of the level of faith, an explanation of dogmas, doctrines and monuments solely on the basis of social determinisms. One can maintain that 'the essential transcends the level of weights and measures',[25] that 'religious situations will always retain something beyond mere numbers', and that belief and charity can never be fully translated into figures, and yet at the same time admit the inevitable presence of what is quantitative in religious history. Therefore it is a question of measuring not intimate spiritual states, but the effects and signs of belief and the attitudes it inspires.

(b) Registers of pastoral visitations and the private records of parish clergy

1. Registers of visitations

The most suitable documents[26] on past religious practice are in-contestably the registers of pastoral, archdiaconal or deanery visits and the reports of parish clergy to their bishop in reply to his request for in-formation on the spiritual and temporal welfare of their parishes (in preparation for a synod, for example). In France these documents are usually kept in series G of the departmental archives or, for the old diocese of Paris, in series L of the National Archives. G. Le Bras has synthesized the information in these files as follows:[27]

I. *Church property*
A. The church and its adjuncts (sacristy, presbytery)
B. The cemetery: extent, form of enclosure, plan, local customs
C. Rural chapels
II. *The clergy*
A. Parish priest: appointment, origin, residence, culture, mores
B. Assistant priests
C. Chaplains and vicars (The French term [*prêtre*] *habitué* refers to a priest without an official responsibility who provides assistance in a parish. It might be used to cover the various categories of *vicarii*: *adiutores, cooperativi, oeconomi, substituti*. A very loose English translation would be supply priest, although no one term will cover all the meanings. Tr): appointments, way of life
III. *Worship and instruction*
A. Patron saint
B. Furniture: statues, paintings, frescoes, ornaments, sacred vessels, liturgical books
C. Ceremonies: personal, liturgical, feastdays, processions, pilgrimages
D. Homily, catechism, missions
IV. *Material life*
A. Sources: gifts and legacies, foundations, taxes
B. Composition: lands, houses, furniture
C. Administration: vestry (vestry members, budget, accounts)
D. List and methods of investment
V. *Establishments*
A. Monasteries and convents
B. Hospitals, hospices, leper colonies
C. Schools
VI. *Society*
A. Demography
B. Hierarchy: lords, officers, notabilities
C. Surveyed professions: midwives, doctors, inn-keepers
D. Associations: corporations and sodalities
VII. *Spiritual and moral state*
A. Beliefs: superstitions, witchcraft, dissidences, Protestants, recent converts, Jansenists
B. Practice: mass attendance, confessions and communions outside Eastertide

C. Mores: social virtues (charity, mutual help); dominant vices: concubinage, adultery; theft, trespass, quarrels; swindling; dances and public houses.

G. Le Bras is right when he says that in this list 'nearly all the human sciences parade before us: geography and toponomy, archaeology and chronology, liturgy and canon law, demography, sociology and collective psychology, history of culture and mores, history of art, history of technology and history of popular traditions'.

Accounts of pastoral, archdiaconal and deanery visits are not rare in European archives. They have already contributed a great deal to our knowledge of the clergy and religious life in England at the end of the middle ages. They are particularly numerous in Italy, where the study of them has already made a serious start. L. V. Pastor analyses twenty-seven pastoral visitations carried out in Italy in 1573 and 1574.[28] The visits by the former advisor to Clement VII, Gian Matteo Giberti, who became bishop of Verona, from 1528 onwards deserve particular mention. P. Tacchi-Venturi[29] and G. Alberigo[30] give ample documentation on the first pastrol visits to be made in Italy in the immediate post-Tridentine period. Mgr Roncalli (later Pope John XXIII) has published the *Acta* of St Charles Borromeo's apostolic visitation to Bergamo in 1576.[36] The interesting study by F.Mellano on the Counter-Reformation in the diocese of Mondovi is largely based on the reports drawn up subsequent to the episcopal visitations of 1574, 1582–3 and 1590–1.[32] Utilizing the account of an apostolic visitation, a Croat historian has been able to clarify the religious situation in Dalmatia (which was then under Venetian rule) in 1579.[33] Nevertheless there is still an enormous amount of work to be done before the extraordinary wealth of this type of document in Italy is fully exploited. It could perhaps explain why Italy rejected the temptation of Protestantism. A similar remark could be made of Spain.

Religious sociology has tapped the bishops', archdeacons' and deans' reports the most intensely in France.[34] The first task was to draw up a complete catalogue, and this is in progress.[35] It is now known where the finest dossiers are to be found.[36] The diocesan archives of Coutances are of particular value: they contain 147 registers of records of archdiaconal and pastoral visitations between 1634 and 1789.[37] Important recently-published works in religious sociology, such as J. Ferté's study of the rural archdeaneries in the diocese of Paris during the seventeenth century, and L. Pérouas' study of the diocese of La Rochelle,[38] have made extensive use of the accounts of parish visitations. Shorter but very detailed monographs have also drawn on this type of document. G. Le Bras himself gave a lead when he published articles on 'The canonical control of the Christian life in the diocese of Auxerre under Louis XIV'[39] and 'The religious state of the diocese of Châlons in the last century of the *Ancien Régime*'.[40] These were followed by a series of extremely penetrating studies, of which we may mention three: M. Join-Lambert's on the religious practice in Rouen under Louis XIV and from 1707 to 1789,[41] and P. Flament's on lay mores in Sées from 1699 to 1710.[42] These researches are yielding mines of information on mass attendance, Easter duties, the residence of parish priests, the teaching of the catechism, the relations between the people and the clergy, the local nobility's disdain of the cloth, the neglect of Church fabric, the insubordination of the peasantry, the rusticity of mores, popular incredulity, and so forth. 'For the history of marriage, folklore and social life, what racy and instructive data we have here!'[43] There has even been an article on the ecclesiastical archives of the *Ancien Régime* as a source of folklore.[44]

2. Private records of parish priests

The accounts of parish visitations must evidently be completed by other documents. The records of parish clergy are of particular interest. These 'manuscript newspapers' provide an abundance of information on the daily life of a population. We may make an especial mention here of the records left by: François Hébert, who was curé of Notre-Dame de Versailles from 1686 to 1704;[45] P. Beurrier, curé of Saint-Étienne-du-Mont in Paris, who heard Pascal's last confession;[46] Alexandre Dubois, curé of Rumegies (in the diocese of Tournai) from 1686 to 1739;[47] and Jean Meslier, curé of Etrépigny in Champagne between 1689 and 1729.[48] In all these cases the writers were relatively educated men: this makes their observations and information on their age and their parishes all the more valuable. The curé of Rumegies, who comes to life again in the inspired pages of Henri Platelle's book, was a Gallican and Jansenizing pastor who wrote a *liber memorialis* for the information of his successors. He was zealous, indefatigable in the service of his people, scrupulous in the financial and administrative matters of his parish. His diary shows that the curé of a rural parish of 750 souls knew and could assess the political events and great religious quarrels of his time. More than this, it reveals the mores and attitudes of a peasant population. Dubois gives the following account of the religious state of his parishioners: '... As regards religion and the articles of the faith, there is no one capable of sustaining the contrary of what is preached; but . . . there are some who harbour ancient errors in their hearts which they justify only by saying that their fathers thought thus, and which they stoutly abide by, for example, that

DIRINOU

PLOUGASTEL •Loperhet
•Irvillac
DAOULAS
ROSCANVEL ○ LOGONNA Hanvec S!-F
•Rumengol
Camaret Landevennec Le Faou B
•Crozon •Rosnoën
•Telgruc ~S!-Segal
•S!-Nic Pl
Chateaulin
○ PLOMODIERNE

Beuzec- DOUARNENEZ •■ Plounevez-Porzay
Cleden-- Cap Sizun
Cap Sizun TREBOUL○ ■(18) •Kerlaz ○LOCRONAN •Br
S!-Theis Goulien (8) Plogonnec N-D. DE
Sein Kersent PONT-CROIX Poullan •■ PLOARÉ ○QUILINEN
POULDAVID Le Juch
Plogoff ■(5) •Heilars ■POULDERGAT(5) La
S!- AUDIERNE MAHALON ○GUENGAT
TUGEAN •Gourlizon PLONEIS KERFEUTEUN
Primelin Esquibien PLOUHINEC •Kermaria (8)○ ○ TY MAND
Landudec QUIMPER■& ○CUZON ERGU
Plozevet Plogastel Plugufan■ ○ GABER
Lababan S!-Germain Penhars Maria •Loc S!-Gi
Pouldreuzic Peumerit Kerlagatu ○ ERGUE
•Plovan■ Plomelin S!- ARMEL
Treogat Evarzec• L
•Plouneour Pleuven
TREMEOC Clohars •■ A
N-D, Benodet •Fouesnant
de Treminou Perguet Concarnea
•Plomeur La
PENMARC'H ○ •Trefiagat

MAP II: *P. Manoir's missions in the diocese of Quimper* (E. Petitjeans)

one may be saved in any religion. The second defect of the Rumegies parishioners is a certain neglect or tepidity in the affairs of salvation, for example in frequenting the holy sacraments and the holy offices in the parish; they have no scruple about missing holy mass or even disdaining to attend vespers, particularly when the weather is fine ... From this stems the third defect, or rather the third defect is the cause of the others, namely that they are excessively partial to temporal riches ... Still, there are good people, and many of whom one could not speak ill, and in particular one may say of almost the entire parish that they have great charity for the poor. I believe God will save them for that'.[49]

In Alexandre Dubois' diary, the picture of village mores is not without its tart features. The inhabitants of Rumegies, desultory in their attendance at church but on the whole of a charitable disposition, spend money on looking nice for going out on Sunday when they have sold food for extortionate sums to campaigning armies, but otherwise they live wretchedly and emit unpleasant odours.[50] 'You have to see the children of these people selling their produce, dressed in a very unpeasant-like fashion: the young men with hats braided with gold or silver, and so forth; the girls with hair-dos a foot high and clothes to match. And as their fathers and mothers are rich, they are insolent enough to frequent taverns on Sunday, despite the synodal statutes and all the preaching on the subject ... Yet nearly all of them live wretchedly at home. I have seen the richest in the village sell a miserable pig and so go without meat for the rest of the year ... You can see them eat soft cheese with their bread, to be able to sell their butter. And as for the other commodities of life, they have none. Their houses are in a state of intolerable filth. Most of them have one shirt on their bodies – and the other at the wash; and apart from Sundays, when they are either at the church or at the tavern, they are so dirty that the girls cure the men of their concupiscence, and vice versa'.

As a general rule, the curé of Rumegies got on well with his parishioners, whom he served with devotion and selflessness, but material problems sometimes roused flashes of anticlericalism in the village which partly explain future events. The parish of Rumegies depended on the neighbouring abbey of Saint-Amand which levied the tithes. The abbot of Saint-Amand took seven sheaves of corn out of every hundred, and the curé one. The abbey had leased its share to the village community, and this placed the curé in a difficulty, because he went without his modest solitary sheaf. He therefore thought himself shrewd when in 1702, at the expiration of the lease of the tithes, he bought the farming lease for the abbey's tithe. Immediately he could receive his quota without any embarrassment, because it was a question of only 'one tither, one cart, one lot of trouble'; but the populace felt that its curé was imposing a burden from which it believed itself freed. There was widespread anger in the village against the curé: 'There were outspoken threats to burn him, kill him, insult him, chase him from the parish! And even his best friends in the parish attacked him. And unless the good Lord favours them with a miracle, they will never forgive him! If the curé had thought he would have to endure so much, he would never have considered taking that tithe'.[51]

We shall have occasion later to speak of the curé Meslier, 'atheist, communist and revolutionary', in the chapter on dechristianization. Also Meslier is much less representative of the average French pastor of the seventeenth and eighteenth centuries than Alexandre Dubois. The latter's diary is a typical document.

(c) Other sources giving information on the secular clergy and places of worship

1. On the episcopate

The diaries of curés are rather rare,[52] and many of the accounts of pastoral visits have disappeared. Even where they are extant, recourse to other ecclesiastical sources is evidently advisable, because they too can shed light on the day-to-day religious life of the Christian people. These other sources include the bishops' *ad limina* reports,[53] the registers of the Church courts (which deal with both laity and clergy), and synodal statutes. 'The double – and considerable – merit of synodal statutes is that they give us an idea of how common law was adapted to the various peoples of Christendom, and afford glimpses into the realities of daily life'.[54] They fulfil this latter function by the complaints and sanctions they mention, which reflect the whole spectrum of parish life. For some years now theses and dissertations based on synodal statutes have dealt with matters such as religious practice,[55] confraternities[56] and marriage.[57] In Poland J. Sawicki has published ten volumes of synodal statutes. Specific studies on this category of document have been written for England by Cheney and for Sweden by Kroon. In France, although many of them are still unpublished, A. Artonne, L. Guizard and O. Pontal have written a *Catalogue of synodal statutes*,[58] which is a very useful source book. For example, it shows that the most important collection of synodal statutes in France under the *Ancien Régime* is for a diocese

(Angers) for which we have practically no accounts of pastoral visitations.

Synodal statutes shed light both on the sociological reality they were attempting to transform, and on their authors. A reforming bishop frequently published more of them than a less zealous prelate. The religious tone of a diocese depended to a very large extent on the activity and lifestyle of the bishop, and that is why the episcopate is subjected to systematic study. (Non-hagiographical) monographs on individual bishops[59] are important, but group studies even more so. P. Broutin has attempted one in his *La réforme pastorale en France au XVIIe siècle*. Concentrating on reformist bishops, he distinguishes six groupings:

(i) the bishops of a Borromean stamp: François de La Rochefoucauld (bishop of Clermont 1585–1610, then of Senlis 1610–22), Alain de Solminihac (Cahors 1636–54), and Francis de Sales;

(ii) those who used administrative means to reform the religious spirit: François de Sourdis (Bordeaux 1600–28), Sébastien Zamet (Langres 1615–54), Richelieu, Henri de Sponde (Pamiers 1628–34);

(iii) those of an Oratorian stamp: Barthélemy de Donadieu (Comminges 1626–37), Jean-Baptiste Gault (Marseilles 1642–3), Étienne de Vilazel (Saint-Brieuc 1637–77);

(iv) those who followed the narrow way of Port-Royal: Nicolas Pavillon (Alet 1637–77), Félix Vialart (Châlons-sur-Marne 1642–80), Étienne Le Camus (Grenoble 1671–1707);

(v) those who remained prisoners of the century's worldly spirit: François de La Fayette (Limoges 1627–76), Claude Joly (Agen 1665–78), Gabriel de Roquette (Autun);

(vi) and lastly those who, like Louis de Lascaris d'Urfé (Limoges 1676–95), followed the spirituality and methods of Saint-Sulpice. Before publishing this book, P. Broutin had translated and adapted Mgr Jedin's *Bischofsideal der katholischen Reformation* (The ideal of the bishop in the Catholic Reformation).[61]

However, it is not sufficient to classify bishops according to their spirituality. They must be examined from a properly sociological point of view: what was their social milieu, their university curriculum, their income etc.? G. Alberigo[62] has provided a model of this sort of study in his work on the Italian secular bishops who participated in the first sessions of the Council of Trent. It transpires that most of the prelates had studied in faculties of canon law and not theology, and that therefore their strictly dogmatic knowledge was brittle. That is why, at the council, they were happy to let the regulars do the talking.

2. On the material situation of the clergy

After the council as before it, the bishops' reforming zeal encountered a number of obstacles mentioned above (privileges of the cathedral chapter, exemptions of the regulars, independence of those who awarded benefices etc). On the question of benefices, another category of documents — polyptychs — gives the benefices which remained at the disposition of the bishop and those that did not. The polyptychs are lists of the benefices of a cure, abbey or diocese giving the title, patron, locality and annual revenue. The oldest of them date from the thirteenth century, but most come between the fourteenth and the seventeenth. In France publication began in 1903.[63] The systematic use of the polyptychs not only enables the historian to measure the limitations imposed by the benefice system on the authority of the bishop, but also reveals important economic data. For example, Charles-Édouard Perrin drew up two tables which give respectively the areas and total income of the benefices of the various French bishoprics in the early fourteenth century, in 1516 and in 1760, and the index of the average benefice wealth at the same three dates. The bishoprics of the province of Bourges were considerably less well off (as far as benefice wealth is concerned) than the provinces of Rheims, Sens and Rouen. The diocese of Paris was the richest. It also transpires that in the country as a whole, the indices of 1760 are much higher than those of 1516, and the latter than those of the early fourteenth century. The devaluation of currency undoubtedly absorbed a part of the increased revenues, but it cannot be too strongly emphasized that in the period of the Catholic Reformation the material situation of the lower clergy improved immeasurably, both in France and in Europe as a whole.[65] The increase in tithes referred to by E. Le Roy-Ladurie,[66] the obligation of a clerical 'title' imposed by Trent and then in France by the ordinance of Orleans (1581: no one shall be promoted to holy orders without 'temporal goods or a benefice sufficient to keep him'), and the drop in the number of supply priests (who held no benefices) which was very marked after 1648 in a diocese like La Rochelle all helped to raise the standard of living of the curés (and curates) of the *Ancien Régime*. Polyptychs, documents from the *Agence du Clergé* and the diocesan clergy-tax offices, registers of ecclesiastical appointments,[67] fiscal declarations of the parish priests in 1790–1, statements of Church property sold under the Revolution: these various categories of archival documents have led students of them in these last years to the same conclusion: the majority of French curés in the eighteenth century were comfortably off, and enjoyed an important position in their parishes. The phrase 'congruous portion' (in connexion with 'congruist curés') was misunderstood by many historians who forgot that its original and proper meaning was 'appropriate and sufficient income'.[68] A tonsured cleric of twelve was not worried about going to stay in a presbytery in 1764: 'I had several times heard it said, somewhat flippantly, that *Dominus vobiscum* never lacked for bread, and I could see for myself that there was no dearth of tasty dishes and wine − good wine at that'.[69]

3. On the material state of places of worship

In our own time, therefore, no adequate study of religious life can afford to exclude as exhaustive an analysis as possible of the material conditions which gave the clergy their living and worship its shape − two connected features. All the information which can shed light on the state and number of places of prayer at the various stages of a historical development is therefore of interest. In France a large number of religious buildings, statues and paintings were damaged or destroyed in the wars of religion. It would be helpful to have a catalogue province by province which would ultimately give a geographical picture of the sackings in the kingdom from 1562. As long ago as the 1930s, V. Carrière pointed out the urgent need for this,[70] and he proposed as a model the *Petit tableau des ravages faits par les huguenots de 1562 à 1574 dans l'ancien et nouveau diocèse de Sées* (Brief list of the Huguenot ravages from 1562 to 1574 in the old and new diocese of Sées) by Fr Blin (1888). It is really a matter of assembling for any given district a number of different documents 'which would, when compared, complete, verify and interpret each other'.[71] Appropriate documents would be the decrees of parliamentary courts, reports on damage drawn up on command of the king by bailiffs and seneschals, evaluations by beneficiaries for the purpose of assessing the damage caused in the wars, and tax reductions conceded to ecclesiastics whose benefices had been destroyed. These requests for exoneration or reduction of tax are in general conserved in the papers of the *Agence du Clergé de France* (series G8 of the National Archives).

The partial or total destruction of churches and chapels in France during the Hundred Years War,[72] then the wars of religion and then the Fronde,[73] as well as the ravages of time and sometimes demographic changes, explain the importance of the rebuilding of places of worship in France during the whole of the modern period.[74] Church accounts (series H of the National Archives, series G of the Departmental Archives), complemented by the reports of pastoral visitations, can help to date and map this massive reconstruction programme and thereby provide valuable information on the religious renovation between the sixteenth and eighteenth centuries.

The documents can also be the buildings themselves, their altars, reredorses, paintings and statues. Historians will now examine with the greatest interest the indexes and photographic dossiers at present being methodically assembled, canton by canton, by the *Inventaire des monuments historiques et richesses artistiques*.[75] This is one of the most important undertakings to identify, date and conserve the monumental and iconographic past that has ever been started in France. Parallel with this ambitious and long-term project, the *Centre de Recherches sur la civilisation de l'Europe moderne*, headed by Roland Mousnier, has for some years been subsidizing the research of Victor L. Tapié and his collaborators into the reredoses of the three old Breton dioceses (Rennes, Dol and Saint-Malo. Similar surveys have been started for Aquitaine, Seine-et-Marne and Roussillon). The questionnaire is spread over forty-six columns with up to ten possible answers in each column. It would take us too long to give a detailed analysis of it, but we may usefully give a general outline. Let us say that a place of worship is under examination. The researchers try to determine the population of the village or town, the building's function (parish church, chapel, centre of pilgrimage etc.), its date of construction, its position with relation to the roads, the sea, the next big town, and its situation with regard to the nearest available raw materials (wood, stone, marble). They then define the materials of the reredos they have studied, its central and collateral themes and its style, and they also try to discover who ordered it, who made it, whether missions were given when it was being built, whether one or more confraternities prayed in front of it, the dates of pastoral visitations, and so on.

(d) Characteristics and manifestations of religious devotion

1. Veneration of local saints and pilgrimages

The index that the above-mentioned researches are gradually building up should make a systematic study of patterns of worship in the past much easier, and clarify the devotions and saints[76] which retained their popularity with the faithful, those that died out over the centuries and the new ones that were introduced. The necessary cataloguing of the sanctuaries, chapels, altars, statues and paintings dedicated to a particular saint makes sense only when expressed in cartographical terms. Maps show the privileged zones in which that particular dulia predominated, the ebb and flow of devotion. Drawing on research into the Breton religious mentality of the sixteenth to eighteenth centuries and the *Inventaire des monuments*, monographs are being written in Ille-et-Vilaine and Finistère to try to determine the fortunes of traditional local saints during the Catholic Reformation, to what extent St Yves and St Anne gained in popularity, and how well supported the confraternities of the Blessed Sacrament and of the Rosary were in the province.[77] To be complete a study of local saints would also have to include indications of the main elements in the folklore of the region under consideration and a map of their distribution.[78]

It goes without saying that a piece of research in religious sociology, into the past or present, must pay particular attention to places of pilgrimage, which are the privileged foci of popular devotion. The archives of certain Roman confraternities are full of information on the faithful who came to pray on the tombs of the apostles in holy years and who lodged with these confraternities for their three-day pilgrimage. At Sainte-Anne-d'Auray there are records from the seventeenth century noting the miracles attributed to our Lady's mother who has been venerated here since a statue was discovered in 1625.[79] From these we can gain some knowledge of the types of miracle and their frequency, and also of the cultural level, social background and geographical origin of those cured, and therefore of the sanctuary's influence.[80]

2. Geography and religion

Geography and religion are connected realities not only globally – Islam, for example, occupies a more or less coherent geographical area – but also within any one country and within any one denomination. Studies have been published on the religion of the Basques,[81] the Bretons,[82] the Ardennais[83] and the Normans.[84] These, of course, are not just repetitions of the same clichés about 'the mystic Bretons' or the 'critical and brutal climate' in which the ceremonies of Rouergue (= approximately Aveyron today) took place; nor is it simply a question of uncritically adopting Corinne's view that the Italians at the beginning of the nineteenth century enjoyed a 'lively, sentimental religion' full of easygoing joy, pageantry and exuberance.

Geographical history cannot be satisfied with such vague approximations. It must be able to give adequate answers to detailed questions. One of the most interesting of these is the missions which proliferated under the Catholic Reformation in the towns and – this was new –

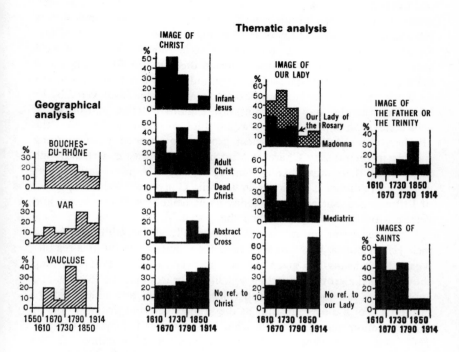

FIG. 1: Holy Souls altars (Altars of Purgatory) in Provence (G. & M. Vovelle).

(The percentages in the geographical analysis refer to the total for the *Département* (County); those in the thematic analysis to the total number in the tables chronologically represented.)

country villages of Europe during the seventeenth and eighteenth centuries. To what extent did they transform or correct the popular piety of this or that region? It has long been held that St Louis Grignion de Montfort (1673–1716) 'made the Vendée', 'was the Father of the Vendée'. There is no doubt that his missions staggered Catholic Europe; but the real question here is surely whether the sense of shock which he induced lasted. In the mid-eighteenth century, referring to taverns open during High mass and work on Sundays, the curé of Malaucène stated: 'These are abuses which missions eradicate for some months, but they always recur'.[85] L. Pérouas has happily examined this question of the impact of the missions on the people, using a method which has become a model for subsequent efforts. He compared the map of the areas covered by Fr Montfort with the map of present-day religious practice, and his pertinent conclusion is that: 'No one would think of calling Fr Montfort the "Father of the Aunis" (an ancient province of France, corresponding roughly to present-day Charente-Maritime, on the west coast), although he preached there more than in Vendée, because in Aunis today the level of religious practice is mediocre, indifferent. Conversely, the Retz district of Brittany is about as fervent today as its neighbour·Pontchâteau, and yet Fr Montfort hardly preached there at all'.[86]

When discussing an age in which practically all the faithful observed their Easter duties, how can we assess the religious vitality of a region? Again Fr Pérouas has given the best answer to this question. A map showing all the groups of certain sodalities, for example the Rosary, and another with the home towns and villages of priests give a clear picture of the faith of a diocese insofar as they reflect certain spiritual works of supererogation over and above what was commanded by the Church. They clarify the depth of faith. The number of vocations to the priesthood cannot be an absolutely determinative criterion for the religious vitality of a region at that time, because ordination meant not only an acceptance of the service of God but also the acquisition of a benefice. Benefices frequently passed from uncle to nephew. Material interests and spiritual motives were therefore inextricably interwoven in the mind of the future pastor.[87] Where, however, there is coincident growth in the number of priestly vocations and the number of judiciously chosen sodalities, the converging probabilities carry conviction. This is the case, for example, in the diocese of La Rochelle between 1648 and 1724. The confraternity of the Rosary spread and multiplied because of the ministry of the Dominicans. Now the Dominican converts were situated not in the regions where their influence was the most fruitful, but at La Rochelle, Fontenay-le-Comte and La Châtaigneraie, that is, where they could more easily wage war on Protestantism. This dearth of confraternities round the convents is extremely significant. They were particularly numerous in the Mauges and then, some way behind, in Gâtine.[88] If one then adds to the map the figures for ordinations to the priesthood (where they are known), again the Mauges is in the lead, followed by Gâtine, and again the plains and fens of the south are near-desert.[89] For our own day religious practice presents the same pattern. In his interpretation of these concordant data, Fr Pérouas speaks of 'religious dimorphism'. Even when religious practice was the accepted thing, the diocese of La Rochelle included vast areas which were religiously luke-warm and districts whose faith was livelier.

This idea of dimorphism could well serve as a working hypothesis in a systematic study of the question, and it can be verified in many ways. J. Ferté has shown that the Paris region under Louis XIV had to call in many priests foreign to the diocese: in the archdeaconry of Paris in 1672, out of ninety-five assistant priests mentioned in the reports of archdiaconal visitations, twelve only belonged to the Paris diocese, and thirty-one came originally from Coutances.[90] Going further back in time trying to explain the unequal success of the Reformation in the various regions, the historian must endeavour to calculate the unequal distribution of priests and religious. In fifteenth-century France, as J. de Font-Réaux discovered, there were considerable differences on this point between the 'high pressure areas' of the Paris basin and the districts of the south. For example, the entire clergy of the diocese of Fréjus was less than the clergy of the town of Amiens on its own. Similarly there were practically no third orders in the southern Mediterranean regions of France.[91] There are other facts which support these conclusions. In the seventeenth and eighteenth centuries, the inhabitants of coastal regions and of the Loire valley[92] seem to have been more independent and religiously less fervent than the inland populations, and the peasants of the wine-growing areas more sceptical than those of other rural districts. And both the Protestant Reformation and unbelief began in the towns.

All this clearly proves the need to rediscover the religious geography of the past: the zones of heresy in the Middle Ages (did they correspond with the zones of heresy at the beginning of the modern era?),[93] the districts in which, in Germany[94] and France,[95] the revolts against tithing broke out, the itinerary of the 'iconoclastic Furies' in the sixteenth century, the countries which remained hostile to images, the spread of Jansenism in Europe,[96] the seedbeds of anticlericalism under the *Ancien Régime*, the paths of faith, and also the routes by which the enlightenment philosophy travelled, for example from France to Spain[97] in the eighteenth century.

Other dimorphisms deserve a mention. Sexual dimorphism – the

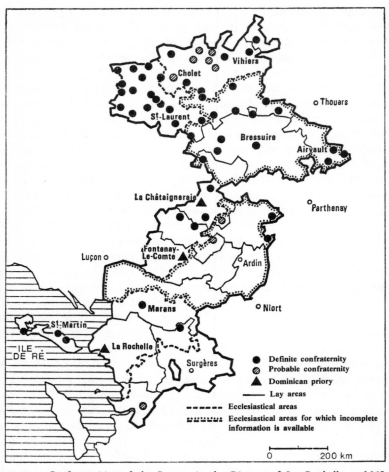

Definite confraternity
Probable confraternity
Dominican priory
Lay areas
Ecclesiastical areas
Ecclesiastical areas for which incomplete information is available

MAP III: *Confraternities of the Rosary in the Diocese of La Rochelle c. 1648.* (*L. Pérouas*)

difference in religious practice between male and female members of the population – is a recent thing. Professional dimorphism, on the other hand, seems to have been common under the *Ancien Régime*, when certain of the professions apparently felt little attraction for religion: theatre groups, for example, which the Church frowned on, inn-keepers whose establishments traditionally vied with the Church during solemn masses and vespers, and 'travellers': domestic servants, pedlars, soldiers[98] and above all sailors. The latter, by the very trade they plied, were frequently deprived of mass and the sacraments. In 1623 the Jesuits set up a naval mission in the Spanish fleet based on Flanders.[99] Although these missioners were few in number – in principle eight of them, or two priests for every naval squadron – they certainly ensured some level of religious vitality among Philip IV's seamen. However, many sailors at the time had no such chaplains and religiously speaking were more or less left to themselves. Present researches at Rennes on Saint-Malo between 1681 and 1789 prove that the chaplains who embarked on ships bound for the New World could be counted on one hand (almost), and that they were a species of sacerdotal misfit: only those priests became naval chaplains who could not find themselves a niche elsewhere.

3. Soundings in depth: from parish registers to the structures of religious language

A geographical history of the Christian people in the past cannot overlook the irreplaceable documentation furnished by baptismal, matrimonial and funeral registers. The thesis of P. Goubert on Beauvais and the Beauvaisis,[100] and the methodological approach to the use of parish registers adopted by M. Fluery and L. Henri[101] have been the inspirations for a series of full-scale demographic inquiries into the past. These inquiries reveal a large amount of information of considerable use to religious sociology and the history of ideas. First of all, in a town like Rotterdam in which the population was divided among several denominations, they indicate the respective adherents of Catholicism and Protestantism(s).[102] In a French port like Saint-Malo, on which research is in progress, they give an idea of the large number of Reformation abjurations round about 1685. More importantly, however, parish registers throw light on the attitudes and behaviour of a population and their degree of obedience to the moral commandments of the Church. They record prenuptial births, the baptisms of illegitimate and foundling children, and shot-gun weddings celebrated (with dispensation) during Advent and Lent. A calculation of the number of baptisms shows the birth-rate and therefore the existence (or not) in a given group of voluntary family planning.[103] The 'certificates of Catholicity' give the Christian names and therefore the popularity of certain saints in a particular community. Finally, with the signatures, they witness to some extent to the level of education in a village or town. It is interesting to establish the relationship between the cultural abilities and the religious practice of a group.[104]

Another category of documents that can help the historian of religious feeling and collective mentality is the files of the Inquisition and ecclesiastical courts, and the archives of lay courts, notably those of the urban police. On the one hand the pleas and defences reflect the average moral conceptions of a population. On the other the categorial and serial study of criminality can establish the relationship between crime and famine,[106] crime and periods of time, and crime and religion. One question the historian of Europe in the sixteenth to eighteenth centuries must consider is whether, as the Catholic Reformation advanced, violence decreased in the towns and countryside. As far as duelling is concerned, there does seem to be a causal relationship; but what about the other forms of delinquency?[107]

The list of sources that can be of use to the historian of social groups from the sixteenth century onwards is inexhaustible. It includes confession manuals and works of casuistry, notarial files, particularly wills, diaries, for example of Amiens citizens,[108] library lists and all documents to do with publishing. A word may be added on the latter. Hawked literature and the Blue Library at Troyes – the largest collection of popular pocket-editions in France – is an irreplaceable source of information on popular belief and piety. Under the *Ancien Régime,* lives of the saints, collections of psalms, devotions and indulgences, catechisms and carols were 'quantitatively speaking the biggest single category of hawked literature: nearly a quarter of it'.[109] The increasing number of studies currently appearing[110] on printing and publishing give a good idea of what the different classes of society were reading in the past. They describe the development of tastes and interests and the growth of a more secular, less religion-centred culture from the time of the eighteenth century. The sociological 'reading' of printed works[111] therefore has no particular preference for well-written books: it encompasses all types of literature; and it is more interested in the readers than in the authors, or to put it more accurately, it tries to locate the latter in relation to the former whose mentality is the object of the study. 'Tell me what you read and I will tell you who you are'. Sociologists are also interested in themes either in the literature of a period – for example, death, fatality and suicide in the sixteenth century – or in a particular sector of literature. A useful study would be of the most popular subjects preached from the pulpit[112] when the missions were in full swing in Europe, provided that the themes themselves were placed in a wider context. Another would be an analysis of religious vocabulary, key words and popular images for each period, social level and school of spirituality, and statistical studies showing the mathematical structures of the languages of faith:[113] the manifestations of the collective unconscious must be the concern of the historian of prayer.

Now that we have said something on the documents available and on the principles of research, we may proceed from the methodology to the problematic and apply the former to the latter. There are three main questions: a) what human material did the Catholic Reformation try to transform? b) how did it set about its work of Christianization? and c) what is meant by the 'dechristianization' of the eighteenth century?

CHAPTER 3

THE LEGEND OF THE
CHRISTIAN MIDDLE AGES

(a) The shortcomings of the clergy before Trent

1.   The morals of the parish clergy: sacerdotal concubinage

It is impossible to understand the aims and methods of the Catholic
Reformation without first trying to grasp something of the religious life
of a parish in western Christendom before the changes of Trent and its
aftermath. With what sort of curés and what sort of assistant priests did
the faithful have to deal? In the early fifteenth century, Nicolas de
Clamanges stated that 'in many dioceses' there were priests living in concubinage.[1] Gerson feared that not all lewd priests could be deposed
because there were so many of them. Pierre d'Ailly gave evidence at a
synod to the effect that 'a large number of ecclesiastics *passim et publice
concubinas tenent*'. Jean de Varennes (who was, it must be said, of a
flamboyant and unbalanced disposition) was emphatic that in the course
of his travels he had met 'vast numbers of "married" priests'.[2] These in-
dictments from theologians of the 1400s are paralleled, two centuries
later (but before the Catholic Reformation had really had time to bite),
by the contents of the Book of Complaints (the 'cahiers de doléance'
[books of complaints] were prepared by the three estates [clergy,
nobility, commons] to be presented to the king on the occasion of the
general estates' [= periodic national parliaments]. They comprised the
separate *cahiers* of the parishes, bailiwicks and estates) presented by the
parishes of the bailiwick of Troyes at the assembly of the 'general
estates' in 1614:[3]

'The said inhabitants (of Bouilly, in the generality [basic administrative unit under the *Ancien Régime*. They numbered sixteen in 1542, thirty-three in 1789] of Châlons) also complain against the curés, curates and chaplains in the said cure and surrounding cures that they lead evil lives and give bad example; these curés and curates keep servant-girls and mistresses, by whom some of them have a child or even quite a number of children, and in greater comfort than the wives of the well-to-do tradesmen and merchants ... they keep the said servants and their children in the presbyteries and in their rooms without any pretence at concealment, to the great scandal of the public ...'

Protest against the loose morals of the lower clergy topped the list of complaints put forward by the inhabitants of La Loupierre (again in the bailiwick of Troyes, 1614[4]): 'In the first place, men of the Church commit many abuses against the holy decrees and ordinances in dissolute habits, gaming, taverning, possessing arms and in hunting. Furthermore, they spend most of their time scandalously, and have women and girls in their houses under pretence of domestic service, by whom they have children'.

These recriminations against the morality of the parish clergy should not be taken entirely at their face value. It is extremely difficult to determine the proportion of concubinary priests in a diocese or deanery. The bishop's court register for Cérisy in Normandy, which, with some lacunae, covers the period 1315–1406, records only fifteen accusations of immorality against as many priests. And the jurisdiction of this court included a dozen parishes in which the clergy were far more numerous than they would be today.[5] Six pastoral visitations in the diocese of Grenoble between 1340 and 1414 discloses only twenty-seven cases of concubinage out of several hundred parishes inspected, many of them more than once.[6] These figures are probably on the low side, because many villages, unlike Bouilly and La Loupierre in 1614, must have treated their clergy with some indulgence and not denounced them to the bishop or his *officialis*. Nonetheless, even when the reports of pastoral visitations are more detailed – in the sixteenth century – the proportion of concubinary priests to the whole parish clergy of the diocese does not rise above a quarter (Low Countries) or a third (Rhineland).[7] These were probably the correct percentages. Another point is worth making. There were two categories of 'concubinary' priests: those whose private lives were dissolute, and those, far more numerous, who lived with women and were faithful to them. Jean de Varennes said he had met many priests and women 'who had exchanged vows, as married persons do',[8] and the registers of the Cérisy court refer to priests whose concubines were 'as it were their wives and by whom they had several children'.[9] For a long time the episcopal tribunals contented themselves with imposing fines on guilty priests, without demanding the dismissal of the concubine. It has to be said in extenuation that concubinage was almost inevitable where the priest had to work for a living and therefore needed a woman to keep house. The canonical age for a housekeeper was sixty, except where she was a relation. 'It is not hard to imagine the faded state of a country woman of sixty in the Middle Ages, and anyhow how many women reached that age? Housekeepers of the correct canonical age were probably the exclusive preserve of bishops and popes'.[10] The curés who had fathered children used their sons to serve mass, despite the proscriptions of diocesan synods, and taught them the rudiments of reading, writing and Latin, hoping to be able to hand over their benefice or vicariate in due course. It was not difficult to buy at Rome the necessary dispensation for a bastard son to be ordained priest; and so clerical dynasties emerged passing a benefice on from father to son. It was not so much the sins of the flesh, 'which were viewed with tolerance by the masses at that time, just as indelicacy in money matters is today',[11] which provoked local scandal and bitterness, as the threat of monopoly of a benefice by the pastor's sons at the expense of the parish's legitimate children, and the life-style of the 'priest's wife' however little it infringed on that of the other village women. It is this which lies behind the complaints of the inhabitants of Bouilly in 1614.

Finally, contrary to what has been accepted for a long time, it was not the misconduct of the clergy, and notably the lower clergy with whom the faithful came into most contact, which tipped a large part of Europe over to the Protestant Reformation. Inquiries into this aspect of the matter should concentrate more on religious and not moral factors, and ask rather why the Church met the people's religious expectations so inadequately, distributed the sacraments, said mass and prayed so incompetently. Even though priests had women and children, if they had celebrated mass devoutly, been enlightened confessors and above all instructed their people in the catechism, there is every chance that the Protestant Reformation would never have happened.

2. Non-residence

The non-residence of many parish curés, especially in country areas, had far more serious consequences for the religious life of the faithful than the moral delinquencies of the clergy. Either because the titular of a benefice was a student at some university (in which case he had the right to appoint a replacement in his cure for seven years), or quite simply because he preferred to live in a town even without authorization and quite happy just to receive the income from his benefice, many parishes between the fourteenth and seventeenth centuries found themselves without a real pastor. In the diocese of Angers in 1413, 103 parishes out of a total of 436, in other words twenty-three per cent, were in the charge of curés who were pursuing university studies far from their flocks.[12] In the deanery of Oudenburg, near Bruges, there were fifty-four cures in 1455 and only twelve resident curés.[13] An unpublished inquiry into the diocese of Sens in 1495 reveals that fifty to sixty per cent of pastors were absent from their parishes:[14] this is more serious than the position at Aix-en-Provence in the early fifteenth century (thirty to forty per cent non-resident[15]), but comparable to the diocese of Narbonne at the same time (fifty-eight per cent[16]). Of 241 parishes in the diocese of Liège, seventy-two cures were without resident pastors in 1501 and ninety-five in 1521; in 1526 nearly half the parishes were staffed by priests who had no charge.[17]

Yet Christendom was not lacking in priests. Clerics abounded because there were enough priorships, chaplaincies, chapelries and so forth to provide a living, however measly, for a whole clerical proletariat. In the diocese of Vannes in 1633, the average number of priests per parish was nine.[18] In La Rochelle, a diocese less well provided with clergy, there were still 110–115 priests in 1650 who had no ministerial charge, out of 600 secular priests altogether.[19] The diocesan clergy was also very probably badly distributed, as future studies will no doubt show. For example, in the diocese of Krk, an island off the Dalmatian coast, in 1579, there were ninety-five priests for seven parishes, whereas at the same date the diocese of Split had twenty-eight for five parishes and the diocese of Sibenik thirty-three for eleven parishes.[20]

The evidence suggests that far from being an advantage, the undue expansion of the clerical corps was an excrescence that bordered on the anarchical. On the other hand, it would be a mistake (as well as naive) to believe that residence necessarily implied a professional conscience on the part of the pastors. E. Catta, who has made a special study of the diocese of Nantes in the sixteenth century, writes judiciously: '. . . even where curés were resident in their parishes (and this was not too often), it was far from being because of their greater zeal. Regrettably it was frequently an indication of even worse excess: priests buried themselves in the country to lead a life of ease far from the Argus eye of authority'.[21]

3. The responsibilities of the episcopate

We have noted two apparently opposed facts: non-residence, and the un-pastoral conduct of resident curés far from the surveillance of the hierarchy; but they both reflect the inadequate concern of the bishops for the spiritual needs of the Christian people.

Prior to the Catholic Reformation, bishops were certainly not so bad as has sometimes been made out, with particular reference to their private lives. One must beware of over-hasty generalizations on the episcopate before Trent: 'One is undoubtedly tempted', writes R. Aubenas, 'to pass collective judgment on the higher clergy of the time ... ; but one should not deceive oneself that this would be possible, even for a particular nation ... because in fact the episcopate of the late fifteenth and early sixteenth centuries offers a spectrum which is extremely rich in personalities, reflecting the infinite variety of human types in which the best rub shoulders with the worst'.[22]

However, one cannot but feel that the Renaissance bishop had little contact with his clergy and people. Certainly, if he had appointed the curés himself he would (might) have known them better. In the early sixteenth century, 452 parishes out of 506 in the diocese of Tournai were not filled by the bishop,[23] and this was the general rule. But because too many prelates were non-resident and involved in preoccupying worldly affairs, particularly service of the state, because even when they *were* resident they regarded the management of their dioceses as a matter of routine administration and because they did not hold synods regularly and seldom carried out pastoral visitations, they were barely aware of the enormous religious problems, of the change in the mentality of the Christian people in the towns and of the difference in Christian needs compared with two or three hundred years before. To have an easy conscience they thought it was enough to maintain Christian society as it was and to look to (or have looked to) the temporal welfare of their dioceses.[24] They lacked pastoral concern and this in turn had a detrimental effect on the lower clergy.

The replacement of non-resident curés by supply priests (badly paid by the titulars of benefices) meant that the salvation of whole sections of the Christian people was entrusted, frequently after much unseemly haggling over prices, to a proletariat of temporary vicars. These replacements, many of them of no fixed abode, and all of them ordained without an ecclesiastical title, were generally ignorant and indifferent. To live they had to take on manual work (as did many curés whose benefices did not provide them with a living wage). The German synodal statutes laid down the authorized trades: gardener, nurseryman, shepherd, cowherd, farm labourer, painter, scribe, 'bookseller', apothecary, fisherman (to which were added barber and tailor in the diocese of Tournai). The priest was forbidden to be a fuller, weaver, bailiff, merchant, money-lender, innkeeper, butcher, horse-dealer or lawyer.[25] The pastor of a parish was therefore at the same level as his parishioners, and this must have been welcome, but having attended no seminary course he was scarcely more educated in religion than they. It is useful to recall how St Vincent de Paul decided on his vocation. In 1617 he was at Folleville, in Picardy (which was then Gondi country). He discovered that the curé did not even know the words of absolution.[26] He later founded the Mission because from this first experience he had some idea of the gargantuan mediocrity of the rural clergy. This was a scourge Nicolas de Clamanges lamented in the early fifteenth century: 'Very few priests indeed are capable of reading even slowly, syllable by syllable, much less of understanding the words and their meaning. What fruit can they produce in others when they themselves find what they read gibberish? How will they manage to obtain God's grace for others when they themselves offend him and dishonour their ministry by their ignorance and the unworthiness of their lives'?[27]

If the parish clergy were really that ignorant — and it was true of many of the resident curés in the country areas as well as for supply priests — how could they hope to offer the faithful substantial spiritual nourishment? J. Toussaert has brilliantly shown the aptness of this hypothesis in the case of Flanders[28] where it transpires that the catechism was taught seldom and badly to Christians of the fourteenth and fifteenth centuries. Dogmas and the sacraments in fact figure very little in the contemporary sermons which have come down to us, and the historian is positively astounded at the few books of hours which include scriptural texts. The (summary) examination for admission to the priesthood put Peter Lombard before St Paul, and canon law before the Fathers of the Church. We must therefore agree with J. Toussaert when he refers so pertinently to 'this skeletal character of the presentation of the Catholic religion and of a knowledge that was orientated towards a purely moral, legalistic and external practice, without any dogmatic framework, without any guidance on how to make the sacraments personally alive, and without any solid spirituality even among those whom education and culture should have made more amenable. On what was their religious life based? It is easy to understand the Protestant emphasis on religion as an activity of faith and an intimate relationship with God'.[29]

4. A new problematic

We have already moved some way towards a conclusion which many still find hard to accept:[30] the 'golden age' of medieval Christianity is a legend. The religion of the mass of people in the west has been confused with the religion of a clerical élite. Starting from the supposition of a Christian peak in the twelfth and thirteenth centuries, many have concluded to an ensuing decadence against which the Protestant, then the Catholic Reformations subsequently reacted. What is the validity, however, of that initial supposition?

If we take the clergy, there are facts which would suggest the contrary. It is true that the papacy and higher clergy did not always edify by their example in the fourteenth and fifteenth centuries, but J. Janssen, who has amassed an impressive documentation on pre-Lutheran Germany, quotes many testimonies to the 'good superiors', 'competent prelates' and 'pious bishops' who were a credit to the Church in the empire.[31] It is also true that from John XXII, the popes gave dispensations of nonresidence too freely to the bishops, and the bishops to the lower clergy. But was the clerical body overall worse in 1500 than in 1074, when, under Gregory VII, the Council of Rome condemned simony, the traffic of benefices, the marriage and dissipation of ecclesiastics? Furthermore, whenever the historian can attempt a detailed study of the thirteenth century – the golden age of cathedrals! – for example using the records of pastoral visitations by Eudes Rigaud archbishop of Rouen, he does not discover a clergy that was significantly better than the clergy of the following period.[32] More positively, J. Toussaert concludes from his study of Flanders in the fifteenth and sixteenth centuries that the Flemish clergy had made some progress between 1450 and 1520 from the point of view of both morals and residence.

If we now turn to the overall religious life of the West during the fourteenth and fifteenth centuries, we can see that church buildings multiplied rapidly in France, Germany and England, that a more personal religion developed among the élites with the Brothers of the Common Life and the *Devotio moderna*, and that new and popular forms of piety blossomed (albeit a shade confusedly). It is as if the masses, at least in the towns, had awakened – *and not reawakened* – to the Christian spirit. Are not the vogue in stations of the cross, the cavalcades of flagellants, the processions behind the Blessed Sacrament and representations of the passion, the proliferation of schools of church music, the extraordinary success enjoyed by preachers (Vincent Ferrier, Bernardino of Siena, Olivier Maillard, Savonarola) irrefutable evidence of the religious thirst of the masses?

In the face of these increased spiritual needs, the parish clergy, especially in the countryside, were still as undereducated and undertrained. The drama of the Church was the lack of theological solidity in too many pastors, which meant that they were incapable of meeting the new religious demands of their faithful. In these conditions Luther's admirable and highly instructive sermon of 1512 is readily understandable: 'Someone will say: the crime and scandal of all this fornication, drunkenness, unbridled lust for gambling, all these vices of the clergy! Grievous scandals, yes, I admit it ... But alas, what an incomparably more harmful and crueller plague is the organized silence on the Word of God, or its adulteration; being not grossly material, it is quite overlooked: no one is moved and appalled by it. ... How many priests would you find today who think it less sinful to err against chastity, to forget a prayer, to commit some fault in reciting the canon than to neglect preaching and the correct interpretation of the Word of Truth'?[33]

Religious thirst does not necessarily imply a solid and structured faith. It is therefore necessary, if we are to understand the period of the Pre-Reformation and inquire into it, to maintain two only apparently contradictory statements: 1) the spiritual anxieties of an élite and the activities of wandering preachers provoked a religious ferment, mainly in the towns, of course; 2) but at a time when priests went through no seminary and the parish clergy did not teach the faithful the catechism, the people remained religiously undernourished, particularly in the country. Using the classification proposed by R. Mandrou,[34] we may distinguish three cultural levels in past populations: an élite; a sizeable proportion of town-dwellers among whom at least rudimentary education spread between the fifteenth and eighteenth centuries, with the growth in publishing and schooling; and the rustic population who were more often than not sunk in ignorance and illiteracy. Now the vast majority of Europeans were country-dwellers. The hypothesis, therefore, which we should like to propose as a direction for research is the following: on the eve of the Reformation, the average westerner was but superficially christianized. In this context the two Reformations, Luther's and Rome's, were two processes, which apparently competed but in actual fact converged, by which the masses were christianized and religion spiritualized. To support this hypothesis, we are going to try, in the following pages, to sound the pre-Christian level in the mentality and conduct of the average European of the past. We may confidently assert beforehand that this level will be more accessible in the rustic than in the educated classes.

(b) The world of witchcraft

1. An animist mentality

Fr Michel Le Nobletz, who preached in lower Brittany from 1610 onwards, encountered 'disorders and superstitions which brought tears to his eyes':[35] 'He found great numbers of women carefully sweeping the nearest chapel in their village, and then collecting the dust and throwing it into the air, hoping by this means to procure a favourable wind for their husbands or sons who were at sea. Others took the statues of the saints in the same chapels and threatened them with the direst consequences if they did not effect the prompt and happy return of their dear ones: and in fact they carried out their threats, whipping the holy statues or throwing them into the water when they failed to obtain all they had asked for. . . . Some people were noticed emptying all the water when there had been a death in the house for fear that the soul of the departed might drown in it, and putting stones near the fire which each family lit on the eve of the feast of St John the Baptist so that their fathers and ancestors could come and warm themselves in comfort. . . . It was an accepted thing in the same regions to kneel down to the new moon and say the Lord's Prayer in its honour; and to make a sort of sacrifice to the public fountains on New Year's Day, each individual offering a piece of bread and butter to his or her own village fountain. Elsewhere, on the same day, the people offered these fountains as many pieces of bread as there were persons in their families, and drew conclusions, from the way the bits they had thrown in in their name floated or not, as to who would die during the coming year. However, the offerings some people made to the evil spirit were far more abominable. These wretched souls, thinking, like the Manichaeans, that there were two principles, one of good and one of evil, believed that the devil had made fagopyrum or buckwheat, and when they had harvested this sort of grain on which the poorest in some provinces of the kingdom regularly fed, they threw some handfuls of it into the ditches round the fields as a gift to the one to whom they thought they were indebted for it'.

Fr Boschet, who published *Le parfait missionaire ou la vie du R. P. Julien Maunoir* (The perfect missioner, or the life of Fr Julian Maunoir) in 1697, wrote that the faith in seventeenth-century Brittany was 'as in the primitive age of the Church': a revealing statement for the historian. Would it not have been equally true for provinces other than Brittany? In Friuli between 1580 and 1650, *Benandanti* claimed to fight a group of sorcerers on ember days. The harvests of the region depended on the outcome of the fight. In a discerning study based on the documents of the Inquisition, C. Ginzburg has connected the myth of the *Benandanti* with a whole collection of agrarian rites and primitive beliefs from Alsace to the Balkans and Lithuania.[36] E. Delcambre has collected a particularly important documentation on Lorraine at the end of the sixteenth and during the seventeenth centuries. With him we may recall (amongst other facts) the offerings at St Benedict's Church in Brecklange.[37] A peasant from Saint-Dié had dislocated his hip, and his neighbour promised to mend it by begging manure from nine different stables, filling the peasant's breeches which he had been wearing at the time of the accident with it and hanging them up in the church. In the same sanctuary a woman healer (*guérriseuse*) brought in pilgrimage, for the cure of a sick person, a man's stocking containing five eggs and three handfuls of horse-dung put there by the patient's daughter.[38] A rite like this is explained on the hypothesis that the sickness was like a poison, represented here by excrement. The saint would destroy the sickness via the offerings. This is a far cry from orthodox Christianity (indeed, any Christianity at all!).

To glean a knowledge of the intimate mentality of the average man of the past, and in particular of the peasant, nothing can replace the study of folklore manuals,[39] in which patient researchers have described the popular practices and traditions which are now dying out. These manuals reveal mental structures radically different from our own in that our ancestors had not at all the same conception of the universe. They believed that every body, living or inanimate, was composed of matter and a spirit. This idea was shared by eminent minds right up to the scientific revolution in the seventeenth century; it underlay the neo-Platonic belief of the Renaissance in the souls of stars and justified the persistence of astrology. The vitalist philosophy of the neo-Platonists was only the conscious expression of a fundamentally primitive, synthetic mentality which could not make a clear distinction between nature and supernature, and which believed the world was ruled less by coherent laws than by the caprice of beings and things. This was a notion which reflected man's profound sense of anguish in the face of a world which threatened him on all sides and over which he had but scant control. In such a universe, ultimately nothing is natural, particularly not sickness and death. Because he is almost incapable of systematic mental analysis, the primitive person cannot see clearly any distinction between what is visible and what is invisible, between the part and the whole, the image and the model. He attributes beings and things with an essential ambivalence, tending to imagine powerful 'souls' in everything that exists. All the evidence assembled by folklore specialists, by E. Delcambre in his admirable book *The concept of witchcraft* and by all those who study Europe's past at its most basic level points to one conclusion: the average European of the early seventeenth century was largely imbued with an animist mentality. It was impossible for his religion not to suffer from the effects.

2. Three laws dominating the world of witchcraft

The three laws are contact, similarity and contrast. One has only to read Delcambre's work to see the extent to which they were still accepted and lived by the Lorrains at the beginning of the classical epoch. We must say a word on each of them here.

Law of contact. E. Delcambre refers to magicians who cured just by touching the patient or even breathing on him, and to a divineress from Saint-Dié who made the patient eat cress. The cress had to come from her own garden because what grew elsewhere was 'worthless for the purpose': the shadow of the healer, passing again and again over the garden, had communicated something of her power to the herbs. A young girl was suffering from jaundice: her treatment was to drink the witch's urine (mixed, one hastens to add, into a cake with flour, butter and honey). The urine was supposed to be the vehicle of the mysterious force possessed by the healer. The universally accepted belief in the 'evil eye' was part of the law of contact. People were persuaded that there was a contact between the maleficent fluid in the eye and the person or thing 'touched' by the witch's glance. The same law also explains the frequent habit of wearing talismans, precious stones, magic formulae (often called 'characters') and other mysterious life-savers. Many pious objects were in fact used as talismans.

Law of similarity. This was the most widely invoked law in the world of witchcraft. It was believed that witches could bring rain or fog by stirring the waters of a marsh, or destroy vineyards by shaking the bines, or damage wheat-crops by touching the ears with 'certain white wands', or make a man impotent or sterile (sometimes both at once) by tying a knot in a shoe-lace or a piece of string. A Eudist missionary travelling round Normandy in 1672 complained that all he ever heard about was 'knotted shoe-laces'.[41] In all these cases the witch performed an imitative rite which was thought to effect what it symbolized. Similarly cures were worked by associating the power of sacred words with a sympathetic magic rite which was, if necessary, based on comparisons as artificial as they were unexpected. For example, a Lorrain sorcerer prayed that the swelling which affected certain horned animals begin to go down 'as surely as our Lady is the daughter of St Anne, and St Anne of St Susanna'.

Law of contrast. All forms of magic played on contraries, cold and hot, water and fire and so forth. The idea of antipathy enabled people to invent a host of counter-charms and amulets. Sometimes, however, the law of contrariety was merely a particular case of the law of similarity: like banished like and conjured up the contrary. In seventeenth century Lorraine, the use of bones as medicaments was frequent: 'Roman bones

bought from apothecaries', 'sea bones brought from Santiago de Com-
postella'. For many people corpses were the incarnation of the devil and
a principle of death. Whether affection was aroused by spells and
charms or not, evil was neutralized by evil: two like poles repelled each
other.

3. Incantations and rites

The three laws just described ignore distance, and the same is true of the
'evil eye' and 'evil breath'. Distance is no obstacle in the world of magic
where thoughts and words are endowed with concrete power. To desire,
to look, to speak is to act. In this totally vitalized world in which nothing
is really material, there is no natural difference between material
causality and the causality of spiritual forces. This is why incantations
and rites are so important. Because words were supposed to exert influence in their own right, a meticulous formalism was always noticeable
in incantatory speech. Any error of omission or any slip would rob the
'prayer' of its force. Because rites were attributed with an external effect,
often Catholics in the past had to perform certain pilgrimages in a
precise way. The technique for this was a secret transmitted from mother
to daughter, aunt to niece, with initiatory significance. Similarly, certain
female healers specialized in going on pilgrimage for other people, and
not only to assist a bed-ridden or house-bound patient.

When it ceased to be the preserve of a profoundly spiritualized élite
and became the religion of an essentially rural civilization, Christianity
camouflaged rather than suppressed the beliefs and actions transmitted
by millennia of obscure history. Fern and vervain were thought by many
to have magical properties, at the time of Louis XIV as for the contemporaries of Virgil. Fr Le Nobletz discovered that Bretons addressed
prayers to the moon. The worship of fountains in the classical age itself –
and since – prolonged pre-Christian practices. In the department of
Charente alone, Marc Leproux counted more than 200 curative springs
which until quite recent times were centres of devotion.[42] A certain
number of them are known to have been venerated in pre-Christian ages.
The sacralization of springs is a legacy from an extremely remote past.

Another relic of an archaic mentality was the attitude of the Catholic
hierarchy and faithful to a suicide. Not only was the corpse taken to
prison, tried and hanged on a gibbet, but while being carried from the
room where it lay to the prison it was not allowed across the door of the
house it had profaned by its crime. Either it was thrown out of the window or – as at Lille in the seventeenth century – it was 'carried through a

hole under the threshold with its face to the ground like a beast'.[43] It was a ritual recalling the evil properties of a dead man in the eyes of primitive peoples. If the corpse were not taken over the threshold they thought it would not easily find its way back into the house.[44] An extremely archaic level of collective mentality is also revealed by the attitudes of sixteenth- and seventeenth-century Europeans to blood (especially menstrual blood), sperm, saliva, urine, excrement and other body wastes like nail parings and loose hair from the head. They held an essential place in the philtres which, according to Pietro Aretino, the Roman courtesans gave their lovers, and more generally in witches' magic potions[45] and healers' remedies. To the primitive mind everything from the human body had a particular power and was to some extent taboo because it contained not only an individual's soul but also the collective soul of the group to which that individual belonged.

(c) The 'folklorization' of Christianity

1. Relics of paganism and the process of paganization

These reminders and comparisons help the modern reader to understand why a certain number of Christian feasts and rites have often been regarded as a dressing-up of pre-Christian religion. The best-known French specialist in folklore, Arnold Van Gennep (d.1957), modified this seductive but facile idea. Although he accepted it in the case of rogations,[46] he rejected the notion that Christmas and the feast of St John the Baptist were survivals of pagan solstitial festivals in Christian garb. 'These days', he writes, 'you cannot read a book or an article on the feast of St John without finding the cliché: "this is a remnant of sun worship from pre-Christian times" with the rider: "sun worship existed in all peoples from the very remotest times" . . . The feast of St John cannot be either solar in general or solstitial in particular by its essence and origin because it does not coincide with the longest day of the year which all peoples could have determined'.[47] A similar observation applies to Christmas, which does not coincide with the winter solstice (on or about 21 December).

A. Van Gennep's approach is a fruitful one for research because it invites the historian to examine ancient Christian feasts in a new light. Despite the resistance of the hierarchy, the Christian festivals tended to be 'folklorized' because they were addressed to a populace that was in general uneducated, and concretized in a civilization impregnated until a relatively late period by an animist mentality. This warping process is particularly evident in the case of the feast of St John, which for Europeans was one of the great days of the year. The celebration of the Precursor's memory had become an occasion for gathering magic herbs and lighting fires to ward off evil spirits (it was quite common, at Paris for example, to throw cats, the devil's familiars, into the flames[48]). Because St John had baptized the Saviour, it was believed, in the region of Metz and elsewhere, that 'whoever bathed on St John's night before dawn was immunized from fever for the period of one year'.[49]

The mental structures and the sluggishness of a still-archaic civilization encouraged the folklorization not only of ceremonies and feastdays but also of beliefs, and thereby brought about a species of relapse into paganism. There is a chasm between the Christian doctrine of final resurrection and eternal life and the world of ghosts which peopled the nights of our ancestors not only in Brittany, but in Charente and Charente Maritime, Provence, Friuli etc. Night-riding washerwomen, officiating priests, movers of milestones, tormented spirits, tombless dead (especially those who died at sea) all haunted Christians in the past, far from the comforting paths of orthodoxy.[50] Magic numbers invaded religion. Because the organs and parts of the human body generally go in pairs, to uneven numbers were ascribed abnormality, and therefore a sacred power, from the earliest times. As it established itself, Christianity gave great prominence to uneven numbers: there were three theologal virtues, three members of the Trinity, seven gifts of the Spirit, seven capital sins and so on. Magic numbers held an even greater place in the pseudo-religious ceremonial of white witchcraft. For instance, the application of hellebore mentioned by E. Delcambre was effective only if accompanied by the recitation, 'five days in succession, of the Pater Noster and as many Ave Marias in the name of our Saviour's passion and death'.

Catholics in the classical era applied this magic ritual efficacy to the ceremony of baptism. It was then thought, following St Augustine,[51] that infants who died without baptism go to hell. Conversely baptism was enough to change the eternal destiny of an infant who would not reach the age of reason. Parents despaired when their child was still-born; and in response to a psychological need, certain sanctuaries were dedicated to our Lady (for example, round Lille and in the Paris region[52]) for the presentation of still-born babies: the infants were laid on the altar, and when colour rose to the cheeks, the lips moved and nostrils quivered, baptism was quickly administered, and the parents and god-parents, reassured, then let them relapse into the stiffness of death.

Many other facts – regrettably we cannot detail them all here – help the modern reader to understand how much the popular mind unconsciously folklorized Christianity. For example, the veneration of the saints. Officially models of virtue and spiritual intercessors with God the saints had become, and have sometimes remained up to our own day, almost specialized divinities in the cure of a particular disease or the warding off of a possible misfortune. In the sixteenth-century church at Saint-Thégonnec (Finistère), the visitor can still read the phrase: 'Look on St Christopher and go your way assured', which meant, if you look on St Christopher and pray to him today, you are sure (for some time at least) of not suffering sudden or accidental death. Nevertheless the saints sometimes caused considerable anxiety to many Catholics trapped in this primitive mentality. The Letters of Remission (official letters conveying pardon for a crime at the king's or judge's discretion) in the Treasury of Charters (royal archives) for the period of the Hundred Years War,[53] judicial documents of the duchy of Lorraine in the late sixteenth and early seventeenth century, and research into folklore in the Charente departments reveal that a maleficent influence was sometimes attributed to the saints. They mention sick people 'touched' or 'affected' or 'held and vexed' by saints. An accused woman from Saint-Dié deposed that when the 'holy saints take a disliking to a person, they make him languish, and if they do not hate him all that much they bring him to a rapid death'. At Berry people referred to the saints as 'jealous'. Hence in the witchcraft trials examined by E. Delcambre, a distinction is drawn between the 'evil caused' and 'saint's evil', the former being attributed to the devil and sorcerers' spells, the latter to the activity of a saint who, although he could cure it if he wanted to, in fact sent it. Another even more aberrant fact in a supposedly Christian society was that our Lady herself was suspected of harming humans. An accused woman from Bazezney in Lorraine[56] wanted to know which one it was, our Lady, our Lady of Sion, our Lady of Fricourt or our Lady of La Maix, who had brought evil on a woman, as if there were as many Virgins as sanctuaries dedicated to her name. In his *Demonolatry* (published in Latin at Lyons, 1595), Nicolas Rémy refers to belief in maleficent saints, and he compares this myth, not without reason, to the religion of pagans who held their gods responsible for their misfortunes.

2. The magic power of exorcisms

That Christianity should undergo a process of folklorization and paganization was hardly avoidable in a civilization where education was a rare commodity, technological and scientific know-how in desperately short supply, and consequently the fear of hunger, the threat of the elements, the imminence of sickness and death everywhere rampant. Is an intelligent, spiritual religion possible when one's daily bread is not assured and when fear is one's habitual companion? How could Christianity, at the level of ordinary people of those times, fail to be first and foremost a system of rituals designed to wrench abundant harvests from heaven and persuade the Divinity to avert calamity, ward off sickness and postpone the dreadful hour of death?

Four times a year, on 25 March and the three days preceding Ascension Thursday, the clergy and faithful went in procession round the fields to implore heaven's protection against climatic scourges. There were special prayers and processions for the cessation of drought and the discontinuance of rain. The relics of St Genevieve and St Marcellus were paraded in procession round Paris in the seventeenth century (with parliamentary permission): four times to ask for rain (1603, 1611, 1615, 1694), twice to ask for the rain to stop (1625 and 1675).[57] In many wine-growing areas, for instance round Paris,[58] the Blessed Sacrament was carried through the vineyards to protect the vines from harmful worms and insects. Exorcisms used to be very common: they banished evil and misfortune. Portuguese sailors caught in a storm recited the prologue to St John's Gospel (which was part of the Roman rite for exorcism). The inhabitants of Chamonix ('Chamoniards'), who in the seventeenth century watched the glaciers creep into the valley and destroy or threaten houses and fields, several times begged successive bishops of Geneva-Annecy to come and exorcize the 'ice mountains':[59] 'The inhabitants of a parish called Chamonix showed singular confidence in their bishop's blessing. Chamonix includes large mountains covered in ice ... (which) is a constant threat of ruin to the surrounding areas; and as often as the bishop (Jean d'Arenthon, bishop of Geneva-Annecy 1660–95) visited that district, the people begged him to go and exorcize and bless these ice mountains. About five years before the death of our bishop, these people sent him a deputation to ask him to come just once more, so afraid were they that in his approaching old age senescence might rob them of this happiness ... They assured him that since his last visit the glaciers had withdrawn more than twenty-four paces. Charmed by their faith, the prelate replied: "Yes, my friends, I will come, even if I have to be carried. ..." He went ... and did as they asked. I have a sworn statement of the most prominent of the inhabitants in which they declare that since the blessing by Jean d'Arenthon the glaciers had receded until they were half a quarter of a league from where they had been before the blessing, and that they had ceased to cause the destruction they had caused before.'

Exorcism was a familiar weapon to civilizations that lived in fear:

G. Le Bras has counted 120 documents in the archives of the department of Doubs for the years 1729–62 which contain requests to the archdiocese for formulas of exorcism against insects and rodents.[60]

(d) The resurgence of Manichaeism

1. Wizards and witches as scapegoats

Liturgical conjurations were utilized as described above because storms, glaciers and rodents were thought to be possessed, or at least manoeuvred, by Satan. The prince of darkness and his legions of demons began to obsess the west from the fourteenth century. Resorting to the style and argumentation of the Old Testament prophets and the misfortune-as-punishment theme already developed by the tenth-century councils of the Church,[61] preachers and theologians showed Christians that the scourges they suffered from (plagues, famine, wars, the Great Schism, then the religious rupture of the sixteenth century) were punishments sent by the Most High in his wrath at man's iniquity. This persistant leitmotif certainly developed the sense of sin in the western mentality and encouraged the notion of individual responsibility: it therefore contributed to the progress of European civilization in the Renaissance period, and this contribution becomes more impressive when one realizes that individual morality was barely adverted to by the classical Greeks.[62] The spokesmen of God tried to bring about a mental conversion and convince the faithful that their concern should be less for the physical evil than for its cause, moral evil. These shock tactics undoubtedly brought about a change: instead of fearing plagues against which he was powerless, man now feared the devil against whom improved behaviour and prayer were effective. However, the cure went beyond the physicians' intentions (unconsciously). If daily life was a web of hazards and misfortunes, it was because Satan was everywhere and his innumerable agents ceaselessly at work. The wizard- and especially witch-hunts which began in Europe in 1326 (Bull of John XXII making witchcraft a heresy) reached their climax in the late sixteenth century and early seventeenth, and did not die out until after 1650. At Douai witch trials were chronologically distributed as follows:[63] fifteenth century, eight; first half of the sixteenth century, thirteen; second half, twenty-three; first half of the seventeenth century, sixteen; second half, three; eighteenth century, one. In the county of Namur 401 wizards and witches were sentenced between 1500 and 1650: 182 between 1500 and

1565, 176 from 1565 to 1620, forty-three from 1621 to 1650.[64]

These and similar figures are quite staggering. In the canton of Lucerne there were 600 witch trials between 1400 and 1675, half of which ended in the death sentence.[65] De Lancre, who was a councillor in the Bordeaux parliament of the late sixteenth and early seventeenth centuries boasted that he had discovered more than 500 sorcerers and had them all burned alive.[66] In the early seventeenth century, Boguet stated that more than 1500 witches had been executed in his time by the tribunal of Saint-Claude (Jura). Between 1570 and 1630 'from 30,000 to 50,000 stakes were set up in Europe. The number of heretics burnt on both sides of the confessional barrier is infinitesimal in comparison with this massive holocaust . . .'[67] The hunt for wizards and witches seems to have been even more violent in Protestant than in Catholic countries. While the city of Rome itself had hardly any witch trials,[68] Luther had written: 'No quarter must be shown to witches and sorceresses who steal eggs from nesting-boxes or butter and milk; I should willingly light their stakes myself, as the priests in the old Law themselves stoned malefactors'.[69] Other Reformers (Melanchthon, Bullinger, Calvin, Peter Martyr [Vermigli]) thought like Luther. The spread of Protestantism thus brought witch-hunting in its train (or where it existed already, intensified it), and witch trials became common in Denmark, Bohemia and Transylvania. In reformed Germany and Protestant Switzerland in the late sixteenth and early seventeenth centuries there were mass executions of people alleged to have concluded a pact with the devil and to have resorted to casting evil spells. In the canton of Berne more than 300 witches were burnt between 1591 and 1600; more than 240 between 1601 and 1610; and in 1613 there were twenty-seven executions in one bailiwick alone.[70] The evidence suggests that like Jews, Moors, heretics, madmen and vagabonds, wizards and witches — that is, alleged wizards and witches — were the scapegoats on which the west cast the responsibility of its sins.[71]

2. The priest and the magician

We must also consider another aspect of the fight against witchcraft at the dawn of modern times: the opposition between priest and magician. No civilization can do without healers. In country areas in the past, where doctors were seldom seen, the people had no choice but to resort to the expertise of magicians. At the Renaissance, however, theologians and judges became increasingly suspicious of magicians. As Nicolas Rémy wrote, 'All Christians are agreed that the presence of soothsayers in the Church is intolerable, and every Sunday preachers denounce and curse them'.[72] Judges in Lorraine declared to accused witches that 'this soothsaying art is a fruit of the Evil Spirit', and that 'all these superstitions are just sorcery fabricated by the Devil'.[73] If an accused woman had tried to cure a bull by tracing signs of the cross on it with her left hand, if another (from Saint-Dié) had practised therapeutic ablutions with water taken 'at night ... from the river', these 'recipes' were held to have been taught 'not by a mortal person, but by an evil spirit', because only Satan who 'hates nothing so much as the light and is called Prince of darkness' could have suggested such remedies.

There is a basic antipathy between magic and religion,[74] even though in history their two domains have frequently overlapped and for a long time the reasons and nature of this antinomy were not clearly seen. There were sanctuaries and liturgies of magic, and it is not always accurate to state that the magic rite exerts force and influence in its own right while the religious rite is merely propitiatory. Magic is in fact sometimes ambiguous: it can incorporate sacrificial ceremonies and like religion make use of vows, prayers and hymns. Conversely, certain religious rites, as rites, are claimed to exert force. However, magic and religion are essentially hostile. The former tends to what is concrete, the latter to what is transcendent; one tries to satisfy 'the lower needs of domestic life', the other to raise man above himself. 'Whereas the religious rite in general is at home in an open gathering, in the broad daylight of publicity, the magic rite flees publicity and concentrates on the individual. Even when perfectly legal, it hides ...'[75] Magic and religion are vitalized by opposing poles: malefice on the one hand, sacrifice on the other.[76] The promoters of spiritualization in the west during the period under study in this book sensed this structural antipathy. They wanted to snatch their contemporaries who had remained in many ways pagan from a false religion which was dragging them down to the earth, that is, to hell. Witchcraft, once it was classed as heresy, was ultimately seen to be the pre-eminent anti-religion and so the work of Satan himself. During the religious Reformations, the promoters of western Christianization, following St Augustine, called Satanism what was really residual paganism – a paganism whose tenacious survival they discovered to their amazement. An inquisitor affirmed that 'a third of Christendom is infected with witchcraft'.

3. The power of Satan

In a society still impregnated with sorcery, it was the judges and theologians who originated the myth of demonic witchcraft by drawing on elements from folklore and beliefs and practices handed down from the most ancient times.[77] The fight against witchcraft was therefore a part of the depaganization of the west, but a part which resulted by overdose in the revival of a Manichaeism which had not entirely disappeared.

It was understood that Satan could do nothing without the permission of the Almighty and that 'evil sprites serve . . . the glory of God as executors and executioners of his consummate justice'.[78] But this stated, a whole literature sparked off by the Bull *Summis desiderantes* (1484) and the *Malleus maleficarum* (Hammer of the witches, 1487) exalted the power of Lucifer. A random statistic is revealing: in the catechism of the Jesuit Canisius, the name of Satan is quoted sixty-seven times – and the name of Jesus only sixty-three! Previous to this Luther had written in his *Great Catechism* of 1529: 'The Devil makes ceaseless attempts on our lives and discharges his anger by causing accidents and bodily hurt. In several cases he has broken a person's neck or made him lose his reason. At other times he has drowned people, and frequently he has pushed them to suicide or other atrocious misfortunes'.

Since God does only what is good, the devil, in Luther's mind, initiated and nourished what was evil. The devil was so powerful that he could cause death by the leaf of a tree. He poisoned the air, caused plague and French disease. He possessed more drugs and more phials of poison than all the apothecaries in the world. It was as if God had abandoned the world to the 'Prince of this world'. As Jean Bodin observed: '. . . the Word of God cannot fail which says that there is no power on earth which can resist the power of Satan. As it is said in Job (chap. 41), so that one may have recourse to God and God alone'.[79]

Bérulle follows the same reasoning as Luther and Bodin. Since the original sin, 'Satan, who before had no rights over the world or any power over man, has despoiled him victoriously of his kingdom and arrogated to himself the power and empire of the world which had been man's from his birth . . . He even sometimes invades his very body so that where, before sin, he was incarnated in the serpent, now he is incarnated in man'.[80] In such a psychological climate, it is not surprising that 'possessions' proliferated. They were the assiduous topic of rumour and conversation in seventeenth-century France, notably at Aix-en-Provence (1609–11), Loudun (1631–8) and Louviers (1643–7).[81]

Theologians as well as popular opinion in the late middle ages and early classic period acknowledged Satan's power to spawn the lower animals: vermin, insects, lizards, toads and so forth. It was believed that sorcerers affected their victims with powders made up of crushed earthworms, ground snail-shells, decomposed toads, bees etc. The devil was able to change these powders into fleas, bugs or spiders. For the majority of westerners at the start of the classic age, Satan was the personification of death; he could take hold of corpses; and he could change himself (or a sorcerer) into a goat, a wolf or a cat. There was nothing in the hidden treasures of the earth of which he was not the master; he knew all the secrets of nature. He was, in short, the god of evil, served by some seven million evil spirits,[82] just as God was served by legions of angels. Sorcery was a sort of Christianity turned inside out, 'the rites of diabolic initiation corresponding to the baptism of Christians with reverse effects, the sabbath being the opposite of the mass and the sacrament of penance, the stigma or devil's mark being the opposite of the baptismal "character" or stigmata of the mystics, etc.'.[83] Because salt was used in exorcisms, non-salted food was eaten at the sabbaths, and because saints of the time had the gift of tears, wizards and witches were said to be incapable of shedding tears (unless they repented).

Trials for witchcraft became less frequent and belief in witchcraft waned after 1650 with the emergence of a new mentality. The critical spirit developed in the educated classes, but at the same time the masses no doubt felt more reassured than before. Fear of the devil diminished as the two Christian Reformations began to filter down to parish level (second half of the seventeenth century). Was this merely coincidence? It would be strange if it were. The people were better served by a worthier, more educated and more accessible pastoral body, and better protected by the Bible (especially in Protestantism), the sacraments (especially in Catholicism) and the catechism (in both). They naturally felt less threatened by the wiles and snares of the devil. In the combat between priest and magician, the former carried the day, but less, probably, because of the stake than because of the renewed devotional life of Christendom and the new-style men of God.

CHAPTER 4

CHRISTIANIZATION

(a) The fight against paganism

1. The ban on popular festivals

Fr Boschet's life of Fr Maunoir, published in 1697,[1] includes the following passage: 'One must not be surprised to see in the missions something akin to what the pagans experienced when the first Apostles preached to them, because in many places of lower Brittany the mysteries of Religion were so little known it was a question of establishing the faith (kerygma) rather than of teaching Christian doctrine (paranesis)'.

Are we to think, from this, of a Land's End (Finisterre) which the breakers of innovation reached only to die exhausted on the beach? It seems not. One of the main sources for superstitions in seventeenth-century France concerns not Brittany at all but Chartres,[2] and it was in the diocese of Autun that in 1686 the peasants sacrificed a heifer to our Lady to obtain protection for their herds against the 'plague'.[3] Truth to tell, before the Catholic Reformation gained momentum there seems to have been extreme religious ignorance in most of the country areas of the kingdom. When Fr Beurrier arrived at Nanterre (where he had been appointed curé-prior) in 1637 he was stupefied by the dearth of Christian education in 'the local dignitaries of advancing years' who were ignorant 'of even the commonest things that have to be known before one can receive the sacraments and be saved'.[4] In the second half of the seventeenth century, a bishop of Autun told the pope in a letter that the people in his diocese were 'quite uneducated, hardly initiated in even the rudiments of the faith' and that they lived 'in crass and deeply rooted ignorance'.[5]

As the classical age, then, dawned in France, and in Europe as a whole,[6] the intellectual and psychological climate of the people was characterized by a profound unfamiliarity with the basics of Christianity, and by a persistent pagan mentality with the occasional vestiges of pre-Christian ceremonial. It would be an admirable historical exercise to group together, without regard for confessional barriers, the varied aspects of European churchmen's fight against superstition and paganized folklore at the time. Here we may content ourselves with selecting and comparing one or two of the more significant facts.

In 1579, a council at Milan forbade the manifestations of *calendimaggio* (Mayday festivities) in the north of Italy. These festivities included 'cutting down trees, branches and all, parading them in the streets and squares of the towns and villages, and then planting them with wild and ridiculous ceremonies'.[7] These May-day antics were fairly widespread in Europe, and seem to have been, in Italy at least, a survival of the ancient *Floralia* on the calends of May. The consecration of the month of May to Mary (in the early eighteenth century) was probably not an attempt to Christianize the folkloric manifestations of that period of the year, but it may well have been a reaction against the widely-held belief that this month was an unlucky one: for example, it was considered unlucky to get married in May.[8]

Still on the subject of May, and still in the late sixteenth century, 'the dean, canons and other clergy' of Chalon-sur-Saône used to process on Whit Monday to a meadow, where they 'went several times round a dome in which was a mass of rounded stones with stone images round about it'. This 'dance of the canons' was abolished between 1593 and 1624 by bishop Cyrus de Thiard.[9] At about the same time archbishop Pierre de Villars suppressed the so-called ceremony of the Blacked Men which took place at Vienne on 1 May. The four Blacked Men were chosen respectively by the archbishop, the chapter of Saint Maurice and the abbots of Saint-André and Saint-Pierre. Naked and blackened all over, they issued forth from the archiepiscopal palace early in the morning, ran round the whole city and then returned to the palace: on completion of which feat, the archbishop gave them a 'king' and a guard. The cortege then went to the town hall to find St Paul, dressed as a hermit, then to the abbey of the Dames of St Andrew where the abbess gave them a 'queen', decked out, like the king, in a quite grotesque fashion. 'This ridiculous court processed round the city, the whole people running after it shouting and hallooing in the most fearful way'.[10] The prohibition of this masquerade may be compared with the action against the feast of fools taken by the Council of Basle in 1436, the synodal statutes of Lyons in 1566 and 1577, and the archbishop of Cologne in 1617,[11] and with this *Addendum* of 1683 to the constitutions of the diocese of Annecy: 'Although the zeal of the reverend clergy has abolished the superstitions which the people's ignorance had introduced into the diocese, we must still exhort them to persevere until the last vestiges are stamped out, and we order the people, under pain of excommunication, to suppress and abolish entirely the torches and fires customarily lit on the first Sunday of Lent . . . and the masquerades . . . which are merely shameful relics of Paganism'.[12]

2. Restrictions to the Fires of St John

In the seventeenth century the Church was particularly vigilant in the matter of the many superstitious manifestations surrounding the St John liturgical cycle.[13] It was the custom for the canons of Chalon-sur-Saône − again − to repair to the place called L'Etoile-à-forêt on the eve of St John. There they cut down branches, especially willow branches, and took them back to the cathedral. All the clergy of the city took part in the procession. The inhabitants, who also had foliage in their hands, threw leaves and flowers as the procession went by. The ceremony was suppressed in 1648.[14]

In different places the religious authorities adopted different attitudes to the Fires of St John. In several dioceses there was an absolute ban as on 'ceremonies redolent of superstition'. In others efforts were made to channel the popular tendencies by Christianizing them. At the time of Bossuet, the *Catéchisme de Meaux* is informative on this point:

'Q. Why does the Church display such joy at the birth of St John the Baptist?
A. It displays such joy to perpetuate the joy foretold by the angel . . .
Q. Is this why fires of joy are lit?
A. Yes.
Q. Does the Church share in these fires?
A. Yes, because in several dioceses, including our own, several parishes light a so-called ecclesiastical fire.
Q. What reason is there for making this fire "ecclesiastical"?
A. To banish the superstitions practised at the Fires of St John.
Q. What are these superstitions?
A. Dancing round the fire, playing, holding feasts, singing vulgar songs, throwing grasses over the fire, gathering grasses before midnight or before breakfast, wearing grasses, keeping them for the whole year, keeping brands or cinders from the fire, and the like'.[15]

Bossuet's approach to this delicate question of the Fires of St John seems to have been the most widespread among the clergy of France, as is evidenced by a *Popular instruction on the origin and ritual of the Fire of the Nativity of St John the Baptist to remove its abuses and superstitions* (1665).[16] This instruction is built up like a catechism on the question-and-answer system:

'Q. What are the abuses which have crept into this ceremony in the course of time?

A. ... Superstitions like executing certain circuits of the fire and making animals do the same, taking small firebrands, bits of charcoal and ashes, wearing belts of grass, throwing bunches of grass on to and over the fire ...

Q. With regard to the materials for this ceremony, what preparations or decorations are made?

A. ... In the middle (of the square) a small stake of eight or nine faggots is erected without heavy wood so that the fire will not last longer than the chanted prayers, and no brands will be left to serve superstitious practices ...

Q. What is the routine for the ceremony?

A. ... While the fire is burning, a lay officiant pokes the wood to speed up the burning, and a prominent ecclesiastic stays by the fire to hold the people back and prevent them from snatching and carrying off even the smallest pieces of wood or charcoal with which they would minister to their superstitious leanings and other disorders. When everything is over, what is left of the fire is doused with a couple of buckets of water, the ashes are immediately removed, the square is swept clean, and the carpet and picture of St John are put away, all this being the responsibility of the person in charge of the fire'.

As well as controlling, sanctifying and limiting the number of Fires of St John, the Instruction of 1665 asked the local dignitaries to tolerate 'no private fires': an indication of the suspicion of paganism in which this folkloric manifestation was held, and the effort made to christianize it in the seventeenth century and afterwards. It is only one case, although a particularly revealing one, of the war on several simultaneous fronts waged by religion against a tenacious mentality of superstition. One last fact amongst many others sheds light on this incessant struggle. It is mentioned by T. J. Schmitt in his study of the diocese of Autun: 'The inhabitants of Reclesne', he writes, 'came during pregnancy to invoke a papier mâché statue of our Lady in one of the chapels of their local church. After some set prayers and an offering, they opened the belly of the statue, gazed at an Infant Jesus there, and then closed the statue hoping for a happy birth. When the curé was ordered not to tolerate this superstition (1689), he put an iron band round the statue, and then assured his superiors, prematurely perhaps, that the devotion was no longer practised'.[17]

This attempt to spiritualize religion, which was very marked in several French theologians of the eighteenth century,[18] was also one of the main aspects of the Catholic *Aufklärung*. The German priests who opted for an 'enlightened' Christianity were reproached with caring little for dogma and the sacraments and preaching morals rather than the faith. As a pastoral 'examination of conscience', the Catholic *Aufklärung* cannot be fully appreciated unless it is seen in the context of the excesses against which it was reacting. It was fighting for a purified Christianity against the 'baroque' piety of 'devotionettes'. It declared war on belief in witches, indulgences, curative pilgrimages, unintelligible masses to which the faithful attributed a sort of magic power, and the bric-à-brac of statues, pictures and reliquaries which turned churches into piety stalls. We now have some good accounts of pre-*Aufklärung* popular devotion in Germany which enable us to do full justice to the effort to depaganize Christianity there at this time.

(b) *The typology of the new priest*

1. The demands of the faithful

In this war on superstition, the Church needed a parish clergy who were more detached than in times past from the traditional world of witchcraft, more detached too from involvement in daily affairs, and more open to the demands of true religion. In Europe during the classical age, and especially in France, such a clergy effectively emerged, but not without a struggle. The historian can rely here on several recent large-scale studies in religious sociology[20] dealing with some of the French dioceses under the *Ancien Régime*. However, the work needs extending so that dioceses, and later whole countries, can be compared. The aim is ultimately to gauge not only the diffusion of the Catholic Reformation in the various regions, but also its varying intensity in different times and areas, and the emphases in the various mentalities. Studies like this should help to clarify the present. For example, a systematic inquiry into the religious life and limits of Christianization from the sixteenth to the eighteenth century in the Marches of Ancona, Emilia and Romagna would perhaps explain why these regions, which were part of the papal states, are the least practising in Italy today.

Religious hunger was certainly not the same from one town or province to another, but one fact is important: all over the place populations whose mores and beliefs were still unformed demanded new-style clergy who would bestow a feeling of greater security: they wanted pastors different from themselves who would be models of Christian living. The need for such clergy was expressed in the books of complaints presented by the bailiwick of Troyes to the general estates of 1614. The people ask that: 'the clergy be forbidden all base actions: the company of suspect women, taverns, dissolute games, blasphemies, hunts and all the other things which bring disgrace and dishonour on their dignity and provoke public scandal'.[21]

In 1662 the inhabitants of a village in Brie lodged a complaint with the archdeacon on their alcoholic curate: 'He is frequently drunk, usually on Sundays and feastdays, and he has several times had to be carried off in a state of advanced intoxication. He refuses to fulfil his charge and administer the sacraments, and on St Bartholomew's eve he threatened the said churchwarden with a pistol, vowing in God's name to blow his brains out. He does not sing vespers and lives a disorderly life'.

Eleven years later, the inhabitants of Montmélian (in the archdeaconry of Paris) denounced their curé to the archbishop's visitor: 'He does nothing but hunt'. 'The squire's warden and game-keepers have orders to take his gun on sight'. He had turned the cemetery into a rabbit-warren, and 'encouraged the rabbits to eat the grass in the graveyard, and there they burrow down to the very coffins of the dead'. He had, furthermore, locked the cemetery so that all the game should be his. A lot of these accusations were probably just gossip,[22] but from the point of view of collective psychology, they pinpoint the faithful's need for a worthier pastoral body. It is true that our prime source of information here is the religious claim of the writers of *cahiers,* therefore of the élite of rural parishes; but this élite fashioned and carried the opinions of the anonymous uneducated masses. The history of the Catholic Reformation proves that the new effort to evangelize the masses made headway only when the episcopate decided to supervise the parish clergy more keenly than theretofore. On the other hand may one not think that the renewal of the Church, and so of the priesthood, was ultimately the demand of an unsatisfied and disorientated people of which the hierarchy took increasing note?

2. A worthier clergy

The ecclesiastical authorities began to make more frequent demands for austerity and dignity of life from the priest. Even before Trent, the rugged bishop of Verona, Giberti, imprisoned parish priests and curates whose lives were evil. In Belgium[23] in the late sixteenth and early seventeenth centuries, the heads of dioceses drew up lists of their parish clergy with comments on each one, imposed fasts of bread and water on prevaricators, and removed from the ministry those whose scandalous lives brought dishonour on the clergy. In France the weight of episcopal authority began to be felt in the second half of the seventeenth century. In 1660 the curé of Bondy, accused of acts of violence and of frequenting undesirable localities, was condemned to be stripped of his benefice and forbidden to exercise any curial function in the diocese of Paris for three years. In the same year the curé of Andrésy was condemned by the episcopal court of Paris to go on retreat to Saint-Lazare (with the St Vincent de Paul missioners) 'on two separate occasions . . . for ten days on each occasion'. Ten years later another pastor in the same diocese who had flaunted himself in public with his housekeeper, was condemned to 'proceed forthwith to the seminary of Saint-Nicolas-du-Chardonnet in this city of Paris, and there remain for the uninterrupted space of three months . . . during which time he will be forbidden all his curial functions and held to provide an approved priest as a replacement in his cure at his own expense'. Steps like these were not without their effect. In the archdeaconry of Paris in 1672–3, the visitor (Ameline) came across only eleven priests out of 302 deservous of serious reproach for their conduct: this is less than four per cent, a figure similar to the percentage calculated by L. Pérouas for the diocese of La Rochelle (five per cent in about 1724, as opposed to twenty-five per cent in about 1648).

Misconduct, however, was not solely concubinage. The abuse of wine seems to have been prevalent amongst the parish clergy before the rigorous times of the Catholic Reformation. In 1652 the bishop of Autun declared that 'the frequentation of taverns and wineshops is customary with the said priests, and there they blaspheme and utter vulgar words, commit indecencies, and take wine to such excess that they render themselves incapable of administering the sacraments'. Some dioceses, Arras for example, seem to have been positively plagued with clerical drunkenness. The position was so bad that two pastoral letters (1673, 1696) were entirely devoted to exposing the ills of drink and decreeing prohibitions and sanctions for abuse. What steps did the hierarchy as a whole take? In Belgium from 1590 to 1630,[24] the bishop of Ruremonde forbade his priests to enter wineshops and fined those who celebrated mass 'the morning after', except when it was absolutely necessary. In the archdiocese of Malines, parish clergy were forbidden to attend the receptions after weddings, baptisms etc., and to participate in public games. In France too the episcopate, especially after 1650, issued severe and repeated decrees against the over-frequent intemperance of the parish clergy. In 1658 the archbishop of Sens decided that the priests of his diocese found in a state of inebriation would have to expiate their fault by a public penance. In 1672, the archbishop of Paris issued the following interdict: 'We forbid under pain of suspension all ecclesiastics with domicile or semi-domicile in this city, or in the other cities, towns and villages of this diocese, to enter inns for the purposes of eating and drinking unless they are travelling and more than a league (= four kilometres) from their place of residence'.

Synodal statutes in Paris at the end of the century fixed the distance at two leagues. Throughout France in the classical epoch there were similar imperatives against frequenting taverns under pain of suspension. In the statutes of the bishops of La Rochelle on the conduct of the clergy in the second half of the seventeenth century, 'no feature', writes L.Pérouas, 'recurs so often as the prohibition to enter wineshops'. The episcopate had to deal with those who twisted the prohibitions by going outside the boundaries of their parish, one or two leagues distant from their place of residence, and drinking in taverns there. In some cases the hierarchy imposed an 'irregularity' on recidivists and thus obliged them to have recourse to the Holy See. The ecclesiastical authorities also tried to stop priests hunting. Clerics have not the right to spill blood. More importantly, hunting encouraged priests 'to eat and drink to excess and to be too familiar with worldly people'. In fact it was a long time before the custom was eradicated, but eradicated it eventually was.

This new priest, to whom hunting, drunkenness, public feasting and unchastity were now extraneous, needed some form of dress which would mark him off from the world. The Counter-Reformation brought in the universal wearing of the soutane or cassock, not without opposition. One day Louis XIII met Bourdoise, the founder of Saint-Nicolas-du-Chardonnet seminary, walking near Garches 'in a cassock and long cloak, with a very short hair-style'. The King, taking him for a religious, asked him to what order he belonged. ' "Sire", M. Bourdoise replied, "I am a simple priest and consequently a member of the order of St Peter". The King, not understanding this reply and surprised at his exterior, said he had never heard of this order and that he did not know it existed in his kingdom. Whereupon M. Bourdoise took the opportunity of discoursing on the excellence and obligations of the ecclesiastical state; and he did so with such unction and modesty that the King was very edified'.

The astonishment of Louis XIII is not surprising. Wearing the cassock was still exceptional in France in the early seventeenth century, and Bérulle was one of those instrumental in extending it. In 1600 the bishop of Autun still thought it sufficient to recommend his priests to wear clothes which were 'not fancy or gaudy, but sober'. Later on the episcopate insisted on the need to wear the cassock and present a dignified exterior. In 1620 Henri de Gondi, bishop of Paris, commanded his priests to 'be always dressed in a long, neat and decent soutane', and 'to have a tidy beard and hair-style, with a neat tonsure'. These admonitions were constantly repeated.

In 1673 synodal statutes for Paris include the following passage: 'We order all ecclesiastics in both the rural and urban areas of this diocese to retain at all times a clerical modesty in their tonsure, hair and general external appearance, in accordance with the holy canons, and always to wear the cassock in their place of residence.' The 1697 statutes added: 'We forbid all ecclesiastics to wear jerkins, ties and all clothes of a hue other than black. . . . We forbid all priests to say mass in a periwig without permission'.

These prohibitions, which would probably be the same in all the dioceses of the kingdom, were, we repeat, in answer to the people's wishes. In 1671 the inhabitants of Châtillon-sous-Bagneux complained to the *officialis* that their curé frequently went about without a cassock, 'wearing only a jerkin'. For a long time the parish clergy were reluctant to comply. Some priests retained a secular affectation about their dress, and thought it sufficient to add frills to the sleeves of lay attire. Others continued to dress in peasant fashion with a linen jacket, a kerchief round the neck, and sabots. In 1696 an episcopal visitor for the diocese of Autun noted: 'There are few curés who wear the cassock in the country, while others have cassocks which extend no further than the knees; they have been asked to lengthen them and remove the pockets on the front'. By dint of the close scrutiny, reprimands and sanctions of the bishops, the cassock became the accepted clerical dress.

3. The obligation of residence

Public opinion and the hierarchy, then, the one reinforcing the other, imposed on the clergy a new image and new standards of behaviour, but this was of use only if the parish priests and curates resided among their parishioners. First the Council of Trent, then Pope Pius V from 1565 to 1570 had insisted on this necessary pastoral reconversion, but it was slow to become a reality.[25] By way of example to illustrate the methodology here, we may again take France, which is at present the country best studied. In the books of complaints from the bailiwick of Troyes for the general estates of 1614, charges of non-residence were still frequent. 'In the first place', wrote the inhabitants of Chaource, 'may it please His Majesty to make ecclesiastics reside in their benefices, so that they may perform in person the office for which they are responsible'.[26] The inhabitants of the castellany of Isle-Aumont wrote: 'So that God may be served and honoured and the people exposed only to good example, may His Majesty be pleased to enjoin that all curés and acting rectors of parishes reside in their parishes, minister there in person to proclaim the glory and word of God, see to the scrupulous and meticulous administration of the Holy Sacraments and exalt their singular virtues'.

The war on the absenteeism of pastors was necessarily a long-term undertaking, so ingrained were the habits of non-residence. No less a person than St Vincent de Paul left his parish of Clichy after a year's residence — against his will, it is true — to take up a post as tutor to the Gondis. For thirteen years he remained curé of that parish and yet hardly set foot in it, and when in 1626 he resigned his cure to his assistant he still kept for himself an annuity of 400 francs. It therefore comes as no surprise to learn of cases of absenteeism in the Paris region as late as the mid-seventeenth century. The people of Villaines declared in 1648 that it was 'about ten months' since their curé took possession of his cure, and so far 'they had seen nothing of him'. They wanted their children 'to be instructed and educated particularly in Christian doctrine and the things necessary to salvation'. At Bondy in 1649, the people disclosed to the archdeacon that their curé 'was never in the said parish, but resided mostly in Paris and elsewhere' and that he did not want an assistant. The people, however, would undertake 'to guarantee a curate's salary and to support him if he would fulfil the ministerial functions, administer the sacraments and teach the children of the parish as there was no schoolmaster'.

Such cases decreased in frequency as the authorities mounted their combined offensive. The general estates of 1614 had decided that in the case of unjustified absence on the part of the curé, the lay authorities would appropriate the temporal revenue of the parish. In 1695 this sanction was mitigated, at the request of the clergy themselves, when the abuse was very much less in evidence: it was limited to the confiscation of a third of the benefice income. The bishops, too, declared war on non-residence. Instructions from the bishop of Autun dated 1597 and 1600 obliged parish priests to return to their benefices within three months. Another instruction, dated 1603, deploring the circumstance that some parish priests had disobeyed orders and were ministering in parishes other than their own 'in the hope of increased gain and profit and to be able to live elsewhere in licentiousness', gave them only a month in which to regain their cures. When the month was up, the benefice would be declared vacant. In 1614, archpriests were ordered to send to Autun, under pain of sanctions, a list of non-resident parish priests. In 1538 the king's attorney was commissioned 'to seize the goods of curés not resident in their cures'. It would serve no useful purpose here to extend the account of these steps and of others like them in all the other dioceses. According to J. Ferté, even before the Fronde the absenteeism of pastors had become uncommon in the Paris region; it became more uncommon still once the civil war ended: out of 138 parishes visited in 1672–3 by the archdeacon of Paris, only six were marked 'curé hardly ever resident' in the visitation reports. In the diocese of La Rochelle, inspections between 1648 and 1667 revealed only seven cases of non-residence, whereas in the same parishes in 1601 the abuse of 'confiding' as it was called (from the fact that the curé received the parish revenues but *confided* the ministry to a 'mercenary' priest) was widespread. It is possible that some curés made sure they were in their cures when the bishop or archdeacon came round, and then felt free to go off again for another long period. Even so, by 1700 non-residence in parishes, which had been a common practice in France in the early 1500s, was very much the exception.

Recent studies in religious sociology, then, make it clear that at least in France one of the most important results of the Counter-Reformation was firmer support for the faithful from the clergy. Such support was strengthened as the number of assistant priests grew. L. Pérouas calculates that in about 1648 the diocese of La Rochelle had 155–170 vicars and in about 1700 175–200. In the archdeaconry of Paris in 1641, eighty-five parishes out of 138 had a curate, and in 1672 the number had risen to 101. In the diocese of Brie, thirty-five parishes out of ninety-nine had curates in 1653, and forty-two in 1662. Another revealing fact reported by L. Pérouas is that in the diocese of La Rochelle in the early eighteenth century, the proportion of priests to faithful was as high as one to 500.

4. The religious training of pastors

It was of little use, however, for a pastor to live among his flock and evince greater worthiness in his life than in the past if he did not then impress the faithful with his theological knowledge. The pastoral visitations between 1535 and 1553 in the diocese of Mantova furnish us with fifty-seven comments on parish clergy: twenty-seven of them positive as regards the priests' mores and ability, twenty-two decidedly negative on both morals and education (*nihil sciens*; *ignarus litterarum*), and eight middling because although the conduct was acceptable the theological knowledge was not (*illiteratus; superficialiter intellegit; non multum sufficiens*).[27] A hundred years later the situation in the diocese of Liège was hardly better.[28] About the mid-seventeenth century the intellectual mediocrity of the majority of priests in the Parisian countryside is scarcely open to doubt, despite the presence among them of university graduate priests. In 1653 the good people of Cossigny complained to the archdeacon of Brie that their curé was 'incapable of fulfilling his office'. Even in the middle of Louis XIV's reign there were still curés in the villages near Paris who did not know a word of Latin. The post mortem inventories throughout the seventeenth century show up the poverty of some parish priests' libraries. In 1630 only four books were found in the rooms of the curé of Dampierre (diocese of Paris): an almanac, a martyrology, the *Paradise of Prayers* (a collection of meditations for different hours of the day) and the *State of the Church militant*, a vaguely historical work published in 1555. In 1686 the library of the curé of La Chapelle-Milon (again diocese of Paris) comprised precisely 'three books bound in vellum, one being the lives of saints, the second being lives of the saints too, and the third being homilies on the Gospel, and another little volume called *Counsels and theological reasons for peace of soul*'.

The seminaries made a decisive contribution to raising the intellectual standards of the clergy: they engineered what amounted to an 'ecclesial revolution' at the time of the Counter-Reformation. However, in France and most Catholic countries it was a long time before they were established on a really firm footing, and as a consequence their influence was almost unnoticeable until the late seventeenth century. While the seminaries were taking shape, the bishops had to resort to various other expedients to ensure the theological education of their parish clergy. In 1602, for example, the bishop of Nice obliged his priests to own at least twelve books. In 1654, Godeau bishop of Vence (Alpes-Maritimes) included with his pastoral letters lists of books to be read by his priests. In 1658 Gondrin archbishop of Sens ordered his curés to procure forty-seven stipulated books which they must produce at parish visitations if asked, and among them he included a Bible, the *Roman Catechism*, the *Decisions of the Council of Trent*, Aquinas' *Summa theologiae*, the *Imitation of Christ*, St Charles Borromeo's *Instructions to Confessors*, and St Francis de Sales' *Introduction to the Devout Life*. In 1681–91 the bishop of Autun systematically inquired into libraries in presbyteries.

'Clergy conferences' also set out to stimulate the intellectual activity of the lower clergy. The archbishop of Paris, Harly de Champvallon, decreed in 1672 that 'all the curés, vicars, confessors and other supply priests and priests residing in the parishes' of the diocese must attend a conference once a month, even when the weather was inclement or farms short-staffed. Almost everywhere that year the directors of the conference complained to the archbishop about the curés in their deaneries, 'saying that it was impossible to make them all come'. At Angers, Mgr Le Peletier gained himself the reputation of a tyrant because he imposed retreats and conferences on his clergy.[29] The hierarchy, however, persisted, and gave the conferences a firmer and firmer structure. The net results were an improvement in the religious standards of the parish clergy, the emergence of a common spirit among the priests of a deanery and a tightening of the bonds between lower clergy and the local ordinary. This is why most of the curés of the Parish diocese followed their archbishop, Cardinal Noailles, in September and October 1718 when he opposed the Bull *Unigenitus* and the pontifical letters condemning the appellants.

Different approaches enable us to gauge the rise in academic standards among the parish clergy during the seventeenth and eighteenth centuries. In the diocese of Autun, the tart marginal comments in the reports of pastoral visitations gradually disappear (on twenty-two occasions between 1650 and 1689, according to T. J. Schmitt, reports of pastoral visitations included marginal notes such as 'extremely stupid and ignorant', 'ignorant and imbecile', 'uncouth and very ignorant'). From an inquiry conducted between 1681 and 1691 in the same diocese, it transpires that only one curé did not have on his shelves the twelve books declared indispensable by the bishop. In 1729 the inquiry was renewed in eight out of the ten deaneries in the archdeaconry of Autun and again only one curé failed to produce the statutory number of books; two had no more than the stipulated dozen; nine had twenty to fifty works, and five had a hundred to three hundred. The triumphant cry of the curé of Rumegies quoted earlier is significant: among the people of his parish there was 'no one capable of sustaining the contrary of what is preached'.[30] It is true, as the provincial administrator of Rochefort opined in 1724, that the clergy of the La Rochelle diocese were 'of an advanced ignorance', but in making this severe judgment he probably had in mind above all the lack of profane culture in ecclesiastics. A curé of Les Epesses in 1775 had fifty-nine works in his library, but only four on secular subjects. This gap in the parish clergy between profane and strictly religious culture in the eighteenth century is an interesting question which has still to be properly studied. However that may be, the theological education of parish priests and curates certainly progressed during the

Catholic Reformation. Around 1724 there were ten times more clerics from the diocese of La Rochelle graduating from Angers University than in 1680. L. Pérouas thinks that the majority, or at least a good half, of the younger priests in the diocese were completing faculty courses in 1724.

5. Improvement in the material situation of the lower clergy

These worthier, better educated lower clergy were also more comfortably off. The combined rise in spiritual fervour and material life-style of the parish priest and his assistant under the *Ancien Régime* have recently been stressed: soundings in the late seventeenth century have revealed a relatively high standard of living not suspected twenty years ago. Earlier on we mentioned certain contributory factors: an increase in tithes, the obligation of a clerical title, a drop in the number of casual priests. To these we may add the re-assessment of mass stipends, burial fees, and stole fees in general, the reorganization of some benefices with the annexation of priories and chaplaincies, and finally the steady increase by the authorities of the 'congruous portion' (for parish priests it was 300 francs in 1686, 500 in 1768, 750 in 1786). Of course the position varied from province to province. In the dioceses of Autun and Bourges, the parish clergy were less well off than in Paris. For Paris at any rate the figures given by J. Ferté need give rise to no anxiety on the clergy's living. A statistic for the year 1666 on 386 cures gives the following results:

12 curés provided less than 300 francs per annum;
259 curés provided between 300 and 1000;
101 curés provided between 1000 and 1500;
14 curés provided more than 1500.

L. Pérouas is of the opinion that the parish priests in the diocese of La Rochelle enjoyed an adequate living in the late seventeenth century. Whereas in about 1648 some sixty cures (out of 300) brought in less than 300 francs a year, there were only two or three in 1700. At that date an average cure in La Rochelle brought in between five and six hundred francs. Despite this improvement in his living standards, the parish priest under the *Ancien Régime* was close with his money and careful of his rights. If the congruist envied the 'great tither' on whom he was dependent, the tither himself was scrupulous in collecting his share of the harvest*. He looked out for cheating in the delivery of sheaves or wine, and competed with the pastors or peasants of the neighbouring parishes. One thing, however, of basic importance was that he no longer sold the sacraments of penance, the eucharist and the anointing of the sick.

We may now briefly sketch in the typology of the new parish priest in early eighteenth-century France. The improvement in the pastor's standard of living and a deeper theological training raised him on the social ladder and, in the country, gave him entry into the élite of rural society. The continuously repeated recommendations of the episcopate succeeded in cutting the priest off from secular life. He no longer danced on public holidays, was a stranger to the tavern, wore the tonsure and the cassock. He was imbued with the eminent dignity of the priesthood on which St Charles Borromeo, Bérulle, Bourdoise, St Vincent de Paul and the Sulpicians had insisted so much. He was no longer 'of the world', he was above his parishioners. The clerical state was upgraded with relation to the lay state. On the other hand the near-disappearance of the casual priest meant that, particularly in the country, the faithful began to identify priesthood and ministry. And in fact the parish priest *was* applying himself to the spiritual care of his flock. He restored and maintained the fabric of the church, took an active interest in church property, taught the catechism, tried to add lustre to the ceremonies, fostered or created sodalities and elementary schools, and dedicated himself to the service of the poor.

(c) Efforts to remodel the religious life of the faithful

1. Missions: their popular and rural aspect

If Catholic Europe in the Tridentine period hummed with travelling missioners, it was because the parish clergy inherited from the previous period were so deficient. This was why Vincent de Paul founded the Lazarists. Here again France was the country in which the itinerant messengers of the faith worked most zealously and above all most methodically. However, their activity must ultimately be seen in a vast geographical and multiconfessional context in which Quakers and Methodists rubbed shoulders with Jesuits, Capuchins and Oratorians; and so far there has been no comprehensive survey of this. Outside

The 'tither' ('décimateur'*) was the titular of the benefice to whom the tithes were paid. He in his turn gave a 'congruous portion' of the tithe to the priest who actually ministered in the benefice (the 'congruist'). In fact in France the 'tithe' was never more than a fourteenth or fifteenth part of the total. Tithing was abolished under the Revolution (Tr.).

France, too, particularly in the seventeenth century, Catholic missioners spent themselves in the process of 'evangelization' – a term to be taken here in its proper sense. Undoubtedly the most active of them were the Jesuits: Schacht and Jeningen in Germany, the two Segneris[31] in Italy, Lopez and Tirso Gonsalez[32] in Spain, to name but a few. The methods used by the fifteenth-century prophets remained alive in the seventeenth century and even in the early eighteenth: the Italian Pietro Ansalone (d. 1713) self-administered the discipline in public, and like Savonarola burnt jewelry and undesirable literature in public squares.[33] St John Eudes ended his missions with similar 'joy fires'.[34] The Augustinian hermit Abraham a Sancta Clara (Ulrich Megerle, d. 1709) was the pillar of Vienna and Graz during the plagues and the Turkish peril. Caustic and moving by turns, he had a brilliant imagination and a facility in story-telling. He has been called the 'greatest writer of German prose in the baroque'.[35] The 'century of lights', particularly in Italy, was not the end of evangelization by mission. Two of the most famous popular preachers in Italy lived in the eighteenth century: Leonardo da Porto Maurizio (d. 1751),[36] who encouraged devotion to the Way of the Cross, and Alphonsus de Liguori (d. 1787) the founder of the Redemptorists.[37] One remarkable aspect of this which has not been properly studied is that the Italian missioners preached particularly in the kingdom of Naples. There is reason to think that the *Mezzogiorno* was the least Christianized part of the country . . . and the most superstitious. There, as in the Brittany of Fr Maunoir, the spreaders of the Gospel no doubt understood the divide between magic and religion.

If the seventeenth century was the golden age of Christianization, especially in France, it was because the missionaries tried to reach the rural world, whereas the preachers of the fourteenth and fifteenth centuries had contacted above all the urban public. The Oratory had hardly been founded, in 1613, when it set up a foundation of 500 francs to provide missions to prepare for the four main feasts of the year (Easter, Pentecost, All Saints, Christmas) in the villages of the Paris diocese. An Oratorian was to repair to a village near Paris for a fortnight, 'going from one archdeaconry to another, and changing from year to year'. The Oratorian Jean Eudes, who himself founded several congregations, was one of the best-known preachers of the seventeenth century.[38] He gave celebrated missions in towns such as Rennes, Caen and Paris, but it has been calculated that about sixty-five per cent of his ministry was to rural parishes. He once said: 'Mission being necessary everywhere, we shall preach everywhere, but with preference in the country'. This programme illumines a whole sociological and religious panorama of which St Vincent de Paul probably had the clearest vision in his own time. It was he who brought into being the first properly missionary congregation, and its prime mission, as he saw it, was to the 'poor people of the fields'. The Lazarists were told not to preach in places which were seats of an 'archbishop, bishop or bailiwick court'. This was a novelty all the more remarkable in that a Capuchin missionary like Fr Honoré de Cannes, a member of the Franciscan religious family whose rise had been tied up with the growth of urbanization since the thirteenth century, continued to go from town to town between 1670 and 1692.

Although all social classes in seventeenth-century France were the object of the missionary apostolate, it was particularly the popular strata that the propagandists of the faith tried to reach (an additional proof that these were considered the least christianized, both in the towns and in the country). This explains St Vincent de Paul's advice to adapt the horary of the missions to the rhythm of peasant life. The first instruction of the day had always been early, before work started, and the 'great catechism' (for adults only) late, at the end of the day's work. In the country areas the Lazarists preached in principle only from November to June, when there was least agricultural activity. The more spectacular side of the missions was evidently to impress a public whose mentality had retained its country roughness and who could learn most quickly from a direct, simple approach to religious teaching. There were autos-da-fé of books and superstitious objects, grandiose plantings of wooden crosses, allegorical pasteboard representations used by Fr Maunoir, and 'living pictures' in his processions which evoked the principal scenes of the Bible and the gesta of eminent saints. Hymns were composed in the vernacular and made easy to remember by being set to the melodies of well-known popular songs. Grignion de Montfort specialized in this pious plagiarism. Some examples are:[39]

Popular songs	*Hymns on them*
You thought, by loving Collete	Carol for spiritual souls
My sweetheart is pretty	The true devotee of Mary
Let us pass the heath, my Jeanne	The love of God
My father, marry me off	The spur of fervour
At last I'm in love	The soul delivered from purgatory
A duck stretching its wings	The sufferings of our Lady
I don't know if I'm drunk	Invocation to the Holy Spirit
Friends, let us drink	Our Lady of gifts
One of our poor drunks is ill	Abandonment to Providence
Good, how good the wine is	The esteem and desire of virtues
Pay for the beer-mug, neighbour	The specific remedy for tepidity.[40]

2. Missions: their methodical approach

Unlike the great preachers of the fifteenth century, the missioners of the seventeenth were men of method. They descended on a parish in groups of four, six or eight, and would not leave until the entire population of the village or quarter had received the sacrament of penance. The daily exercises were numerous – sometimes four a day – and there would need to be quite a few religious to organize them properly. They were reminiscent of the exercises recommended by St Ignatius: both were 'put together like the parts of a machine'[41] so that the faithful would be encouraged, listening to a judiciously graded series of instructions, to undergo an inner revolution. It is a significant thing, in the age of Descartes, that *Mission manuals*, giving the correct ways of setting about converting the crowds, were written in large numbers. These manuals dealt with every aspect and detail: the frequency and timing of exercises, the themes of preaching, the type of language to be used, and so on; and all of them recommended lengthy missions. St Jean Eudes wrote: 'Our missions in the smaller parishes never last less than six weeks: otherwise you conceal the wickedness but do not cure it; you snap the weeds, but do not uproot them; you make a lot of noise, but have not much to show for it.' This preference for long missions reveals an awareness that for many years, perhaps since the beginning, the religious instruction of the faithful had been sadly neglected. The missioners were not to be led astray by their own eloquence: the purpose was not to declaim but to instruct. St Vincent de Paul recommended the simple, direct 'little method', and the catechism rather than the homily: 'The people need the catechism more . . . and they reap more profit from it.' In his *Avis aux jeunes prédicateurs* (Counsels to young preachers, circa 1660), St Jean Eudes gave similar advice: 'However great a preacher you are, do not disdain to catechize the children and poorest people at least two or three times a week'. The reader will have noticed from this passage that the catechism was not only for children, but for adults as well: the reference is to the 'great catechism' at the end of the day.

Because they were methodical, the itinerant preachers of the seventeenth century did not abandon a parish once they had been there. The foundations which contributed to the missioners' expenses were usually in the form of annuities which helped to keep the missions in a parish regular: every four, six or eight years, for example. Of what use was it, however, to work in a village if the surrounding areas and indeed the wider province were neglected? It was important to cover an entire region if it was to be brought to God. Fr Berthelot du Chesnay has furnished a representative example: by drawing diagrams of the Eudist missions in the old diocese of Coutances between 1632 and 1676, with the calculated area covered by each mission (five miles round from the centre), he concluded that almost the whole diocese was covered by St Jean Eudes and his disciples.[42] Religious history must cartograph and quantify here if it is to be convincing. Ninety-four of the 117 missions preached by St John Eudes were in Normandy. Fr Maunoir preached some 375 missions in Brittany alone between 1640 and 1683. Grignion de Montfort's seventy missions (mostly between 1706 and 1716) were limited to western France: higher Brittany, Poitou and Aunis. To be effective missions had to be repeated and apostolic effort concentrated.

The itinerant messengers of the Catholic faith tried in any one parish to achieve limited but definite aims. First of all – and this is really revealing – the purpose was to teach the people four basic prayers: the *Pater Noster*, the *Ave Maria*, the *Credo* and the *Confiteor,* and inculcate the habit of reciting them twice a day, morning and evening: only long missions could do this. Secondly, the idea was to encourage an examination of conscience in the light of Christian doctrine, with special emphasis, and I quote from a Lazarist,

> 'on repentance . . . man's last end . . . the enormity of sin, the severity of God on unrepentant sinners . . . hardening of the heart . . . final impenitence . . . remorse, relapses into sin . . . gossip . . . envy, hatred and enmity, oaths and blasphemies . . . intemperance in food and drink and other similar sins which are usually committed by country folk'.[43]

The fear of God which resulted was meant to be salutary. It was designed to lead the faithful to a general confession, the basic legitimation of the mission. 'Our maxim', Vincent de Paul wrote to Jane Frances de Chantal in 1639, 'is not to leave a village . . . until everybody has made his general confession; and there aren't many in the places we visit who don't'.[44] The Eudist missioners guaranteed to be available for confessions from six o'clock to nine and ten to eleven thirty in the morning, and from two to six thirty in the afternoon; they had therefore to provide quite a team of confessors. 'Lions' in the pulpit, they tried to be 'charming' and 'as mild as lambs' in the confessional. They covered their faces so as not to see the penitents. The mission ended with general communion, a suitable culmination to the purification brought about by the examination of conscience and absolution.

The study of missions in the baroque and classical periods has only just begun. There is no European cartography for this religious phenomenon. Other directions of research would be to compare the various methods of evangelization, picking out the similarities and the different emphases, spiritualities (and indeed doctrines) in the various countries and in the different orders. The historian will also try to assess the quality and extent of results achieved by the missions. The foregoing will, it is hoped, offer a method.

3. The parish framework: a sacramental life

The missions induced a sense of religious shock. Only a solid parish framework, however, could transform that shock into a durable spiritual life. As St Vincent de Paul wrote to the bishop of Périgueux in 1650: 'We know by experience that the fruits of missions are very great, corresponding to the extreme needs of country people; but as their minds are generally rather rough and little educated, they readily forget what they have learnt and their good resolutions, unless they have good pastors who maintain the high standards they have reached'.[45]

St Vincent here exposes the nub of the Catholic Reformation: its permeation of the average Christian's daily life. This could be a grand theme of historical inquiry, paralleled by research into countries where the Christianization process was the work of the Protestant Reformation. Tridentine Catholicism gave the faithful a feeling of security by surrounding them with protective sacraments, and consequently giving the sacraments a new depth. There was no difficulty in persuading the people of the need for baptism because there was general adherence to Augustine's view that 'no one could be saved unless he were baptized' (in the wording of a catechism printed in Paris by order of Mgr de Péréfixe): this meant hell (limbo) for infants who died without baptism. Tirelessly synodal statutes of the seventeenth century repeated the duty of parents to have their infants baptized within three days of birth. If necessary, negligent parents could find themselves refused entry into the church. Surveillance of midwives was increased, less, probably, to limit abortions than because they were obliged to baptize the newly-born in danger of death. Chosen by the female élite of the village, the midwife gave an oath with her hands between the curé's, and she also had to prove that she could administer baptism. During a pastoral or archdiaconal visitation, the visitor never failed to question the midwife. French parish registers reveal that lapses in the administration of baptism became rarer and rarer from the late seventeenth century onwards. Also the seriousness of the ceremony was brought out more; godparents had to be 'practising Catholics' (which meant Catholics who fulfilled their Easter duties), and candidates who were 'incapable or unsuitable because of their conduct and bad example' were to be turned down; the rush of volunteer campanologists was forbidden (traditionally bell-ringers at baptisms received a tip from the godparents).

More so than baptism, confirmation needed re-evaluating. According to J. Toussaert,[46] in fourteenth- and fifteenth-century Flanders either the sacrament was a semi-superstitious rite or else no notice was taken of it. In 1665 Mgr de Péréfixe stated in a pastoral letter that 'the people in the (Parisian) country areas and the poor have no knowledge of confirmation, either because of their pastors' negligence in omitting the relevant instructions, or because of their own laziness in not attending instructions'. He did not say that the lack of visitations from the bishop was the chief reason why the sacrament had sunk into semi-oblivion. It was a lot to ask the faithful to go to the bishop's or archbishop's palace to receive confirmation on the appointed days (usually ember days). St Margaret Mary Alacoque, for instance, was not confirmed until she was twenty-two. Confirmation, then, did not begin to play a regular role in ordinary parish life until pastoral visitations became more frequent. From the late seventeenth century, the lists of confirmees which we have for the Parisian countryside include adults only by way of exception, which presumably proves that the sacrament was now being conferred systematically on children without undue delay. On the other hand, in a backward diocese like Autun regular administration of confirmation did not become the rule for a long time, because of both general inertia and the geographical fragmentation of the area. As late as 1690, 200 communicants out of 350 in the parish of Saint-Nazaire at Bourbon-Lancy had not been confirmed.

In the fourteenth and fifteenth centuries, the veneration of the Blessed Sacrament had developed enormously. However, the grandiose Corpus Christi processions and the magnificent monstrances that the late Gothic period has left us should not be allowed to give a false impression. Religious instruction being so deficient, the people venerated in the eucharist primarily a 'miraculous object' and a 'sensational element';[47] and such veneration was not necessarily extended into regular Easter duties. From his researches into Flanders prior to the Protestant Reformation, J. Toussaert believes that making Easter duties was much less common than is generally imagined today.[48] Further, even when the obligation to go to communion once a year 'at Easter time or thereabouts' was observed, it was not necessarily matched with frequenting the sacrament at the other feasts of the year. Some figures given by J. Ferté for the early seventeenth century are revealing. From 1604 to 1626 the parish priest of Lagny kept a record of the number of communions distributed in his parish on the great feasts. In 1618, for example, there were 297 communions at Easter, 140 at Christmas, 43 on All Saints, 23 at Whitsun, 20 on the feast of the Assumption. The figures are much the same for the other years. Similar data are furnished by the much more important parish of Colombes in 1626: of the 1195 Easter communicants, only a quarter went to communion at the Assumption and All Saints, and a tenth at Whitsun.

The Catholic Reformation tried to introduce regular Easter duties everywhere. It reminded the faithful that the Easter communion should be in one's own parish church (to make surveillance easier). The posting-up of the names of non-communicants on the church door, the threats of excommunication, the refusal of ecclesiastical burial amounted to so much social pressure that the number of those who did not fulfil their Easter duties does not seem to have exceeded one per cent of the Catholic population in the diocese of La Rochelle in 1648, and 0.22 per cent in the (rural) archdeaconry of Paris in 1672. Still, it is probable that the defaulters were more numerous than this in the towns, where surveillance anyway was more difficult. Of more interest from the point of view of gaining some ideas of the religious vitality of a population is the number of communions outside Easter time. It is certain that they increased, bringing with them a more frequent use of the confessional. At the beginning of his ministry at Ivry, Jean Jollain, who was curé there from 1669 to 1686, complained that even with his two curates he could not 'manage to see to all the offices on feast days and confess 400 or 500 people who are accustomed to do their devotions at the big feasts such as the feasts of our Lady and the parish's patron saint, the parish comprising nearly 800 communicants and 400 souls who do not as yet go to communion'.

The combined action of the Jesuits, new congregations of nuns (Visitation nuns, Ursulines etc.), sodalities (especially the Blessed Sacrament and the Rosary) and missions, counterbalancing Jansenist reticence, brought in a change in the faithful's attitude to communion and confession. In 1687 at Lille, the Jesuits distributed more than 3000 hosts on some feast days.[49] The constitutions of the Visitation nuns stipulated that the sisters would go to communion on Sundays, holidays of obligation and Thursdays. In the early 1700s in the diocese of La Rochelle (and the same may certainly be said of other dioceses in the kingdom), the obligation of monthly confession and communion was written into the statutes of new confraternities. With reference to the confraternity of the Blessed Sacrament, the curé of Mauges wrote in 1715: 'I enrolled men only in this sodality to encourage them to frequent the sacraments, and I have had the consolation of seeing them respond even more than I could ever have hoped'. It was to strengthen devotion to the eucharist that Bourdoise, Bourgoing, Olier and all the French 'home missioners' of the seventeenth century — Oratorians, Lazarists, Eudists etc. — introduced and fostered the solemn ceremony of first holy communion (although it was not the general usage until about 1750).

4. The parish framework: Sunday mass

The new insistence on sacramental life was paralleled with an effort to make the mass more important in the estimation of the faithful. Attendance at Sunday mass, which had formerly been a pious custom, gradually became a positive law;[50] but to what extent was it observed before the Catholic Reformation filtered down to parish level? And what meaning did attendance at mass have in a generally slack and careless atmosphere? People sat on the altar-steps or chatted during the service; hats and coats were left lying around anywhere; gentlemen brought their hounds into church; the buildings in the country were often too small, and became crowded giving rise to 'a thousand inconveniences and immodesties'; the lower people, excluded from the pews which the gentlemen and burghers had hired for their own use, had frequently to stand or sit on the floor; many of the men were content to attend mass from the porch, or divide the time of mass between this rather theoretic presence under the 'roof' of the church and the neighbouring wineshop; even inside the church, scuffles and brawls were not uncommon (usually over precedence in seating); finally, the faithful were permitted no active participation in the liturgy. This is the picture that emerges from Jeanne Ferté's study on the religious life of the Paris country districts in the seventeenth century, before the impact of the renewal had made itself felt.

To personalize the sanctification of feastdays on which attendance at mass was obligatory, their number was reduced: from the thirteenth century onwards, holidays, different from diocese to diocese, had been added to the calendar at an alarming rate. Religiously, biologically and economically matters had reached a sorry pass. In 1657 the bishop of Autun wrote: 'It is not appropriate to multiply holidays of obligation for fear of multiplying the occasions of sin', Christian festivals being the usual occasions of fairs, revels and debauches. Fasting or abstinence (or both at once) were the obligatory preliminaries to the carousings, and the alimentary imbalance which resulted got steadily worse as the number of these vigils grew in number. Finally, the prohibition of servile work on holidays disrupted agricultural activities, and in both town and country it was the poor who suffered most. A cobbler lamented that 'we're being ruined by feastdays . . . M. le Curé's sermon has a new saint in it every time'. When, in 1700, Mgr Colbert suppressed a third of the holidays in his diocese (Rouen) – which reduced their number to seventy-eight! – he stated in his pastoral letter that 'the poor had complained that the multiplicity of feasts had adverse effects on their misery'.[51] Throughout the kingdom under Louis XIV, the bishops reduced the number of holidays (in Autun in 1657, Paris 1666 etc.). At the same time they tried to see that the remaining feasts were more strictly observed: that no work was done, and that taverns were closed during 'the divine service, the homily and the catechism'.

Although the measures gave more dignity to the mass, they did not standardize the form of celebration. In a conference he gave in 1659, St Vincent de Paul recalled the masses he had seen in the diocese of Paris forty years previously: 'Some priests started with the *Pater Noster*, others took the chasuble, recited the *Introibo* and then put the chasuble on. Once at Saint-Germain-en-Laye I noticed seven or eight priests all saying mass quite differently; it was a scene to weep over'.

In practice liturgical usages continued to vary from one diocese to another. Local traditions were respected, and some of the more Gallican bishops departed as a matter of principle from Roman customs. They enjoined on their clergy and the parish councils the purchase of new missals and breviaries published in the diocese.[52] In the diocese of Paris, the modifications to the breviary (1680) and the missal (1685) were inspired by a concern for historical accuracy: more than forty pious legends were excised from the missal. In the sung sections bits were added and suppressed so that only the words of scripture were used. Did the mass of the faithful appreciate these changes? Even more importantly, did they take a greater part in the mass than before? Over a long period the best of the spiritual writers, and this applies to St Francis de Sales as to Mgr de Péréfixe, were content to recommend Catholics to recite a certain number of prayers (especially the rosary) during mass. This was not, however, the only reason why mass books spread slowly, even among the educated public: the hierarchy, fearing Protestantism, several times condemned French translations of liturgical books. Even so such translations appeared to be indispensable when, after the Revocation, the Gallican Church tried to bring into its fold the 'Newly Converted'. Two hundred thousand copies of an Ordinary of the Mass in French were then printed.

Likewise in the late seventeenth and early eighteenth centuries, some Jansenizing parish priests in the Paris region and United Provinces – and there not even the educated classes knew Latin – took some interesting liturgical initiatives: they began to read the Gospel in the vernacular, recite the canon out loud, omit the repeated *Confiteor* before the communion etc. Such avant-garde curés were always a minority. A more numerous category of priests were those who raised their altars and at the cost of artistic sacrifices of which they were little aware replaced the Gothic rood-screens with simple altar-rails. At least now the faithful were less cut off physically from the eucharistic liturgy. Finally, a doctrine emerged encouraging a more active share in the mass. In 1651, François de Harlay, uncle of the future archbishop of Paris, wrote a work entitled *La manière de bien entendre la messe de paroisse* (Towards fruitful attendance at mass): 'All the different private prayers should cease when the priest prays and offers the sacrifice in the name of all those present. You should be attentive to the prayer he is about to address God for you and for the whole congregation, and think of the sacrifice there present, by offering it – and yourself – through the priest with the mind of the Church and in union with the Church'. The preface to a complete translation of the Paris Missal of 1701 expressed the same sentiment: 'Although one would not like to condemn those who say their own mental or vocal prayers during the divine sacrifice, as their devotion inspires them, it will always be best to hear mass by uniting oneself with the priest and entering into the spirit of the words he is uttering'.

Despite these strong recommendations, congregations, especially in the country, remained more often than not passive, except during the congregational prayers and notices for the week. The latter, which effectively interrupted the service, were probably for centuries the basic part of the Sunday liturgy as far as the average Catholic was concerned. The parish priest mounted the pulpit, commented on the feast of the day and then led public prayers for the pope, the king and the local aristocracy. A *De profundis* was said for the dead, a Credo (in French), the Our Father and the commandments. Then the celebrant announced the religious calendar for the week, published the banns of marriage, gave out the burials, processions and pilgrimages, read the pastoral letter if there was one and any decisions from lay authorities affecting the inhabitants,[53] proposed various measures and obtained the people's agreement. Sometimes he attacked the scandalous behaviour of this or that parishioner. Then he continued with the mass.

5. The parish framework: catechism

The importance the congregational prayers and notices assumed in the mind of the faithful just shows how necessary preaching and catechism were. Yet it was only in the sixteenth century that the Protestant and Catholic Reformers – Luther, Calvin, Peter Canisius[54] and the fathers of Trent – felt the urgent need for catechetical instruction. Even then it was slow to infiltrate religious habits, because it was unpopular with both clergy and laity. In Italy and the Low Countries, from the second half of the sixteenth century, sodalities of Christian doctrine multiplied, often at the initiative of the Jesuits who started catechism classes in the urban parishes. At Anvers in about 1610, 4000 children from nine to sixteen attended these religious instruction classes under sixty male and female teachers.[55]

In the early seventeenth century in a diocese like that of Paris it was frequently foundations by pious laity which enabled a priest (effectively a curate) to be appointed to a parish with the specific role of teaching the catechism. The episcopate insisted and kept on insisting that parish priests should provide systematic religious instruction for the children. In 1652 Mgr de Ragny bishop of Autun urged his parish priests and curates to lay on religious instruction for the children every Sunday, 'charitably' (without demanding payment), as he said. This is the first allusion to catechetical teaching in the diocese. Three years later the new bishop, Mgr d'Attichy, told his clergy that people had complained to him because their pastors were neglecting the catechism. He therefore ordered them to teach children at least the Our Father, the Apostles' Creed, the commandments and the substance of the main mysteries of the faith. This religious instruction must be given on Sundays at midday, preceded by a long peal on the church bells to alert the people. The members of the parish council were to denounce defaulting curés to the archpriest and they would be fined $3\frac{1}{4}$ francs, the sum to go towards the upkeep of their church. In 1672 Mgr Roquette again reminded his clergy of their obligation to provide catechism classes every Sunday from All Saints to 24 June 'at the most convenient hour'; and the threat of a fine levied on uncompliant clergy was renewed. The threat was again mentioned in 1690, when the bishop stated that most pastors still limited catechism to 'a few days in Advent and Lent'. He therefore ordered them to teach the catechism every single Sunday of the year 'except during the harvest and the grape-gathering'. These repeated menaces show how novel catechism teaching still was, how it disrupted the traditional attitudes of parish clergy and faithful alike. To persuade the faithful that catechism was to their ultimate advantage, the archpriests of the diocese of Autun – in 1690–3 – resorted to a variety of expedients: they chose the most convenient time of day; attracted the children with small rewards, kindness and friendliness; put pressure on reluctant parents by threatening to bar them from the sacraments; in fact refused absolution and communion to parents and masters who did not send their children and young domestics to catechism; and limited the lessons to half an hour.

In the Low Countries and France, to take only these two examples, the seventeenth century saw the appearance of many catechism manuals. The Belgian ones were mostly off-shoots of Canisius' famous catechism; the French ones relied heavily on the experience of Bourdoise, who for forty years developed a catechetical method at Saint-Nicolas-du-Chardonnet. Between 1670 and 1685, a score of diocesan catechisms were published in France. One of the best-known was the one written by 'the three Henrys': Henry de Laval, bishop of La Rochelle, Henry de Barillon, bishop of Luçon, and Henry Arnauld, bishop of Angers. It was first published at La Rochelle in 1676. Despite the Jesuits it was never condemned at Rome because it was more Augustinist than Jansenist. It included a 'little catechism' of twenty-seven pages for young children, a 'medium catechism' of ninety-three pages as preparation for first communion, and finally a 'great catechism' of 382 pages for educated adults and priests, who could find in it sermon material in abundance. It was, in short, a theological vade-mecum for all ages and all levels of instruction, and a sign, among many others, of the new religious mentality thirsting for dogmatic clarity and doctrinal guidance.[56]

6. The 'primary schools'

The effect of regular catechism classes was reinforced by the 'primary schools' which aimed at teaching children 'both religion and human letters'. At Bagneux towards the close of the seventeenth century, the schoolmaster was to 'provide the catechism instruction himself twice a week in the school'. At Ivry, as stipulated in an endowment clause of 1696, the master was to take 'all the scholars into the church of the said place Ivry to make them hear mass, every day as school finished, without fail'. The hierarchy, who were so anxious about the teaching of the catechism, did not take much interest in the primary schools (and even when they did, it was tardy). In the towns these schools were founded by the Company of the Blessed Sacrament, the Jansenists, charitable sodalities and various teaching communities of which the chief were the Ursulines for girls and later, the Brothers of St John Baptist de la Salle for boys.[57] In country areas many of the schools were the work of the parish priests, who left money in their wills for the upkeep of a teacher, and even more often of prominent laity: local aristocracy, burghers wanting to contribute to the villages where they owned land, parish councillors concerned for the education and training of the village children. Frequently a school was the fruit of a mission. And frequently it was the Sisters of Charity of St Vincent de Paul – the 'grey sisters' – who administered the schools for the country girls.

Two questions suggest themselves to the historian, indicating two lines of research: how far did elementary schooling spread in France and Europe during the seventeenth and eighteenth centuries? and how much did it contribute to effective Christianization? The answer to the first question will be different for different regions. In Paris round about the turn of the eighteenth century, a free, popular school system existed in practically all the parishes. In the archdeaconry of Brie, pastoral visitation reports for 1673 record that out of 127 parishes (plus three chapels of ease) visited, only sixteen had no school. The situation was much less encouraging in the early eighteenth century in the diocese of La Rochelle. According to Fr Pérouas, if one excepts the large towns, 'which were always well-endowed', and the Ile de Ré, more than half the parishes of Aunis had no school in 1732. Education was even less common in the rest of the diocese where, even though schoolmistresses were less rare than in 1648, the number of boys' schools had not risen much since the mid-seventeenth century. At the outbreak of the Revolution, barely twenty per cent of the population in the Angevine parishes dependent on La Rochelle could sign their names. The map of schools under the *Ancien Régime* which Fr de Dainville is drawing up will certainly enrich our knowledge of French history. At the same time the inquiry should be extended to other countries to show up the zones of obscurantism and the zones of enlightenment. A comparatively recent study of the province of Grosseto[58] throws light on one of the latter. It reveals that in 1676, out of fifty-four 'lands and castelli', forty-six had a schoolmaster. Some of these forty-six villages, Arcidosso for example, spent some six per cent of their resources on teaching, against three and a half per cent on worship. In others, for example Roccatederighi, fifty out of the 473 inhabitants were children at school.

The second question mentioned above − how much did elementary schooling under the *Ancien Régime* contribute to the country's christianization? − could be answered accurately for any given diocese only by comparing the map of schools with many other elements in the picture: the movement of vocations, the density of the new-style confraternities (the Blessed Sacrament, the Rosary), statistics of construction and reconstruction of places of worship, successive maps of religious practice from the Revolution onwards etc. A particularly interesting set of documents on the problem of education and religion is that relating to the Catholic *Aufklärung*.[59] At the parish level, the *Aufklärung* was at once the rejection of superstition, an attempt to purify worship and give the faithful a more active part in it, and a determination to instruct the faithful. What was the extent of the schooling it aimed at? And in countries affected by the Catholic *Aufklärung*, was it ultimately a factor for or against the faith? These are fascinating questions.

CHAPTER 5

DECHRISTIANIZATION?

(a) The customary view

1. The attack on religion

On a bird's-eye view – and only that – the contrast between the Christian fervour of the seventeenth century and the religious tepidness of the following centuries is so abrupt as to be almost brutal. At least one historian has thought it necessary to postulate a 'European crisis of conscience' to try and explain the sudden change.[1] In fact with the sixteenth century 'Paduans' – Pompanazzi, Etienne Dolet, Jean Bodin – without going back as far as the 'ill-thinking' Averroists of the middle ages, a free-thinking current began in certain western intellectual milieux.[2] In the seventeenth century it developed in France to the point of alarming Fr Garasse, author of the *Curious Doctrine of the contemporary wits*[3] (1623), Mersenne, author of *The impiety of the deists, atheists and free-thinkers overthrown and confounded*[4] (1624), and then Pascal, Nicole, Bossuet and La Bruyère. From the *Parnasse satyrique* (1622) of the poet Théophile de Viau, which provoked an indignant condemnation, to the *Testament*[5] of the Reverend Meslier (d. 1729) which reviled the name of Jesus, numerous writings in the golden age of Tridentine Catholicism attacked Christian dogma – more often than not indirectly – and expressed the free-thinking appropriate to 'strong minds': the anonymous quatrains signed by 'The Antibigot' (see below, p. 230), the poems on death by Chaulieu, priest and poet, the utopias of Cyrano de Bergerac, Naudé's *Considérations politiques* and philosophical dialogues like the *Orasius Tubero* of La Mothe Le Vayer.[6] The 'turncoats' were deists like Saint-

Evremond, 'doubters' like Gassendi and downright unbelievers like Naudé and Cyrano, Mme Deshoulières and the Reverend Meslier. In the seventeenth century sceptical comments on Christianity were not confined to France. They emerged in the teaching of the Italian Cremonini (d. 1631), the materialist sensualism of Hobbes (d. 1679) and the pantheism-cum-positive rationalism of Spinoza (d. 1677).

In the 'age of lights' which coincided with an increased influence from Britain in all areas of human endeavour, British intellectuals diffused a basically adogmatic conception of religion as evidenced in Locke's *The Reasonableness of Christianity* (1695), Toland's *Christianity not Mysterious* (1696), Collins' *Discourse of Free Thinking* (1713) and Tindal's *Christianity as Old as the Creation* (published anonymously in 1730). The titles of these works are significant: they equate tolerance with the abandonment of revelation, and retained Christianity only by turning it into a natural religion from which tension towards salvation was extruded. British deism passed to the continent, but in the process lost its island serenity and in France took on an aggressive pungency.

In this Bayle had already set an example. One must correct the view, for a long time current, that Bayle was an unbeliever.[7] Nonetheless his *Historical and Critical Dictionary* (1695–7) was, before Diderot's *Encyclopaedia* of 1751–72 and Voltaire's *Philosophical Dictionary* of 1764, the arsenal whence free-thinkers of the time liberally drew arguments against belief and authority. Bayle's caustic style set the tone for a whole literature. What is more, his affirmation that 'atheism does not necessarily lead to the corruption of mores' swept away in a sentence the apologetics of 1000 years. The way being thus opened, the deism of Montesquieu, Fontenelle[8] and Voltaire[9] proceeded to positive ridicule of Christianity. The two latter did not conceal that they wished to 'crush the Beast', and Voltaire even signed himself 'Mocker of Christ'. It is true that in the second half of the century Rousseau, who had inherited the Socinian tradition, relinquished the polemical tone of his predecessors, gave deism a soul and rehabilitated religious fervour; but it was also then that the *Encyclopaedia* was channelling minds towards positivism and that Diderot himself was changing from natural religion to atheism. After La Mettrie's *Homme machine* (Man the Machine, 1748) came the materialist manifestos of Claude Helvétius (*De l'esprit* – On the Mind – 1758, 'a staggering blow to every kind of prejudice' was Diderot's affectionate comment) and Baron d'Holbach (*Le christianisme dévoilé*– Christianity unmasked – 1767). In his main work, *Le système de la nature*, Holbach held that 'matter acts by itself without the need of any external impulse to set it in motion'. Newton had seen in the law of universal attraction a decisive proof for the existence of God and he thought of the Creator as an engineer ready to repair breakdowns in the machine of the universe. 'Transplanted into France', as J. Ehrard has written, 'Newtonian theism faded into an insipid deism'.[10] At the end of the century, Laplace showed how 'the celestial mechanism' is self-adjusting, without the intervention of Providence.[11] As Louis XIV came to the end of his long reign, atheism, at least in the higher echelons of society, had already ceased to be exceptional and a slur on those who professed it. Seventy-five years later it was positively acceptable.

The eighteenth century, then, delivered against religion in general, and Christianity (as it was then understood and practised) in particular, a whole series of converging broadsides — direct and indirect, rarefied and full-bodied — and coupled with those, but from within, rose a number of disturbing doubts. The facile teleology proposed by the Reverend Pluche in his *Spectacle de la nature* (1732) — the melon has ribs so that it can be more easily divided among a family — was demolished by the Lisbon earthquake of 1755. And Maupertuis (whom Frederick II yet found one day saying his prayers) asked that difficult question: the workings of a snake are wonderful to behold, but of what use is a snake?[12] Then the doubts about the historicity of the early chapters of Genesis could not fail to make a lively impression. Fontenelle proposed to replace theological belief in the flood with the secular theme of 'revolutions of the globe'. With Maillet's *Telliamed* (1748) and Buffon's *Théorie de la terre* (1749), the idea of continuity in nature began to gain currency. The cosmogony of the Bible and the strict hierarchy of creatures yielded to the new idea of a 'chain of beings' in which, according to Buffon, man 'should class himself among the animals'.[13] The Christian Churches took nearly two centuries to accept evolutionism.

As R. Mauzi has noted,[14] 'one of the original features of the eighteenth century, from Montesquieu to Rousseau, is to have discovered the happiness of existence'. Tired of asceticism, Christian authors, especially before 1750, tried to present an 'amiable' religion to an enlightened public who were rehabilitating the joy of life. Fr Calmel proposed an *Easy method to be happy in this life and assure one's eternal beatitude* (1727),[15] while Mme Aubert described *The charms of the society of a worldling* (1730).[16] In his very popular *Le traité du vrai mérite* (Treatise on true merit, 1734), Le Maître de Claville vaunted 'the pleasures of devotion' and discovered 'a consubstantial intimacy between pleasure, virtue and religion'. Philosophical criticism was not convinced, and radically opposed earthly happiness, creative activity and Christian morality.[17] 'Who can deny', asked the article on 'Christianity' in the *Encyclopaedia*, 'that the arts, industry, a taste for fashion, everything which extends the branches of commerce, are of real profit to states? Now

Christianity, which proscribes luxury and stifles it, destroys and does away with these things, which are its necessary adjuncts. With its spirit of abnegation and its renunciation of all vanity, it replaces them with idleness, poverty, neglect, in a word, with the destruction of the arts. It is therefore, by its constitution, little suited to advancing the happiness of states'.

In his *Pensées philosophiques*, Diderot was much more virulent and gave an almost demented description of Christian 'happiness': 'What cries! what shrieks! what groans! Who has imprisoned all these woeful corpses? What crimes have all these wretches committed? Some are beating their breasts with stones, others are tearing their bodies with hooks of iron; remorse, pain and death lurk in their eyes'.

2. The crisis in the Roman Church

Faced with attacks like these, ranging from ironic comment on the super-stitions of the faithful to criticism of dogma and even denial of God, Catholicism, on the defensive, began to show signs of fatigue. Of the eight popes between 1700 and 1800, all of them but one from the nobility, 'only the fifth in the series, Benedict XIV (1740–58) exceeded mediocrity'.[18] The time of the great fighters, Pius V, Sixtus V, Innocent XI, seemed to have receded. The nepotism combatted by the last named pontiff resurfaced; the 'ecclesiastical State' was, in the opinion of De Brosses (first president of the Dijon parliament, d. 1777), the worst governed in Europe, and Rome the capital of *dolce far niente*. The Italian Genovesi, exalting the ideal of a pure and simple faith, wrote with melancholy: 'Go to Rome and see those cardinals' palaces, those enchanted villas, those tables glistening with fine gold. Poor Church, so worldly, so impure! Where is the *vos non estis de hoc mundo*'?[19] The Roman example was followed by an episcopate monopolized by the nobility and prisoner of wealth almost everywhere. Many of the bishops were ostentatious aristocrats, many gave scandal. Posterity has remembered their names to cast them reproachfully in the Church's face: Rohan, Talleyrand, von Callen. Some, who were otherwise pious and worthy bishops, forgot the instructions of Trent on residence and pastoral visitations. Recent studies show that the latter were neglected in the diocese of Rouen[20] as of Poitiers. Not one bishop of Poitiers visited Niort, county town of Deux-Sèvres, between 1713 and 1743, and there was only one other visitation before the Revolution, in 1769.[21] This is one example among many, illustrative of a reality that was all too fre-quent.

Paralyzed by money, the force of inertia and conservatism, the Catholic Church also suffered from internal tensions, which the Bull *Unigenitus* did nothing to assuage. As we recalled earlier on, it was in the eighteenth century that a widely-diffused Jansenism spread through the French provinces and then outside France altogether, in particular to Tuscany where Grand Duke Leopold was a subscriber to the *Ecclesiastical News*. It is true that in 1730 Louis XV declared *Unigenitus* state law; and that the archbishops of Malines and the prince-bishops of Liège waged a relentless war on the doctrine and disciples of Jansen in the Low Countries from the end of the 1600s; but the spirit of opposition to Rome had not vanished from the Church. It was less theological, more juridical, and its name was episcopalism. In 1700 a canonist from Louvain, Zegen Bernard Van Espen, who was not long afterwards to refuse to accept *Unigenitus*, published a work which did the tour of Europe: *Jus ecclesiasticum universum* (Universal Church Law). In this book he preached conciliarism and accorded the pope a primacy of honour only. Now it was Van Espen, coming after Quesnel, who some years later pushed the vicars apostolic and the secular clergy of Holland to schism, so irritated were they by the denunciations and initiatives of the Jesuits, who would accept orders only from Rome. In 1723 the rupture was completed by the election of an archbishop of Utrecht consecrated by a missionary bishop who had emigrated from France because of his Jansenist sympathies. Circa 1800, there were only some 10,000 Old Catholics in the 'Church of Utrecht' . . . but the Church exists to this day.

In 1763, a former pupil of Van Espen's, Johann Nikolaus von Hontheim, usually known as Justinus Febronius, published his famous *Liber singularis de statu Ecclesiae* (Work in one volume on the state of the Church). What henceforward came to be known as Febronianism was, in substance, the defence of national churches against Rome, and more particularly, since Hontheim was coadjutor bishop of Trier, of the Germanic episcopate against the centralizing despotism of the curia and the repeated interventions of the nuncios. Taking up the theses of Richerism, Febronius thought of each bishop as pope in his own diocese, and concluded to the superiority of an ecumenical council over the sovereign pontiff. He was condemned by Rome, and retracted. It is significant, however, that out of the twenty-six German bishops, sixteen refused to publish the condemnation of his book; and that in 1786 the four archbishops of Cologne, Trier, Mainz and Salzburg signed a joint statement, of a clearly episcopalist thrust, in which they invited Rome to renounce the conferment of offices, to oblige nuncios to confine their activities to diplomacy, to publish neither Bulls nor briefs without the agreement of the German episcopate, and to cede to themselves all jurisdiction over the regular clergy. In that same year the synod of Pistoia, whose bishop was the Jansenizing Scipione de' Ricci, protested against the usurpations which emptied episcopal authority of its meaning, objected to the independence of the regulars, adopted the Gallican declaration of 1682 and commended the doctrine of St Augustine and the purification of worship. We must not exaggerate either the extent or the volume of these gestures, but they do prove that the decisions and style of Rome were not universally accepted in the Catholic Church without protest: the condemnations of Free Masonry (by Clement XII in 1738 and Benedict XIV in 1751) were not published in France and not even applied in the Papal States themselves. And they reveal a persistent suspicion of the papacy shared and encouraged by the 'enlightened despots'.

The weakness of Rome in the eighteenth century can be seen in its attitude to the Jesuits. Innocent XIII and Benedict XIV mistrusted the Company, despite its special vow of obedience to the pope; but the Company really went under because the popes sacrificed it to the combined hostility of the Franciscans and Dominicans, the anxiety of all shades of Augustinists inimical to its 'laxism', the jealousy of the secular clergy and the suspicion of governments fearful of its latent power. The calvary of the Jesuits extended chronologically over most of the eighteenth century, and geographically from China to the Americas. In 1759 Pombal engineered the suppression of the Company in all Portuguese territories: eighty fathers were executed, several hundred thrown into prison, and a thousand or more deported to the Papal States. Three years later a complaint from the Marseilles shipowners against Fr Lavalette (of Martinique) and the French Jesuit province gave the parliaments an excuse to confiscate all the Company's possessions in the kingdom. In 1764, against his own convictions, Louis XV dissolved the Company in France. The same step was taken in 1767 by Charles III and his minister Aranda in Spain and the Spanish colonies, where the Jesuits were accused of fomenting popular insurrection. Five thousand fathers living in the Company's 240 houses in Spain and its colonies were arrested. It was the end of the famous 'reductions'. Finally, in 1773 Clement XIV decided to suppress the Company altogether. The superior general was imprisoned in Castel Sant'Angelo and there he died.

There was a further symptom of the crisis which seems to have affected the Roman Church at this time. In many of the Catholic states of Europe action was taken against depopulated convents and flagging congregations. In about 1750 the craze for the contemplative life had waned and mysticism become suspect (as its name suggested, it started by being misty and ended in schism, or so it was said). The spirit of the time was unfavourable to monastic life, which it judged to be useless and idle (a judgment widely shared by the secular clergy). The young generation of religious was sparse. The gap that therefore existed between the large revenues, vast lands and buildings of the monasteries on the one hand, and the ageing, dwindling communities who enjoyed them on the other was distressing to many observers. (The difficulties experienced by these communities did not prevent internal quarrels, the recriminations of the monastic proletariat against the aristocracy who exploited the abbeys, and the proliferation of the *appels comme d'abus* to parliaments.) A distaste for the advanced theological and historical study which had been the glory of seventeenth century monastic life added to this decadence. As indicative of this general disaffection, it is interesting to note that when the Constituent Assembly of 1789 secularized the orders and congregations, there was a mass exodus from the Benedictines, the Cistercians, the Canons of St Genevieve and the Dominicans: at Cluny, thirty-eight out of the forty monks returned to civilian life. The 'Commission for Regular Clergy' (1766–1784) under the presidency of Étienne Charles de Loménie de Brienne, archbishop of Toulouse, therefore had a purpose. Despite his friendship with Choiseul and d'Alembert, Loménie de Brienne was not the anti-monk he is sometimes thought.[22] He and his collaborators – bishops and parliamentarians – undeniable weaknesses notwithstanding, wanted less the ruin than the reform of the monastic orders, to whom they proposed to give genuine social 'utility'. They had no wish to act without the co-operation of the congregations themselves and, despite their Gallicanism, without the ultimate approval of the Holy See. The Commission admittedly prepared the way for the general suppression of the regulars in 1790, but its underlying spirit was not the same as that of the Constituent Assembly. Its decisions were of some importance. The age for final vows was brought back to twenty-one for men, eighteen for women. The minimum number of religious in any one house was fixed at nineteen for monks and fifteen for nuns. No order could have more than one house in a town. Monastic exemption was to all intents and purposes abolished. Finally, the Commission suppressed no less than 426 convents, 108 of them Benedictine and 69 Augustinian.

There is an evident affinity between the attitude of the bishops and the French government as we have just described it and the attitudes to the regulars at that time of many of the sovereigns of Europe, especially of Maria Theresa and Joseph II in Austria and the Low Countries, Grand Duke Leopold in Tuscany and the archbishop-elector Joseph von Erthal at Mainz. The desire to make the Church more tractable by a centralized state, animus towards mysticism, concern for the utilitarian and the effective, a species of indignation at the scandal of over-wealthy abbeys badly run by decayed communities explain Joseph II's brutal religious policies. His mother Maria Theresa, who was nonetheless a woman of great piety, had already, in 1750, set up a commission to look into the financial administration of ecclesiastical institutions. She had also, in 1770, forbidden solemn vows to be taken before the age of twenty-four (this was extended to the Low Countries). In 1783, with a stroke of his pen, Joseph II suppressed all the contemplative monasteries in Austria and the Low Countries.[24] His example was contagious: in 1789 the archbishop of Mainz turned the city's Dominican convent into a house for aged priests.

In the 'age of lights', then, the Roman Church seemed to be undergoing something of a crisis. The papacy was powerless, religious orders grew old and went into decline, the energy of the clergy slackened, theological sciences stagnated, religious fervour shrank, sodalities turned lay,[25] and Christian dogmas were being openly challenged. Had the Christianization programme of the preceding age, with all its effort and enthusiasm, foundered so swiftly?

(b) A revision of the traditional problematic

The traditional picture just presented, in which the emphasis is on the opposition between enlightenment philosophy and Christian theology and on the tensions within the weakened Roman Church itself, is certainly not false; but recent researches, which must be extended, prove that it has to be nuanced, completed and re-interpreted.

For example, the struggles between pro-clerics and anti-clerics in the Latin countries, especially France, during the nineteenth century and in the early twentieth, have induced an error of judgment with regard to the Free Masonry of the enlightenment, which is now being corrected.[26] In the first place it is quite clear that *British* Free Masonry was never antireligious. On the contrary, the existence of God has always been taken as a fundamental axiom. The same is true of France up to 1877. The rapid growth of lodges in the eighteenth century in Europe and even beyond, especially in America, must not, therefore, be taken as a sort of tidal wave bearing down on religion. Admittedly Clement XII condemned Free Masonry in 1738 after a series of scandals in Florence, for reasons unspecified (*aliisque de justis ac rationabilibus causis nobis notis*),[27] but the masters of the 700 or so lodges in France in 1787, with their 70,000 initiates of all grades, were frequently canons or regulars

(Oratorians, Benedictines, Cistercians etc.). Most of the lodges had chaplains. On Masonic feastdays, the Masons attended mass with great solemnity. Joseph de Maistre, a most ardent Catholic, was initiated into the 'Three Mortars' Lodge at Chambéry in 1773. Mystics like Martinez Pasqualis and Claude de Saint-Martin were likewise members of this secret society.[28] Cambracérès, who had been prior of the White Penitents at Montpellier in 1790–1, was a practising Catholic and Grand Master of French Free Masonry under the Empire.[29] Conversely, a mere handful of the 150 editors of the *Encyclopaedia* were Masons.

Another point on which revised ideas are overdue is the eighteenth-century episcopate, who have been summarily judged on one or two scandalous cases. It cannot be denied that in France the bishops contemporary with Louis XV and Louis XVI were less dynamic and energetic than their immediate predecessors, but is that to deny them a genuine spirit of piety? Monographs like M. Levré's on *Louis-François-Gabriel d'Orléans de la Motte (1683–1774)*[30] would help to correct a probably erroneous view of religious life in the eighteenth century. We may particularly recall here the observations of E. Préclin:[31] 'As a whole the episcopate of 1789 was good. No diocese seems to have suffered unduly from successive mediocre prelates, and some ecclesiastical provinces had only good bishops: Brittany, for example, with its nine sees, Gascony with its thirteen . . . Paris likewise, from 1695 to 1789, had none but good archbishops. Among the great bishops we may mention: at Marseilles Mgr de Belzunce, the hero of the 1720 plague, at Carcassonne Mgr Bazin de Bezons, sprightly, charitable, a martyr resigned to suffering, at Besançon Mgr de Durfort, charitable, charming and mischievous, and at Paris Christophe de Beaumont, champion of the faith against the Jansenists and scoffers. He distributed practically all his wealth among the poor. Mgr de La Motte at Amiens had the reputation of a saint'.

In the death registers of Saint-Malo, under 5 February 1767, the decease of the bishop, Mgr Fogasse de La Bastie[32] is followed by this comment: '. . . a prelate whose enlightened wisdom merited him the reputation of one of the greatest bishops of the French Church; whose pure and unshakable faith ever dictated to him the soundest doctrine; whose exemplary life was the finest model of virtue to his flock; whose inexhaustible charity made him distribute two-thirds of his income annually to the poor; whose zeal tempered with prudence reanimated and maintained discipline in his clergy; whose constant study has brought so precious a life to such an untimely close. He lived too short a time for the good of his flock, but long enough to merit the most ample reward . . .'

E. Préclin's hagiographical insistence on the 'good' French bishops of the eighteenth century perhaps brings a smile to the reader's lips. Further, the funerary eulogy just reproduced smacks of a stereotype: it is in fact found, with minor variants, in the registers of Saint-Malo for the encomiums of other deceased bishops of the city. Nevertheless it is undoubtedly true that if the French episcopate of the seventeenth century, as a corpus, is compared with that of the eighteenth, the latter very definitely emerges the leader from the triple point of view of worthiness, piety and doctrine. Studies still have to be undertaken for countries other than France.

What is true of the bishops is also true, mutatis mutandis, of the parish clergy. M.-L. Fracart reaches the following conclusion in her excellent study on Niort:[34] 'In short, this Niortais clergy at the end of the *Ancien Régime* displayed real intellectual competence, zeal and goodwill, and a generally serious approach to things. On the other hand, one can detect a sort of creeping lukewarmness and torpor which to some extent paved the way for the defections of 1791. Among the latter, many were spur-of-the-moment defections, due either to inadequate information or to a lack of courage in the face of the option presented. Many were later corrected'.

In the election (a financial subdivision of the 'generality' under the *Ancien Régime*) of Niort, she continues, the people in general esteemed 'these venerable pastors who bore the heat of the day and frequently exposed their health and life to aid the dying', these country priests who, well off or not, 'had to share their soup and provide their parishioners with medicaments'. Similar deference is to be found in the books of complaints.

Pérouas has made a sociological study of the *Diary of the Montfortist missions in the west* (of France) kept by a Montfortist priest, F. Hacquet, from 1740 to 1779.[35] Over a period of thirty-nine years, this preacher met more than 1000 priests in the dioceses from Vannes to La Rochelle. In his *Diary* Hacquet does not usually criticize the moral behaviour of the clergy – the most he does is to mention 'differences' between priests or between priests and laity – but as he came to be better acquainted with ecclesiastical circles, he adopted the habit, from 1753, of adding a word or two of commendation on the priests who seemed to him to be the best. He called them 'worthy' and 'zealous'. The proportion of parish priests who came up to his standard increased as the years went by: between 1753 and 1760, thirty per cent; between 1761 and 1770 thirty-seven per cent; and in the last decade of his apostolate nearly fifty per cent. A comparable situation obtained in Normandy, studied by M. Join-Lambert. 'The little we know', he writes, 'seems to prove that as the number of priests dropped their quality rose. The seminary, which was now attended by most clergy, had its full effect only in the course of the eighteenth century'. Although unfortunately deficient, the documents for Normandy reveal 'a first class clergy, probably the best seen for three centuries'.[36] Tocqueville passed a similar judgment in the last century on the French clergy prior to the Revolution: 'I do not know whether, taken all in all and despite the glaring vices of some of its members, there was ever in the world a more remarkable clergy than the Catholic clergy in France as Revolution broke out, more enlightened, more national, less entrenched in its own private virtues, better furnished with those virtues and with greater faith: the persecution demonstrated it. I embarked on this study of society in the past full of prejudices against the clergy; I have finished it full of respect. . .'[37]

Among the most zealous of these French priests were the home missioners who throughout the eighteenth century preached in the towns and country villages. Between 1700 and 1789 there were very few parishes in Brittany not visited by the missioners.[38] Over 2000 missions have been counted, certainly far more than in the seventeenth century. Religious life under the enlightenment needs, therefore, to be reassessed. To return to the measures taken by Joseph II: having suppressed all the contemplative orders, he pooled their secularized goods in a 'Religion Fund'; but then he used this money to give pastors an increase in salary and create more than 800 new parishes.[39] From then on there was one priest for every 600 faithful, as opposed to one for every 1000 under Maria Theresa. The emperor also created four new dioceses and twelve seminaries in his empire. It would be helpful to have a study of the Catholic *Aufklärung* in the wide sense, not only in Germany but in Europe as a whole, and this would reveal, in Italy as in France and Germany, a new pastoral concern evidenced, for example, by the publication of numerous prayer-books.[40]

We can say, then, that a total, careful history of Christianity, from the eighteenth century at least, must clarify two intersecting curves. The one rises, the other descends; the one expresses a qualitative religion, the other a quantitative adherence; the one translates fidelity to a better understood Gospel message, the other a conformism that cracked as civilization changed. On the one hand, there was a zeal, less spectacular certainly than that of the sixteenth- and seventeenth-century Polyeuctes, but less tied to individuals, too, more widespread among an élite of clergy and laity, and on the other the growing disaffection for a religious practice corroded by social pressures. A gap between the two curves can be discerned as early as the eighteenth century, with the pastoral effort of the *Aufklärung* and the increase in vocations to the secular priesthood, after a drop in the preceding period, at Rouen, Rheims and Mainz in the 1780s as revealed in recent studies.[41] This renewal is also evinced, on the eve of the Revolution, in several religious orders after the depression which was characteristic of the period in which the Commission for Regular Clergy was active (1766–1784).[42] This renaissance was expressed in the first place as reform (the Maurists, Cluniac monks, Dominicans), then subsequently as a rise in vocations. The year 1788 was a record for vocations to the Congregation of St Genevieve. In that order, when the *Ancien Régime* crumbled, fifty-three per cent of the religious were under fifty, and seventeen per cent were between twenty and thirty. The older, slightly lax monks, clinging to their ancient usages, resented the young partisans of a recently reformed observance, and many of the latter became 'deserters'. In France the Revolution revealed in all its nakedness the abyss that separated faith and conformism. Pastors left the ministry, many of the laity lapsed. Catholicism emerged from the ordeal quantitatively reduced but qualitatively purified. Using the term 'dechristianization', on which, with G. Le Bras, we shall shortly express our reserve, as a convenient shorthand, we may say that in the new world which began in the eighteenth century, christianization and dechristianization followed parallel, simultaneous paths: the christianization of the minority, the dechristianization of the majority.

(c) *The weakening of conformism*

1. The 'socialization of habit'

What is too frequently referred to as 'dechristianization' was often, as far as the masses were concerned, no more than a *refusal to conform*, which in France (here as before the country on which most studies have been done) appeared in the eighteenth century, particularly after 1750.

In the Christian attitude of the past, what were the respective roles of faith, custom and constraint? There was certainly constraint, exercised jointly by the ecclesiastical and civil authorities.[43] Since the fourth Lateran Council (1215), every member of the Church who had reached the age of discretion had to go to confession and communion at least once a year in his own parish church '*in Pascha*' (that is, between Ash Wednesday and Trinity Sunday), under pain of exclusion from the Church and privation of Christian burial. If Trent put such emphasis on pastoral visitation, it was especially to provide more effective surveillance over the religious practice of the faithful. After the council, synodal statutes prescribed a register of those who did not fulfil their Easter duties, and the lists of defaulters were sent to the bishop or presented at synods. In late seventeenth-century France, it was not rare for the bishop to put the curés a questionnaire, one item of which was devoted to Easter confessions and communions, before he set off on his pastoral rounds. Félix Vialart, bishop of Châlons from 1640 to 1680, suggested to pastors the attitude they should take towards the refractory and the scale of sanctions to be applied: two private warnings, then a public warning, followed by a denunciation to the bishop, who could decide to excommunicate, or at the very least forbid the recalcitrant Catholic solemn engagement, marriage and sponsorship in church, the presentation of the offerings and reception of ashes.

The civil power had nothing to do with the surveillance and punishment of those who contravened the law of Easter duties, that being a purely spiritual matter, but it did ensure and favour Sunday attendance at mass. Delamare's *Traité de la police* (the second edition of which was published in 1722), devoted the whole of the first book to religion, and stated that religion was the first and principal object of the police. The state supported the ecclesiastical order, forbade innkeepers to open during the parish mass, and in principle prohibited markets and fairs, servile work and profane entertainments on Sundays and other religious feast-days.

In practice religious and civil sanctions seem to have been relatively rarely applied, at least in the eighteenth century. Of course there were a certain number of condemnations: the diocesan archives of Nantes (1670), Tréguier (1704 and 1709), and Maurienne (1744, 1754 and 1756) all mention them,[44] but then when, in 1746, Languet, the archbishop of Sens, opened a seventy-six-page register for private suits in church law, 'particularly those concerning persons who have not made their Easter duties and who have been cited to appear before him at the request of the diocesan *promotor iustitiae*', only four cases were ever entered in the book. 'It appears', writes G. Le Bras, 'that in the eighteenth century denunciation was irregular and in general resulted only in warnings'.[45] The state intervened only intermittently, to ensure respect for Sunday observance; the convictions were therefore of publicans, people causing scandal and the intractable. On the other hand the police frequently rejected the complaints of curés about taverns unless the curés were prepared to foot the bill for the judicial proceedings. Almost everywhere the parish clergy bewailed the slackness of the judiciary. So although there was a certain amount of juridical constraint, it was never the principal factor in religious conformism. Social pressures, particularly in the country, were far more effective, and they included village and family customs, the authority of the local clergy and the attitude of the *seigneur* 'who, even though perhaps an encyclopaedist himself, deemed it fitting for the people to practise'. All in all, then, obedience to Easter duties was almost universal in the country areas under the *Ancien Régime* – and over three-quarters of the population were still rural. G. Le Bras has some pertinent remarks again:[46] 'The number of rural parishes on which I have been able to gather information tops the 8000 mark. In the large majority of these parishes the proportion of inhabitants who distinguished themselves by neglecting their Easter duties rarely exceeded a dozen. ... Round Paris the archdeacon of the metropolitan diocese encountered almost total observance.[47] The archdeacons of Chartres discovered a few isolated defaulters, five or six at Chatenay and three at Saint-Aubin-des-Bois in 1716. In 1757, Canon Louis Bouras, the vicar general of Sens, registered only a very small number of abstentions at Paron and in the whole of the north of the diocese in 1758–9; Jean-Joachim de Gabriac registered rare lapses at Saint-Martin-du-Tertre, Saint Denis and Voisines; the only place at which they were at all numerous was Bussy-le-Repos. Subsequent visitors recorded no serious cases at all. Similarly in 1756 archdiaconal visitations in the vicariate of Pontoise noted tiny groups of people not going to communion, except in parishes like Saint-Martin-la-Garenne where "there were many who did not go". The same is true of the whole of Normandy: Rouen, Coutances, Sées; of Goële and Picardy. Limousin, Mâconnais and Champagne were the same as Brittany and the Massif Central; Toulouse, Rieux and Comminges in the south the same as Arles and Grasse'.

Naturally observance of Easter duties did not always mean regular attendance at mass during the year. Many parishes had only one mass on Sundays, and that was not enough to enable all the population to go to church. They could not leave a house or farm empty. This was explained in 1660 by the peasants of Grégy (near Paris), who regretted not all being able to hear mass on Sundays 'as some of us have to stay behind to look after the houses'.[48] Many villages consequently demanded a curate. At Quilleboeuf (a port at the mouth of the Seine) in 1664, 'the parishioners requested another priest, there being only one, which means that many of the sailors miss mass on Sundays and feastdays'.[49] A single mass, parishes that were too large, difficult roads, urgent jobs at the farm were all (mostly legitimate) reasons for not being able to attend mass every Sunday in the country No conclusions may be drawn as to dissatisfaction with religion. The clergy were not alarmed by such intermittent attendance: they were satisfied if any one parishioner put in an appearance one Sunday out of every three.[50]

2. From lukewarmness to hostility

On the eve of the French Revolution, then, ninety-five per cent of the rural population observed their Easter duties, even if they were not assiduous attenders at regular Sunday mass. However, recent researches, which are only in their initial stages, have brought to light zones of lukewarmness in an apparently monotonous countryside of religious conformity and socialized habit. Some mission accounts here are revealing. Those kept by the Lazarists who preached round Montauban between 1683 and 1714 register two zones of exceptionally fruitful missions – Beaumont-de-Lomagne and Salvagnac with Rabastens – and two zones of signal unsuccess – the valley of the Garonne, from Verdun-sur-Garonne to Saint-Nicolas-de-la-Grave, and the valley of the Tarn, from Villebrumier to Lafrançaise. 'These regions show the same characteristics today', observes F. Boulard.[51]

We may quote from part of the missioners' reports: 'Gasseras, 1686: some 300 communicants. Old as well as new Catholics are very badly instructed. Sundays and feastdays are days when the least people come, because most of them go to the town nearby to sell their produce; few new converts went to confession. – Corbarieu, 1686: the inhabitants, old as well as new Catholics, were very uninstructed and undevout'.

Regional temperaments emerge: in this village or town Catholics and Protestants were zealous for religion; in that they were passive or even resistant. L. Pérouas has studied this for the diocese of La Rochelle, in which the vigorous faith of people in the Mauges and Gâtine contrasted as early as the seventeenth century with the sluggishness evident in lower Poitou, the Aunis plain and the fens. Fr Hacquet's diary of his missions in the west during the eighteenth century confirms the geographical differences to be found in collective religious attitudes. The people of Champagné-les-Marais (diocese of La Rochelle) are, he wrote, 'a hard, close, undevout lot. If Easter had come before the mission instead of after it, I don't think we should have had any customers at all. When you've said they live on the plain, you've said it all. . . .'[52] Other remarks of this Montfortist missioner are worth recalling. At Bignon (diocese of Nantes) 'the people are hard, undevout and wine-bibbing';[53] at Saint-Julien-de-Vouvantes (same diocese) they are 'hard' and 'not very keen on attending the mission exercises, so effective is the influence of the numerous local ciders'.[54] Wine-growing and cider-apple cultivation therefore, in his view, had a deleterious effect on a population's piety. The valley of the lower Loire near the sea was always the scene of a brisk circulation of men and ideas, and this, too, did not help popular religious fervour: at Savenay, 'the parishioners don't attend the exercises very much';[55] at Paimboeuf, 'the sea air and the constant arrival of strangers taint the people with free-thinking ways. . . .' The inhabitants would be capable of good if they were not republican.[56] Another factor militating against religious fervour was large numbers of people: at Vertou 'the populace are too influenced by the nearness of the town (Nantes) and are not devout, not much interested at all'.[57] However, reticence in piety was not only geographical; it was also professional. Hacquet noted that the people of Riaillé (diocese of Nantes), 'who are predominantly smiths, are not noticeably devout',[58] that the 'reputation of the bargees (of Vertou) does not stand very high',[59] that the 'mussel-farmers ... who are very numerous' at L'Hermenault (diocese of La Rochelle) 'seem to form a corpus on their own, (and) enjoy some scandalous practices for which one must watch out'.[60] The missioners, therefore, came up against human blocks centred round a trade or line of business who never exceeded the most mediocre conformism.

However, in the eighteenth century conformism sometimes cracked, even in the country. G. Le Bras has proved it for the diocese of Châlons, where from the 1740s chinks appeared in the Christian armour: 'At Mesnil-sur-Oger in 1746, there were some hundred abstentions (at Easter) out of a possible 588 communicants; at Moëlain in 1741, nineteen out of a hundred; at Givry in 1748, more than 108 out of 400; at Villers-le-Sec, ninety out of three hundred; at Gigny in 1751, two hundred out of six hundred; the same proportion at Ecury in 1747; at Larzicourt in 1741, all the faithful bar one went to confession, but as many as two-thirds did not present themselves for communion'.[61]

From indifference the people sometimes passed to hostility. In 1747 it was reported that at Sompuis '... a considerable band of free-thinkers regularly assemble at the cemetery and at the doors of the church before the Divine Service and by their attitude, gestures and words insult the persons of the opposite sex ... (who) dare not, in consequence, go near the church or into it'.[62] We need more local studies to gain a clearer idea of the contours of this drop in religious practice in the eighteenth century which was almost always accompanied by anticlericalism. A model of such study is furnished by Alain Molimier's work on the parish of Sérignan in lower Languedoc where the inhabitants suffered from 'a republican spirit'.[63] In 1740 the consuls (the consular system was peculiar to certain towns of southern France, and flourished from the twelfth century to 1789. The consul was a municipal magistrate representing a guild [eg, mercers, drapers] or other social group [eg, the aristocracy]) noted with some anxiety a drop in Sunday attendances. Three years later the danger was confirmed: 'One sees very few people in church, and notably yesterday Sunday 24 March and today the feast of the Annunciation'. Apparently bowls and the taverns were in victorious competition with the Church, and many peasants worked on Sundays. The curé and consuls decided on a counter-offensive: the widow

Combescure, who ran the tavern and who served twenty customers during benediction, was fined; a public announcement was made 'through the streets, at cross-roads and at the four corners of the village' forbidding frequentation of the tavern during services and servile work on Sundays; a sally on to 'the plain' on a holiday of obligation discovered 'four individuals cutting wheat, or getting foreign workers to cut wheat'. Muted hostility against the curé broke out. His flower-beds were trampled in the night; his chickens were let out; his wheel-barrow smashed; one bucket of his well was dropped to the bottom, and the other filched 'pulley, chain and all'. These facts prove, contrary to over-simplified accounts, that the lapse in religious practice and the process of 'dechristianization' were not the product solely of industrialization, proletarianization and urbanization.

This is not to say that the drop in observance and hostility to religion were not very soon much more in evidence in the towns than in the country. Concordant evidence suggests that the 'degenerate' in Paris were, already at the time of Louis XIII, a relatively important body, and that they grew subsequently. In his *Quaestiones in Genesim* (1623), the priest-philosopher and scientist Mersenne declared that 'Paris alone is plagued with at least 50,000 atheists'.[65] This is a lot out of 600,000 inhabitants! A more moderate estimate is given by a free-thinking lawyer who was visited by Fr Beurrier, curé of Saint-Etienne-du-Mont from 1653 to 1675. The lawyer told the priest: 'Sir, I am in no state to confess my sins or receive the sacraments, although you were good enough to clarify my difficulties on the Christian religion which I have professed externally to avoid notice and save appearances. In the bottom of my soul I feel it is all a fairy-tale. And I am not alone in this: 20,000 other people in Paris share my views. We know each other, we hold secret meetings, and we strengthen each other in our irreligious resolve'. The lawyer added that 'many of his friends in irreligion did not stop going to the sacraments and attending the parish masses so as not to be found out, but that he himself did not wish to be so hypocritical. That was why he had not been to confession or communion for thirty or forty years'.[66]

One should not give too much credit even to the relatively modest figure reported by Fr Beurrier. On the other hand, once Louis XIV was dead (1774), and religious surveillance in the towns slackened and social pressures decreased, it became easier and easier not to practise. In high society it was considered U to scoff at religion or drop it altogether – and this created its own type of conformism. In the golden age of little masters, fashionable marriages and lightness of artistic style, the Princess Palatine said (in 1772): 'I do not believe that there are a hundred persons in Paris, whether among the churchmen or among people of the

219

world, who have real faith or even who believe in our Lord'.[67] At the approach of the Revolution, the tragic poet Jean Ducis, in his usual honest way, stated with emotion: 'Religion has been so badly damaged in this capital that purity of morals has gone, nobility of opinion is no more'.[68] These cries are no doubt alarmist, but to some extent they are confirmed by other evidence. In 1753, Argenson, councillor of state and friend of Voltaire, remarked that the number of communicants at Saint-Côme and Saint-Sulpice parishes had sadly declined.[69] In 1766 it was reported to Voltaire that the faithful had not celebrated St Genevieve.[70] In the urban areas of the provinces, too, religious practice went down. In 1772 the bishop of Châlons wrote: 'In the towns, the divine offices . . . are hardly frequented any more'.[71] Researches on Auxerre, Clamecy, Rouen and Bordeaux make it quite clear that even before the Revolution, half, a third, perhaps even only a quarter of those who could legally go to communion were in fact doing so with any regularity.[72]

3. Confraternities, vocations and birth control

Even more significant are the discoveries of recent researches on sodalities, vocations to the clergy and sexual behaviour in the eighteenth century. They reveal a general lack of wind in traditional piety, a drop in interest in the priesthood as a career, and less fear of the Church's moral prohibitions. The framework of conformist religion was slowly and discreetly coming apart at the seams.

On the subject of confraternities, it is interesting to recall the words of the parish priest of Ingoville (Normandy) who wrote when two 'Charities' in the bailiwick of Le Havre were disbanded: 'Laxity gradually affected the Confraternities of Saint Fiacre and the Holy Saviour. They went from indifference to distaste, from distaste to contempt for the religious functions which their numerous engagements obliged them to fulfil. For two whole years Holy Viaticum was taken to the sick without a single Brother in attendance with the canopy, as was customary . . . A total stoppage is, I suppose, preferable to the indecency and scandal the confraternities brought to their pious practices'.[73]

M. Join-Lambert, who has happily brought this document to light, adds: 'There were probably exceptions: more than one sodality survived the Revolution, although most of them, in 1789, needed only one jolt to keel over'. In his study on the *Penitents and Free Masons in old Provence*,[74] M. Agulhon comes to a similar conclusion: at the end of the *Ancien Régime*, the fervour of the Provençal confraternities had diminished, and their activities had been laicized, to such an extent that the associations of 'penitents' had often become just municipal undertakers.

We said earlier that there was a partial recovery in ordinations to the priesthood circa 1780 in regions on which quantitative studies for this have been published: the dioceses of Rouen, Rheims, Mainz and the Alsatian part of the old diocese of Basle.[75] However, this – temporary – recovery cannot conceal (and could not correct) the general downward trend.[76] This is proved by the following figures given by D. Julia which, calculating a quinquennial turnover of students, express the theoretical effective strength of the seminary of Rheims between 1749 and 1788:[77]

Year	Effectives	Year	Effectives	Year	Effectives	Year	Effectives
1749	94	1759	164	1769	88	1779	79
1750	97	1760	135	1770	89	1780	82
1751	100	1761	126	1771	85	1781	92
1752	111	1762	125	1772	80	1782	103
1753	104	1763	125	1773	92	1783	94
1754	120	1764	111	1774	87	1784	104
1755	126	1765	119	1775	90	1785	99
1756	150	1766	100	1776	80	1786	96
1757	143	1767	96	1777	75	1787	93
1758	158	1768	78	1778	79	1788	90

Hence, in the diocese of Rheims, the graph dipped from the 1760s exactly as at Rouen and in upper Alsace. To explain this phenomenon one must evidently include reference to 'the definitive suppression of the Jesuits, Jansenist exhaustion and the spread of philosophical ideas in the middle classes',[78] but in a wider context one must also say that minds more open than before to lay affairs were feeling less attraction for traditional religion, and that the Church was having less purchase on people's minds.

Finally, the statistics of demography provide irrefutable evidence of the simultaneous falling off in morality and in the fear inspired by the Church. As the eighteenth century progressed, the desertion of infants in the towns assumed alarming proportions. In Paris, for example, the yearly average of admissions to the Foundling Hospital increased from 1786 in 1700–9 to 5713 in 1780–9.[79] This 219 per cent growth is evidently much larger than the corresponding growth in Paris's population for the same period. In 1772, 7676 foundlings were reported in Paris, and this represented forty per cent of the total of baptized infants. In Milan 405 children were found annually in 1660–9, 684 in 1705–9, and 959 in 1780–9. At Aix-en-Provence, the yearly average went from 107 in 1722–67 to 249 in 1768–78. The increase in Protestant countries was no different. In 1739 the philanthropist Thomas Coram opened a home for 400 foundlings: thirty years later it was catering for 6000. In Amsterdam the figures for abandoned children in 1726–70 are low: they fluctuate between seven minimum and thirty-one maximum; between 1771 and 1784 the jump was sudden and sustained: forty-one minimum, 257 maximum; between 1785 and 1805 the increase continued: all but one of the yearly figures rose above 300, and in 1800 the highest figure, 488, was reached.[80] It is certain that women living in the country near enough to urbanized areas came into the towns to abandon their infants. The phenomenon we are dealing with, then, goes beyond the urban framework. On the other hand, in certain years at least it can be traced to conditions approaching serious food shortage. Nevertheless, the regularity (and universality) of the upward trend would suggest a change in the people's mentality, and this is borne out by a parallel increase in illegitimate births.

At Toulouse[81] there was one illegitimate birth in every ninety-four births in 1650–87; one in fifty-nine in 1668–75; one in thirty-six in 1676–99; one in seventeen in 1700–19; one in 10.6 in 1720–31; one in 8.4 in 1732–43; one in 7.2 in 1751; one in four in 1788. At Bordeaux[82] on the eve of the Revolution, the proportion was one in 5.8. Present studies on Saint-Malo give lower figures, but reveal a similar tendency, particularly for the second half of the eighteenth century. Between 1651 and 1700 the average rate of illegitimacy was 0.66 per cent. During the following half-century it was still low, at 1.73 per cent, but from 1751 it rose regularly, decade by decade: 1751–60, 3.03 per cent; 1761–70, 3.68 per cent; 1771–80, 4.42 per cent; 1781–90, 4.58 per cent; 1791–1800, 6.47 per cent.[83] Here again the phenomenon was international, even though it might appear in one town much later or in another more markedly. At Frankfurt-on-Main there was one illegitimate child out of every 113 baptized in 1635–49, and one out of every eighty-seven in 1700–9; but in 1750–9 the proportion rose to one in twenty-one, and in 1780–9 it had risen again to one in ten. At Leipzig the figures were: one in thirty-three, 1696–1700; one in seven, 1751–60; and one in five, 1781–90.[84] F. Dreyfus writes: 'In the parish of St Emmeran in Mainz, there were never more than fourteen illegitimate births in any one year between 1760 and 1783. In 1784 there were twenty-four; in 1785 fifty-six; in 1786 seventy-one; in 1787 seventy-two; in 1789 seventy-six; in 1790 seventy-nine; in 1791 eighty-three; in 1792, seventy-seven'.[85] Even in quite small towns – Bad Tölz in Bavaria, Schwäbische Hall in Wurtemburg, Engelberg in Obwalden, Ath in Hainaut, Theux in the bishopric of Liège – there was a considerable increase in illegitimate births in the period immediately preceding the Revolution.

It might be objected that the phenomenon was confined to the towns, and the objection would be sustained. On the other hand, as demographic studies multiply, there is every probability that they will disclose a similar if less marked breakdown in traditional moral standards in rural areas as well. Preliminary researches at Crulai (in the Perche), Port-en-Bessin and Troarn (Normandy) show, for the eighteenth century, coefficients of illegitimacy of 1.4 per cent, 2.5 per cent, even 3 per cent, while the highest figure for the country areas of Beauvaisis, Anjou and Languedoc was 0.5 per cent.[86] At Troarn the increase in premarital conceptions and illegitimate births after 1750 is massive.

Finally, the study of legitimate fertility proves that, especially in the towns, voluntary birth control started to spread, and that a contraceptive mentality emerged in circles outside those of prostitution and dissolute high society. The published works of P. Ariès[87] have emphasized the subtle changes in attitude to the family unit in Europe, the deepening concern for children and the increasing female objections to repeated pregnancies, as evinced by the letters of Mme de Sévigné to her daughter and the avowals of the Princess Palatine. The result of this slow evolution was that in the eighteenth century a Malthusian mentality developed among the leisured classes. L. Henry proved it statistically for Geneva.[88]

This drop in the birth-rate in Calvin's city during the eighteenth century could perhaps be the result merely of greater sexual continence, but if the use of the 'English riding-coat', which seems to have begun in the early eighteenth century, was restricted to free-thinking circles, there is no doubt that the *coitus interruptus* was adopted by a certain number of families, even respectable families, despite religious prohibitions – the Jesuit Sanchez had admitted no more than the *amplexus reservatus*[90] – and the anxieties of the 'populationists'. It seemed to observers that a high standard of living brought oliganthropy with it and led to 'infamous economy': 'Nature', wrote the Marquis de Mirabeau, 'bewails the means wealth suggests to avoid the encumbrance of a numerous family' (1756). And the Reverend Moy went one better: 'It is the taste for wealth which, sullying the very holiness of the nuptial bed, has now limited the number of children whose affection a couple should receive' (1776).[91]

In the second half of the eighteenth century, the contraceptive mentality began to affect the rich classes and urban milieux. Writing in 1756, the Reverend Coyer observed in his *Bagatelles morales:* 'A rumour is going round, perhaps with only too much foundation, that coarse men have found a means to deceive nature in the very bosom of marriage'.[92] Twenty-two years later the 'populationist' Moheau was more affirmative: 'The baneful secrets unknown to all animals but man have already penetrated the countryside: nature is deceived even in the villages'.[93] If this was true, it was because the fear inspired by the Church had weakened, for according to Moheau religion favours 'the conservation and reproduction of the human species, since it proscribes with threats of eternal punishment all excesses contrary to health, the tastes which seduced Greece and Italy at their most brilliant hour, and other tastes which dishonour humanity; it wrests from Man the disposal of his own being and forbids a use of his powers without their natural object; it penetrates the intimacy of marriage and prohibits all acts of pleasure which do not tend to generation . . .'.[94]

A curious and significant episode was that occasioned by Fr Féline, an enthusiastic missionary, whose *Catechism for married people* (1782) was banned by the ecclesiastical authorities. Full of good intentions, he had set out to counter 'the ignorance of young couples' and alert them to the 'infamous crime of Onan'. He knew from experience that after a certain period of life together, husbands and wives avoided speaking about their conjugal relations in confession, and that *coitus interruptus* was practised. The reasons he gave for the prevalence of a 'crime' which 'is enormous and very common among married people' merit attention, because they reveal a new concern of a man for his wife and an anxiety for the health of young children: 'The first reason (why people resort to the "crime of Onan") is that husbands show too much indulgence to their wives. They take too much notice of the complaints their wives make about the pain and trouble of bringing children into the world. They humour their excessive delicacy, agree to spare them the suffering of childbirth, but are unwilling to renounce the right of self-satisfaction which they think is theirs. The second is that the wives are afraid of being pregnant again too soon after their confinements; they do not wish to prejudice the children they are already suckling. This is a frequent cause'.[95]

Despite the fears of Moheau and Féline, voluntary birth control in marriage seems to have been relatively little practised in the country areas of pre-1789 France. At Crulai, for example, it was practically non-existent before the Revolution. The Revolution liberated consciences and from that moment, at Crulai, legitimate fertility dropped rapidly. E. Gautier and L. Henry draw this important conclusion: 'The fact that this change came about so quickly under the impulse of the Revolution suggests that *people's minds were already prepared to accept it*'.[96]

(d) 'Dechristianization'

Is 'dechristianization' the most appropriate word to describe this break in religious and moral conformism – the two were linked – which we have been trying to trace in its early stages? As the present work comes to a close, it invites the reader to rethink an all too common understanding. Certainly dechristianization exists, and it existed in certain circles well before the Revolution. The free-thinkers of the seventeenth century – Cyrano, Naudé and others – and later of the enlightenment – Fontenelle, Voltaire, Diderot, La Mettrie, Helvétius – consciously rejected the essentials of Christian dogma: Jesus' divinity and resurrection, the immortality of the soul. Although most of them were alumni of religious schools and colleges, they left the Church and made no secret of it. On the other hand, it is well known that many nobles who played fast and loose with the commandments of God and the Church at a time when 'life was sweet and fair' were led back to religion by the turbulence of the Revolution. But to understand one of the most important and intriguing phenomena of modern times, two questions must be asked: 1) to what extent were the masses christianized when the Revolution broke out? 2) what Christianity had they been taught, and how faithful was it to the Gospel?

1.   How christianized were the people?

In the preceding chapter, we emphasized the serious effort on the part of the Catholic Church – and of Protestantism in the Reformation countries – to christianize the mass of people in the sixteenth, seventeenth and eighteenth centuries. The relatively large number of practising Christians in France today, at a time when to conform means to be religiously indifferent, proves that that effort, with its preliminary pre-Reformation attempts and its post-Revolution continuation, did much to eliminate a deep-seated and persistent paganism frequently camouflaged with the most superficial veneer. However, all the evidence suggests that when the political and economic revolutions swept over the West and plunged it into confusion, the process of christianization was very far from being complete. How could it have been when half the inhabitants could neither read nor write? In France the national average of literates between 1786 and 1790 has been calculated at forty-seven per cent for men and twenty-seven per cent for women.[97] This means that the majority of people's acquaintance with the catechism was oral and nothing more, without the support of books to refresh, consolidate and correct the knowledge learned. It would certainly not be very difficult to gather numerous documents on the religious ignorance of the masses and the survival of superstition in the final century of the *Ancien Régime*. In the diocese of Châlons, for example, the parish priest of Triaucourt lamented the 'crass ignorance' of his people in 1748, the parish priest of Villers-le-Sec called it 'frightful ignorance', and the parish priest of Reims-la-Brûlée referred to his parishioners as 'baptized Jews'.[98] M.-L. Fracart clarifies a vast mental landscape, for too long unfamiliar to historians, when she writes on Niort in the eighteenth century: 'The clergy had to teach the catechism to children who were only too often illiterate, and this did not make it any easier. One must not therefore be surprised at the profound religious ignorance of the time, despite the outwardly Christian habits of the majority'.[99] In fact the history of evangelization has still to be written.[100]

In the nineteenth century, when industry developed and the towns began to grow rapidly, what elements of the population left the over-populated country to become workers in the suburbs of the large towns? The first people to go were the farm labourers, the manual workers, and in general the least privileged, least educated and most superficially christianized of the rural population. Uprooted as they were, living in quarters where there were few churches, subject to inhuman working hours which made attendance at Sunday mass a work of heroism, it is scarcely surprising if they did not always retain the religious conformism of the rural world. They dropped out of a religion which was much more of an external life-structure than an inward, living faith.

Since Constantine's time, Christianity had gradually become Europe's official religion. As Lucien Febvre has stressed,[101] it dominated the whole of existence, from baptism to burial; the whole year, with its Sunday masses and liturgical feasts; and the whole day, with the regular ringing of the angelus. For centuries successive authorities at every level had imposed beliefs and practices on the people: and they called it 'Christendom', by which was meant a system in which the civil and the religious were part and parcel of each other. The king, it was said in the Middle Ages, was not just a layman. As the Lord's anointed, he joined the ranks of miraculous saints. Did he not every year touch thousands of sick people? He was even *plus quam sacerdos*, as evidenced by the 'divine right of kings' accepted by Catholics and Protestants. 'The royal throne', said Bossuet, 'is not a man's throne, but the throne of God himself. Princes therefore act as God's ministers and lieutenants on earth'. Pastor Merlat was no less categorical when he wrote: 'Sovereigns, to whom God has allowed absolute power, are bound by no law which would limit their influence over their subjects. Their will alone is their law ... although God will one day call them to account and punish their injustices if there have been any'. Although these extravagant claims were made of the summit of the pyramid, it was understandable that although the parish priest was the minister of worship responsible for bringing God's grace to the faithful, he should also to some extent be a controller of religious practice, an agent of the police and a steward of the civil authority. It was inevitable, therefore, that when Sunday mass and Easter communion ceased to be compulsory, when the crown toppled, when a lay state was set up, when the parish clergy no longer included royal edicts and other official texts in the notices for the week, traditional Christianity should be profoundly affected. Clergy and laity were completely disorientated.

G. Le Bras' remarks[102] are extremely pertinent here. 'Dechristianization', he says, 'is a fallacious term, practice of the faith being only one sign, the most visible certainly, but also the most superficial, (of religious adherence)'. 'Christian society and the official Church' have been confused. 'Christianization is attested' by personal religion and not merely external practice. 'To speak of dechristianization is therefore to pose a problem of history' and imply that the mass of the population before the industrial era was effectively christianized. He goes on: 'We must insist on this frequently neglected truth: the fulfilment of periodic duties does not constitute genuine, deep-rooted Christianity. The man who believes in the divinity of Christ and eternal life, the man who observes the commandments even by habit is better than the regular mass-goer who observes the law by habit but does not practise the virtues. Attitudes like these can characterize entire populations. To be dechristianized, they must at some stage have been "christianized". The measure of the latter will give us the measure of the former'.

2. What was the quality of the Christianity taught?

Leaving behind us politico-religious structures and religious conformism, we come, finally, to the level of theology. The Christianity of the classical age, which was impregnated with Augustinist pessimism, regarded Church and world as 'irreconcilable enemies'.[103] Now the eighteenth century, recovering and amplifying the attitudes of the Renaissance, opened people's eyes to the universe and expressed an esteem for man, the joy of living and scientific investigation. This secularization of interests, particularly in the second half of the eighteenth century, is attested by recent statistics on printed literature – one indication among many, but a sure one because supported by figures. The results of J. Quéniart's research on Rouen are as given in the table on p. 228.[104]

The new interest in the external world would not have drawn people away from God if the Church too had appropriated this different mentality. The more fervent Christians seemed to many of their contem-

Dates	Total production of book titles	Religious books[105]	Percentage of religious books
1701–10	 145	50	34.5%
1711–20	 103	34	33
1721–30	 126	47	37
1731–40	 119	44	37
1741–50	 65	12	18.5
1751–60	 88	13	15
1761–70	 112	22	19.5
1771–80	 142	28	20
1781–89	 133	16	12

poraries 'like men of austere and insensitive temperament'. 'Boring' and 'pious' were taken as synonyms. To generations of increasing curiosity, religion frequently offered no more than 'a melancholy and mortifying practice'. People's greatest fear was to 'fall into devotional ways'. This gap between faith and profane culture is seen in the library of the curé of Les Epesses (diocese of La Rochelle) in 1775: out of fifty-nine works, only four were on religion.[106] The two Reformations had struggled to restore its sacredness to Christianity; as a consequence they dehumanized it by forgetting to christianize the profane. 'This general unawareness of earthly and human values was their congenital weakness', writes L. Pérouas.[107] They forced people who lived 'in the world' to choose between God and the world, and when certain priests and religious tried to bridge the gap – as the Jesuit casuists, the German clergy who welcomed the *Aufklärung,* and the Oratorians, keen to give their pupils a complete human culture, did – they fell foul of the hierarchy, and not, sometimes, without reason: they were often very close to the wind, so difficult was it to integrate daily life and the aspirations of human knowledge with the traditional religious universe. How could the Church have accepted nascent science when Genesis was still held to be a faithful account of creation? When men were beginning to suspect that the appearance of the human race on earth was preceded by an incalculably long pre-human history, and that the whole universe was evolving and changing, the leaders of religious life, who had already condemned Galileo in the name of the Bible, outlawed the slightest violence to fixist tradition, the smallest doubt on the literalness of the sacred texts.

This rejection of the world and science was accompanied by a theology of the 'terrible God'. The unsettled and insecure religion of the fifteenth century had stressed the redemptive sufferings of Christ, which did not, however, prevent it from trying to deflect divine justice with indulgences and pilgrimages and appeals to our Lady and the saints. Justification by faith on the Protestant side, increased frequentation of

228

the sacraments on the Catholic side tried to reassure the faithful, but if they had to reassure, it meant that there was a fear of the punishing God. This God loomed large in the minds of the Marseillais decimated by the plague in 1720. The idea that 'calamities are the soldiers with whom God fights hardened hearts, the cannons with which he shatters human boldness'[108] was for ages one of the most widely held ideas in the West and one of the ideas most dear to men of the Church. It was still very much alive in France after the defeat of 1870, and again after 1940.

In 1720, a contemporary of the plague wrote: 'Marseilles became at once opulent and criminal: the weight of its pleasures dragged it down into the greatest disorders, and those disorders brought on it the just scourge afflicting it today.... The Lord saw arrogance trampling the poor underfoot, avarice setting up families on the ruins of the widow and orphan, unrestrained ambition grasping for position and influence, impurity resorting to the blackest intrigues to feed its infamous desires, lust gloriously reigning from top to bottom of the social ladder, and vice thrusting through the very rails of the altar. He saw fraudulence in trade, chicanery at the bar, irreverence in the sanctuary. Is it any wonder that such excess and disorder should oblige him to unleash his justice and chasten the city without stint as it had delivered itself to vice without stint'?[109]

But why Marseilles rather than Genoa, Leghorn or Barcelona, which were certainly as sin-ridden? God alone knows when he must punish, replied the author of a *Discourse on the chief events of the contagion at Marseilles*:[110] '... I can see here no cause but the Supreme Cause who manages all events according to the designs of His Providence to reward, punish and put to the test.... The hour of His vengeance was appointed, and arrive it must, despite all the efforts to evade the execution of His decrees, which are as just as they are infallible'.

Mgr Belsunce knew, to his own satisfaction at any rate, who were the chief guilty parties: the 'appellants'. 'If the evil continues to increase', he said, '... I am very tempted to excommunicate all the appellants whose many sacrileges are, I believe, the main cause of the plague from which we are presently suffering'.[111] Hence to save the city what was needed was 'an entire submission of mind and heart to the sacred decisions of the Church, which are the sure and only means of staving off the hand of a wrathful God'.[112]

Had this wrathful God not condemned the whole human race after the original sin? Up till very recent times, Christian orthodoxies presented the first fault as a veritable cosmic catastrophe which had condemned humanity and every living being to suffering and death, thrown the harmonious laws of the universe out of gear and would have entailed the eternal punishment of hell for all Adam and Eve's posterity had God not saved some of these unfortunate people by sending his Son on earth to die on a cross and thus appease the divine anger. Giovanni Pico della Mirandola, the Spanish doctor and theologian Servet and later the Socinians[113] rejected this God of wrath. In the early seventeenth century (before 1624), the *Deist's Quatrains* tried to defend the goodness of God against the doctrine of original sin and the eternity of the pains of hell:

'Since God cares infinitely more for us
Than any caring mother for her children
Could he impose an infinite misfortune
To satisfy an anger that is make-believe? (6)

Can one conceive an infinite torment
To please the Eternal and satisfy his ire,
Without supposing him infinitely cruel
And worse to us than the worst of tyrants? (12)

If from the infinite Being nothing may be taken
Nothing subtracted from the scope of his almighty power
How did he lose, and then redeem,
What never belonged but to his divine essence? (27)'[114]

It has not, perhaps, been sufficiently adverted to that the revolt against Christianity in the seventeenth, eighteenth and subsequent centuries was mainly a rejection of the 'cruel God' whom Chaulieu contrasted with a 'beneficent' and 'merciful' Father. Was this tyrant the God of Christians? The Socinians denied it, and proclaimed 300 years in advance the discovery of a God of Love which is the principal feature of Christianity today. In his *Philosophical Dictionary*, Voltaire offered them this tribute: 'They say that it is an outrage on God to accuse him of the absurdest barbary that he created all the generations of men to torment them with eternal tortures, on the pretext that their first father ate a fruit in the garden. This sacrilegious imputation is the more inexcusable in Christians in that there is not a single word on this invention of original sin[115] either in the Pentateuch, or in the Prophets, or in the Gospels, whether canonical or apocryphal, or in any of the writers commonly referred to as the first Fathers of the Church'.[116]

If everything in the Christianity of the *Ancien Régime* that was constraint, conformism and official worship, everything that was rejection of the world despite the fact that it was the only world men had, everything that was magic, Manichaeism and fear, had been excised, what, for many people, would have remained? Have we not for too long called 'Christianity' what was in fact a mixture of practices and doctrines with frequently but little connexion with the gospel message? If this is so, can we still properly talk of 'dechristianization'? This fundamental question seems to us to be the most important conclusion of this book.

NOTES

(INTRODUCTION)

[1]Thus in A. G. Dickens, *The Counter–Reformation* (London, 1968); H. O. Evennett, *The Spirit of the Counter-Reformation* (Cambridge, 1968).

[2]See the two collections of essays edited by Peter Burke: *Economy and Society in Early Modern Europe: Essays from Annales* (New York, 1972); *A New Kind of History: from the Writings of Lucien Febvre* (London, 1973).

[3]See the as yet incomplete volume 3 of the *History of Irish Catholicism*, edited by P. J. Corish (Dublin, 1967–   ), and my own 'The Counter-Reformation and the People of Catholic Ireland', in T. D. Williams (ed.). *Historical Studies VIII: Papers read before the Irish Conference of Historians* (Dublin, 1971), pp. 155–169.

[4]"Four Catholic congregations in rural Northumberland, 1750–1850', *Recusant History*, ix (1967), pp. 88–119; also ibid., x (1969), pp. 1–29; *The English Catholic Community* (London, 1976).

[5]As in Evennett, *The Spirit of the Counter-Reformation* (above, n.1).

[6]Norman Sykes, *Church and State in England in the Eighteenth Century* (Cambridge, 1934), chaps. iii & vi: W. R. Ward, 'The Religion of the People and the Problem of Control, 1790–1830', in G. J. Cuming & D. Baker (eds.), *Studies in Church History, viii: Popular Belief and Practice* (Cambridge, 1972), pp. 237–57, or *Religion and Society in England, 1790–1850* (London, 1972).

[7]For Ariès, see Bibliography; the point is argued in my 'The Counter-Reformation and the People of Catholic Europe', *Past and Present*, no. 47 (1970), esp. pp. 64–70.

[8]Oxford, 1971; cf. *Past and Present*, no. 47, pp. 58–60.

[9]London, 1971, e.g., pp. 560–7.

[10]*Religion, The Reformation and Social Change* (2 ed. London, 1972), pp. 90–192.

CHAPTER ONE (p. 1)

[1]Cf. on this point see my *Naissance et affirmation de la Réforme* (Paris, 1968[2]).

[2]We do no more here than recall the main ones. The reader will find fuller documentation in F. RAPP, *L'Église et la vie religieuse en Occident à la fin du Moyen Age* (The Church and religious life in the west at the end of the middle ages), *Nouvelle Clio* No. 25 (Paris, 1971).

[3]For the *Devotio moderna*, cf. notably *Dictionnaire de spiritualité ascétique et mystique*

(Dictionary of ascetical and mystical theology), Paris 1937ff, III, col. 727–47, and *Courants religieux et humanisme à la fin du XVe siècle et au début du XVIe* (Religious currents and humanism at the end of the fifteenth and beginning of the sixteenth centuries) (Paris, 1959).

[4]Cf. A. FLICHE-V. MARTIN, *Histoire de l'Eglise:* Vol. 16: *La crise religieuse du XVIe siècle* (by E. de MOREAU, P. JOURDA, P. JANELLE), 1950: Vol. 17: *L'Église à l'époque du concile de Trente* (by L. CRISTIANI), 1948; Vol. 18/1: *La restauration catholique 1563–1648* (by L. WILLAERT), 1960; Vol. 19/1 and 2: *Les luttes politiques et doctrinales aux XVIIe et XVIIIe siècles* (by E. PRÉCLIN and E. JARRY), 1955–6. The present reference is to Vol. 14/2, pp. 629–56.

[5]The University and the Parliament of Paris did not see in 1516 that the concordat confirmed the Gallican mentality and structure which the *Pragmatique Sanction* had helped to create. The *Sanction* in fact re-instituted the election of bishops and abbots only to make the king's 'benign and benevolent' recommendations easier. Cf. J. THOMAS, *Le concordat de 1516, ses origines, son histoire au XVIe siècle*, 3 vols. (Paris, 1910).

[6]Cf. A. RENAUDET, *Préréforme et humanisme à Paris pendant les premières guerres d'Italie* (Pre-Reformation and Humanism in Paris during the first Italian wars) (Paris, 1916), pp. 178f.

[7]H. JEDIN, *A History of the Council of Trent*, trans. Graf (London, 1957), I, p. 152.

[8]Paul III approved the founding of the Company of Jesus in 1540.

[9]*Histoire de l'Église* (see note 4 above), XVII, p. 279.

[10]The *Interim* of Augsburg authorized the marriage of priests and communion from the chalice for the laity.

[11]This letter is printed in the *Oeuvres* of Bossuet, ed. LACHAT, Paris 1862–8, XVIII, pp. 198–9.

[12]Apart from the voting bishops, there were some fifty theologians who had no vote.

[13]G. ALBERIGO, *I vescovi italiani al concilio di Trento 1545–1547* (The Italian bishops at the Council of Trent) (Florence, 1959), pp. 350–2.

[14]Ibid., pp. 274ff.

[15]J. DELUMEAU, *Naissance* (see note 1 above), first and last chapters.

[16]Fourth Session. The council sat for twenty-five sessions, nine of them preparatory.

[17]H. STROHL, *Luther jusqu'en 1520* (Luther up to 1520) (Paris, 1962), p. 270.

[18]Fifth Session.

[19]Sixth Session.

[20]P. RICHARD-A. MICHEL, *Le concile de Trente* (in HEFELE-LECLERCQ, *Histoire des conciles*), IX/1, pp. 303–5.

[21]Ibid., X/1, p. 85. *Decree on justification*, chap. 4.

[22]Ibid., p. 91, chap. 7.

[23]Ibid., p. 161.

[24]Ibid., p. 92. *Decree on justification*, chap. 7.

[25]They were studied in the 7th, 13th, 14th and 21st Sessions.

[26]*Histoire des conciles* (see note 20 above), X/1, p. 203.

[27]Ibid., p. 553.

[28]TITTMANN, *Libri symbolici Ecclesiae evangelicae* 1827, p. 253.

[29]*Dictionnaire de théologie catholique* (Paris, 1923ff), V/2, col. 1342.

[30]*Institution chrétienne* (last ed.), IV, chap. 17: E. T. Allen, *Institutes of the Christian Religion* (Philadelphia, 1936), II, p. 648. Cf. J. DELUMEAU, *Naissance* (see note 1 above), pp. 130ff.

[31]Thirteenth Session, can. 2: *Histoire des conciles* (see note 20 above), X/1, p. 273.

[32]Ibid., p. 242.

[33]Ibid., p. 430.

[34]Twenty-second Session.

[35]It will be noticed that the Roman Church believed in purgatory, which was rejected by the Protestants. Further, it continued to maintain the perfect legitimacy of masses in honour of the saints offered to obtain their intercession with God. The council left it to the pope to give or refuse the chalice to lay people in certain central European countries. Rome chose to refuse it.

[36]As before, the translation of the council texts is directly from the Latin.

[37]Reform decree of the 7th Session: *Histoire des conciles* (see note 20 above), X/1, p. 233.

[38]Twenty-fourth Session: ibid., p. 567.

[39]Twenty-third Session: ibid., p. 496.

[40]Sixth Session: ibid., p. 163.

[41]Cf. the thesis, still in manuscript, of Cardinal Gouyon, *L'introduction de la réforme disciplinaire du concile de Trente dans le diocèse de Bordeaux, 1582–1624* (Introduction of the disciplinary reforms of the council of Trent in the diocese of Bordeaux), typed extracts in the University Library, Bordeaux.

[42]Fifth Session: *Histoire des conciles*, X/1, p. 63.

[43]Twenty-first Session: ibid., p. 424.

[44]Seventh Session: ibid., p. 235.

[45]Fourteenth Session: ibid., pp. 385 and 390.

[46]Twenty-first Session: ibid., p. 422.

[47]Seventh Session: ibid., p. 235.

[48]Fourteenth Session: ibid., p. 386.

[49]Fourteenth Session: ibid., p. 385.

[50]Thirteenth Session: ibid., pp. 284–5.

[51]Thirteenth Session: ibid., p. 286.

[52]Fourteenth Session: ibid., pp. 385–6.

[53]Twenty-fourth Session: ibid., p. 568. The visit of the whole diocese was to be completed in two years.

[54]Twenty-third Session: ibid., p. 495.

[55]Fourteenth Session: ibid., p. 388.

[56]Twenty-second Session: ibid., pp. 460–1.

[57]Fourteenth Session: ibid., p. 288.

[58]Twenty-fifth Session: ibid., p. 622.

[59]Twenty-second Session: ibid., p. 461.

[60]Twenty-second Session: ibid., p. 457.

[61]Twenty-first Session: ibid., p. 421.

[62]Twenty-first Session: ibid., p. 420.

[63]For this and the following regulations, 23rd Session: ibid., pp. 494–505.

[64]Ibid., p. 501.

[65]Ibid., p. 607.

[66]Ibid., p. 609.

[67]G. ALBERIGO, 'The council of Trent: New Views on the Occasion of its Fourth Centenary', *Concilium* Vol. 7, No. 1 (September, 1965), pp. 38–48.

CHAPTER TWO (p. 24)

[1]The 25th Session of the Council had asked the pope for both of these.

[2]*Dictionnaire de théologie catholique* (see chap. 1 above, note 29), XV/1, col. 1485.

[3]L. V. PASTOR, *Storia dei papi* (History of the popes), 16 vols (Rome, 1910–34), translated from the original German: *Geschichte der Päpste seit dem Ausgang des Mittelalters* (History of the popes from the end of the middle ages) (Freiburg, 1886–1933): Vol. 8 of the Italian edition, pp. 441–2.

[4]Quoted in A. FLICHE–V. MARTIN, *Histoire de l'Eglise* (see chap.1, note 4), XVIII, pp. 392–3.

[5]Clement VIII laid down as one of the conditions of his absolution of Henry IV that the decrees of Trent were to be accepted in France.

[6]P. BLET, *Le clergé de France et la monarchie. Études sur les assemblées générales du clergé de 1615 à 1666,* 2 vols. (Rome, 1959), I, p. 129.

[7]*L'Alsace du passé au présent* (Alsace from the past to the present), Bull. No. 7: *L'Alsace au XVIIIe siècle,* (Strasburg, 1969), pp. 17–8.

[8]H. SÉE, *La France économique et sociale au XVIIIe siècle* (Paris, 1946), p. 57. The disadvantages of the benefice sysem could to some extent be offset by the choice of zealous commendatory abbots.

[9]The political authority in the countries under the crown of Spain opposed provincial synods. Philip II has been called the 'gravedigger of synods'; *Histoire de l'Église,* XVIII/1, p. 71.

[10]They were impossible to observe anyway in the vast areas of Latin America.

[11]J. FERTÉ, *La vie religieuse dans les campagnes parisiennes 1622–1695* (Religious life in the country areas around Paris) (Paris, 1962), p. 23.

[12]Ibid., p. 22

[13]Ibid., p. 13.

[14]M. JOIN-LAMBERT, 'La pratique religieuse dans le diocèse de Rouen sous Louis XIV, et de 1707 à 1789' (Religious practice in the diocese of Rouen under Louis XIV, and from 1707 to 1789), *Annales de Normandie* 1953 and 1955: 1953, p. 262.

[15]E. BIRAUD, *Le clergé séculier à Nantes à la fin du XVIIe siècle* (The secular clergy at Nantes in the late seventeenth century), unpublished thesis (Rennes, 1963), p. 53.

[16]C. HIGOUNET (ed.), *Bordeaux de 1453 à 1715* (Bordeaux, 1967), p. 385.

[17]F. LEBRUN, *Cérémonial (1692–1721) de R. Lehoreau* (Paris 1967), p. 54.

[18]He had founded a first seminary in 1658.

[19]J. DELUMEAU, *Vie économique et sociale de Rome dans la seconde moitié du XVIe siècle* (Social and economic life in Rome in the second half of the sixteenth century), 2 vols, (Paris, 1957–9), I, pp. 223ff.

[20]Ibid., I, p. 172.

[21]M. ROMANI, *Pellegrini e viaggiatori nell'economia di Roma dal XIV̊ al XVIĬ secolo* (Pilgrims and travellers in the economy of Rome from the fourteenth century to the seventeenth century) (Milan, 1948), pp. 331ff.

[22]P. SARPI, *Istoria del concilio tridentino* (History of the council of Trent) (London, 1619: French Translation: Amsterdam, 1686), preface. Cf. G. GETTO, *Paolo Sarpi* (Florence, 1967²), pp. 261–332.

[23]Bibliography in *Revue Historique,* 1961, no. 460; J. DELUMEAU, *Les progrès de la centralisation dans l'Etat pontifical au XVIe siècle* (Progress in the centralization of the pontifical States in the sixteenth century), p. 399: and *Históire de l'Eglise,* XVIII, pp. 57–8.

[24]In 1567 Pius V revoked all pontifical edicts allowing cardinals to confer churches, convents and benefices as they pleased: L.-V. PASTOR, *Storia* (see note 3 above), VIII, p. 102.

[25]Ibid., p. 145.

²⁶Ibid., pp. 148–9, and *Dictionnaire de thélogie catholique* (see chap. 1, note 29), XV/1, col. 1490.

²⁷E. de MOREAU, *Histoire de l'Élise en Belgique* (History of the Church in Belgium), (Louvain, 1952), V, pp. 13–31.

²⁸Cf. L. PÉROUAS, *Le diocèse de La Rochelle de 1648 à 1724. Sociologie et pastorale* (The social and pastoral history of the diocese of La Rochelle) (Paris, 1964).

²⁹J. PROKES, *Histoire tchécoslovaque* (Prague, 1927), and V.–L. TAPIÉ, *Monarchie et peuples du Danube* (Paris, 1969), pp. 149 and 243.

³⁰L.–V. PASTOR, *Storia* (see note 3 above), p. 147.

³¹*Enciclopedia Universal ilustrada*, (Bilbao, 1930–55), LV, pp. 142–3.

³²The following information is from *Histoire de l'Église* (see chap. 1, note 4), XVIII, pp. 88–9 and 194–5.

³³Ibid., XVII p. 341.

³⁴Cf. M. MARCOCCHI, *La riforma dei monasteri femminili a Cremona* (The reform of nuns' convents in Cremona), (Cremona, 1966).

³⁵These and the following details in T.–J. SCHMITT, *L'organisation ecclésiastique et la pratique religieuse dans l'archidiaconé d'Autun de 1650 à 1750* (Ecclesiastical organization and religious practice in the archdeaconry of Autun (Autun, 1957), p. 32.

³⁶A. GUILLERMOU, *Les Jésuites* (Paris, 1963), pp. 40 and 73.

³⁷P. MOISY, *Les églises des Jésuites de l'ancienne Assistance de France* (Jesuit churches in the old Assistance de France) (Rome, 1958), p. 6.

³⁸H. PIRENNE, *Histoire de Belgique* (History of Belgium), 1948–51 ed., II, p. 462, according to the *Imago primi saeculi*, (Anvers, 1640).

³⁹Ibid., p. 463.

⁴⁰G.HERMANT, *Histoires des odres religieux et congrégations*, 2 vols. (Rouen, 1710), under 'Capucins'; A. de LUTERA, *Compendio degli ordini regolari esistenti* (Compendium of existing orders of regulars), 4 vols (Rome, 1790), II, p. 105; F. d'AVERSA, *Quatre siecles d'apostolat dans l'ordre des freres mineurs capucins (1528–1928)* (Four centuries of apostolate in the Capuchins) (Rome, 1928); R. M. de POBLADURA, *Historia generalis fr. min. capuc.* (General history of the Capuchins), 3 vols, (Rome, 1924–51).

⁴¹Cf. C. CHESNAU, *Le P. Yves de Paris et son temps (1590–1678)*, 2 vols, (Paris, 1948).

⁴²'Missionnaires catholiques de la France pendant le XVIIe siècle' (French Catholic missionaries in the seventeenth century), in *XVIIe siècle* No. 41, 1958, pp. 349ff.

⁴³'Colloque d'histoire religieuse, Lyon 1963' (Colloquium on religious history, Lyons 1963), in *Cahiers d'Histoire* 1964, I, p. 32.

⁴⁴L.–V. PASTOR, *Storia* (see note 3 above), XI, pp. 284–5 and 301.

⁴⁵P. PISANI, *Les compagnies de prêtres des XVIIe et XVIIe siècles* (Companies of priests in the seventeenth and eighteenth centuries) (Paris, 1928), pp. 50–4.

⁴⁶Ibid., pp. 57–8; cf. also *Congrégation de la Mission. Répertoire historique* (Paris, 1900).

⁴⁷*Dictionnaire de theólogie catholique* (see chap. 1, note 29), II, col. 1784–8.

⁴⁸On the Ursulines, cf. ibid., I, col. 2481; *Lexikon für Theologie und Kirche* (Freiburg, 1957ff²), X, col. 455. Cf. also *Niveaux de culture et groupes sociaux* (Levels of culture and social groups), (Paris, 1967), p. 143 (paper by Fr de DAINVILLE).

⁴⁹*Dictionnaire d'Histoire et de Géographie ecclésiastiques* (Paris, 1912), V, col. 614; HERMANT, *Histoire des ordres religieux et congrégations* (see note 40 above), III, p. 143.

236

[50]Its statutes were approved by the archbishop of Paris only in 1655, and by the pope in 1668.

[51]P. COSTE, *Saint Vincent de Paul, correspondance, entretiens et documents*, (Paris, 1920–3), X, p. 661.

[52]A. HELYOT, *Dictionnaire des ordres religieux*, 8 vols. (Paris, 1714–24) reproduced in MIGNE, *Encyclopédie théólogique*, XX, p. 819.

[53]P. GOUBERT, *Beauvais et le Beauvaisis de 1600 à 1730* (Beauvais ¡and district) (Paris, 1960), p. 233.

[54]F. LEBRUN, *Cérémonial* (see note 17 above), p. 47.

[55]C. ÉTIENNE, *La population d'Angers en 1769* (thesis), (Rennes, 1967).

[56]H. PIRENNE, *Histoire* (see note 38 above), II, p. 468.

[57]Cf. for example E. LE ROY-LADURIE, *Les paysans du Languedoc* (The peasants of Languedoc) (Paris, 1966), I, pp. 474–7.

[58]Cf. M. MARCOCCHI, *La riforma* (see note 34 above).

[59]J. VIVÈS, *Historia económica y social de Espãna y América* (Economic and social history of Spain and America) (Barcelona, 1957ff), III, pp. 81, 310.

[60]Ibid., p. 308.

[61]For the following, see *Histoire de l'Église* (see chap. 1, note 4), XVIII, pp. 99ff.

[62]*Histoire littéraire de la France, Historiens des Gaules, Gallia christiana* etc.

[63]*Histoire de L'Église*, XIX, p. 371.

[64]H. BREMOND, *Histoire littéraire du sentiment religieux en France depuis la fin des guerres de religion* (Literary history of religious feeling in France from the end of the wars of religion), 11 vols, re-edited (Paris, 1967), I, p. 225.

[65]R. RAPIN, *Mémoires 1647–1669*, 3 vols, (Paris, 1865–9), I, p. 95.

[66]Ibid.

[67]H. J. MARTIN, *Livre, Pouvoirs et société à Paris au XVIIe siècle. Une analyse de psychologie historique* (The book, the authorities and society in seventeenth century Paris. A historico-psychological analysis), 2 vols, (Paris, 1969). After Anvers and Venice, Paris was the third city in Europe for the publication of books. Rome came fourth.

[68]Ibid., I, pp. 76–88.

[69]Ibid., I, p. 153.

[70]Ibid., II, p. 750.

[71]This is the remark of a Dominican humanist in 1520. Cf. *Histoire de l'Église* (see chap. 1, note 4), XVIII, p. 223. The following remarks, ibid., pp. 222–6.

[72]J. T. NOONAN, *Contraception. A History of its treatment by the Catholic theologians and canonists* (Camb., Mass., 1965), pp. 336–8.

[73]Ibid., pp. 447–75.

[74]See below, pp. *115*.

CHAPTER THREE (p. 43)

[1]*Scripta*, I, 379, quoted by RIBADEAU–DUMAS, *Grandeur et misère des Jésuites*, (Paris, 1963), p. 153.

[2]*Autobiography*, chap. 32: *The Complete Works of St Teresa of Jesus*, trans. Peers, (London, 1943), 3 vols, I, pp. 215–6.

[3]*Dark Night of the Soul*, quoted in Y. PELLE-DOUËL, *Saint Jean de la Croix et la nuit mystique* (Paris, 1960), p. 65. The standard edition of St John of the Cross in English is *The Complete Works of St John of the Cross*, trans. Peers, (London, 1935) (3 vols), 1964 (1 vol.).

⁴*Opuscule* XVII.

⁵*Oeuvres complètes* (Complete Works), ed. Migne, 2 vols, (Paris, 1857): I, p. 967.

⁶A. DODIN, *Saint Vincent de Paul. Entretiens spirituels aux missionaires* (St Vincent de Paul. Spiritual talks to missioners) (Paris, 1960), pp. 636–7.

⁷H. BREMOND, *Histoire* (see chap. 2, note 64), II, p. 506.

⁸This quotation and the complete story of Marie de l'Incarnation, ibid., VI, pp. 3–72.

⁹*Autobiography,* chap. 27, Peers trans. (see note 2 above), pp. 176–7.

¹⁰On Philip Neri see L. PONNELLE–L. BORDET, *Saint Philippe Neri et la société romaine de son temps* (Paris, 1955²).

¹¹M. MANSIO, *Vita del Letterato* (Life of the Letterato) (Rome, 1625), p. 36.

¹²Cf. H. BREMOND, *Histoire* (see note 7 above), VI, pp. 84–91.

¹³A. BUTLER, *The Lives of the Saints,* 12 vols, (London, 1931), III, p. 273; Saint Jean de BREBEUF, *Les relations de ce qui s'est passé au pays des Hurons 1635–1648* (Account of what happened in the country of the Hurons), introduction by T. BESTERMAN (Geneva, 1957), pp. xxiv–xxvii.

¹⁴Quoted in Y. PELLE–DOUËL, *Saint Jean de la Croix* (note 3 above), p. 65.

¹⁵Ibid., p. 43.

¹⁶ M. de CERTEAU, *J. J. Surin, Correspondance,* Paris 1966, p. 10.

¹⁷Cf. J. BARUZI, *Saint Jean de la Croix et le problème de l'expérience mystique* (Paris, 1931²), pp. 378–448.

¹⁸Ibid., p. 396.

¹⁹Ibid., p. 405.

²⁰*Treatise on the Love of God,* 7, 6, quoted in E. M. LAJEUNE, *Saint François de Sales et l'esprit salésien* (Paris, 1962), p. 119.

²¹P. de BÉRULLE, *Oeuvres complètes* (Complete Works), pp. 1180–1 and 1358, quoted in H. BREMOND, *Histoire* (see note 7 above), III/1, pp. 79–80.

²²Ibid., V, pp. 24–8.

²³*Poems,* trans. Campbell (Harmondsworth, 1960), p. 51.

²⁴*Les justifications de Mme J. M. B. de la Mothe Guion, écrites par elle même* (Cologne, 1720), II, p. 276, note B.

²⁵M. de CERTEAU, *Correspondence* (see note 16 above), pp. 15 and 133.

²⁶H. BREMOND, *Histoire* (see note 7 above), V, p. 265.

²⁷*Autobiography* (see note 2 above), p. 65.

²⁸*Treatise on the Love of God,* 6, 9.

²⁹H. BERGSON, *Les deux sources de la morale et de la religion* (The two sources of morality and religion), 1961 ed., pp. 259–66.

³⁰J. BARUZI, *Saint Jean de la Croix* (see note 17 above), p. 510.

³¹Ibid., p. 705.

³²Cf. *Le traité historique de Jurieu contenant le jugement d'un Protestant sur la theólogie mystique* (Historical treatise by Pierre Jurieu [1637–1713] containing the judgment of a Protestant on mystical theology).

³³On Molinos and Mme Guyon, cf. the remarkable study of L. KOLAKOWSKI, *Chrétiens sans Église* (Paris, 1969).

³⁴*Oeuvres complètes* (Complete Works), (Paris, 1828), IX, *Dialogue second sur le Quiétisme,* pp. 258–9, (Translator's English version).

³⁵J. DELUMEAU, *La civilisation de la Renaissance* (Paris, 1967), p. 507, and 'Réinterprétation de la Renaissance: les progrès de la capacité d'observer, d'organiser et d'abstraire' (A reinterpretation of the Renaissance: progress in the ability to observe, organize and abstract), *Revue d'Histoire Moderne et Contemporaine* 14 (1967), pp. 296–314.

[36]J. DELUMEAU, *I protagonisti (22): Ignazio di Loyola* (Milan, 1965), pp. 85–112.

[37]On St Ignatius, cf, A. GUILLERMOU, *La vie saint Ignace de Loyola* (Paris, 1956); H. RAHNER, *Ignatius von Loyola als Mensch und Theologe* (Ignatius of Loyola as man and theologian) (Freiburg, 1964).

[38]See below, p. 189.

[39]P. ARIÈS, *L'enfant et la vie familiale sous l'Ancien Régime*, (Paris, 1960), 318ff (ET: *Centuries of Childhood*, London, 1962). Cf. also G. SNYDERS, *La pédagogie en France aux XVIIe et XVIIIe siècles* (Paris, 1965).

[40]Cf. G. RIGAULT, *Histoire générale de l'Institut des Frères des écoles chrétiennes*, 6 vols. (Paris, 1937f); Y. POUTET, *Le XVIIe siècle et le origines ,lasalliennes*, (Rennes, 1970).

[41]M. ARON, *Les Ursulines* (Paris, 1937), pp. 50–64 and 113. Cf. also M. CHALENARD, *La promotion de la femme á l'apostolat 1540–1650* (Paris, 1950); I. de AZCARATE RISTORI, *El origen de las ordenes femeninas de enseñanza y la Compania de Maria* (The origin of female teaching orders and the Company of Mary) (San Sebastian, 1963); and *Niveaux* (see chap. 2, note 48), ibid.

[42]C. FANUCCI, *Trattato di tutte l'opere pie dell'alma città di Roma* (Treatise on all the pious works in the immortal city of Rome) (Rome, 1601), pp. 54–5.

[43]Cf. p. 46.

[44]J. DELUMEAU, *Vie économique* (see chap. 2, note 19), I, pp. 408–11, on the rise in the number of hospitals in Rome during the sixteenth century.

[45]Cf. G. LA TARCHE, *Saint Camille de Lellis* (Paris, 1907); ESCOBAR, 'Storia dell'Ordine degli Chierici regolari ministri degli infermi 1586–1607' (History of the Order of the Clerks regular ministers of the sick), in *Domesticum 1937–45*. St Camillus was ordained priest by Bishop Goldwell, the last English bishop of the Pre-Reformation hierarchy.

CHAPTER FOUR (p. 60)

[1]Francis Xavier left for Goa four years before the council opened.

[2]Above all because of the work of G. SCHÜRHAMMER, *Franz Xaver. Sein Leben und seine Zeit* (Francis Xavier. His life and times), (Freiburg, 1955); J. BRODRICK, *Francis Xavier, 1506–1552*, (New York, 1957). There is an excellent account by H. BERNARD–MAÎTRE, in S. DELACROIX, *Histoire universelle des missions catholiques*, Symposium, 2 vols. (Paris, 1956–7), I, pp. 269–84.

[3]According to C. R. BOXER, *The Christian Century in Japan 1549–1650* (Berkeley-London, 1951).

[4]Cf. J. L. PHELAN, *The Hispanisation of the Philippines 1565–1700* (Madisan, 1959).

[5]F. BRAUDEL, *Civilisation matérielle et capitalisme*, (Paris, 1967), I. p. 28. (ET: *Capitalism and Material Life*, London, 1974).

[6]Cf. H. BERNARD, *Aux portes de la Chine. Les missionaires du XVIe siècle* (On the threshold of China. The sixteenth century missionaries) (Paris, 1937); Id., *Le P. Matthieu Ricci et la société chinoise de son temps 1552–1610* (Matteo Ricci and the Chinese society of his time), (Tientsin, 1937); V. CRONIN, *The Wise Man from the West* (London, 1955); P. D'ELIA, *Fonti ricciane* (Riccian sources), 3 vols, (Rome, 1942–9); Id., *Storia dell'introduzione del cristianesimo in China* (History of the introduction of Christianity into China), 3 vols, (Rome, 1957); and *Opere storiche del P. Matteo Ricci* (Historical works of Fr Matteo Ricci), 2 vols. (Macerata, 1911–13).

[7]*Nouvelle Histoire de l'Englise:* Vol. III, *Réforme et Contre–Réforme* (by H. TÜCHLE

et al.); Vol. IV, *Siècle des Lumières, Révolutions, Restaurations* (by L. J. ROGLER et al.) (Paris, 1966–8): III, p. 341.

[8]Destroyed six times, this seminary emigrated successively to Burma, Cochin China and India. It is now in Penang (Malay Straits).

[9]Figures in R. RICHARD, *La 'conquête spirituelle' du Mexique* (The 'spiritual conquest' of Mexico) (Paris, 1933), pp. 110–2.

[10]Text in L. HANKE, *Colonisation et conscience chrétienne au XVIe siécle* (Paris, 1957), p. 102.

[11]Metropolitan of Lima from 1581 to 1606.

[12]Cf. A. MÉTRAUX, *La civilisation matérielle des tribus Tupi-Guarani* (Paris, 1928); *La religion des Tupinamba et ses rapports avec celle des autres tribus Tupi-Guarani* (The religion of the Tupinambas and its relation to that of other Tupi-Guarani tribes) (Paris, 1928).

[13]Quoted in S. DELACROIX, *Histoire* (see note 2 above), p. 273.

[14]For the latter, cf. J. DELUMEAU, *Civilisation de la Renaissance* (see chap. 3, note 5), pp. 355–73.

[15]P. CHAUNU, *L'Amérique et les Amériques,* (Paris, 1964), p. 108.

[16]Ibid., p. 109.

[17]J. H. RODRIGUES, *Brasil,* (Mexico City, 1953).

[18]'So-called from the banderole carried by each gang' (P. Chaunu).

[19]For Fr Vieira, see R. CHANTAL, *Prophétisme et messianisme dans l'oeuvre d'Antonio Vieira* (Paris, 1959), and the bibliography in F. MAURO, *L'expansion européenne 1600–1870* (Paris, 1964).

[20]For Marie de l'Incarnation, see above, p. 45; J. BRODRICK, *A Procession of Saints* (London, 1957), pp. 174–201 (originally an article in the *Clergy Review* 1945). Three Ursulines and three Hospitallers of Dieppe reached Canada in 1639.

[21]See above p. 46.

[22]The Antilles are included in these figures.

[23]Excluding the Near East, where dioceses were created on paper.

[24]The name Melkite was given by the Monophysites to their opponents who accepted the decisions of the council of Chalcedon sanctioned by the emperor Marcion in 480.

[25]The Nestorians denied that Mary is the Mother of God: she is mother of the man Jesus only.

[26]F. BRAUDEL, *Civilisation* (see note 5 above), I, pp. 28–30.

[27]Ibid., p. 26.

[28]Ibid.

[29]Mary of the Incarnation and the Ursulines settled in Canada, but did not do strictly missionary work. Even the Creoles who became nuns in America became contemplatives.

[30]F. CHEVALIER, *La formation des grands domaines au Mexique. Terre et société aux XVIe et XVIIe siècles* (Paris, 1952), p. 317.

[31]A first vicar apostolic had been appointed previously, in Europe to govern the Church of Utrecht.

[32]In his *Treatise on the enslaved Indians*, published in 1552: M. MAHN-LOT, *Las Casas. L'Evangile et la force* (Las Casas. The Gospel and violence) (Paris, 1964), p. 201.

[33]The bull of 1493 divided the non-European world between the Spaniards and the Portuguese.

[34]Memorandum of 1513, reproduced in L. HANKE, *Colonisation* (see note 10 above), p. 32.

[35]Text from the *History of the Indians,* quoted by L. HANKE, loc. cit., p. 126.

[36]Quoted ibid., p. 4.

[37]Phrases of Lewis Hanke's.

[38]For a bibliography on Las Casas, see M. GIMENEZ FERNANDEZ-L. HANKE, *Bartlomé de Las Casas, Bibliografía crítica* (santiago, Chile, 1954).

[39]Letter, 1555, trans. in M. MAHN–LOT, *Las Casas* (see note 32 above), p. 167.

[40]J. F. GRONER, *Kardinal Cajetan* (Fribourg–Louvain, 1951), p. 29.

[41]Cf. M. BARBIER, *Francisco de Vitoria. Leçons sur les Indiens et sur le droit de guerre* (F. de V. Readings on the Indians and the right of war) (Geneva, 1966).

[42]Ibid., pp. 69–70.

[43]Trans. in L. HANKE, *Colonisation* (see note 10 above), p. 102.

[44]Analysis in ibid., pp. 136–7.

[45]Cf. F. CHEVALIER, *La formation* (see note 30 above).

[46]M. MAHN-LOT, *Las Casas* (see note 32 above), p. 28.

[47]A. J. SARAIVA, 'Le P. Antonio Vieira et l'esclavage des Noirs au XVIIe siècle' (Fr Antonio Vieira and the slavery of the blacks in the seventeenth century), in *Annales [Economies. Societes. Civilisations]* 1967, p. 1290.

[48]Ibid., p. 1294.

[49]Published only in 1829. Recent edition by A. M. GARIBAY: Bernardino de SAHAGUN, *Historia de las cosas de Nueva España* (History of the affairs of New Spain) (Mexico City, 1956).

[50]Cf. below, p. 161.

[51]Quoted in S. DELACROIX, *Histoire* (see note 2 above), II, p. 156.

[52]In 1615, Paul V had allowed future Chinese priests to celebrate mass, recite the breviary and administer the sacraments in literary Chinese. This 'Pauline privilege' was never in fact conceded because the curia and certain Asian elements were opposed to it: cf. F. BONTINCK, *La lutte autour de la liturgie chinoise aux XVIIe et XVIIIe siècles* (The struggle over Chinese liturgy in the seventeenth and eighteenth centuries) (Louvain-Paris, 1962), pp. 21–56, 389–402.

[53]See below, p. 177.

[54]See above, p. 64.

[55]*Dictionnaire historique et critique* (Historical and critical dictionary), Vol. III (article 'Milton'), p. 1991.

PART TWO

CHAPTER ONE (p. 99)

[1]L. WILLAERT, *Bibliotheca janseniana belgica,* 3 vols. (Paris, 1949–51), gives 13,000 titles, but his list does not include all the French works or works on Pascal and Racine.

[2]J. ORCIBAL–A. BARNES, *Les origines du Jansénisme,* 5 vols. (Louvain-Paris, 1947–62); Idd., *Saint Cyran et le Jansénisme* (Paris, 1961).

[3]Idd., *Relation de la captivité d'Angélique de saint Jean Arnauld d'Andilly* (Paris, 1954); Idd., *Port-Royal entre le miracle et l'obéissance . . .: Flavie Passart et Angélique de saint Jean Arnauld d'Andilly* (Paris, 1957).

[4]L. WILLAERT, *Les origines du Jansénisme dans les Pays-Bas catholiques* (Gembloux, 1948).

⁵L. CEYSSENS, *Sources relatives aux débuts du Jansénisme et de l'antijansénisme 1640–1643* (Louvain, 1957); Id., *La première bulle contre Jansénius. Sources relatives à son histoire 1644–1653*, 2 vols. (Brussels, 1961–2); Id., *Sources relatives à l'histoire du Jansénisme et de l'antijansénisme des années 1661–1672* (Louvain, 1970).

⁶J. TANS, *P. Quesnel et les Pays-Bas* (Groningen, 1960).

⁷L. GOLDMANN, *Correspondance de Martin de Barcos, abbé de Saint-Cyran* (Paris, 1956).

⁸G. NAMER, *L'abbé Le Roy et ses amis. Essai sur le Jansénisme extrémiste intramondain* (Paris, 1964).

⁹B. NEVEU, *Sébastien-Joseph Du Cambout de Pontchâteau 1634–1690* (Paris, 1969).

¹⁰B. PLONGERON, 'Une image de l'Église d'après les "Nouvelles Ecclésiastiques" 1728–1790', in *Revue d'Histoire de l'Église de France*, 1967, pp. 241–68.

¹¹See above, pp.

¹²H. MARROU, *St Augustine and his influence through the ages* New York–London, 1957), p. 91 (texts translated by Edmund Hill).

¹³This formula was proposed by fifteen French bishops in 1655, accepted by the Assembly of Clergy in 1656, approved by the pope in the following year, and actually imposed from 1661.

¹⁴It is thought today that the distinction between right and fact was suggested by Pierre Nicole, the moralist who translated the *Provincial Letters* into Latin.

¹⁵Brother to Mère Angélique and the great Arnauld.

¹⁶The Cistercian convent of Port-Royal-des-Champs had moved to Paris in 1626. Although the 'Hermits' moved into the old abbey buildings in the Chevreuse valley in 1638, nuns returned to the Champs ten years later. From 1665, the Paris convent was distinct from its country sister-house, and was governed by anti-Jansenist abbesses.

¹⁷A. LATREILLE, *Histoire du catholicisme en France*, II (Paris, 1960), p. 468.

¹⁸Ibid.

¹⁹Quoted in J. ORCIBAL–A. BARNES, *Les origines* (see note 2 above), p. 105.

²⁰P. PITHOU, *Les libertés de l'Église gallicane*, 1594.

²¹In 1749, the archbishop of Paris Christophe de Beaumont demanded from the dying a note attesting their submission to the Bull *Unigenitus*. Parliament reacted by giving appellants the last rites and burying them in consecrated ground. Louis XV exiled him for fifteen months, but finally, in 1754, imposed silence on both sides.

²²Louis-Isaac Le Maître de Sacy, a nephew of the great Arnauld and Mère Angélique, and one of the Port-Royal hermits.

²³In fact printed by the Elzevier family in Holland.

²⁴1617–90. He left the Sorbonne after the condemnation of Arnauld.

²⁵*Mémoires sur l'histoire ecclésiastique du XVIIe siècle*, ed. A. GAZIER (Paris, 1905), I, p. 67.

²⁶*Les origines* (see note 2 above), II, pp. 477–595.

²⁷A. ADAM, *Du mysticisme à la révolte. Les Jansénistes du XVIIe siècle* (From mysticism to revolt. The Jansenists in the seventeenth century) (Paris, 1968), p. 191.

²⁸Ibid.

²⁹*Mémoires*, IV, p. 533.

³⁰R. TAVENEAUX, *Le Jansénisme et politique* (Jansenism and politics) (Paris, 1965), p. 15.

³¹J. ORCIBAL, *Saint-Cyran* (see note 2 above), p. 138.

³²*Instructions chrétiennes tirées par M. Arnauld d'Andilly ... des lettres de M. Jean Duvergier de Hauranne* (Christian instructions taken by M. Arnauld from the letters of M. Duvergier) (Paris, 1672), p. 118.

[33]Ibid., pp. 69–70.

[34]R. TAVENEAUX, *Jansénisme* (see note 30 above), p. 41.

[35]Ibid., p. 43.

[36]*Pascal*, 2 vols. (Paris, 1949–54).

[37]*Le Dieu caché* (Paris, 1955) (ET: *The Hidden God*, London, 1962).

[38]Ibid., especially pp. 115–57.

[39]R. MOUSNIER, *La vénalité des offices sous Henri IV et Louis XIII* (Paris, 1946); and 'Le conseil du Roi, de la mort de Henri IV à l'avènement du gouvernement personnel de Louis XIV' (The King's Council, from the death of Henri IV to the start of the personal rule of Louis XIV), in *Études d'Histoire moderne et contemporaine*, 1947–8.

[40]M. CROUZET, article in *Nouvelle Critique* No. 70.

[41]J. DELUMEAU, *Naissance* (see Part I, chap. 1, note 1), pp. 275–80.

[42]R. MANDROU, 'Tragique XVIIe siècle' (The tragic seventeenth century), in *Annales Econ. Soc. Civil.* 1957, pp. 305–13.

[43]R. TAVENEAUX, *Jansénisme* (see note 30 above), p. 21.

[44]R. MANDROU, loc. cit., p. 308.

[45]*Pascal* (see note 36 above), I, p. 53.

[46]Ibid., p. 41.

[47]Ibid., p. 55.

[48]Ibid., p. 80.

[49]H. MARROU, *St Augustine* (see note 12 above), p. 171.

[50]Cf. H. GOUHIER, *La philosophie de Malebranche et son expérience religieuse* (Paris, 1926).

[51]Letter to M. Daudin, loyally quoted by H. LEFEBVRE, *Pascal* (see note 36 above), II, p. 244.

[52]Ibid., I, p. 92.

[53]Letter to M. Daudin, ibid., II, p. 246.

[54]*Histoire* (see Part I, chap. 2, note 64), IV.

[55]J. ORCIBAL, *Les origines* (see note 2 above), II, pp. 595–685, and *Saint Cyran* (ibid.), pp. 114–7.

[56]1607–64, a disciple of Vincent de Paul, and then confessor to the Port–Royal nuns for nearly twenty years.

[57]*Le Dieu caché* (see note 37 above), pp. 212–4.

[58]*L'abbé Le Roy* (see note 8 above).

[59]A development discussed by L. COGNET in the introduction to his edition of the *Provincial Letters* (Paris, 1965), p. lxvii.

[60]L. GOLDMANN, *Le Dieu caché* (note 37 above), pp. 347–447.

[61]Cf. B. PLONGERON, 'Une image' (see note 10 above), pp. 248–68.

[62]M. JOIN-LAMBERT (see Part I, chap. 2, note 14), 1953, pp. 247–74; 1955, pp. 35–49.

[63]Cf. J. MAHUAS, *Le diocèse de Vannes et le Jansénisme*, 2 vols., cyclostyled (Rennes, 1967).

[64]*Le Jansénisme en Lorraine 1640–1789* (Paris, 1960).

[65]Henri Grégoire, French ecclesiastic and statesman, first at the University of Nancy and then as parish priest of Emberménil adopted Gallican, Jansenist and presbyterian views which were current in several regions of Lorraine after the suppression of the Jesuits: ibid., pp. 714–20.

[66]E. APPOLIS, *Le Jansénisme dans le diocèse de Lodève;* 'A travers le XVIIIe siècle: entre Jansénistes et Constitutionnaires, un tiers parti', *Annales Econ. Soc. Civil.* 1951, pp. 154–71.

[67]P. JANSEN, *De Blaise Pascal à Henry Hammond: les 'Provinciales' en Angleterre* (Paris, 1954).

[68]A. de LA GORCE, *Wesley, maître d'un peuple* (Paris, 1940).

[69]M. VAUSSARD, *Jansénisme et gallicanisme aux origines religieuses du Risorgimento* (Jansenism and Gallicanism at the religious origins of the Risorgimento) (Paris, 1959). The French Jansenist library of Scipione de'Ricci, Jansenist bishop of Pistoia, is given in *Revue d'Histoire de l'Église de France*, 1967, pp. 292–9.

[70]On Jansenism in Italy, besides the works mentioned by M. VAUSSARD (see previous note), cf. P. STELLA, *Giuridizionalismo et Giansenismo all'università di Torino nel secolo XVIII°* (Juridicism and Jansenism at the University of Turin in the eighteenth century) (Turin, 1958), and especially Nuove ricerche storiche sul Giansenismo' (New historical researches on Jansenism), in *Analecta gregoriana* 1954, LXXI, 1.

[71]In *Revue historique* 1938, pp. 46ff.

[72]E. APPOLIS, *Le 'tiers parti' catholique au XVIIIe siècle* (The Catholic 'Third Party' in the eighteenth century) (Paris, 1960); *Les Jansénistes espagnols* (The Spanish Jansenists) (Bordeaux, 1966).

[73]'Third party' members, like Amort, did not hesitate to dispute with strict Jansenists.

[74]C. COZZI, *Il doge Contarini* (Rome–Venice, 1958).

[75]Cf. P. CHAUNU, 'Jansénisme et frontière de catholicité' (Jansenism and the frontiers of Catholicism), in *Revue historique* 227 (1962), p. 116.

[76]L. CEYSSENS, *Sources* (see note 5 above), introd.

[77]Cf. A. BONNAR, 'The English Franciscans and Jansenism', *Clergy Review* 1931, pp. 122–32; A. de SERENT, 'Les Frères Mineurs en face du Jansénisme 1607–1754' (The Friars Minor and Jansenism), *Études franciscaines* 1951, 213–39, 321–33.

[78]This is the sentiment of the Oratorian LE VASSOR in his *Traité de la veritable religion* (Treatise on the true religion): cf. A. LATREILLE, *Histoire* (see note 17 above), II, p. 446.

[79]P. CHAUNU, 'Jansénisme et frontière de catholicité' (see note 75 above), p. 133; cf. V. DURAND, *Le Jansénisme au XVIIIe siècle et Joachim Colbert évêque de Montpellier 1698–1738* (Toulouse, 1907).

[80]For a bibliography of these sociological studies, see the following chapter, and P. CHAUNU's article in the previous note, pp. 121–2.

[81]Ibid., p. 123, note 1.

CHAPTER TWO (p. 129)

[1]This has been understood by the editors of the new collection *Histoire des diocèses de France*, the first volume of which, *Le diocèse de Marseille*, by J. R. PALANQUE, appeared in 1968 (Paris). It is no longer a 'history of bishops and bishoprics', but a history of the whole Christian people.

[2]Cf. H. DESROCHE, *Sociologies religieuses* (Paris, 1968), and the Groupe de Sociologie des Religions in *Archives de Sociologie des Religions* 1969, pp. 3–92.

[3]In 1912 he published a book called *Les formes élémentaires de la vie religieuse: le système totémique en Australie*.

[4]'Statistique et histoire religieuses. Pour un examen détaillé et pour une explication historique de l'état du catholicisme dans les diverses régions de France' (Religious statistics and religious history. Towards a detailed examination and historical explanation of the state of Catholicism in the different regions of France), *Rev. d'Hist. de l'Église de France*, October 1931, pp. 425–49.

[5]G. LE BRAS, *Études de sociologie religieuse,* 2 vols (Paris, 1955–6).

[6]Y. DANIEL–L. GODIN, *La France, pays de mission* (Paris, 1943).

[7]*Problèmes missionaires de la France rurale,* 2 vols 1945; *Essor ou déclin du clergé français* (The rise or fall of the French clergy) (Paris, 1950); *Premiers itinéraires en sociologie religieuse* (First steps in religious sociology) (Paris, 1954).

[8]G. LE BRAS, *Études* (see note 5 above), II, p. 767.

[9]Ibid, II, p. 490.

[10]P. de GRANDMAISON, *La religion personnelle* (Paris, 1930), pp. 7–8.

[11]G. LE BRAS, *Études,* II, p. 416.

[12]Cf. *Année Sociologique,* Vol. V, p. 189, and Vol. VII, pp. 217–9.

[13]G. LE BRAS, loc. cit., II, p. 774.

[14]Cf. E. CALLOT, *L'histoire et la géographie au point de vue sociologique* (History and geography from a sociological point of view) (Paris, 1957).

[15]These remarks are in G. LE BRAS, loc cit., II, p. 777. Cf. also W. HELLPACH, *Grundriss der Religionspsychologie* (Outline of the Psychology of Religion) (Stuttgart, 1951).This is an extreme position: the sociological school dependent on M. Mauss identifies the mental with the social, psychological formulation being merely the translation of a properly sociologial structure: cf. M. MAUSS, *Sociologie et anthropologie* (introduction by C. LÉVI-STRAUSS) (Paris, 1966 ed.), especially pp. 285–309.

[16]R. MANDROU, *Introduction à la France moderne* (Paris, 1961); *Magistrats et sorciers en France au XVIIe siècle. Une analyse de psychologie historique* (Paris, 1968).

[17]P. ARIES, *L'enfant et la vie familiale sous l'Ancien Régime* (Paris, 1967).

[18]M. FOUCAULT, *Folie et déraison. Histoire de la folie à l'âge classique* (Paris, 1961) (ET: *Madness and Civilization,* London, 1971).

[19]A seminar under M. MOLLAT at the Sorbonne was dedicated to the theme of poverty: cf. *Rev. d'Hist. de l'Église de France* 1966, pp. 6–27: 'Recherches sur la pauvreté' (Researches into poverty).

[20]J. TOUSSAERT, *Le sentiment religieux en France à la fin du Moyen Age* (Religious feeling in France at the end of the Middle Ages) (Paris, 1963).

[21]L. PÉROUAS, *Le diocèse* (see Part I, chap. 2, note 28).

[22]J. FERTÉ, *La vie religieuse* (see ibid., note 11).

[23]J. TOUSSAERT, *Le sentiment* (note 20 above), mainly pp. 122–95.

[24]R. MOLS, 'Emploi et valeur des statistiques en histoire religieuse' (Use and value of statistics in religious history), in *Nouvelle Revue Théologique* 86 (1964), pp. 388–410.

[25]R. MOLS, loc. cit. p. 409.

[26]Despite the reservations judiciously presented by R. SAUZET in his *Les visites pastorales dans le diocèse de Chartres pendant la première moitié du XVIIe siècle* (Pastoral visitations in the diocese of Chartres during the first half of the seventeenth century), cyclostyled (Sorbonne, 1970).

[27]G. LE BRAS, *Études* (see note 5 above), I, pp. 101–2.

[28]*Storia* (see Part I, chap. 2, note 3), VIII, pp. 441–2.

[29]*Storia della Compagnia di Gesù in Italia* (History of the Company of Jesus in Italy), 3 vols (Rome, 1951²).

[30]'Studi e problemi relativi all'applicazione del concilio di Trento in Italia' (Studies and problems concerning the application of the Council of Trent in Italy), *Rivista Stor. Ital.* 70 (1958), pp. 239–98.

[31]*Gli atti della visita di S. Carlo Borromeo a Bergamo 1576* (The acta of St Charles Borromeo's visitation to Bergamo in 1576), 6 vols. (Milan, 1936–49).

[32]M. F. MELLANO, *La Controriforma della diocesi di Mondovì* (The Counter-Reformation in the diocese of Mondovì) (Turin, 1955); F. CHABOD, *Per la storia*

religiosa dello stato di Milano (Towards the religious history of the state of Milan) (Bologna, 1938), has drawn on pastoral visitations, pp. 33–41.

[33]J. VITEZIĆ, *La prima visita apostolica posttridentina in Dalmazia nell'anno 1579* (The first post-Tridentine apostolic visitation in Dalmatia, 1579) (Rome, 1957).

[34]L'histriographie contemporaine du Catholicisme en France' (Contemporary historiography of Catholicism in France), in *Mélanges P. Renouvin*, pp. 23–32.

[35]G. LE BRAS, *Études*, I, pp. 203–7, and J. GADILLE, D. JULIA and M. VENARD, 'Pour un répertoire des visites pastorales' (Towards an inventory of pastoral visitations), *Annales Econ. Soc. Civil.* 1970, pp. 561–6.

[36]These dossiers deal notably with the parishes of Paris, Chartres, Rheims, Amiens, Châlons, Sens, Auxerre, Lyons, Langres, Autun, Mâcon, Tarentaise, Moutiers, Grenoble, Die, Besançon, Saint-Claude, Gap, Grasse, Vence, Nîmes, Alès, Avignon, Toulouse, Rodez, Mende, Limoges, Clermont, Bordeaux, Périgueux, Rouen, Coutances, Sées, Nantes, Tréguier, Léon, Quimper.

[37]Under current analysis on the initiative of P. CHAUNU.

[38]Similarly R. SUAUDEAU, *L'évêque inspecteur administratrif sous la monarchie absolue, d'après les archives du centre de la France* (The administrative inspecting bishop under the absolute monarchy, according to the archives of central France) (Paris, 1940); and T.–J.SCHMITT, *L'organisation* (see Part I, chap. 2, note 35).

[39]"Le contrôle canonique de la vie chrétienne dans le diocèse d'Auxerre sous Louis XIV' (Canonical control of the Christian life in the diocese of Auxerre under Louis XIV), in *Études* (see note 5 above), I, pp. 38–53.

[40]"L'état religieux du diocèse de Châlons au dernier siècle de l'Ancien Régime' (The religious state of the diocese of Châlons in the last century of the Ancien Régime), ibid., I, pp. 54–68.

[41]"La pratique religieuse dans le diocèse de Rouen sous Louis XIV' and 'de 1707 à 1789', *Annales de Normandie* 1953, pp. 247–74 and 1955, pp. 35–49.

[42]"Les moeurs des laïques au diocèse de Sées sous l'épiscopat de Mgr d'Aquin 1699–1710'(Lay mores in the diocese of Sées during the episcopate of Mgr d'Aquin), *Revue d'Histoire de l'Église de France* 1955, pp. 235–92. Cf. also M. L. ROSTAGNET, 'Les visites pastorales de Mgr C. de Neufville dans le diocèse de Lyon au XVIIe siècle', *Cahiers d'Histoire* 1960, and R. SAUZET, *Les visites pastorales dans le diocèse de Chartres pendant la première moitié du XVIIe siècle* (Pastoral visitations in the diocese of Chartres during the first half of the seventeenth century), cyclostyled (Paris, 1970). For his excellent work *Amiens, capitale provinciale, étude sur la société urbaine au XVIIe siècle* (Amiens, provincial capital, a study in urban society in the seventeenth century) (Paris, 1967), P. DEYON used the records of episcopal visitations in the city and its suburbs.

[43]G. LE BRAS, *Études* (see note 5 above), I, p. 203.

[44]G. JEANTON–E. MAURIANGE, 'Les archives ecclésiastiques de l'Ancien Régime, source de folklore', *Revue du Folklore français* 1941.

[45]Cf. *Revue d'Histoire de l'Église de France* 1963, p. 244.

[46]J. FERTÉ, *Saint-Étienne-du-Mont à la mi-XVIIe siècle. Mémoires d'un curé génovéfain* (Saint-Étienne-du-Mont in the mid-seventeenth century. The memoirs of a canon regular of St Genevieve), cyclostyled.

[47]H. PLATELLE, *Journal d'un curé de campagne au XVIIe siècle* (Diary of a seventeenth-century country priest) (Paris, 1965).

[48]M. DOMMANGET, *Le curé Meslier, athée, communiste et révolutionnaire sous Louis XIV* (The curé Meslier, atheist, communist and revolutionary under Louis XIV), (Paris, 1965). A typical diary of an *English* country priest might be *The Diary of Benjamin*

Rogers, rector of Carlton 1720–1771, Bedfordshire Historical Record Society, 1950.
[49]H. PLATELLE, *Journal* (see note 47 above), pp. 76–7.
[50]Ibid., p. 114.
[51]Ibid., p. 139.
[52]But cf. the remarks of C. BERTHELOT DU CHESNAY, 'Le clergé diocésain français au XVIIIe siècle et les registres d'insinuations ecclésiastiques' (The French diocesan clergy in the eighteenth century and the ecclesiastical registers of promotions, appointments and translations), *Revue d'Histoire moderne et contemporaine* October–December 1963, pp. 241–69.
[53]These are used for example by E. de MOREAU in Vol. V of his *Histoire* (see Part I, chap. 2, note 27), pp. 275ff.
[54]A. ARTONNE, *Répertoire des statuts synodaux des diocèses de l'ancienne France* (Catalogue of the synodal statutes of the dioceses of ancient France) (Paris, 1963).
[55]E. DIEBOLD, *La pratique religieuse d'après les statuts synodaux du IVe concile du Latran au concile de Trente* (Religious practice according to the synodal statutes from Lateran IV to Trent), cyclostyled thesis, E.P.H.E.
[56]S. POTONNIÉE, *Recherches sur les confrèries sous l'Ancien Régime* (Research into confraternities under the Ancien Régime according to the synodal statutes), typescript thesis (Paris, 1960).
[57]C. PIVETEAU, *La pratique matrimoniale en France d'après les statuts synodaux (du concile de Trente à la Révolution),* typescript thesis (Paris, 1957).
[58]See note 54 above.
[59]Eg. L. VERBIRIOU, *Jean-François de La Marche, évêque-comte de Léon 1729–1806* (Paris-Quimper, 1924); X. AZEMA, *Un prélat janséniste: Louis Foucquet, évêque et comte d'Agde (1656–1702)* (Paris, 1923). Shorter monographs on French bishops of the seventeenth and eighteenth centuries are mentioned in the already quoted works of L. PÉROUAS, *Le diocèse* (see Part 1, chap. 2, note 28), J. FERTÉ, *La vie* (ibid., note 11), T.–J. SCHMITT, *L'organisation* (ibid., note 35), and in L. WELTER, *La réforme ecclésiastique du diocèse de Clermont au XVIIe siècle* (Paris, 1955). See also the recently published histories of Bordeaux and Besançon: B. POCQUET DU HAUT-JUSSÉ, 'Les évêques de Bretagne dans la Renaissance religieuse du XVIIe siècle' (The Breton bishops in the religious renaissance of the seventeenth century), *Annales de Bretagne* 54 (1947), pp. 30–59, and M. LÈVRE, *Louis-François Gabriel d'Orléans de La Motte* (1638–1744) (Abbeville, 1962). For Corsica: F. J. CASTA, *Evêques et curés corses dans la tradition pastorale du concile de Trente (1570–1620),* n.p., 1964: the spirit of St Charles was predominant here.
[60]2 vols. (Paris, 1956).
[61]Under the title *L'évêque dans la tradition pastorale du XVIe siècle* (Bruges, 1953).
[62]See Part I, chap. 1, note 13.
[63]Nine volumes of the *Collection des pouillés* (Collection of polyptychs) have been published so far. The latest one, *Pouillés de la province de Bourges,* 2 vols. (Paris, 1961–2), was edited by J. de FONT-RÉAUX.
[64]Preface to the work mentioned in the previous note.
[65]See p. 00 below.
[66]*Les paysans* (see Part I, chap. 2, note 57), I, pp. 474–80.
[67]The diocesan registrar (a royal official) transcribed from day to day the letters of ordination (from tonsure to priesthood), the acquisitions of benefices, the mandates to resign them at the Roman court, the notifications and reiterations of university grades to the ecclesiastical patrons of benefices etc. These registers are particularly numerous for the dioceses of Bayeux, Lisieux and Saint-Malo.

[68]For information on the material position of the clergy, see the already quoted works of T.–J. SCHMITT, J. FERTÉ and L. PÉROUAS (see note 59 above). Cf. also M. E. VIVIER, 'La condition du clergé séculier dans le diocèse de Coutances au XVIIIe siècle', *Annales de Normandie* 1952, pp. 3–27; C. H. GIRAUT, 'L'aisance du curé sarthois à la fin de l'Ancien Régime' (The affluence of the curé in the Sarthe at the end of the Ancien Régime), in *La Province du Maine* 1953, and *Les biens de l'Église de la Sarthe à la fin du XVIIIe siècle* (The wealth of the Church in the Sarthe at the end of the eighteenth century) (Laval, 1953); J. BINDET, 'La vie d'un curé de campagne de basse Normandie au XVIIIe siècle' (The life of a country curé in lower Normandy in the eighteenth century), in *Revue de l'Avranchin* 1953; A. SCHAER, *Le clergé catholique en Haute-Alsace sous l'Ancien Régime 1648–1789* (Paris, 1966); D. JULIA, 'Le clergé paroissial dans le diocèse de Reims à la fin du XVIIIe siècle' (The parish clergy in the diocese of Rheims at the end of the eighteenth century), *Revue d'Histoire mod. et contempt.* 1966.

[69]F.-Y. BERNARD, *Souvenirs d'un nonagénaire* (Paris, 1880), I, p. 70, quoted by C. BERTHELOT DU CHESNAY, 'Le clergé' (see note 52 above), p. 254.

[70]*Introduction aux études d'histoire ecclésiastique locale*, III (Épreuves de l'Église de France aux XVIe siècle) (Paris, 1936): III, pp. 353–95.

[71]Ibid., p. 354.

[72]H. DENIFLE, *La guerre de Cent Ans et la désolation des églises, monastères et hôpitaux de France*, 2 vols (Paris, 1899).

[73]J. FERTÉ, *La vie* (see Part I, chap. 2, note 11), pp. 77ff.

[74]Cf. for example ibid., p. 85, note 68.

[75]The inventory for the canton of Carhaix was published in 1970 under the editorship of A. MUSSAT.

[76]Two examples of studies on the veneration of saints: B. KLEINSCHMIDT, *Die heilige Anna, ihre Verehrung in Geschichte, Kunst und Volkstum* (St Anne: her veneration in history, art and popular devotion) (Düsseldorf, 1930); L. d'ANCONA, *The iconography of the Immaculate Conception in the Middle Ages and early Renaissance* (Princeton, 1955).

[77]Eg. M.-C. LE ÑEVÉ, *Le culte des saints dans les cantons de Châteauneuf-du-Faou, Carhaix, Mael-Carhaix, Gourin, Le Faouet du XVe siècle, au XVIIIe siècle*, thesis (Rennes, 1969).

[78]Cf. particularly M. LEPROUX, *Dévotions et saints guérisseurs. Contribution au folklore charentais* (Devotions and healing saints. A contribution to the folklore of Charente) (Paris, 1957); *Saint Roch dans l'art et le folklore en haut Limousin et basse Marche* (St Roch in the art and folklore of upper Limousin and lower Marche), Bellac 1964 (an index preceded by an interesting study by J. DECANTER); J. FOURNÉE, *Le culte des saints dans le canton de Flers* (Flers, 1961). On French folklore in general, see especially A. VAN GENNEP, *Manuel de folklore français contemporain* (Manual of contemporary French folklore), 12 vols. (Paris, 1943–58); and P. SÉBILLOT, *Le folklore de France*, 4 vols. (Paris, 1968²).

[79]On the miracles recorded in the diocese of Lille in the seventeenth century, cf. H. PLATELLE, *Les chrétiens devant le miracle* (Paris, 1968).

[80]Cf. for the methodology here, P.-A. SIGAL, 'Maladie, pèlerinage et guérison au XIIe siècle: les miracles de saint Gilrien à Reims' (Illness, pilgrimages and cures in the twelfth century: the miracles of St Gilrien at Rheims), *Annales Econ. Soc. Civil.* 1969, pp. 1522–39.

[81]In the periodical *Gure Henia*: G. REICHER, 'Le sens du sacré chez les Basques', 1961, pp. 282–6; 1962, pp. 1–18, 285–311, 321–8. Cf. also M. PERRUSQUI, *La*

religion des Basques; esquisse historique (The religion of the Basques: a historical outline) (Bayonne, 1964).

[82]*Revue de Psychologie des Peuples,* 1948, study by F. STROWSKI.

[83]Ibid., 1950 (HARDY).

[84]Ibid., 1951 (LECHANTEUR).

[85]M. VENARD, 'Les missions des Oratoriens d'Avignon aux XVIIe et XVIIIe siècles', *Revue d'Histoire de l'Église de France* 1962.

[86]L. PÉROUAS, 'Saint L.-M. Grignion de Montfort', in *XVIIe siècle* 41 (1958), pp. 393–4. Another recent study on missions in seventeenth-century France: C. BERTHELOT DU CHESNAY, *Les missions de saint Jean Eudes* (Paris, 1968).

[87]L. PÉROUAS, 'Le nombre des vocations sacerdotales est-il un critère valable en sociologie religieuse historique aux XVIIe et XVIIIe siècles' (Is the number of vocations to the priesthood a valid criterion in historical religious sociology for the seventeenth and eighteenth centuries?), *Actes de LXXXVIIe Congrès national des Sociétés savantes* (*Hist. Mod.*), *de Poitiers,* 1962 (Paris, 1963), pp. 35–40.

[88]L. PÉROUAS, *Le diocèse* (see Part I, chap. 2, note 28), particularly the maps on p. 501.

[89]L. PÉROUAS, 'Le nombre' (see note 87 above), and 'Problèmes de sociologie religieuse', *Revue du bas Poitou* 1961, pp. 1–12.

[90]J. FERTÉ, *La vie* (see Part I, chap. 2, note 11), p. 59, note 171. On the question of recruitment to the priesthood, cf. also D. JULIA, 'Le clergé paroissial dans le diocèse de Reims à la fin du XVIIIe siècle', *Revue d'Histoire moderne et contemporaine* 1966; and M. VENARD, 'Recherches sur le recrutement sacerdotal dans la province d'Avignon au XVIe siècle', *Annales Econ. Soc. Civil.* 1968.

[91]*Acta* of the International Congress of historical sciences (Rome, 1955), p. 364.

[92]Cf. L. PÉROUAS, *Fr Hacquet. Mémoire des missions des Montfortains dans l'Ouest 1740–1779* (Fontenay-le-Comte, 1964).

[93]Cf. *Histoire de Languedoc* (general editor P. WOLFF) (Toulouse, 1967), pp. 197–204, 313–9.

[94]One of the facets of the German peasants' revolts in 1524–5.

[95]V. CARRIÈRE, *Introduction* (see note 70 above), III, pp. 287–352.

[96]Cf. *Histoire* (see Part I, chap. 1, note 4), XIX/1, pp. 84, 124; and R. TAVENAUX (see chap. I above, note 64), p. 570.

[97]M. DEFOUREAUX, *L'inquisition espagnole et les livres français au XVIIIe siècle* (Paris, 1963).

[98]A. CORVISIER, in his work on *L'armée française de la fin du XVIIe siècle au ministere de Choiseul* (The French army from the end of the seventeenth century to the ministry of Etienne duke of Choiseul, 1761–70) (Paris, 1964), concludes that 'the army and the Church are two worlds which seldom meet'.

[99]E. HAMBYE, *L'Aumônerie de la flotte de Flandre au XVIIe siècle 1623–1622* (The chaplaincy of the Flemish fleet in the seventeenth century) (Louvain-Paris, 1967).

[100]See Part I, chap. 2, note 53.

[101]M. FLEURY–L. HENRY, *Nouveau manuel de dépouillement et d'exploitation de l'état civil ancien* (New manual of the despoiling and exploitation of the old civil state) (Paris, 1965).

[102]A. VAN DER WOUDE–G. J. MENTINK, 'La population de Rotterdam au XVIIe et au XVIIIe siècle', *Population* 1966, pp. 1165–90.

[103]Cf. H. BERGUES–P. ARIES. *La prévention des naissances dans la famille. Ses origines dans les temps modernes* (Birth control in the family. Its origins in modern times) (Paris, 1960).

[104]For his excellent study on Valladolid, *Valladolid au siècle d'or* (Valladolid in the golden age) (Paris, 1967), B. BENNASSAR checked the parish registers, and tried in this way to define the religious attitudes of the people. The same goes for P. DEYON, *Amiens* (see note 42 above).

[105]C. GINZBURG's book, *I Benandanti* (The Benandanti) (Turin, 1966), shows just what can be done with the Inquisition investigations and trials.

[106]In seventeenth-century Mexico, the average number of condemnations per year rose from 250–300 in 1765–81 to 1023 in 1782–7 (years of serious agricultural crisis): P. N. F. MARTIN, *Los vagabundos en la Nueva España* (Mexico City, 1957).

[107]On criminality, see particularly P. DEYON, 'Mentalités populaires: un sondage à Amiens au XVIIe siècle' (Popular mentalities: a sounding at Amiens in the seventeenth century), *Annales Econ. Soc. Civil.* 1962, pp. 448–58, and the researches of P. CHAUNU, 'De la violence au vol; en marche vers l'escroquerie' (From violence to theft; the path to fraud), *Annales de Normandie* 1962, pp. 235–62; H. MOREL, 'La fin du duel judiciaire en France' (The end of legal duelling in France), *Revue d'Histoire du Droit français et étranger* 1964, pp. 594–639; F. BILLACOIS, 'Pour une enquête sur la criminalité dans la France d'Ancien Régime', *Annales Econ. Soc. Civil.* 1967, pp. 340–50.

[108]P. DEYON, 'Mentalités' (see previous note).

[109]R. MANDROU, *De la culture populaire en France aux XVIIe et XVIIIe siècles. La bibliothèque bleue de Troyes* (Popular culture in France in the seventeenth and eighteenth centuries. The Troyes Blue Library) (Paris, 1964).

[110]The exemplary study is L. FEBVRE–H. J. MARTIN, *L'apparition du livre* (The emergence of the book) (Paris, 1958). Cf. also D. POTTINGER, *The French Book Trade in the Ancient Régime* (New York, 1958); A. DUPRONT, *Livre et société dans la France du XVIIIe siècle* (The book and society in eighteenth-century France) (Paris, 1965); M. VENTRE, *L'imprimerie et la librairie en Languedoc dans le dernier siècle de l'Ancien Régime 1700–1789* (Printing and publishing in Languedoc during the last century of the Ancien Régime) (Paris, 1958); J. QUÉNIART, *L'imprimerie et la librairie à Rouen au XVIIIe siècle 1701–1789* (Printing and publishing at Rouen in the eighteenth century) (Paris, 1969); H. J. MARTIN, *Livre* (see Part I, chap. 2, note 67).

[111]For French printed works, apart from the books mentioned in the previous note, see: A. KOLB, *Bibliographie des französischen Buches im 16. Jahrhundert* (Bibliography of French books in the sixteenth century) (Wiesbaden, 1966); A. CIORANESCU, *Bibliographie de la littérature française du XVIe siècle* (Paris, 1959); *Bibliographie de la littérature française du XVIIe siècle,* 3 vols. (Paris, 1965–8); *Bibliographie de la littérature française du XVIIIe siècle,* 3 vols. (Paris, 1970).

[112]On the themes of Bossuet's preaching, see J. TRUCHET, *La prédication de Bossuet,* 2 vols. (Paris, 1960).

[113]A tentative study on the books of the New Testament will be found in R. MORGENTHALER, *Statistik des Neutestamentlichen Wortshatzes* (Statistics of the treasury of words in the New Testament) (Zürich, 1958).

CHAPTER THREE (p. 154)

[1]This quotation and the two following are from P. ADAM, *La vie paroissiale en France au XIVe siècle* (Parish life in France in the fourteenth century) (Paris, 1964), pp. 155–6.

[2]Ibid., p. 152.

Y. DURAND, *Cahiers de doléances des paroisses du bailliage de Troyes pour les états généraux de 1614* (Paris, 1966), pp. 87–8.
Ibid., p. 205.
P. ADAM, *La vie* (note 1 above), p. 156.
Ibid., p. 157.
Nouvelle Histoire de l'Église (see Part I, chap. 4, note 7), III, p. 34.
P. ADAM, *La vie* (note 1 above), p. 152.
Ibid., p. 153.
J. TOUSSAERT, *Le sentiment* (see chap. 2 above, note 20), p. 571.
J.LESTOCQUOY, *La vie religieuse d'une province. Le diocèse d'Arras* (Arras, 1949), p. 59.
According to Mme C. ÉTIENNE (thesis, directed by P. Riché, Rennes).
J. TOUSSAERT, loc. cit., p. 561.
J. MINARD, *La vie religieuse dans le diocèse de Sens dans le deuxième moitié du XVe siècle*, Sorbonne thesis, 1966, p. 71.
N. COULET, 'La désoation des églises de Provence à la fin du Moyen Age', *Provence historique* 1956, pp. 34–52, 123, 141.
V. CHOMEL, 'Droit de patronage et pratique religieuse dans l'archévêché de Narbonne au début du XVe siècle' (The right of patronage and religious practice in the archbishopric of Narbonne in the early fifteenth century), *Bibliothèque de l'Ecole des Chartes* 1957, pp. 58–138.
E. de MOREAU, *Histoire* (see Part I, chap. 2, note 27), IV, p. 202.
G. LE BRAS, *Études de sociologie religieuse*, 2 vols (Paris, 1955–6), II, p. 505.
L. PÉROUAS, *Le diocèse* (see Part I, chap. 2, note 28), pp. 194–6.
J. VITEZIĆ, *La prima visita* (see chap. 2 above, note 33), p. 19.
E. CATTA, 'Les évêques de Nantes des débuts du XVIe siècle aux lendemains du concile de Trente' (The bishops of Nantes from the early sixteenth century to the aftermath of the council of Trent), *Revue d'Histoire de l' Église de France*, 1965, p. 67.
Histoire de l'Église (see Part I, chap. 1, note 4), p. 313. And for the good German bishops of the fifteenth century, cf. J. JANSSEN, *L'Allemagne et la Réforme* (Germany and the Reformation), 9 vols (Paris, 1887–1914), I, p. 554.
J. TOUSSAERT, *Le sentiment* (chap. 2 above, note 20), p. 554.
Still, the English bishop Richard Foxe (1448–1528) confessed towards the end of his life: 'Of four cathedral churches of which I have gained successive possession, two, Exeter and Wells, I never see, and there are countless souls whose bodies I never see. If I should live for another twenty years I could do never do enough penance.'
In J. TOUSSAERT, loc. cit., p. 565.
Cf. A. DODIN, *Saint Vincent de Paul et la charité* (Paris, 1960), p. 22.
Quoted by P. ADAM (see note 1 above), pp. 147–8.
Le sentiment (chap. 2 above, note 20), pp. 69–82, 564–82.
Ibid., p. 72.
Although G. LE BRAS contested the legend of the Christian Middle Ages some years ago: 'Déchristianisation: mot fallacieux' (Dechristianization: a deceptive word), in *Cahiers d'Histoire* IX/1, 1964, pp. 92–7.
L'Allemagne (see note 22 above), I, p. 574.
Cf. O. DOBIACHE–ROJDESTVENSKY, *La vie paroissiale en France au XIIIe siècle* (Paris, 1911).
From the French of L. FEBVRE, *Un destin: Martin Luther* (Paris, 1968 ed.), p. 51.
R. MANDROU, 'Spiritualité et pratique catholiques au XVIIe siècle', *Annales Econ. Soc. Civil.* 1961, p. 142.

251

35 Antoine de SAINT–ANDRÉ(alias Fr VERJUS), *Vie de Michel Le Nobletz*, 1666, Bk V, chap. 3. I have to thank Mme Petitjeans for bringing this text to my notice: E. PETITJEANS, *La sorcellerie en Bretagne aux XVIIe et XVIIIe siècles* (Sorcery in Brittany in the seventeenth and eighteenth centuries), thesis (Rennes, 1969).

36 C. GINZBURG, *I Benandanti* (see chap. 2 above, note 105), includes an important bibliography on German witchcraft.

37 E. DELCAMBRE, *Le concept de sorcellerie dans le duché de Lorraine* (The concept of witchcraft in the duchy of Lorraine), 3 vols (Nancy, 1948), III, p. 149.

38 Ibid.

39 For France, cf. especially A. VAN GENNEP, *Manuel* (see chap. 2 above, note 78), and P. SEBILLOT, *Le folklore* (ibid.).

40 Cf. G. LE BRAS, *L'Église et le village* (Paris, 1972).

41 C. BERTHELOT DU CHESNAY, *Les missions* (see chap. 2 above, note 86), p. 114.

42 M. LEPROUX, *Dévotions* (see chap. 2 above, note 78), pp. 222–39.

43 A. LOTTIN, *Vie et mentalité d'un Lillois sous Louis XIV* (Lille, 1968) p. 282.

44 G. WELTER, *Les croyances primitives et leurs survivances* (Primitive beliefs and their present-day vestiges) (Paris, 1960), pp. 62–3.

45 Cf. *Macbeth*, Act IV, sc. 1.

46 A. VAN GENNEP, *Manuel* (see chap. 2 above, note 78), IV/1, p. 1637.

47 Ibid., p. 1734.

48 Ibid., p. 1855–60.

49 Ibid., p. 1948.

50 Cf. P. SÉBILLOT, *Le folklore de la Bretagne* (The folklore of Brittany),2 vols (Paris, 1968 ed.).

51 Cf. H. MARROU, *St Augustine* (see chap. 1 above, note 12), p. 92.

52 H. PLATELLE, *Les chrétiens* (see chap. 2 above, note 79), pp. 48 and 62; and J. FERTÉ, *La vie* (see Part I, chap 2, note 11), p. 299.

53 R. VAULTIER, *Le folklore pendant la guerre de Cent Ans d'après les lettres de rémission* (Folklore during the Hundred Years War according to the Letters of remission) (Paris, 1965), pp. 77–8.

54 E. DELCAMBRE, *Le concept* (see note 37 above), II, pp. 48–51.

55 M. LEPROUX, *Dévotions* (see chap. 2 above, note 78), pp. 61–2.

56 E. DELCAMBRE, loc. cit., II, pp. 49–50.

57 J. FERTÉ, loc. cit., p. 339.

58 Ibid., p. 338.

59 E. LE ROY–LADURIE, *Histoire du climat depuis l'an mil* (History of the climate since the year 1000) (Paris, 1967), pp. 155–6.

60 G. LE BRAS, *Études* (chap. 2 above, note 5), I, p. 245, note 1; Doubs archives G 121 and 122.

61 H. MAISONNEUVE, 'La morale d'après les conciles des Xe et XIe siècles' (Morality according to the councils of the tenth and eleventh centuries), in *Mélanges de sciences religieuses* XVIII, pp. 3–4.

62 J. DUMORTIER, 'Le sens du péché chez les Grecs au Ve siècle' (The sense of sin among the Greeks of the fifth century), ibid., XVII, p. 38.

63 P. VILLETTE, 'La sorcellerie à Douai', ibid., XVIII, p. 129.

64 J. EHRARD, in *Satan* (Études Carmélitaines) (Paris, 1948), p. 376.

65 Ibid.

66 This and the two following items of information in E. ESMONIN, *Études sur la France des XVIIe et XVIIIe siècles* (Paris, 1964), p. 339. The principal work on witchcraft in France is now that of R. MANDROU, *Magistrats* (see chap. 2 above,

note 16). For Germany, J. JANSSEN, *L'Allemagne* (see note 22 above), especially Vol. VIII; J. HANSEN,*Zauberwahn, Inquisition und Hexenprozess im Mittelalter und die Entstehung der grossen Hexenverfolgung* (Witchcraft, the Inquisition and witch-trials in the Middle Ages and the rise of the great witchhunts) (Munich–Leipzig, 1900), and *Quellen und Untersuchungen zur Geschichte des Hexenwahns und der Hexenver-folgung im Mittelalter* (Sources and researches in the history of witchcraft and medieval witchhunts) (Bonn, 1901); N. PAULUS, *Hexenwahn und Hexenprozesse, vornehmlich im 16. Jahrhundert* (Witchcraft and witchhunts, especially in the sixteenth century), 1910; H. ZWETSLOOT, *Fr. Spee und die Hexenprozesse* (Fr. Spee and the witchtrials), 1954. For Italy, M. PETROCCHI, *Esorcismi e magia nell'Italia del cin-quecento e del seicento* (Exorcisms and magic in Italy in the sixteenth and seventeenth centuries) (Naples, 1957), and C. GINZBURG, *I Benandanti* (see chap. 2 above, note 105). For Spain, H. C. LEA, *A history of the Inquisition in Spain,* 4 vols (New York, 1907); S. CIRAC ESTOPANAN, *Los processos de hechiceria en la Inquisición de Castilla* (Witchtrials in the Inquisition of Castille) (Madrid, 1942); F. IDOATE, *Hispania sacra,* 1951, pp. 193–218. For England, B. ROSEN, *Witchcraft* (London, 1970). Cf. also H. R. TREVOR–ROPER, *The European Witch-craze of the 16th and 17th Centuries* (Harmondsworth, 1967, 1969).

[67]P. CHAUNU, *La civilisation de l'Europe classique* (Paris, 1966), pp. 485–6.

[68]The *Instructio pro formandis processibus in causis strigum, malificiorum et sor-tilegiorum* (Instruction for the institution of trials to judge witches, practitioners of the black arts and soothsayers), published by the Holy Office in about 1620, helped to limit the number of witch-trials and condemnations in Italy: cf. C. GINZBURG, *I Benandanti* (see chap. 2 above, note 105), p. 135.

[69]Quoted by J. JANSSEN, *L'Allemagne* (note 22 above), VIII, p. 554.

[70]Ibid., VIII, p. 695.

[71]Cf. H. BARUK, *Psychiatrie morale, expérimentale, individuelle et sociale,* Paris 1945, pp. 256–77.

[72]Quoted E. DELCAMBRE, *Le concept* (note 37 above), III, p. 213.

[73]Ibid.

[74]Cf. G. WELTER, *Les croyances* (note 44 above), pp. 13, 98–9.

[75]M. MAUSS, *Sociologie* (see chap. 2 above, note 16), p. 15.

[76]Ibid.

[77]A counter-proof is that where judges did not believe in witchcraft, or not much, ac-cusations against wizards and witches subsided. Cf. R. AUBENAS, *La sorcière et l'In-quisiteur; épisode de l'Inquisition en Provence 1439* (The witch and the Inquisitor: an episode in the Inquisition in Provence) (Aix-en-Provence, 1956).

[78]J. BODIN, *Démonomanie des sorciers* (Paris, 1580), p. 6R.

[79]Ibid., p. 152R.

[80]*Traité des energumènes* (1599), chap. 2, in *Oeuvres complètes du cardinal de Bérulle* (1644).

[81]Cf. R. MANDROU, *Magistrats* (see chap. 2 above, note 16), pp. 197ff.

[82]An anonymous book published in 1581, the *Cabinet du Roy de France,* mentions seventy-two princes and 7,405,920 demons at Satan's beck and call.

[83]P. VILLETTE, 'La sorcellerie' (note 63 above), p. 166.

CHAPTER FOUR (p. 175)

[1]*Le parfait missionnaire, ou la vie du R. P. Julien Maunoir,* 1697, Bk. 3, p. 214.

[2]J.-B. THIERS, *Traité des superstitions selon l'Écriture sainte, les décrets des conciles*

et les sentimens des Saints Pères et des Théologiens (Treatise on superstition according to Holy Scripture, council decrees and the doctrine of the Holy Fathers and Theologians) (Paris, 1679); *Traité des superstitions qui regardent tous les sacramens* (Treatise on superstitions about all the sacraments), 3 vols (Paris, 1703–4).

[3]T.-J. SCHMITT, *L'organisation* (see Part I, chap. 2, note 35), p. 183.

[4]J. FERTÉ, *La vie* (see ibid., note 11), pp. 219–20.

[5]T.-J. SCHMITT, loc. cit., p. 217.

[6]For the struggle against paganism in the sixteenth and seventeenth centuries, cf. K. THOMAS, *The Decline of Magic* (London, 1971).

[7]A. VAN GENNEP, *Manuel* (see chap. 2 above, note 78), IV/1, 2, p. 1426.

[8]M. LOUIS, *Le folklore et la danse* (Paris, 1963), p. 143.

[9]A. VAN GENNEP, loc. cit., p. 1624.

[10]Ibid., pp. 1663–4.

[11]M. LOUIS, loc. cit., p. 79.

[12]A. VAN GENNEP, loc. cit., p. 1818.

[13]On religious pamphlets against the fires of St John, cf. H. J. MARTIN, *Livre* (see Part I, chap. 2, note 67), II, p. 796.

[14]Ibid., p. 1741.

[15]J. B. BOSSUET, *Catéchisme de Meaux*, p. 267, reprinted in A. BERTRAND, *La religion des Gaulois* (Paris, 1897), pp. 115–6, and in A. VAN GENNEP, loc. cit., pp. 1818–9.

[16]*Instruction populaire touchant l'origine et la façon de faire le feu de la Nativité de saint Jean-Baptiste pour en oster les abus et les superstitions*, in a *Receuil de divers traitez concernant l'office des Prestres* (Collection of divers treatises on the office of priests), National Library D. 49744, and reprinted in A. VAN GENNEP, loc. cit., pp.1818–9.

[17]*L'organisation* (Part I, chap. 2, note 35), p. 181.

[18]Cf. J. EHRARD, *L'idée de nature en France dans la première moitié du XVIIIe siècle*, 2 vols (Paris, 1963), I, pp. 27–38.

[19]There are some excellent comments on the *Aufklärung* in *Nouvelle Histoire* (see Part I, chap. 4, note 7), IV, pp. 137–62, and a bibliography on pp. 508–9 and 518–9. Cf. in particular C. SCHREIBER, *Aufklärung und Frömmigkeit* (Enlightenment and Piety) (Munich, 1940), and L.-A. VEIT–L. LENHART, *Kirche und Volksfrömmigkeit im Zeitalter des Barock* (Church and popular piety in the Baroque) (Freiburg, 1956).

[20]Basically the works of L. PÉROUAS, J. FERTÉ and T.-J. SCHMITT already quoted.

[21]Y. DURAND, *Cahiers* (see chap. 3 above, note 3), p. 140.

[22]On the mediocrity of the Parisian clergy in the first half of the seventeenth century, see the remarks of Fr. Beurrier in H. J. MARTIN, *Livre* (see Part I, chap. 2, note 67), I, pp. 42–3.

[23]E. de MOREAU, *Histoire* (see Part I, chap. 2, note 27), V, pp. 319–25.

[24]Ibid., V, pp. 321–5.

[25]L.-V. PASTOR, *Storia* (see Part I, chap. 2, note 3), VIII, p. 131.

[26]Y. DURAND, loc. cit., p. 113.

[27]Quoted in F. CHABOD, *Per la storia religiosa* (see chap. 2 above, note 32), p. 34, note 1.

[28]E. de MOREAU, loc. cit., V, p. 324.

[29]F. LEBRUN, *Cérémonial* (see Part I, chap. 2, note 17), p. 98.

[30] See p. 137.

[31]Cf. *Histoire de l'Eglise* (see Part I, chap. 1, note 4), XIX, p. 48, note 2, and G. MARZOT, *Un Classico della contrariforma: Paolo Segneri* (Palermo, 1950).

[32]E. REYERO, *Misiones del M. R. P. Tirso Gonzalez de Santalla* (Santiago, 1913).

[33] Article 'Ansalone' in the *Dict. d'Hist. et Géogr. ecclés.*, III, col. 1328.

[34] C. BERTHELOT DU CHESNAY, *Les missions* (see chap. 2 above, note 86), p. 98.

[35] F. LOIDL, *Abraham a Sancta Clara. Ueber das religiös-sittliche Leben in Oesterreich 1670–1710* (Abraham of St Clare. On religious and moral life in Austria) (Vienna, 1939).

[36] G. GUASTI, *Vita di san Leonardo da Porto-Maurizio* (Milan, 1951).

[37] P. CHARTON, *Saint Alphonse de Liguori* (Paris, 1947).

[38] On missions in seventeenth-century France, cf. especially 'Missionnaires' (see Part I, chap. 2, note 42), pp. 299–395, and on the missions of St Jean Eudes, C. BERTHELOT DU CHESNAY, *Les missions* (see chap. 2 above, note 86).

[39] V. BOUCARD, 'Un poète réaliste et satirique: saint Grignion de Montfort', *Bulletin de la Soc. Archéol. et Hist. de Nantes et de la Loire-Inférieure*, 1952, p. 109.

[40]

Popular songs	Hymns on them
Tu croyais en aimant Colette	Noël des âmes spirituelles
Ma maîtresse est jolie	Le véritable dévôt de Marie
Passons la lande, ma Jeanne, ma Jeanne	L'amour de Dieu
Mon père, mariez-moi	L'aiguillon de la ferveur
Enfin, je suis amoureux	L'âme délivrée du purgatoire
Un canard étendant ses ailes	Les souffrances de la sainte Vièrge
Je ne sais si je suis ivre	Invocation au Saint-Esprit
Amis, buvons à tasse pleine	Notre-Dame des dons
Un de nos pauvres ivrognes est malade	Abandon à la Providence
Bon, bon, bon, que le vin est bon	L'estime et le désir des vertus
Paie chopine, ma voisine	Le remède spécifique de la tiédeur

[41] C. BERTHELOT DU CHESNAY, loc. cit., p. 99.

[42] Ibid., map 6.

[43] L. ABELLY, *La vie du vénérable serviteur de Dieu, Vincent de Paul* (Paris, 1664), II, pp. 12–3.

[44] 'Missionnaires' (see note 38 above), p. 326.

[45] Ibid., p. 320. On mission literature, cf. H. J. MARTIN, *Livre* (see note 13 above), II, p. 795.

[46] *Le sentiment* (see chap. 2 above, note 20), pp. 102–4.

[47] Ibid., p. 201.

[48] Ibid., especially pp. 160–95.

[49] A. LOTTIN, *Vie et mentalité d'un Lillois sous Louis XIV* (Lille, 1968), p. 231.

[50] J. TOUSSAERT, loc. cit., pp. 124–5.

[51] M. JOIN-LAMBERT, *La pratique* (see Part I, chap. 2, note 14), p. 251.

[52] On the works spread by the neo-Gallican liturgy, cf. H. J. MARTIN, *Livre* (see note 13 above), II, pp. 778–9.

[53] It was not until 1695 that a royal edict dispensed the priest from announcing the 'acts of justice and other acts regarding the people's interests' from the pulpit.

[54] Cf. *S. Petri Canisii Catechismus*, ed. F. STREICHER, 2 vols (Munich, 1933–6).

[55] E. de MOREAU, *Histoire* (see Part I, chap. 2, note 27), V, p. 345.

[56] Catechisms began rolling off the French printing-presses in significant numbers in about 1640. In the second half of the seventeenth century they were published in copious quantities, but most of them were for catechists to use as a basis for their lessons: H. J. MARTIN, loc. cit., II, p. 789.

[57] Cf. Y. POUTET, *Le XVIIe siècle* (see Part I, chap. 3, note 39).

[58] I. IMBERCIADORI, 'Spedale, scuola e chiesa in popolazioni rurali dei secoli

XVI–XVII' (Hospitals, schools and churches in rural populations of the 16th–17th century), *Economia e Storia* 1959, pp. 436–7.

[59]See references in note 19 above.

CHAPTER FIVE (p. 203)

[1]P. HAZARD, *La crise de la conscience européenne*, 3 vols (Paris, 1935) (ET: *The European Mind 1680–1715*, London, 1958).

[2]R. CHARBONNEL, *La pensée italienne au XVIe siècle et le courant libertin* (Italian thought in the sixteenth century and the free-thinking current) (Paris, 1917); R. BUSSON, *Les sources et le développement du rationalisme dans la littérature française de la Renaissance*, 1957[2]; B. NARDI, *Saggi sull'aristotelismo padovano dal secolo XIV al XVI* (Studies in Paduan Aristotelianism from the fourteenth to the sixteenth century (Florence, 1958).

[3]*Doctrine curieuse des beaux esprits de ce temps.*

[4]*Impiété des déistes, athées et libertins renversée et confondue.*

[5]This *Testament*, which was for years in manuscript form, was known to Voltaire and Holbach, who both published extracts from it.

[6]On the question of unbelief in France in the seventeenth century, cf. R. PINTARD, *Le libertinage érudit dans la première moitié du XVIIe siècle* (Erudite free-thinking in the first half of the seventeenth century), 2 vols (Paris, 1943).

[7]Cf. E. LABROUSSE, *Pierre Bayle*, 2 vols (La Haye, 1963).

[8]Cf. J. EHRARD, *L'idée* (see chap. 4 above, note 18), I, esp. p. 88.

[9]Cf. R. POMEAU, *La religion de Voltaire* (Paris, 1956).

[10]Loc. cit., p. 139.

[11]Ibid., p. 175.

[12]P. L. de MAUPERTUIS, *Essai de cosmologie* (Berlin, 1750), Foreword, pp. 22–3.

[13]Cf. J. EHRARD, loc. cit.; E. GUYÉNOT, *Les sciences de la vie aux XVIIe et XVIIIe siècles* (The sciences of life in the seventeenth and eighteenth centuries) (Paris, 1941).

[14]R. MAUZI, *L'idée du bonheur en France au XVIIIe siècle* (The notion of happiness in eighteenth-century France) (Paris, 1968).

[15]*Méthode facile pour être heureux en cette vie et assurer son bonheur éternel.* For what follows, see R. MAUZI, loc. cit., pp. 180–216.

[16]*Les charmes de la société du mondain.*

[17]The quotations which follow are taken from R. MAUZI, loc. cit., p. 205.

[18]L. J. ROGIER, in *Nouvelle Histoire de l'Église* (see Part I, chap. 4, note 7), IV, p. 53.

[19]Quoted in F. VALSECCHI, *L'Italia nel Settecento* (Italy in the eighteenth century) (Milan, 1959), p. 593.

[20]M. JOIN-LAMBERT, 'La pratique' (see Part I, chap. 2, note 14), 1955, p. 40.

[21]M.-L. FRACART, *La fin de l'Ancien Régime à Niort, Essa de sociologie religieuse* (Paris, 1956), p. 43.

[22]Cf. P. CHEVALLIER, *Loménie de Brienne et l'ordre monastique 1766–1789*, 2 vols (Paris, 1959–60).

[23]For the latter, cf. F. DREYFUS, *Sociétés et mentalités à Mayence dans la seconde moitié du XVIIIe siècle* (Paris, 1968), pp. 287–93.

[24]For Josephism, cf. V.-L. TAPIÉ, *Monarchiue et peuples du Danube* (Paris, 1969), pp. 243–7, and the bibliography given on p. 462.

[25]Cf. M. AGULHON, *Pénitents et Francs-Maçons dans l'ancienne Provence* (Penitents and Free Masons in old Provence) (Paris, 1968), pp. 67–161.

[26]Cf. S. HUTIN, *Les Francs-Maçons* (Paris, 1960); A. MELLOR, *Nos frères séparés,*

les Francs-Maçons (Tours, 1961); P. CHEVALLIER, *Les ducs sous l'acacia* (Paris, 1964); J. BAYLOT, *Dossier français de la Franco-Maçonnerie régulière* (Paris, 1965).

[27]This condemnation was probably at the instigation of the pretender James III Stuart, because Freemasonry tended to be a political instrument in the hands of the government in London.

[28]On the Martinist milieu, cf. A. FAIVRE, 'Un martinésiste catholique: l'abbé Pierre Fournié', *Revue d'Hist. relig.* 1965, pp. 33–172.

[29]M. AGULHON, *Pénitents* (see note 25 above), p. 191.

[30]Abbeville, 1962. Cf. also L. KERBIRIOU, *Jean-François de La Marche, évêque-comie de Léon 1729–1806* (Quimper–Paris, 1924).

[31]*Les luttes politiques et doctrinales aux XVIIe et XVIIIe siècles*, Vols XIX/1 and 2 of the *Histoire de l'Église* (FLICHE-MARTIN) (Paris, 1955–6).

[32]He was born at Avignon in 1704, gained his doctorate in theology at Paris, and was bishop of Saint-Malo from 1739 to 1767.

[33]Departmental Archives, Ille-et-Vilaine, GG 187, folio 4. I have to thank Mlles Brigardis and Durand, MM. Gauvrit and Rauxel, who have made a special study of the demography of Saint-Malo from 1751 to 1800, for bringing this document to my attention.

[34]*La fin* (see note 21 above), pp. 101–2.

[35]*P. Fr. Hacquet, Mémoire des missions des Montfortains dans l'Ouest 1740–1779* (Fontenay-le-Comte, 1964).

[36]'La pratique' (see note 20 above), 1955, pp. 37–8.

[37]A. de TOCQUEVILLE, *L'Ancien Régime et la Révolution*, ed. MAYER (Paris, 1952), II, pp. 172–3. I have to thank Fr Frémaux for drawing my attention to this text.

[38]*Histoire de la Bretagne* (symposium) (Toulouse, 1969), p. 437 (contribution of J. MEYER).

[39]*Nouvelle Histoire* (see Part I, chap. 4, note 7), IV, p. 157; V.-L. TAPIÉ, *Monarchie* (see note 24 above), p. 243.

[40]Cf. B. PLONGERON, 'L'*Aufklärung* catholique en Europe occidentale, 1770–1830', in *Revue d'Hist. mod. et contemporaine* 1969, pp. 555–606.

[41]M. JOIN-LAMBERT, 'La pratique' (see Part I, chap. 2, note 14), 1955, pp. 35–6; D. JULIA (see chap. 2 above, note 90), pp. 201–2; F. DREYFUS (see note 23 above), p. 505.

[42]B. PLONGERON, *Les reguliers de Paris*, pp. 63ff, 306. There was also a very important growth in the Foreign Missions seminary: *Histoire de l'Église*, XIX/2, p. 560.

[43]For all that follows, cf. G. LE BRAS, *Études de sociologie religieuse* (Paris, 1955), I, pp. 25, 56, 60, 202–5, 245–7.

[44]Cf. also J. VINOT-PRÉFONTAINE, 'Sanctions prises dans l'ancien diocèse de Beauvais aux XVIIe siècle contre les réfractaires du devoir pascal (vers 1662–1664)', *Revue d'Hist. de l'Église de France* 1959, pp. 79–84.

[45]G. LE BRAS, loc. cit., I, p. 246.

[46]Ibid., pp. 276–7.

[47]This is confirmed by Jeanne FERTÉ, *La vie* (see Part I, chap. 2, note 11).

[48]Ibid., pp. 269–70.

[49]M. JOIN-LAMBERT, loc. cit. (note 41 above), 1955, pp. 269–70.

[50]Many of the faithful preferred low mass at a neighbouring convent to the long high mass at the parish church.

[51]*Premiers itinéraires* (see chap. 2 above, note 7), pp. 44–6.

[52]L. PÉROUAS, *P.Fr.Hacquet* (see note 35 above), p. 67.

[53]Ibid., p. 28.

[54]Ibid., p. 39.
[55]Ibid., p. 28.
[56]Ibid., pp. 65–6.
[57]Ibid., p. 37.
[58]Ibid., p. 21.
[59]Ibid., p. 37.
[60]Ibid., p. 41.
[61]G. LE BRAS (see note 43 above), I, p. 59.
[62]Ibid., pp. 64–5.
[63]A MOLINIER, *Une paroisse du bas Languedoc, Sérignan, 1650–1792*, (Montpellier, 1968), pp. 130–5.
[64]Cf. on this the pertinent remarks of R. RÉMOND, 'Recherche d'une méthode d'analyse historique de la déchristianisation depuis le milieu du XIXe siècle' (Research into a method of historical analysis for dechristianization since the mid-nineteenth century), *Colloque d'Histoire religieuse* (Lyons, 1963): *Cahier d'Histoire* IX/1, 1964.
[65]Cf. R. PINTARD, *Le libertinage érudit* (Erudite free-thinking) (Paris 1943), p. 29, and H. BUSSON, *La pensée religieuse de Charron à Pascal* (Paris, 1933), pp. 36–7.
[66]Text in A. ADAM, *Les libertins au XVIIe siècle* (Free-thinkers in the seventeenth century) (Paris, 1964), pp. 112–3.
[67]Cf. D. MORNET, *Les origines intellectuelles de la Révolution française* (Paris, 1953), p. 53.
[68]Ibid.
[69]Ibid.
[70]Ibid.
[71]G. LE BRAS, *Études* (see note 43 above), I, p. 62, note 2.
[72]Ibid., p. 278.
[73]M. JOIN-LAMBERT, 'La pratique' (see note 41 above), 1955, p. 48.
[74]Note 25 above.
[75]In addition to the references given in notes 41 and 42 above, see A. SCHAER, *Le clergé* (see chap. 2 above, note 68), pp. 100–3.
[76]New studies might modify this outline in its details: for example, M.-L. FRACART (note 21 above), p. 88, calculates some 100 ordinations in Niortais between 1710 and 1750, and more than 140 from 1750 to 1790.
[77]'Le clergé' (see chap. 2 above, note 90), pp. 200–3.
[78]Ibid., p. 202.
[79]R. MOLS, *Introduction à la démographie historique des villes d'Europe du XIVe au XVIIIe siècle*, II, 1955, p. 303.
[80]These and the preceding figures ibid., p. 304.
[81]Ibid., p. 300.
[82]Ibid.
[83]I should like to thank the young researchers who worked out these figures: Mme Creff and Mlle Régent (1651–1700), Mlles Pancarte, Quilleré and Rannou (1701–50), Mlles Brigardis et Durand, MM Gauvrit and Rouxel (1751–1800).
[84]The preceding figures are from R. MOLS, loc. cit., p. 302.
[85]*Sociétés* (see note 23 above), p. 254.
[86]P. CHAUNU, *La civilisation de l'Europe classique*, pp. 196–200.
[87]*L'enfant* (see chap. 2 above, note 17), and (with others) *La prévention* (ibid., note 103).

[88]*Anciennes familles genevoises* (Ancient Genevan families) (Paris, 1956), p. 76.

[89]There was also a drop at Saint-Malo: 4.3 per family in 1651–1700; 4.2 in 1701–50; 3.4 in 1751–1800.

[90]J. T. NOONAN, *Contraception* (see Part I, chap. 2, note 72), pp. 367–70.

[91]These two quotations are from P. ARIES, *La prévention* (see note 87 above), p. 318.

[92]Ibid.

[93]*Recherches et considérations sur la popolation de la France,* 1778, quoted ibid.

[94]Quoted by P. ARIES, loc. cit., p. 318.

[95]Ibid., pp. 227–8.

[96]E. GAUTIER–L. HENRY, *La popolation de Crulai, paroisse normande.* (Paris, 1958), p. 19. Did voluntary birth control begin outside the towns before the Revolution? This question is being discussed and studied. Cf. A. CHARMOUX–C. DAUPHIN, 'La contraception avant la Révolution francaise: l'example de Châtillon-sur-Seine', *Annales Econ. Soc. Civil.* 1969, pp. 662–84; J. DUPAQUIER–M. LACHIVER, 'Les débuts de la contraception en France ou les deux malthusianismes', ibid. 1969, pp. 1391–1406.

[97]M. FLEURY–P. VALMARY, 'Les progrès de l'instruction élémentaire en France de Louis XIV à Napoléon III' (Growth in elementary schooling in France from Louis XIV to Napoleon III), *Popolation* 1957, pp. 71–92.

[98]G. LE BRAS, *Études* (see note 43 above), I, p. 64.

[99]'La fin' (see note 21 above), p. 79.

[100]Cf. F. BOULARD, *Premiers itinéraires* (see chap. 2 above, note 7), p. 49: 'Were all the dioceses of France (and, we may add, of the Catholic world) seriously evangelized? And what was the quality of the Christianity preached?'

[101]L. FEBVRE, *Le problème de l'incroyance au XVIe siècle* (The problem of unbelief in the sixteenth century), 1968², pp. 307–27.

[102]*Cahiers d'Histoire* 1964, IX/1, pp. 92–7.

[103]B. PASCAL, *Opuscule XVIII.*

[104]I am very grateful to J. QUÉNIART for giving me these statistics, which condense the results of his *L'imprimerie* (chap. 2 above, note 110). A similar table would have been welcome in M. VENTRE's *L'imprimerie* (ibid.).

[105]J. Quéniart includes under this heading books of piety and theology, works of canon law and Church history.

[106]L. PÉROUAS, *Le diocèse* (see Part I, chap. 2, note 28), p. 450.

[107]Ibid., p. 470.

[108]Quoted in C. CARRIÈRE, *Marseille ville morte, la peste de 17820* (Marseilles, 1968), p. 199.

[109]Ibid.

[110]*Discours sur ce qui s'est passé de plus considérable à Marseille pendant la contagion,* quoted in C. CARRIÈRE, loc. cit., p. 200.

[111]Ibid., p. 201.

[112]Ibid.

[113]Cf. M. MARTINI, *Fausto Socino et la pensée socinnienne* (Paris, 1967), pp. 77, 115–7.

[114]Quoted in A. ADAM, *Les libertins* (note 66 above), pp. 91–4. Cf. also D. P. WALKER, *The Decline of Hell. Seventeenth Century Discussion of Eternal Torment* (Chicago, 1964).

[115]The 'invention' referred to is the doctrine according to which humanity was condemned to hell because of the first sin.

[116]VOLTAIRE, *Dictionnaire philosophique,* ed. R. POMEAU (Paris, 1964), p. 310.

ABBREVIATIONS

AESC	*Annales (Economies. Sociétés. Civilisations).*
DHGE	*Dictionnaire d'histoire et de géographie ecclésiastiques.*
DSAM	*Dictionnaire de spiritualité ascétique et mystique.*
DTC	*Dictionnaire de théologie catholique.*
HC	*Histoire des conciles* (RICHARD & MICHEL, formerly HEFELE & LECLERCQ).*
HE	*Histoire de l'Eglise* (FLICHE & MARTIN).*
LTK	*Lexikon für Theologie und Kirche.*
NHE	*Nouvelle Histoire de l'Eglise* (ROGER, AUBERT & KNOWLES).*
NRTh	*Nouvelle Revue théologique.*
RH	*Revue historique.*
RHE	*Revue d'Histoire ecclésiastique.*
RHEF	*Revue d'Histoire de l'Eglise de France.*
RHMC	*Revue d'Histoire moderne et contemporaine.*
RSI	*Rivista storica italiana.*
HP	*History of the Popes.*

SOURCES

The main relevant documents in the perspective of traditional historical studies are listed in volume VII/1 (by E. PRÉCLIN and V.-L. TAPIÉ) and volume VII/2 (by E. PRÉCLIN) of the *Clio* series (published by Presses Universitaires of Paris); *L'Histoire de l'Eglise* by A. FLICHE and V. MARTIN, vols. XVII, XVIII, XIX/1 and 2, and especially vol. XVIII by L. WILLAERT; *L'Histoire de l'Eglise* by C. BIHLMEYER and H. TÜCHLE, which offers exhaustive bibliographies at the end of volumes III and IV. Traditional religious history has relied to a considerable degree on the correspondence of nuncios and bishops with Rome. The Vatican has a vast archive of *Lettere di vescovi e prelati* from 1595 to 1797. See in this regard J. BATELLI, 'Le ricerche storiche nell 'archivo vaticano' in the *Relazioni* of the ICHSR, 1955 (Florence, 1955), I, pp. 451–77. An entire chapter (the second chapter of Part II) of the present book is devoted to various kinds of documentation which can aid the progress of the sociology of religion and the study of collective attitudes towards and in interaction with belief. Records of pastoral visitations take pride of place among such documents. In France a systematic research project is under way which is concerned to tabulate and collate references to pastoral visitations in the *Catalogue générale des manuscripts des bibliothèques publiques*, the 'inventaires sommaires' and 'répertoires numeriques' for series G and H, local archives ('archives communales et hospitalieres'), and the printed catalogue of French and Latin manuscripts of the Bibliothèque Nationale (see J. GADILLE, D. JULIA & M. VENARD, 'Pour un repertoire des visites pastorales', in *AESC*, 1970, pp. 561–6). The bibliography that follows gives details of sources for (that is, the main works based on) pastoral visitations made in France in the seventeenth and eighteenth centuries, as well as similarly relevant sources for Italy, Germany and Switzerland.

Principal journals:

(a) Non-specialized: *Amercian Historical Review; Annales ESC; Bibliothèque d'Humanisme et Renaissance; XVIIc.; English Historical Review; Historische Zeitschrift; Revue belge de Philologie et d'Histoire; Revue historique; Revue d'Histoire moderne et contemporaine; Rivista storica italiana.*

(b) Specialized: *Archives de Sociologie des Religions; Church History; Concilium; Les Etudes; Nouvelle Revue théologique; Revue d'Ascétisme et de Mystique; Revista española de Teologia; Revue d'Histoire ecclésiastique; Revue d'Histoire de l'Eglise de France; Revue d'Histoire et de Philosophie religieuses; Rivista di Storia della Chiesa; Theologisch Literarzeitung; Zeitschrift für Theologie und Kirche.*

BIBLIOGRAPHY

A. *RELIGIOUS ENCYCLOPAEDIAS*

Catholic Encyclopedia (New York, 1913 ff).

Ciencia y Fe, S. Miguel (Argentine, 1945 ff).

Dictionnaire de Droit canonique (Paris, 1935 ff).

Dictionnaire d'Histoire et de Géographie ecclésiastiques (Paris, 1912 ff).

Dictionnaire de Spiritualité ascétique et mystique (Paris, 1937 ff).

Dictionnaire de Théologie catholique (Paris, 1923 ff).

Enciclopedia cattolica (Rome, 1929 ff).

Encyclopédie théologique de MIGNE (1844 ff).

Katholieke Encyclopaedie (Amsterdam, 1933 ff).

Kirchenlexicon (Freiburg, 1882 ff).

Lexikon für Theologie und Kirche (Freiburg, 1957² ff).

Religion in Geschichte und Gegenwart (Tübingen, 1957 ff).

Répertoire général des sciences religieuses (Rome, 1950 ff).

The Oxford Dictionary of the Christian Church (London & New York, 1957 ff).

B. *GENERAL*

(i) *THE REFORMATION BACKGROUND*

Histoire de l'Eglise (*HE*) FLICHE (A.)-MARTIN (V.), & JUROSELLE (J.-B.)-JARRY (E.): vol. XVI, *La crise religieuse du XVIe siècle*, MOREAU (E. de), JOURDA (P.) & JANELLE (P.), 1950; vol. XVII, *L'Eglise à l'époque du concile de Trente*, CRISTIANI (L.), 1948; vol. XVIII/1, *La restauration catholique, 1563–1648*, WILLAERT (L.), 1960; vols. XIX/1 & 2, *Les luttes politiques et doctrinales aux XVIIe et XVIIIe siècles*, PRÉCLIN (E.) & JARRY (E.), 1955–1956.

L'Histoire de l'Eglise, BIHLMEYER (C.)-TÜCHLE (H.), vols. III, *L'Eglise des temps modernes* & IV, *L'Eglise contemporaine* (Mulhouse, 1964–1967).

La *Nouvelle Histoire de l'Eglise* (*NHE*), vol. III, *Réforme et Contre-Réforme*, TÜCHLE (H.), BOUMAN (C. A.) & LEBRUN (J.), and vol. IV, *Siècle des Lumières, Révolutions, Restaurations*, ROGIER (L.-J.), BERTIER DE SAUVIGNY (G.), HAJJAR (J.) (Paris, 1966–1968); ET: *The Christian Centuries: A New History of the Catholic Church* (London, 1964 ff) but it has not reached these centuries yet.

The History of the Popes of L. VON PASTOR

1. GENERAL STUDIES BY COUNTRY

Germany

LAMPRECHT (K.), *Allgemeine Staatengeschichte* (Berlin, 1936).

GEBHARDT (B.), *Reformation bis zum Ende des Absolutismus* (Stuttgart, 1955²).

262

RÖSSLER (H.), *Europa im Zeitalter der Renaissance, Reformation und Gegenreformation (1450–1630)* (Munich, 1956).

HUBSCHMID (H.), *Die Neuzeit von der Renaissance bis zum Beginn der Aufklärung* (Erlenbach-Zürich, 1959).

HASSINGER (E.), *Das Werden des neuzeitlichen Europa (1300–1600)* (Brunswick, 1969).

HUBATSCH, *Das Zeitalter des Absolutismus* (Brunswick, 1962).

Britain and USA
Cambridge Modern History (vols. I to VI).
New Cambridge Modern History:
POTTER (G. R.), *The Renaissance, 1493–1520* (Cambridge, 1957).
ELTON (G. R.), *The Reformation Era, 1520–1559* (Cambridge, 1958).
CARSTEN (F. L.), *The Ascendancy of France, 1648–1688* (Cambridge, 1961).
Rise of modern Europe series:
GILMORE (M. P.), *The World of Humanism, 1453–1517* (New York, 1952).
FRIEDRICH (C. J.), *The Age of the Baroque, 1610–1660* (New York, 1953).
NUSSBAUM (F. L.), *The Triumph of Science and Reason, 1660–1685* (New York, 1953).

France
Clio series:
SÉE (H.) & RÉBILLON (A.), *Le XVIe siècle* (Paris, 1950²), vol. VI.
PRÉCLIN (Éd.) & TAPIÉ (V.-L.), *Le XVIIIe siècle* (Paris, 1949²), vol. VII/I.
PRÉCLIN (Éd.) & TAPIÉ (V.-L.), *Le XVIIIe siècle* (Paris, 2 vols., 1952²), vols. VII/2 and VII/3.
Les grandes civilisations series:
DELUMEAU (J.), *La civilisation de la Renaissance* (Paris, 1967).
CHAUNU (P.), *La civilisation de l'Europe classique* (Paris, 1966).
Peuples et civilisations series:
HAUSER (H.) & RENAUDET (A.), *Les débuts de l'âge moderne* (Paris, 1956²).
HAUSER (H.), *La prépondérance espagnole (1559–1660)* (Paris, 1948²).
SAGNAC (Ph.), *Louis XIV (1661–1715)*, (Paris, 1949²).
MURET (P.), *La prépondérance anglaise (1715–1763)* (Paris, 1949²).

Italy
Storia universale series:
BARBAGALLO (C.), *Età moderna*, 2 vol. (VI/1 et VI/2) (Turin, 1958²).
See also:
SPINI (G.), *Storia dell'età moderna dall'impero di Carlo Quinto all' illuminismo* (Rome, 1960).

2. CHURCH HISTORY
Germany
KIRSCH (J. P.), *Kirchengeschichte*, 4 vols. (Freiburg, 1930).
KRÜGER (G.), *Handbuch Kirchengeschichte für Studierende*, 4 vols. (Tübingen, 1923–1931²). Espiral III: HERMELINCK (H.) & MAURER (W.), *Reformation und Gegenreformation*.
PASTOR (L. von), *Geschichte der Päpste seit dem Ausgang des Mittelalters*, 16 vols. (Freiburg, 1886/1933).
TÜCHLE, *Geschichte der Kirche*, III: *Reformation und Gegenreformation* (Einsiedeln, 1965).

Britain etc
HUGHES (P.), *History of the Church*, 3 vols. (London, 1956²).
LATOURETTE (K. S.), *History of the Expansion of Christianity* (New York, 1939).
— *A History of Christianity* (London, 1954).
SCHAFF (P.), *History of the Christian Church*, 7 vols. (New York, 1916–1923).

Belgium and Low Countries
BAKHUIZEN VAN DEN BRINK (J. N.) & LINDEBOOM (J.), *Handbock der Kerkgeschiedenis*, 2 vols. (The Hague, 1942–1945²).
Histoire de l'Eglise, FLICHE–MARTIN & DUROSELLE–JARRY:
DELARUELLE (E.), LABANDE (E.R.), OURLIAC (P.), *L'Eglise au temps du Grand Schisme et de la crise conciliaire* (Paris, 1962).
AUBENAS (R.) & RICARD (R.), *L'Église et la Renaissance (1449–1517)* (Paris, 1951), XV.
DE MOREAU (E.), JOURDA (P) & JANELLE (P.), *La crise religieuse du XVIe siècle* (Paris, 1950), XVI.
CRISTIANI (L.), *L'Église à l'époque du Concile de Trente* (Paris, 1948), XVII.
WILLAERT (L.), *La restauration catholique (1563–1648)* (Tournai, 1960), XVIII.
PRÉCLIN (Éd.) et JARRY (E.), *Les luttes politiques et doctrinales aux XVIIe et XVIIIe siècles* (Paris, 1955), XIX.
Nouvelle Histoire de l'Eglise, vol. III: H. TÜCHLE, C. A. BOUMAN, J. LE BRUN, *Réforme et Contre-Réforme* (Paris, 1968).
DANIEL-ROPS, *L'Église de la Renaissance et de la Réforme* (Paris, 1955).
— *L'Église des temps classiques*: I. *Les grand siècle des âmes* (Paris, 1958); II. *L'ère des grands craquements* (Paris, 1958).
FARGUES (P.), *Histoire du Christianisme*, vols. III, IV & V (Paris, 1936–1938).
LÉONARD (É. G.), *Histoire générale du Protestantisme*: I. *La réformation*; II. *L'établissement* (Paris, 1961).

Italy
BONAIUTI (E.), *Storia del cristianesimo*, 3 vols. (Milan, 1943–1944²).
TODESCO (L.), *Corso di storia della Chiesa*, 5 vols. (Turin-Rome, 1944–1948²).

3. CAUSES OF THE REFORMATION; REFORMATION PERIOD

(a) *General studies*
AUGUSTIN (C.), *Erasmus en de Reformatie* (Amsterdam, 1962).
BAINTON (R. H.), *The Age of the Reformation* (Boston, 1956).
— *The Reformation of the XVIth century* (London, 1966).
BATAILLON (M.), *Érasme et l'Espagne: recherches sur l'histoire spirituelle du XVIe siècle* (Paris, 1937).
BORNKAMM (H.), *Das Jahrhundert der Reformation. Gestalten und Kräfte* (Göttingen, 1961).
BRAUDEL (F.), *La Méditerranée et le monde méditerranéen au temps de Philippe II*, 2 vols. (Paris, 1967²). ET: (London, 1975).
BOUETTE (E.), 'Satan', dans *Études carmélitaines*, 1948.
Colloque d'Histoire religieuse (Lyons, October 1963).
FEBVRE (L.), *Le problème de l'incroyance au XVIe siècle: la religion de Rabelais* (Paris, 1947²).
— *Au cœur religieux du XVIe* (Paris, 1957).

GRIMM (H. J.), *The Reformation Era, 1500–1650* (New York, 1954).

HYMA (A.), *The Christian Renaissance, a History of the 'Devotio Moderna'* (New York, 1924).

— *Renaissance to Reformation. A Critical Review of the Spiritual Influences on Medieval Europe* (Grand-Rapids, Mich., 1951).

IMBART DE LA TOUR (P.), *Les origines de la Réforme*: I. *La France moderne* (Paris, 1905, 1948²); II. *L'Église catholique. La crise et la renaissance* (1909, 1946²); III. *L'évangelisme (1521–1538)* (1914); IV. *Calvin et l'Institution chrétienne.*

JEDIN (H.), *Katholische Reformation oder Gegenreformation?* (Lucerne, 1946).

— *Geschichte des Konzils von Trent,* 2 vols. (Freiburg, 1949–1957).

MACKINNON (J.), *The Origins of the Reformation* (London & Toronto, 1939).

MESNARD (P.), *L'essor de la philosophie politique au XVIe siècle* (Paris, 1939).

MICHELET (J.), *Histoire de France,* vol. VIII: *La Réforme* (Paris, 1855).

RENAUDET (A.), *Préréforme et humanisme à Paris pendant les premieres guerres d'Italie (1495–1517)* (Paris, 1916).

— 'Erasme, sa vie et son œuvre jusqu'en 1517, d'apres sa correspondance', in *RH,* CXI (1912) and CXII (1913).

— *Érasme, sa pensée religieuse et son action d'après sa correspondance (1518–1521)* (Paris, 1926).

— *Études érasmiennes (1521–1529)* (Paris, 1939).

— *Humanisme et Renaissance* (Geneva, 1958).

RITTER (G.), *Die Weltwirkung der Reformation* (Leipzig, 1941; Munich, 1959²).

— *Die Neugestaltung Europas im XVI Jahrhundert* (Berlin, 1950).

TROELTSCH (E.), *Die Soziallehren der Christlichen Kirchen und Gruppen* (Tübingen, 1912).

(b) *Individual Studies (by country)*

Germany and Austria:

ANDREAS (W.), *Deutschland vor der Reformation* (Stuttgart, Berlin, 1932).

BRANDI (K.), *Die deutsche Reformation* (Leipzig, n.d.).

— *Der Augsbürger Religionsfriede* (Berlin, 1928).

— *Gegenreformation und Religionskriege* (Leipzig, 1930).

HAUCK (A.), *Kirchengeschichte Deutschlands,* 5 vols. (Leipzig, 1898–1920²).

JANSSEN (J.), *Geschichte des deutschen Volkes seit dem Ausgang des Mittelalters,* 8 vols. (Freiburg, 1878–1893); 1913–1917².

JOACHIMSEN (P.), et al, *Das Zeitalter der religiösen Umwälzung, 1500–1660* (Berlin, 1950²).

— *Die Reformation als Epoche der deutschen Geschichte* (Munich, 1951).

LORTZ (J.), *Die Reformation in Deutschland* (Freiburg, 1949²); ET: The Reformation in Germany, 2 vols. (London, 1968).

— *Die Reformation als religiöse Anliegen heute* (Trier, 1948).

— *Wie kam es zur Reformation?* 4 vols. (London–New York, 1925–1930).

MACKINNON (J.), *Luther and the Reformation,* 4 vols. (London–New York, 1915–1930).

RANKE (L.), *Deutsche Geschichte im Zeitalter der Reformation,* 6 vols. (Vienna, 1934²).

France:

'Les Protestants en France au XVIIe siècle', nos 76–77 of *XVIIe siècle,* 1967.

GEISENDORF (P. F.), *Liste des habitants de Genève (1549–1560),* I (Geneva, 1957); II (1963).

HAUSER (H.), *Études sur la Réforme française* (Paris, 1909).

— *La naissance du Protestantisme* (Paris, 1940).
JUNDT (A.), *Histoire résumée de l'Église luthérienne en France* (Paris, 1935).
LATREILLE (A.), DELARUELLE (E.), PALANQUE (J. R.), *Histoire du Catholicisme en France*, vol. II (Paris, 1960).
LEMONNIER (R.) & MARIÉJOL (J. H.), vols. V & VI of *Histoire de France*, E. LAVISSE (Paris, 1903, 1904).
LÉONARD (É. G.), 'Les origines de la Réforme en France', in *Calvin et la Réforme; Revue de théologie* (Fac. Théol. Aix) (1944; 1959²).
— *Le Protestant français* (Paris, 1955²).
LIVET (G.), *Les guerres de religion* (Paris, 1962).
MOURS (S.), *Le Protestantisme français au XVIe siècle* (Paris, 1967).
ROMIER (L.), *Les origines politiques des guerres de religion*, 2 vols. (Paris, 1913–1914).
— *Le royaume de Catherine de Médicis: la France à la veille des guerres de religion*, 2 vols. (Paris, 1922).
— *Catholiques et Huguenots à la cour de Charles IX* (Paris, 1924).
VIÉNOT (J.), *Histoire de la Réforme française des origines à l'Édit de Nantes* (Paris, 1926).

Britain:
CONSTANT (G.), *La Réforme en Angleterre: le schisme anglican: Henri VIII (1509–1547)* (Paris, 1930).
CHADWICK (O.), *The Reformation*, vol. III of the *Pelican History of the Church* (Harmondsworth, 1964).
CULKIN (G.), *The English Reformation* (London, 1954).
GAIRDNER (J.), *The English Church in the Sixteenth Century from the Accession of Henry VIII to the Death of Mary* (London, 1904), vol. IV of *History of the English Church*, ed. W. R. W. STEPHENS & W. HUNT.
GASQUET (F.), *The Eve of the Reformation* (London, 1900).
HUGHES (P.), *The Reformation in England*, 3 vols. (London, 1951–1954, 1963²).
— *Rome and the Counter-Reformation in England* (London, 1942).
JANELLE (P.), *Obedience in Church and State* (Cambridge, 1930).
— *L'Angleterre catholique à la veille du schisme* (Paris, 1935).
JORDAN (W. K.), *The Development of Religious Toleration in England*, 4 vols. (London, 1932–1940).
MAYNARD-SMITH (H.), *Prereformation in England* (London, 1938).
MOORMAN (J. H.), *A History of the Church of England* (London, 1953).
RUPP (E. G.), *Studies in the Making of the English Protestant Tradition* (Cambridge, 1947).
THOMPSON (A. H.), *The English Clergy and their Organization in the Later Middle Ages* (Oxford, 1947).
WOODHOUSE, *The Doctrine of the Church in Anglican Theology, 1547–1603* (New York, 1954).
BROWNE (P. H.), *History of Scotland*, 2 vols. (Cambridge, 1899–1902).
— *George Buchanan and his Time*, 2 vols. (Edinburgh, 1906).
BURLEIGH (J. H. S.), *A Church History of Scotland* (London, 1960).
DONALDSON (G.), *The Scottish Reformation* (Cambridge, 1960).

Low Countries:
AXTERS (S.), *Geschiedenis van de vroomheid in de Nederlanden*, vols. II & III (Anvers, 1952, 1953).

BLOK (P. J.), *Geschiedenis van het Nederlandsche Volk*, vols. III & IV (1923–1926³).
COLLINET (R.), *La Réformation en Belgique au XVIe siècle* (Verviers, 1947).
DE MOREAU (E.), *Histoire de l'Église en Belgique*, vols. IV & V (Louvain–Brussels, 1949–1952).
DE PATER (J.), *De tachtigjarige oorlog Geschiedenis van Nederland* (Amsterdam, 1936, vols. III & IV).
GEYL (P.), *The Revolt of the Netherlands, 1555–1609* (New York, 1958).
HALKIN (L. E.), *La Réforme en Belgique sous Charles Quint* (Paris, 1957).
— 'Les martyrologes et la critique. Contribution à l'étude du *martyrologe* protestant des Pays-Bas', in *Mélanges Meyoffer* (Lausanne, 1952).
LINDEBOOM (J.), *De confessioneele ontwikkeling der Reformatie in de Nederlanden* (The Hague, 1946).
MOREAU (G.), *Histoire du Protestantisme à Tournai jusqu'à la veille de la révolution des Pays-Bas* (Liège, 1962).
NAUTA (D.), *Het calvinisme in Nederland* (Francker, 1949).
PIRENNE (H.), *Histoire de Belgique* (Brussels, 1949), vol. II.
POST (R. R.), *Kerkelijke verhoundingen in de Nederland voor de Reformatie van 1500 tot 1580* (Utrecht, Anvers, 1954).
SHORT (R. G.), *Stories of the Reformation in the Netherlands* (Washington, 1948).
TOUSSAERT (J.), *Le sentiment religieux en Flandre à la fin du Moyen Age* (Paris, 1963).
VAN DER ESSEN, *Alexandre Farnèse ..., gouverneur général des Pays-Bas* (Brussels, 1937).
VAN DER ZEE, *Vaderlandsche Kerkeyeschiedenis*, vol. III: *Van de Hervorming tot heden* (Kampen, 1940).
VAN GELDER (H. A. Enno), *Revolutionnaire Reformatie. De vestiging van de gereformeerde Kerk in de Nederlandsche gewesten gedurende de eerste jaren van de opstand tegen Filips, 1575–1585* (Amsterdam, 1943).
VERHEYDEN (A.), *Le Conseil des troubles, 1567–1573* (Brussels, 1961).

Bohemia & Moravia:
BARTOS (Fr.), *Petr Chelcicky, duchovni otec Jednoty Bratrské* (Prague, 1958).
— *Husitska revoluce*, 2 vols. (Prague, 1965–1966).
DENIS (E.), *La fin de l'indépendance de Bohême*, 2 vols. (Paris, 1890).
KLIMA (A.), *Cechy v obdobi kmna* (Prague, 1958).
MACEK (J.), *Tabor v husitkem revolucnim Hnuti* (Prague, 1955²).
— *Jan Hus* (Prague, 1963).
MOLAR (A.), *Boleslavsti bratri, 1421–1627* (Prague, 1952).
RICAN (R.), *Dejiny jednoty bratrské* (Prague, 1957).
SUSTA (J.), 'Chroniques sur l'historiographie tchécoslovaque', in *RH*, 1925, pp. 67–73; 1933, pp. 86–101; 1938, pp. 281–294.
Vingt-cinq ans d'historiographie tchécoslovaque, 1936–1960 (Prague, 1960).
DE VOOGHT (P.), *L'hérésie de Jean Huss* (Louvain, 1960).

Poland and Baltic area:
BAMGART (J.) & MALEC (A.), *Bibliografia historii polskiej za rok 1961* (Warsaw, 1963).
DAVID (G.), *Le Protestantisme en Pologne jusqu'en 1570* (Paris, 1927).
FOX (P.), *The Reformation in Poland* (Baltimore, 1924).
KONIECKI (E.), *Geschichte der Reformation in Polen* (1904³).
S. KOT, 'L'humanisme et la Renaissance en Pologne', *BHR*, 1952 (XIV), pp. 39ff, 1953 (XV), pp. 233ff.

KRAUSE (G.), *Reformation und Gegenreformation in ehemaligen Koenigreich-Polen* (1905²).

POHRT (O.), *Zur Frömmigkeitsgeschichte Livlands zu Beginn der Reformationszeit* (Riga, 1925).

SZEKELI (G.) & FÜGEDI (E.), *La Renaissance et la Réformation en Pologne et en Hongrie, 1450–1650* (Budapest, 1963).

TAZBIR (J.), *Reformacja a problem chlopoki w Polsce XVI wieku* (1953).

— 'Recherches sur l'histoire de la Réforme en Pologne (1945–1948)' in *Acta Poloniae Historica*, vol. II, 1960.

Hungary and Transylvania:

KARACSONYI, *Kirchengeschichte Ungarns* (Nagyvarad, 1915).

KLANICZAY (T.), 'La Renaissance hongroise', in *BHR*, 1964, pp. 439–75.

SZABO (J. S.), *Der Protestantismus in Ungarn* (1927).

SZEKELY (G.) BALAZS (E.) & MAKKAI (L.), *History of Hungary*, I (to 1526), II (1526–1790) (Budapest, 1961–1962).

Mediterranean (Italy):

BUSCHBELLE (G.), *Reformation und Inquisition in Italien um die Mitte des XVI. Jahrhunderts* (Paderborn, 1910).

CHABOD (F.), *Per la storia religiosa dello stato di Milano durante il dominio di Carlo V* (Bologna, 1938).

Ginevra e l'Italia (Florence, 1959).

RODOCANACHI (E.), *La Réforme en Italie*, 2 vols. (Paris, 1921).

RUFFINI (Fr.), *Studi sui riformatori italiani* (Turin, 1955).

Spain:

ARTUS (W.), *Los reformadores españoles del siglo XVI y las bases biblicas de su polemica antiromanista* (Mexico City, 1949).

BATAILLON (M.), 'Alonzo de Valdès auteur du Dialogo de Mercurio y Caron', in *Homenaje a Menendez Pidal* (Madrid, 1925).

BOEHMER (Ed.), *Spanish Reformers of two Centuries from 1520*, 2 vols. (Strasbourg–London, 1874–1883).

LLORCA (B.), *Die spanische Inquisition und die Alumbrados, 1509–1667* (Berlin–Bonn, 1934).

MENENDEZ Y PELAYO, *Historia de los heterodoxes españoles* (Madrid, 1911–1932²).

SCHAEFER (E.), *Beiträge zur Geschichte des spanischen Protestantismus und der Inquisition im sechzehnten Jahrhundert*, 3 vols. (Gütersloh, 1902).

Scandinavia (Sweden):

HOLMQUIST (H.), *Die Schwedische Reformation, 1523–1531* (Leipzig, 1925).

— *Reformationstidevarvet, 1521–1611*, vol. III of *Svenska Kyrkanhistoria*, 2 vols. (Stockholm, 1933).

GREN (N. E.), *Gustave Vasa et l'Église de Suède. Comment on détruit une Église* (Louvain, 1937).

HOFFMANN (J. G. H.), *La Rèforme en Suède (1523–1572), et la succession apostolique* (Neuchâtel, Paris, 1945).

JOHANNESON (B.), *Den svenska Kyrkan och reformationen* (Lund, 1947).

MARTIN (J.), *Gustave Vasa et la Réforme en Suède* (Paris, 1906).

MURRAY (R.), *Olavus Petri* (Stockholm, 1952).

WEIDLING (J.), *Schwedens Geschichte im Zeitalter der Reformation* (1881).

Denmark:
ANDERSEN (N. J.), *Confessio Hofniensis. Den kobenhavnske Bekendelse af 1530. Studier i den begundende Reformation* (Copenhagen, 1954).
DUNKLEY (E. H.), *The Reformation in Denmark* (London, 1949).
KJOER (J. C.), *History of the Church of Denmark* (Blair, Nebr., 1945).
KOCH (H.), *Den danske kirkes historie,* vol. VI (Copenhagen, 1954).

Switzerland:
BLOESCH (E.), *Geschichte der schweizerisch-reformierten Kirchen,* 2 vols. (Berne, 1898–1899).
HADORN (W.), *Die Reformation in der deutschen Schweiz* (1928).
ROGET (A.), *Histoire de Genève depuis la Réforme jusqu'à l'escalade de 1602,* 3 vols. (Geneva, 1883).
STAEHLIN (E.), *Das Buch der Basler Reformation zu ihren 400 jährigen Jubiläum* (Basle, 1929).
VASELLA (O.), articles in *Zeitschrift für Schweizerische Kirchengeschichte* 1939, 1940, 1941, 1942, 1943; in *Jahresbericht des Histor. Antiqu. Gesellschaft für schweizerische Geschichte,* 1944, and *Historisches Jahrbuch,* 1957.
VON MURALT (L.), *Reformation und Gegenreformation,* book III of vol. I. of *Geschichte der Schweiz* (Zürich, 1932).
VUILLEUMIER (H.), *Histoire de l'Église réformée du canton de Vaud sous le régime bernois,* 4 vols. (Lausanne, 1927).

(ii) *THE COUNTER-REFORMATION BACKGROUND*
EDER (K.), *Die Kirche im Zeitalter des Konfessionellen Absolutismus (1555–1648),* dans la coll. *Handbuch der allgemeinen Kirchengeschichte,* III, 2 (Freiburg, 1949).
LATREILLE (A.) ..., *Histoire du Catholicisme en France,* vol. II (Paris, 1960).
LORTZ (J.), *Geschichte der Kirche in ideengeschichtlicher Betrachtung,* II: *Die Neuzeit* (Münster, 1964²¹).
SABA (A.), *Storia delle Chiesa,* 4 vols. (Turin, 1954³).
VEIT (L. A.), *Die Kirche im Zeitalter des Individualismus; Handbuch der allgemeinen Kirchengeschichte,* IV/2 (Freiburg, 1951).
VILOSLADA (R. G.) & LLORCA (B.), *Historia de la Iglesia catolica,* III: *Edad nueva* (Madrid, 1960).

C. *THE COUNCIL OF TRENT*

SARPI (P.), *Istoria del concilio tridentino* (London, 1619); ET: by N. BRENT (London, 1620).
SFORZA PALLAVICINO, *Istoria del concilio tridentino,* 2 vols. (Rome, 1656–1657).
ALBERIGO (G.), *I vescovi italiani al concilio di Trento, 1545–1547* (Florence, 1959).
— 'L'ecclesiologia del concilio di Trento', in *Rivista di storia della Chiesa,* 1964. 'The Council of Trent: new views on the occasion of its 4th century', in *Concilium* Sept. 1965.
CASTRO (J. de), *Portugal no concilio de Trento,* 6 vols. (Lisbon, 1944–1946).
Il concilio di Trento e la riforma tridentina, 2 vols. (Rome, 1965).
CONGAR (Y.), *Tradition and Traditions* (London, 1966).
CONSTANT (G.), *Etude et catalogue critique de documents sur le concile de Trente* (Paris, 1910).
DOUGLAS (R. M.), *Jacopo Sadoleto, 1477–1547. Humanist and Reformer* (London, 1959).

DUPRONT (A.), 'Le concile de Trente', in *Le concile et les conciles* (Paris–Chevetogne, 1960), pp. 345–60.

JEDIN (H.), *Girolamo Seripando*, 2 vols. (Würzburg, 1937): ET (vol. 1): *Papal Legate at the Council of Trent* (St Louis–London, 1947).

— *Der Quellenapparat der Konzilgeschichte Pallavicinis* (Rome, 1940).

— *Krisis und Wendepunkt der Trienter Konzils 1562–1563* (Würzburg, 1941); ET: *Crisis and closure of the Council of Trent* (London, 1967).

— *Das Konzil von Trient. Ein Überblick über die Erforschung seiner Geschichte* (Rome, 1948).

— *Geschichte des Konzils von Trient*, 2 vols. (Freiburg, 1949–1957); ET: Vols. 1–2: *History of the Council of Trent* (London, 1957–61).

— *Tommaso Campeggio (1483–1564). Tridentinische Reform und Kuriale Tradition* (Münster, 1958).

— *Kleine Konziliengeschichte* (Freiburg, 1959): ET: *Ecumenical Councils of the Catholic Church* (London, 1960).

— 'Die Deutschen am Trienter Konzil, 1551–1552', in *Historische Zeitschrift*, 1959.

— *Der Abschluss der Trienter Konzils, 1562–1563* (Münster, 1963).

LUTZ (H.), *Christianitas afflicta* (Göttingen, 1962).

MOBILIA (A.), *Cornelio Musso e la prima forma del decreto sulla giustificazione* (Naples, 1960).

RICHARD (P.) & MICHEL (A.), *Le concile de Trente* (in *Histoire des conciles*, HEFELE-LECLERCQ), IX, 2 vols. (Paris, 1931–1938), and X/1, 1958.

ROGGER (L.), *Le nazioni al concilio di Trento, 1545–1552* (Rome, 1952).

SCHMIDT (A. P.), *Liturgie et langue vulgaire* (Rome, 1950).

SCHREIBER (G.), *Das Weltkonzil von Trient*, 2 vols. (Freiburg, 1951).

SPYKMAN (G. J.), *Attrition and Contrition at the Council of Trent* (Kampen, 1955).

STAKEMEIER, *Der Kampf um Augustin auf dem Tridentinum* (Paderborn, 1937).

— *Das Konzil von Trient über die Heilsgewissheit* (Heidelberg, 1947).

STUPPERICH (R.), 'Die Reformatoren und das Tridentinum', in *Archiv für Reformationsgeschichte*, 1956.

TAVARD (G. H.), *Holy Writ or Holy Church* (New York, 1959).

WALZ (A.), *I Domenicani al concilio di Trento* (Rome, 1961).

D. *THE TRIDENTINE REFORMS IMPLEMENTED*

1. *Religious orders etc.*

BEYER (J.), *Les instituts séculiers* (Paris, 1954).

BONNET (H.), *Histoire des ordres religieux* (Paris, 1950).

ESCOBAR (M.), *Ordini e congregazioni religiosi*, 2 vols. (Rome–Turin, 1951–1953).

HEIMBUCHER (M.), *Die Orden und Kongregationen der Katholischen Kirche*, 2 vols. (Paderborn, 1932–1934²).

HELYOT (A.), *Dictionnaire des ordres religieux*, 8 vols. (Paris, 1714–1724), reproduced in *Encyclopédie théologique*, MIGNE.

HERMANT, *Histoire des ordres religieux et congrégations*, 2 vols. (Rouen, 1710).

PISANI (P.), *Les compagnies de prêtres des XVIIe et XVIIIe siècles* (Paris, 1928).

BECHER (H.), *Die Jesuiten* (Munich, 1951).

BÖHMER (H.), *Die Jesuiten* (Stuttgart, 1957²).

BRODRICK (J.), *The Origin of the Jesuits* (London, 1940).

— *The Progress of the Jesuits* (London, 1947).

CRÉTINEAU-JOLY, *Histoire de la Compagnie de Jésus*, 6 vols. (Brussels, 1845).
GUILLERMOU (A.), *Les Jésuites* (Paris, 1963).
ROSA (E.), *I Gesuiti dalle origini ai nostri giorni* (Rome, 1957).
VAN DE VORST (C.), *Synopsis historiae Societatis Iesu* (Louvain, 1950).

2. *Seminaries*

DEGERT (A.), *Histoire des séminaires français jusqu'à la Révolution*, 2 vols. (Paris, 1912).
MARKHAM (J. J.), *The Sacred Congregation of seminaries and universities of studies* (Washington, 1957).
O'DONOHOE, *Tridentine seminary Legislation. Its Sources and its formation* (Louvain, 1957).

3. *The Catholic Reformation in general*

BENDISCIOLI (M.), *Riforma cattolica. Antologia di documenti* (Rome, 1963).
JEDIN (H.), *Katholische Reformation oder Gegenreformation?* (Lucerne, 1946).
— *Das Bischofsideal der Katholischen Reformation* (1942).
OGGIONI (E.), *Rinascimento e Controriforma. Problemi filosofici dell'odierna storiografia* (Bologna, 1958).

4. *France*

BLET (P.), *Le clergé de France et la monarchie. Etudes sur les assemblées générales du clergé de 1615 à 1666*, 2 vols. (Rome, 1959).
BROUTIN (P.), *La réforme pastorale en France au XVIIe siècle*, 2 vols. (Paris, 1956).
GRANDET (J.), *Les saints prêtres français du XVIIe siècle*, 3 vols. (Angers, 1897).
MOISY (P.), *Les églises des Jésuites de l'ancienne Assistance de France* (Rome, 1958).
PRUNEL (L.), *La renaissance catholique en France au XVIIe siècle* (Paris, 1911).

5. *Spain and Portugal*

CASTRO (J. de), *Bispado de Bragança e Miranda*, 4 vols. (Porto, 1946–1950).
PERREIRA (J. A.), *Fastos episcopais da Igreja primacial de Braga*, 4 vols. (Braga, 1928–1935).
GONI GAZTAMBIDE, *Los Navaros en el concilio di Trento y la reforma tridentina en la diocesis de Pamplona* (Pamplona, 1947).
LOS RIOS (F. de), *Religion y estado en la España del siglo XVI* (Mexico City, 1957).
MARAVALL (J. A.), *La philosophie politique espagnole au XVIe siècle dans ses rapports avec l'esprit de la Contre-Réforme*, trans. L. CAZES & P. MENSARD (Paris, 1955).

6. *Italy*

ALBERIGO (G.), 'Studi e problemi relativi all'applicazione del Concilio di Trento in Italia (1945–1958)', in *RSI*, 1958.

ANGLADE (P.), *Il concilio provinciale di Aquileia celebrato dal patriarca Francesco Barbaro a Udine nel 1596* (Rome, 1949).

CATTANEO (E.), *Storia di Milano*, XI (Milan, 1958).

DELUMEAU (J.), *Vie économique et sociale de Rome dans la seconde moitié du XVIe siècle*, 2 vols. (Paris, 1957–1959).

FANTON (C.), *La riforma tridentina a Vicenza nella seconda metà del secolo XVI* (Vicenza, 1941).

FELC (F.), *Reformation und Gegenreformation im Patriarcha Aquileia* (1955).

PASCHINI (P.), *Eresia e riforma cattolica al confine orientale d'Italia* (Rome, 1951).
Problemi di vita religiosa in Italia nel Cinquecento (Padua, 1960).

SILVINO DA NADRO, *Sinodi diocesani italiani. Catalogo bibliografico, 1534–1878* (Rome, 1960).

TACCHI-VENTURI (P.), *La vita religiosa in Italia durante la prima età della Compagnia di Gesù* (Rome, 1931).
— *Storia della Compagnia di Gesù in Italia*, 3 vols. (Rome, 1951²).

7. *The Netherlands (Low Countries)*

DIERICK (M.), *Documents inédits sur l'érection des nouveaux diocèses aux Pays-Bas*, 3 vols. (Brussels, 1960–1962).

JADIN (L.), *Relations des Pays-Bas, de Liège, de la France-Comté d'après les « Lettere dei vescovi » conservées aux Archives vaticanes, 1566–1579* (Brussels–Rome, 1952).

MOREAU (E. de), *Histoire de l'Eglise en Belgique*, vol. V (Louvain, 1952).

PASTURE (A.), *La restauration religieuse aux Pays-Bas catholiques, 1596–1633* (Louvain, 1925).

ROGIER (L. J.), *Geschiedenis van het Katholizisme in Noord-Nederland in de XVIe en XVIIe eeuw*, 3 vols. (The Hague, 1959).

WILLCOCX (F.), *L'introduction des décrets du concile de Trente dans les anciens Pays-Bas* (Louvain, 1929).

8. *Switzerland*

FRY (K.), *G. A. Volpe, seine erste Nuntiatur in der Schweiz, 1560–1564*, 3 vols. 1931–1946.

MAYER (J.), *Das Konzil von Trient und die Gegenreformation in der Schweiz*, 2 vols., 1901–1903.

MURALT (L. von), *Reformation und Gegenreformation:* vol. III of *Geschichte der Schweiz* (Zürich, 1932).

REINHARDT (H.), *Studien zur Geschichte der Katholischen Schweiz im Zeitalter Karl Borromeos* (1911).

SCHWEGLER (T.), *Geschichte der Katholischen Kirche der Schweiz* (Stans, 1943³).

STEFFENS (F.) & REINHARDT (H.), *Die Nuntiatur von G. Fr. Bonhomini*, 3 vols. (Solothurn, 1906–1929).

9. *Germany and Austria*

ALBRECHT (D.), *Die auswärtige Politik Maximilians von Bayern, 1618–1635* (Göttingen, 1962).

BRANDI (K.), *Gegenreformation und Religionskriege* (1930).

LOJEWSKI (L.), *Bayerns Weg nach Köln. Geschichte der bayerischen Bistumspolitik in der 2 Hälfte des 16 Jahrhunderts* (Bonn, 1962).

LOSERTH (J.), *Akten und Korrespondenzen zur Geschichte der Gegenreformation in Innerösterreich unter Erzherzog Karl II (1578–1590) und Ferdinand II (1590–1637)*, 3 vols. (Vienna, 1898–1907).

REPGEN (K.), *Die romische Kurie und der Westfälische Friede. Idee und Wirklichkeit des Papstums im 16. und 17. Jahrhundert* (Tübingen, I, 1962).

RITTER (M.), *Deutsche Geschichte im Zeitalter der Gegenreformation und des 30 jährigen Krieges*, 3 vols. (Stuttgart, 1889–1907).

SCHMIDLIN (J.), *Die Kirchlichen Zustände in Deutschland vor dem 30 jährigen Krieg nach den bischöflichen Diözesanberichten an den Heiligen Stuhl*, 3 vols. (1908–1910).

— *Kirchliche Zustände und Schicksale des deutschen Katholizismus während des 30 jährigen Krieges nach den bischöflichen Romberichten* (1940).

SIEBERT (F.), *Zwischen Kaiser und Papst. Kardinal Truchsess von Waldburg und die Anfänge der Gegenreformation in Deutschland* (Berlin, 1943).

SPAHN (P.), *Die Reichskirche vom Trienter Konzil bis zum Auflösung des Reiches. Darstellungen und Quellen* (1931ff).

WODKA (J.), *Kirche in Österreich* (Vienna, 1959).

10. *Bohemia and Hungary*

BERENGER (J.), 'La Contre-Réforme en Hongrie', in *Mélanges V.-L. Tapié* (nyp).

GINDELY (A.), *Geschichte der Gegenreformation in Böhmen* (1894).

KARACSONYL, *Kirchengeschichte Ungarns* (Nagyvarad, 1915).

KLIMA (A.), *Cechy v Obdobi temna* (Prague, 1958).

KORNIS (J.), *La personnalité de Pazmany* (Paris, 1937).

STURMBERGER (H.), *Aufstand in Böhmen. Der Beginn des Dreissigjährigen Krieges* (Munich, 1959).

TAPIÉ (V.-L.), *Monarchie et peuples du Danube* (Paris, 1969).

Vingt-cinq ans d'historiographie tchécoslovaque, 1936–1960 (Prague, 1960).

SZEKELY (G.), BALAZS (E.) & MARKAI (L.), *History of Hungary*, II, *1526–1790* (Budapest, 1962) (in Hungarian).

11. *Poland*

BAMGART (J.) et MALEC (A.), *Bibliografia historii polskiej za rok 1961* (Warsaw, 1963) (3,000 publications cited).

BERGA (A.), *Pierre Skarga SJ* (Paris, 1916).

KRAUSE (G.), *Reformation und Gegenreformation in ehemaligen Königreichpolen* (1905²).

LORTZ (J.), *Kardinal Stanislaus Hosius* (Braunsberg, 1931).

WERMTER (E. M.), *Kardinal Stanislaus Hosius und Herzog Albrecht von Preussen* (Münster, 1957).

E. *SPIRITUALITY*

Archivio italiano per la storia della pietà, 5 vols. (Rome, 1951–1968).

AUCLAIR (M.), *La vie de sainte Thérèse d'Avila* (Paris, 1950).

BARUZI (J.), *Saint Jean de la Croix et le problème de l'expérience mystique* (Paris, 1931²).

BATAILLON (M.), *Erasme et l'Espagne* (Paris, 1937); *Erasmo y la España* (Mexico City, 1966).

BERTHELOT DU CHESNAY (C.), *Saint Jean Eudes. Lettres choisies et inédites* (Namur, 1958).

BERTRAND (L.), *Bibliothèque sulpicienne*, 3 vols. (Paris, 1900).

BREMOND (H.), *L'abbé Tempête, Armand de Rancé, réformateur de la Trappe* (Paris, 1929); ET: *The Thundering Abbot* (London, 1930).

— *Histoire littéraire du sentiment religieux en France depuis la fin des guerres de Religion*, 11 vols. (Paris, 1967); ET: vols. 1 to 3: *A Literary History of Religious Thought in France* (London, 1928–36).

— *Le courant mystique au XVIIIe siècle* (Paris, 1943).

BRODRICK (J.), *St Peter Canisius* (London, 1936).

— *St Ignatius of Loyola. The Pilgrim's years 1491–1538* (London, 1956).

BUSSON (H.), *Littérature et théologie* (Paris, 1962).

CALVET (J.), *La littérature religieuse de François de Sales à Fénelon* (Paris, 1938).

— *Saint Vincent de Paul* (Paris, 1949).

— *Louise de Marillac par elle-même* (Paris, 1958).

CHALENDARD (M.), *La promotion de la femme à l'apostolat, 1540–1650* (Paris, 1950).

CHARTON (P.), *Saint Alphonse de Liguori* (Paris, 1947).

CHESNEAU (C.), *Le P. Yves de Paris et son temps (1590–1678)*, 2 vols. (Paris, 1948).

— (= J. EYMARD D'ANGERS), *L'apologétique en France de 1580 à 1670* (Paris, 1954).

COCHOIS (P.), *Bérulle et l'Ecole française* (Paris, 1963).

COGNET (L.), *Les origines de la spiritualité française au XVIIe siècle* (Paris, 1949).

— *De la dévotion moderne à la spiritualité française* (Paris, 1958); ET: *Post-reformation spirituality* (London, 1959).

— *Saint Vincent de Paul* (Paris, 1959).

— '*La spiritualité moderne, I, L'essor: 1500–1650*', in *Histoire de la spiritualité chrétienne* (Paris, 1965).

COSTE (P.), *Monsieur Vincent*, 3 vols. (Paris, 1934).

COURCEL (F.), *La vie et les œuvres du P. L. Lallemand* (Paris, 1959).

CRISOGONO DE JESUS, *Vida y obras de S. Juan de la Cruz* (Madrid, 1955³).

DAGENS (J.), *Bibliographie chronologique de la littérature de spiritualité et de ses sources* (Paris, 1952).

— *Bérulle et les origines de la restauration catholique* (Bruges–Paris, 1952).

DE CERTEAU, *P. Favre. Mémorial* (Paris, 1960).

— 'Mystique au XVIIe siècle', in *L'Homme devant Dieu*, II (Paris, 1964).

— *Concilium* 1965 (Spirituality issue).

— *J. J. Surin, Correspondance* (Paris, 1966).

DEROO (A.), *Saint Charles Borromée* (Paris, 1963).

DERREAL (H.), *Un missionnaire de la Contre-Réforme, saint Pierre Fourier et l'institution de la Congrégation de Notre-Dame* (Paris, 1965).

DODIN (A.), *Saint Vincent de Paul et la charité* (Paris, 1960).

— *Saint Vincent de Paul. Entretiens spirituels aux missionnaires* (Paris, 1960).

DUPUY (M.), *Bérulle, une spiritualité de l'adoration* (Paris, 1964).

GEORGES (E.), *Jean Eudes* (Paris, 1936²).

GRAZIOLI (A.), *Gian Matteo Giberti* (Verona, 1955).

GUIBERT (J. de), *La spiritualité de la Compagnie de Jésus* (Rome, 1953); ET: *The Jesuits: Their spiritual doctrine and practice* (Chicago, 1964).

GUILLERMOU (A.), *La vie de saint Ignace de Loyola* (Paris, 1956).

— *Saint Ignace de Loyola et la Compagnie de Jésus* (Paris, 1960).

GUITTON (G.), *L'âme du bienheureux Pierre Favre* (Lyons, 1960).

HAMON (A.), *Histoire de la dévotion au Sacré-Cœur*, 5 vols. (Paris, 1923–1940).

HEDERER (E.), *Deutsche Dichtung des Barocks* (1955).

IPARRAGUIRRE (I.), *Répertoire de spiritualité ignatienne, 1556–1615* (Rome, 1961).

LAFUE (P.), *Le P. Joseph* (Paris, 1946).

LAJEUNIE (E.-M.), *Saint François de Sales et l'esprit salésien* (Paris, 1962).

LECLERCQ (J.), *Un humaniste ermite. Le bienheureux Paul Giustiniani* (Rome, 1951).

— *Ignatius von Loyola und das geschichtliche Werdern seiner Frömmigkeit* (Vienna, 1947); ET: *The Spirituality of St Ignatius Loyola* (Westminster, Md., 1953).

LEROY (O.), *Sainte Thérèse d'Avila* (Paris, 1962).

LIUIMA (A.), *Aux sources du Traité de l'amour de Dieu de saint François de Sales*, 2 vols. (Rome, 1959–1960).

LOIDL (F.), *Abraham a Sancta Clara. Über das religiös-sittliche Leben in Österreich, 1670–1710* (1939).

MARTIMORT (A.), *L'Église en prière* (Paris, 1961).

MARZOT (C.), *Un classico della controriforma. Paolo Segneri* (Palermo, 1950).

MOLS (R.), 'Saint Charles Borromée, pionnier de la pastorale moderne', in *NR Th*, 1957, pp. 600–22, 715–47.

MONIER (F.), *Vie de Jean-Jacques Olier*, I (Paris, 1914).

MOREL (G.), *Le sens de l'existence selon saint Jean de la Croix*, 3 vols. (Paris, 1960–1961).

MORET (A.), *Le lyrisme baroque en Allemagne* (Lille, 1936).

NICOLINI (B.), *Ideali e passioni nell'Italia religiosa del Cinquecento* (Bologna, 1962).

ORCIBAL (J.), *La rencontre du Carmel thérésien avec les mystiques du Nord* (Paris, 1959).

— *Le cardinal de Bérulle, évolution d'une spiritualité* (Paris, 1965).

ORSENIGO (C.), *Vita di san Carlo Borromeo* (Milan, 1929³); ET: *Life of St Charles Borromeo* (St Louis–London, 1945).

PELLE-DOUËL (Y.), *Saint Jean de la Croix et la nuit mystique* (Paris, 1960).

PONELLE (L.) & BORDET (L.), *Saint Philippe Neri et la société romaine de son temps* (Paris, 1955²).

RAHNER (H.), *Saint Ignace de Loyola et la genèse des Exercises* (Toulouse, 1948).

— *Ignatius von Loyola als Mensch und Theologe* (Freiburg, 1964); ET: *Ignatius the Theologian* (New York, 1968).

RENAUDIN (P.), *Un maître de la mystique française, Benoît de Canfeld* (Paris, 1956).

RIGNAULT (G.), *Saint Louis-Marie Grignion de Montfort* (Tourcoing, 1947).

SELLIER (Ph.), *Pascal et la liturgie* (Paris, 1966).

SHERGOLD (N.) & VAREY (J.), *Los autos sacramentales en Madrid en la epoca de Calderon, 1637–1681* (Madrid, 1961).

TRUCHET (J.), *La prédication de Bossuet*, 2 vols. (Paris, 1960).

VILLARET (E.), *Les congrégations mariales* (Paris, 1947).

VILNET (J.), *Bible et mystique chez saint Jean de la Croix* (Paris, 1949).

VERMEYLEN (A.), *Sainte Thérèse en France au XVIIe siècle, 1600–1660* (Louvain, 1958).

F. *CATHOLICISM OUTSIDE EUROPE*

1. *General*

DELACROIX (S.), *Histoire universelle des missions catholiques* (symposium) I & II (Paris, 1956–57).

DESPONT (J.), *Nouvel atlas des missions* (Paris, 1951).
FREITAG (A.), *Atlas du monde chrétien* (Paris–Brussels, 1959).
GENSIDEN (H.), *Missionsgeschichte der neueren Zeit* (1961).
LATOURETTE (K.), *History of the Expansion of Christianity*, III (1500–1800) (London, 1939).
MAURO (F.), *L'expansion européenne, 1600–1870* (Paris, 1964).
SILVA REGO (A. da), *Curso de missionologia* (Lisbon, 1956).
STREIT (R.) & DINDINGER, *Bibliotheca missionum* (Freiburg, 1916ff).

2. Africa and Asia

ATTWATER (R.), *A. Schall. A Jesuit of the court of China* (London, 1963).
BERNARD (H.), *Aux portes de la Chine. Les missionnaires du XVIe siècle* (Paris, 1937).
— *Le P. Matthieu Ricci et la société chinoise de son temps (1552–1610)* (Tient-Sin, 1937).
BERNARD-MAÎTRE (H.), *S. François-Xavier et la rencontre des religions. Introduction et choix de textes* (Paris, 1960).
BOXER (C.), *The Christian Century in Japan, 1549–1650* (Berkeley–London, 1951).
— *South China in the Sixteenth Century* (London, 1953).
BRASIO (A.), *Monumenta missionaria africana* (Lisbon, 1951ff).
BRODRICK (J.), *St Francis Xavier, 1506–1552* (London, 1952).
CUVELIER (J.), & JADIN (L.), *L'ancien Congo d'après les archives romaines, 1518–1640* (Brussels, 1954).
CHAPPOULIE (H.), *Aux origines d'une Église. Rome et les missions d'Indochine*, 2 vols. (Paris, 1943–1948).
CRONIN (V.), *The Wise Man from the West. M. Ricci* (London, 1955).
— *A Pearl to India. The life of Roberto de' Nobili* (London, 1959).
DUNNE (G.), *Generation of Giants* (Notre-Dame, Ind., 1962).
ELIA (P. D'), *Fonti ricciane*, 3 vols. (Rome, 1942–9).
— *Storia dell'introduzione del Cristianesimo in Cina*, 3 vols. (Rome, 1957).
GHESQUIÈRE (T.), *Matthieu de Castro premier vicaire apostolique aux Indes* (Louvain, 1937).
GONCALVES (S.), *Historia dos religiosos da Companhia de Jesus... nos reynos e provincias da India oriental*, ed. J. WICKI, 3 vols. (Coîmbra, 1957–1962).
LAURES (J.), *Geschichte der Katholischen Kirche in Japan* (Kaldenkirchen, 1956).
PHELAN (J.), *The Hispanisation of the Philippines, 1565–1700* (Madison, 1959).
SA (A. B. de), *Documentaçâo para a Historia des Missioes do Padroado português do Oriente* (Lisbon, 1954ff).
SCHURHAMMER (G.) & WICKI (J.), *Epistolae S. Francisci Xaverii*, 2 vols. (Rome, 1944–1945).
SCHÜRHAMMER (G.), *Die Zeitgenössischen Quellen zur Geschichte Portugiesisch Asiens und seiner Nachbarländer zur Zeit des hl. Franz Xaver, 1538–1552* (Rome, 1962).
— *Franz Xaver. Sein Leben und seine Zeit* (Freiburg, 1955 ff).
— & SCHÜTTE (J. F.), *Valignanos Missionsgrundsätze für Japan*, 2 vols. (Rome, 1951–1958).
SILVA REGO (A. de), *Documençao para a historia das Missôes do Padroado Português do Oriente*, 12 vols. (Lisbon, 1947–1958).
VAN DE WYNGAERT (A.) & MENSAERT (G.), *Sinica franciscana* (Quaracchi–Rome, 1933–1954).

3. *America*

ARMAS MEDINA (F. de), *Cristianización del Peru (1532–1600)* (Seville, 1953).

BARBIER (M.), *Francisco de Vitoria. Leçons sur les Indiens et sur le droit de guerre, 1538–1539* (Geneva, 1966).

BATAILLON (M.), *Etudes sur Bartolomé de Las Casas* (Paris, 1966).

BORGES (P.), *Metodos missionales en la cristianización de América. Siglo XVI* (Madrid, 1960).

CARAMAN (P.), *The Lost Paradise* (London, 1975).

CHAUNU (P.), *L'Amérique et les Amériques* (Paris, 1964).

— *Conquête et exploitation des nouveaux mondes* (Paris, 1969).

CUEVAS (M.), *Historia de la Iglesia en Mexico*, 5 vols. (Tlelpam, 1921–1928).

DE BONNAULT, *Histoire du Canada français* (Paris, 1950).

DECORME (G.), *La Obra de los Jesuitas mexicanos durante la epoca colonial*, 2 vols. (Mexico City, 1949).

DOMINIAN (H.), *The biography of P. Jose Anchieta* (New York, 1958).

ENGELHARDT (Z.), *The Mission and missionaries of California*, 4 vols. (San Francisco, 1908–1915).

ENRICH (F.), *Historia de la Compania de Jesús en Chile*, 2 vols. (Barcelona, 1891).

GIMENEZ FERNANDEZ (M.), *Bartolomé de Las Casas*, 1953 ff.

— & HANKE (L.), *Bartolomé de Las Casas. Bibliografia critica...* (Santiago, 1954).

HANKE (L.), *The Spanish Struggle for Justice in the Conquest of America* (Philadelphia, 1949).

LEITE (S.), *Historia da Compania de Jesús no Brasil*, 2 vols. (Lisbon, 1938).

LEVILLIER (R.), *Organización de la Iglesia y Ordenes religiosas en el Virreinado del Perú en el siglo XVI*, 2 vols. (Madrid, 1919).

LISSON (E.), *La Iglesia de España en el Perú*, 2 vols. (Seville, 1943–1945).

LUGON (Cl.), *La république communiste chrétienne des Guaranis, 1610–1768* (Paris, 1949).

MAAS (O.), *Misiones de Nuevo Mexico* (Madrid, 1929).

MAHN-LOT (M.), *Las Casas. L'Evangile et la force* (Paris, 1964).

MATEOS (E.), *Historia general de la Compania de Jesús en la Provincia del Perú*, 2 vols. (Madrid, 1944).

MAYNARD (Th.), *The story of American Catholicism*, 2 vols. (London, 1961).

OLWER (L. N. d'), *Fray Bernardino de Sahagun* (Mexico City, 1952).

OTRUBA (G.), *Der Jesuitenstaat in Paraguay. Idee und Wirklichkeit* (Vienna, 1962).

PACHECO (J.), *Los Jesuitas en Colombia*, 2 vols. (Bogota, 1959–1962).

PASTELLS (P.), *Historia de la Compania de Jesús en la provincia del Paraguay*, 8 vols. (Madrid, 1912–1949).

RENNARD (J.), *Histoire religieuse des Antilles françaises, des origines a 1914* (Paris, 1954).

RICARD (R.), *Etudes et documents pour l'histoire missionnaire de l'Espagne et du Portugal* (Louvain, 1931).

— *La « Conquête spirituelle » du Mexique* (Paris, 1933); ET: *The Spiritual Conquest of Mexico* (Berkeley, 1966).

SAHAGUN (Bernardino de), *Historia de las cosas de Nueva España*, ed. A. M. GARIBAY (Mexico City, 1956).

TORMO SANZ, *Experiencia misionera en la Florida* (Madrid, 1957).

VARGAS (V.), *Concilios Limenses (1557–1772)*, 3 vols. (Lima, 1951–1954).

4. *Congregation of Faith and Foreign Missions*

Acta SC de Propaganda Fide spectantia, 1622–1649, ed. TÜCHLE (Paderborn, 1962).

BAUDIMENT (L.), *François Pallu, principal fondateur de la Société des Missions Etrangères* (Paris, 1934).

BECKMANN (J.), *La Congrégation de la Propagation de la Foi face à la politique internationale* (Schöneck-Beckenried, 1963).
GUENNOU (J.), *Les Missions Etrangères* (Paris, 1963).
LAUNAY (A.), *Histoire générale des Missions Etrangères*, 5 vols. (Paris, 1894).
PIEPER (K.), *Die Propaganda. Ihre Enstehung und ihre religiödr znrfriyimh* (Aachen, 1922).

G. TENSIONS IN THE CATHOLIC CHURCH

1. Liturgy

BETTRAY (J.), *Die Akkomodationsmethode des P. Matteo Ricci SJ in China* (Rome, 1955).
BONTINCK (F.), *La lutte autour de la liturgie chinoise aux XVIIe et XVIIIe siècles* (Louvain–Paris, 1962).
ROULEAU (F.), 'Maillard de Tournon. Papal Legate at the Court of Peking', dans *Archivum historicum Societatis Jesu* (Rome, 1962) pp. 264–323.

2. Grace and Jansenism

ADAM (A.), *Du mysticisme à la révolte. Les Jansénistes du XVIIe siècle* (Paris, 1968).
APPOLIS (E.), *Le « tiers parti » catholique au XVIIIe siècle* (Paris, 1960).
— *Les Jansénistes espagnols* (Bordeaux, 1966).
CEYSSENS (L.), *Sources relatives aux débuts du Jansénisme et de l'antijansénisme, 1640–1643* (Louvain, 1957).
— *La première bulle contre Jansénius. Sources relatives à son histoire, 1644–1653*, 2 vols. (Brussels, 1961–1962).
— *Sources relatives à l'histoire du Jansénisme et de l'antijansénisme des années 1661–1672* (Louvain, 1970).
— & LEGRAND (A.), *Correspondance antijanséniste de Fabio Chigi* (Rome–Brussels, 1957).
COGNET (L.), *La réforme de Port-Royal* (Paris, 1950).
— *La Mère Angélique et son temps*, 2 vols. (Paris, 1950–1952).
— *Le Jansénisme* (Paris, 1961).
GAZIER (A.), *Histoire générale du mouvement janséniste*, 2 vols. (Paris, 1922–1924).
— *Port-Royal-des-Champs* (Paris, 1951).
GOLDMANN (L.), *Le Dieu caché* (Paris, 1955); ET: *The Hidden God* (London, 1964).
— *Correspondence de Martin de Barcos, abbé de Saint-Cyran* (Paris, 1956).
HAVINGA (J.), *Les Nouvelles ecclésiastiques* (Amersfôôrt, 1925).
JEMOLO (A.), *Il Giansenismo in Italia prima della Rivoluzione* (Bari, 1928).
LAPORTE (J.), *La doctrine de Port-Royal. La morale (d'après Arnauld)*, 2 vols. (Paris, 1951–1952).
LEFEBVRE (H.), *Pascal*, 2 vols. (Paris, 1949–1954).
NAMER (G.), *L'abbé Le Roy et ses amis. Essai sur le Jansénisme extrémiste intramondain* (Paris, 1964).
NEVEU (B.), *Sébastien-Joseph Du Cambout de Pontchâteau, 1634–1690* (Paris, 1969).
ORCIBAL (J.) & BARNES (A.), *Les origines du Jansénisme*, 5 vols. (Louvain–Paris, 1947–1962).

— *Relation de la captivité d'Angélique de saint Jean Arnauld d'Andilly* (Paris, 1954).
— *Port-Royal entre le miracle et l'obéissance* ... : *Flavie Passart et Angélique de saint Jean Arnauld d'Andilly* (Paris, 1957).
— *Saint-Cyran et le Jansénisme* (Paris, 1961).
PRÉCLIN (E.), *Les Jansénistes au XVIIIe siècle et la Constitution civile du clergé* (Paris, 1929).
SAINTE-BEUVE, *Port-Royal*, new ed. 3 vols. (Paris, 1953–5).
STEGMÜLLER (F.), *Geschichte des Molinismus*, I (Munich, 1935).
STEINMANN (J.), *Pascal* (Paris, 1962, ET: London, 1965).
TANS (J.), *P. Quesnel et les Pays-Bas* (Groningen, 1960).
TAVENEAUX (R.), *Le Jansénisme en Lorraine, 1640–1789* (Paris, 1960).
— *Jansénisme et politique* (Paris, 1965).
THIBAUDERIE (I. de LA), *Eglises et évêques catholiques non romains* (Paris, 1962).
THOMAS (J.), *La querelle de l'Unigenitus* (Paris, 1950).
VAUSSARD (M.), *Jansénisme et gallicanisme aux origines religieuses du Risorgimento* (Paris, 1959).
WILLAERT (L.), *Les origines du Jansénisme dans le Pays-Bas catholiques* (Gembloux, 1948).
— *Bibliotheca janseniana belgica*, 3 vols. (Paris, 1949–51).

3. Pure Love and Quietism

COGNET (L.), *Crépuscule des mystiques. Le conflit Fénelon-Bossuet* (Tournai–Paris, 1958).
DUBOIS–QUINARD (M.), *Laurent de Paris. Une doctrine du pur amour en France au début du XVIIe siècle* (Rome, 1959).
DUPRIEZ (B.), *Fénelon et la Bible. Les origines du mysticisme fénelonien* (Paris, 1961).
HUVELIN (H.), *Bossuet, Fénelon, le Quiétisme*, 2 vols. (Paris, 1912).
KOLAKOWSKI (L.), *Chrétiens sans Eglise* (Paris, 1969).
LANGLOIS (M.), *Fénelon. Les origines du Quiétisme avant 1694* (Paris, 1934).
— 'Fénelon et le Quiétisme', in *XVIIe siècle*, 1951 & 1952).
PETROCCHI (M.), *Il Quietismo italiano del seicento* (Rome, 1948).
VARILLON (F.), *Fénelon et le pur amour* (Paris, 1957).

4. Gallicanism

GUITTON (G.), *Le P. de La Chaise confesseur de Louis XIV*, 2 vols. (Paris, 1959).
'L'idée d'Eglise aux XVIe et XVIIe siècles' in the *Relazioni* of the ICHSR, 1955, vol. IV.
MARTIMORT (A.), *Le gallicanisme de Bossuet* (Paris, 1953).
— 'Comment les Français du XVIIe siècle voyaient la Pape', in *XVIIe siècle*, 1955.
MARTIN (V.), *Le gallicanisme et la Réforme catholique... 1563–1615* (Paris, 1919).
— *Le gallicanisme politique et le clergé de France* (Paris, 1929).
— *Les origines du gallicanisme*, 2 vols. (Paris, 1938–9).
— ORCIBAL (J.), *Louis XIV contre Innocent XI. Les appels au futur concile de 1688* (Paris, 1949).

5. Episcopalism, Febronianism and Josephism

JUST (L.), *Der Widerruf des Febronius*, 1960.
KLEEF (A. Van), *Geschiedenis van de oud-Katholicke kerk van Nederland* (Assen, 1953²).

KÜNTZIGER (J.), *Febronius et le Fébronianisme* (Brussels, 1891).
MAAS (F.), *Der Josephinismus. Quellen zu seiner Geschichte in Österreich*, 5 vols. (Vienna, 1951–1961).
MATTEUCI (B.), *Scipione de' Ricci* (Brescia, 1941).
NUTTINCK (M.), *La vie et l'œuvre de Zeger-Bernard Van Espen. Un canoniste janséniste, gallican et régalien à l'Université de Louvain (1646–1728)* (Paris, 1970).
PAC DE BELLEGARDE (G. du), *Histoire abrégée de l'Eglise métropolitaine d'Utrecht* (Utrecht, 1852³).
RAAB (H.), *Die concordata nationis germanicae in der Kanonistischen Diskussion des 17. bis 19. Jahrhunderts* (Wiesbaden, 1956).
SCHEPPER (G. de), *La réorganisation des paroisses et la suppression des couvents dans les Pays-Bas autrichiens* (Louvain, 1942).
VALJAVEC (F.), *Der Josephinismus* (Munich, 1945²).
VIGENER (F.), *Gallikanismus und episkopalistische Strömungen im deutschen Katholizismus zwischen Tridentinum und Vatikanum* (Munich, 1913).

6. *Expulsion of the Jésuits etc.*

BONENFANT (P.), *La suppression de la Compagnie de Jésus dans les Pays-Bas autrichiens* (Brussels, 1925).
CHEVALLIER (P.), *Loménie de Brienne et l'ordre monastique, 1766–1789*, 2 vols. (Paris, 1959–1960).
CORDARA (J.), *Memoria sulla suppressione della Compagnia di Gesù* (Rome, 1774).
LE BRET (J.), *Sammlung der merkwürdigsten Schriften die Aufhebung des Jesuitenordens betreffend*, 4 vols. (Frankfurt, 1773–1774).
MASSON (F.), *Le cardinal de Bernis depuis son ministère, 1758–1794. La suppression des Jésuites* (Paris, 1884).
ROCHEMONTEIX (C. de), *Le P. A. Lavalette à la Martinique* (Paris, 1907).
ROMANO (B.), *L'espulsione dei Gesuiti dal Portogallo* (Città di Castello, 1914).
SAINT-PRIEST (A. de), *Histoire de la chute des Jésuites au XVIIIe siècle* (Paris, 1844).
SARRAILH (J.), *L'Espagne éclairée de la seconde moitié du XVIIIe siècle* (Paris, 1954).
THEINER (A.), *Histoire du pontificat de Clément XIV*, 2 vols. (Paris, 1852).

H. *APOLOGETICS, MORAL THEOLOGY. BIBLE AND HISTORY*

BARONI (V.), *La Contre-Réforme devant la Bible* (Lausanne, 1943).
BRUFAU PRATS (J.), *El pensamiento politico de Domingo de Soto y su concepción del poder* (Salamanca, 1960).
BRODRICK (J.), *St Robert Bellarmine, saint and scholar* (London, 1961).
DELEHAYE (H.), *L'œuvre des Bollandistes, 1615–1915* (Brussels, 1959²).
DÖLLINGER (J.) & REUSCH (F.), *Geschichte der Moralstreitigkeit in der katholischen Kirche seit dem 16. Jahrhundert*, 2 vols. (1889).
GIACON (C.), *La seconda scolastica*, 3 vols. (Milan, 1944–1950).
LECLERCQ (H.), *Mabillon*, 2 vols. (Paris, 1953–1957).
MARCOTTE (E.), *La nature de la théologie d'après Melchior Cano* (Ottawa, 1949).
MERL (O.), *Theologia salmanticensis* (Regensburg, 1947).
NOONAN (J. T.), *Scholastic Analysis of Usury* (Cambridge, Mass. 1957).
PETERS (P.), *L'œuvre des Bollandistes* (Brussels, 1961).

PETROCCHI (M.), *Il problema del lassismo nel secolo XVIII* (Rome, 1953).

POLMAN (P.), *L'élément historique dans la controverse religieuse du XVIe siècle* (Gembloux, 1932).

SAGRADO CORAZON (E. del), *Los Salmanticenses* (Madrid, 1955).

SOLANO (M.), *Los grandes escolasticos espanõles de los siglos XVI y XVII* (Madrid, 1928).

STEINMANN (J.), *Richard Simon et les origines de l'exégèse biblique* (Paris, 1960).

TERNUS (J.), *Zur Vorgeschichte der Moralysteme von Vitoria bis Medina* (1930).

TÜRKS (P.), *Das Gottesbild des L. Lessius* (Munich, 1957).

TURMEL (J.), *Histoire de la théologie positive du concile de Trente au concile du Vatican* (Paris, 1906).

VEREECKE (L.), *Conscience morale et loi humaine selon Gabriel Vasquez* (Paris, 1957).

I. *PASTORAL VISITATIONS*
(for France, see above)

BATTISTELLA (A.), *La prima visita apostolica nel patriarcato aquileiese dopo il concilio di Trento* (Cividale, 1909).

FABIANI (G.), 'Sinodi e visite pastorali ad Ascoli dopo il concilio di Trento,' *Rivista di storia della Chiesa* (1952).

FRANZEN (A.), *Die Visitationsprotokolle der ersten nachtridentinischen Visitation im Erzstift Köln* (Cologne, 1960).

GUERRINI (P.), *Atti della visita pastorale del vescovo Domenico Bollani nella diocesi di Brescia*, 3 vols. (Brescia, 1915–1940).

JUNGNITZ (J.), *Die Visitationsberichte der Diözese Breslau*, I–IV (1902–1908).

MARANI (A.), *La visita pastorale di Minuccio Minucci alla diocesi di Zara (1597) (nyp)*.

MELLANO (M. F.), *La Controriforma nella diocesi di Mondovi* (Turin, 1955).

— *La Controriforma nell'arcidiocesi di Torino*, 3 vols. (Rome, 1957).

MONTI (S.), *Atti della visita pastorale di F. Feliciano Ninguarder vescoco di Como 1589–1593*, 2 vols. (Como, 1892–1894).

MONTICONE (A.), 'L'applicazione a Roma del concilio di Trento. Le visite del 1564–1566,' in *Rivista di storia della Chiesa*, 1953.

PASINI (A.), *Applicazione del concilio di Trento in diocesi di Parma nella visita apostolica di Mons. G. B. Castelli, 1578–1579* (Parma, 1953).

PERICOLI (M.), *La visita apostolica di Pietro Camaiani nella diocesi di Todi, 1574* (nyp).

PIANZOLA (F.), *I decreti della visita pastorale fatta da S. Carlo nella diocesi di Vigevano nel 1578* (Varese, 1938).

RONCALLI (A.) = JOHN XXIII, *Gli atti della visita apostolica di S. Carlo Borromeo a Bergamo, 1576*, 6 vols. (Milan, 1936–1949).

SCHWARZ (W. E.), *Die Akten der Visitation des Bistums Münster aus der Zeit Johanns Von Hoya, 1571–1573* (1913).

VASELLA (O.), *Das Visitationsprotokoll über den schweizerischen Klerus des Bistums Konztanz von 1586* (Berne, 1963).

VITEZIĆ (J.), *La prima visita apostolica posttridentina in Dalmazia nell'anno 1579* (Rome, 1957).

J. *SOCIOLOGY OF RELIGION. RELIGION AND ATTITUDES*

ABOUCAYA (C.), *Le testament lyonnais, de la fin du XVe siècle au milieu du XVIIIe siècle* (Paris, 1961).

AGULHON (M.), *Pénitents et Francs-Maçons dans l'ancienne Provence* (Paris, 1968).

ARTONNE (A.), *Répertoire des statuts synodaux des diocèses de l'ancienne France* (Paris, 1963).

ARIES (P.), *L'enfant et la vie familiale sous l'Ancien Régime* (Paris, 1960); ET: *Centuries of Childhood* (London, 1973²).

BENNASSAR (B.), *Valladolid au siècle d'or* (Paris, 1967)

BERGUES (H.), ARIES (P.) . . . , *La prévention des naissances dans la famille. Ses origines dans les temps modernes* (Paris, 1960).

BERTHELOT DU CHESNAY (C.). *Les missions de saint Jean Eudes* (Paris, 1968).

BOLLÈME (G.), *Les almanachs populaires aux XVIIe et XVIIIe siècles* (Paris, 1969).

BOULARD (F.), *Premiers itinéraires en sociologie religieuse* (Paris, 1954); ET: *An Introduction to Religious Sociology* (London, 1960).

CARRIÈRE (V.), *Introduction aux études d'histoire ecclésiastique locale*, III (*Epreuves de l'Eglise de France au XVIe siècle*) (Paris, 1936).

CHASTEL (A.), 'L'art et le sentiment de la mort au XVIIe siècle,' in *XVIIe siècle*, 1957.

CHORON (J.), *La mort et la pensée occidentale* (Paris, 1969).

CORETH (A.), *Pietas austriaca. Ursprung und Entwicklung barocker Frömmigkeit in Österreich* (Munich, 1959).

DAINVILLE (F. de), *Les Jésuites et l'éducation de la société française. La naissance de l'humanisme moderne* (Paris, 1940).

— *Cartes anciennes de l'Eglise de France. Historique, répertoire, guide d'usage* (Paris, 1956).

— 'Effectifs des collèges et scolarité aux XVIIe et XVIIIe siècles dans le Nord-Est de la France,' in *Population*, 1955.

— 'Collèges et fréquentation scolaire au XVIIe siècle,' in *Population*, 1957.

DELARUELLE (E.). 'La pietà popolare alla fine del medioevo', in *Relazioni del Xe CISHR*, III (Florence, 1955).

DELUMEAU (J.), 'Christianisation et déchristianisation,' in *Mélanges V.-L. Tapié.*

DELCAMBRE (E.), *Le concept de sorcellerie dans le duché de Lorraine*, 3 vols. (Nancy, 1948).

DESROCHE (H.), *Sociologies religieuses* (Paris, 1968).

DEYON (P.), 'Mentalités populaires: un sondage à Amiens au XVIIe siècle', in *AESC*, 1962.

— *Amiens, capitale provinciale. Etude sur la société urbaine du XVIIe siècle* (Paris–The Hague, 1967).

DOMMANGET (M.), *Le curé Meslier, athée. communiste et révolutionnaire sous Louis XIV* (Paris, 1965).

DREYFUS (F.), *Sociétés et mentalités à Mayence dans la seconde moitié du XVIIIe siècle* (Paris, 1968).

DUPRONT (A.), ..., *Livre et société dans la France du XVIIIe siècle* (Paris, 1965).

EHRARD (J.), *L'idée de nature en France dans la première moitié du XVIIIe siècle*, 2 vols. (Paris, 1963).

Etudes carmélitaines, Paris, 1948 & 1950.

FEOUR (A.), 'Reactions des populations atteintes par une grande épidémic,' in *Revue de psychologie des peuples*, 1960.

FERTÉ (J.), *La vie religieuse dans les campagnes parisiennes, 1622–1695* (Paris, 1962).

FLAMENT (P.), 'Les moeurs des laiques au diocèse de Sées spis ;'è-oscp-at de Mgr d'Aquin, 1699–1710.' in *RHEF*, 1955.

FOUCAULT (M.), *Folie et déraison. Histoire de la folie à l'âge classique* (Paris, 1961); ET: *Madness and Civilization* (London, 1967).

FRACART (M.-L.), *La fin de l'Ancien Régime à Niort. Essai de sociologie religieuse* (Paris, 1956).

GENNEP (A. Van), *Manuel de folklore français contemporain*, 12 vols. (Paris, 1943–1958).

GINZBURG (C.), *I Benandanti* (Turin, 1966).

GROETHUYSEN (B.), *Les origines de la bourgeoisie :* I, *L'Eglise et la bourgeoisie*, (Paris, 1956).

HAZARD (P.), *La crise de la conscience européenne*, 3 vols. (Paris, 1935); ET: *The European Mind, 1680–1715* (London, 1964).

JANSSEN (J.), *L'Allemagne et la Réforme*, 9 vols. (Paris, 1887–1914). *Geschichte des Deutschen Volkes seit dem Ausgang des Mittelalters* (Freiburg, 1878ff); ET: *History of the German people at (after) the close of the Middle Ages*, 17 vols. (London, 1896–1925).

JOIN-LAMBERT (M.), 'La pratique religieuse dans le diocèse de Rouen sous Louis XIV, et de 1707 à 1789,' in *Annales de Normandie*, 1953 & 1955.

JULIA (D.), 'Le clergé paroissial dans le diocèse de Reims à la fin du xviiie siècle,' in *RHMC*, 1966.

KNAPP (R.), *Studien zum 16. und 17. Jahrhundert*, I. (Halle, 1934).

LE BRAS (G.), *Etudes de sociologie religieuse*, 2 vols. (Paris, 1955–1956).

— ' "Déchristianisation", terme fallacieux,' in *Cahiers d'Histoire* (Lyons), IX, i, 1964.

— *L'Eglise et le village* (nyp).

LEBRUN (F.), *Cérémonial (1692–1721) de R. Lehoreau* (Paris, 1967).

— *Les hommes et la mort en Anjou aux XVIIe et XVIIIe siècles* (nyp).

LEPROUX (M.), *Dévotions et saints guérisseurs. Contribution au folklore charentais* (Paris, 1957).

LESTOCQUOY (J.), *La vie religieuse en France du VIIe au XXe siècle* (Paris, 1964).

LOTTIN (A.), *Vie et mentalité d'un Lillois sous Louis XIV* (Lille, 1968).

MALE (E.), *L'art religieux après le concile de Trente* (Paris, 1932).

MANDROU (R.), *Introduction à la France moderne* (Paris, 1961).

— *De la culture populaire en France aux XVIIe et XVIIIe siècle. La bibliothèque bleue de Troyes* (Paris, 1964).

— *La France aux XVIIe et XVIIIe siècles* (Paris, 1967).

— *Magistrats et sorciers en France au XVIIe siècle. Une analyse de psychologie historique* (Paris, 1968).

MARTIN (H. J.), *Livre, pouvoirs et société à Paris au XVIIe siècle*, 2 vols. (Paris, 1969).

MAUZI (R.), *L'idée du bonheur en France au XVIIIe siècle* (Paris, 1968).

'Missionnaires catholiques de la France pendant le xviie siècle,' in *XVIIe siècle*, no 41, 1958.

NEVEU (J.-B.), *Vie spirituelle et vie sociale entre Rhin et Baltique au XVIIe siècle* (Paris, 1967).

NISARD (Ch.), *Histoire des livres populaires ou de la littérature du colportage*, 2 vols. (Paris, 1863²).

PAULUS (N.), *Geschichte des Ablasses im Mittelalter*, III (Paderborn, 1923).

PEROUAS (L.), *Le diocèse de La Rochelle de 1648 à 1724. Sociologie et pastorale* (Paris, 1964).

— *P. Fr. Hacquet, Mémoire des missions des Montfortains dans l'Ouest, 1740–1779* (Fontenay-le-Comte, 1964).

PLATELLE (H.), *Journal d'un curé de campagne au XVIIe siècle* (Paris, 1965).

— *Les Chrétiens devant le miracle* (Paris, 1968).

QUENIART (J.), *L'imprimerie et la librairie à Rouen au XVIIIe siècle, 1701–1789* (Paris, 1969).

SAGE (P.), *Le « bon prêtre » dans la littérature française* (Geneva–Lille, 1951).

SCHAER (A.), *Le clergé catholique en Haute–Alsace sous l'Ancien Régime, 1648–1789* (Paris, 1966).

SCHMITT (T.–J.), *L'organisation ecclésiastique et la pratique religieuse dans l'archidiaconé d'Autun de 1650 à 1750* (Autun, 1957).

SCHREIBER (C), *Aufklärung und Frömmigkeit* (Munich, 1940).

SEBILLOT (P.), *Le Folklore de France*, 4 vols. (Paris, 1968²).

SEBILLOT (P.-Y.), *Le folklore de la Bretagne*, 2 vols., (Paris, 1968²).

SILVA DIAS (J. S. da), *Corrantes de sentimento religioso em Portugal* (*seculos XVI a XVIII*), 2 vols (Coïmbra, 1960).

TAPIÉ (V.-L.), *Baroque et classicisme* (Paris, 1957); ET: *The Age of Grandeur* (London, 1961).

— *Le Baroque* (Paris, 1961).

TENENTI (A.), *Il senso della morte e l'amore della vita nel Rinascimento* (*Francia e Italia*) (Turin, 1957).

TOUSSAERT (J.), *Le sentiment religieux en France à la fin du Moyen Age* (Paris, 1963).

VEIT (L. A.) & LENHART (L.), *Kirche und Volksfrömmigkeit im Zeitalter des Barock* (Freiburg, 1956).

VENARD (M.), 'Les missions des Oratoriens d'Avignon aux XVIIe et XVIIIe siècles,' in *RHEF*, 1962.

— 'Recherches sur le recrutement sacerdotal dans la province d'Avignon au XVIe siècle,' in *AESC*, 1968.

VOVELLE G. et M.), 'Ln mort et l'au-delà en Provence d'après les aûtels des âmes du purgatoire' (xve-xxe siècles),' in *AESC*, 1969.

WALKER (D. P.), *The Decline of Hell. Seventeenth Century Discussion of Eternal Torment* (Chicago, 1964).

INDEX*

A

ABRAHAM A SANCTA CLARA
  (ULRICH MEGERLE), 190.
ACADIA, 74.
ACARIE (Mme), 36, 45.
ACOSTA (J. de), 91.
AFRICA, 61–3, 76–9, 81, 92.
AGEN, 142.
AGUESSEAU (H. F. d'), 112.
AILLY (P. d'), 154.
AIN-TOURA, 78.
AIX-EN-PROVENCE, 157, 173.
AKBAR, 79.
ALCALA, 2.
ALDOBRANDINI, 27.
ALEMBERT (J. Le Rond d'), 73.
ALEPPO, 78.
ALET, 103, 142.
ALEXANDRE DE RHODES, 65–6.
ALEXANDRIA, 78.
ALFONSO (Don), 61, 76.
Algonquins, 75.
ALPHONSUS LIGUORI (St.), 42, 190.
ALSACE, 162.
ALTOTTING, 40.
AMAZONAS, 74.
AMBOISE (Cardinal d'), 2.
AMERICA, 68, 74–6.
AMIENS, 149.
AMORT (E.), 125.
AMSTERDAM, 106.
ANCHIETA (P. J.), 74.
ANCONA, 78.

ANDRESY, 181.
ANGERS, 29, 38, 103, 142, 156, 187.
ANGOLA, 77, 89.
ANNAM, 66.
ANNAT (P. F.), 103.
ANNECY, 37, 45, 176.
ANNE OF AUSTRIA, 28.
ANSALONE (P.), 190.
Anticlericalism, 218.
ANTILLES, 67, 86, 90.
ANTIOCH, 78.
ANVERS, 200.
APACHES, 70–1.
AQUITAINE, 35, 145.
ARANDA (P. d'), 80.
ARENTHON (J. d'), 169.
ARETINO (P.), 166.
ARGENTINA, 73.
ARISTOTLE, 87, 120.
ARLES, 216.
ARNAULD (Angelique), 99.
ARNAULD (Antoine), 40–1, 102, 104,
  107–9, 115, 123.
ARNAULD (Henri d'Angers), 29, 103.
ARNAULD (Jacqueline), 39.
ARRAS, 32, 181.
ARTOIS, 59.
ASIA, 61–3.
ASUNCION, 71.
ATTICHY (Mgr d'), 200.
Attitudes (religious), see *Mentalities*.
AUBERT (Mme), 205.
AUGE, 128.

---

*The names of persons and places are printed in capitals; subjects are lower-case. Recent authors are not given here, but are to be found in the bibliography on pages 261–84 and in the notes (p. 232 *et seq.*). For major topic divisions see CONTENTS (p. viii).

CANTON, 64.
CAO (D.), 61.
CAPRANICA (D.), 7.
Capuchins, xi 2, 6, 35, 36, 40, 69, 75.
CARAFFA, (G. P.), see *PAUL IV*.
Carmel, Carmelites, 36, 37, 40, 78.
CARROLL (J.), 76.
Cartesianism, see *DESCARTES*.
CARTAGO, 72.
Carthusians, 2, 40.
CASTILLE, 39.
CASTRO (M. de), 84.
Casuists, Casuistry, 42.
CATEAU-CAMBRÉSIS (Peace of), 8.
Catechism, 174, 199–201.
CAULET (Mgr E. F. de), 103, 110, 123.
CAUX, 128.
CAVELIER DE LA SALLE, 76.
CAYLUS (Mgr D. de), 33, 113.
CERISY, 155.
CERVINI (Cardinal) MARCEL II, II.
CEYLON see *SRI-LANKA*.
CHÂLONS-SUR-MARNE, 104, 128, 142, 155.
CHALON-SUR-SAÔNE, 176.
CHAMONIX, 169.
CHAMPAGNE, 35, 59, 137.
CHAMPLAIN (S.), 74.
CHARENTE, 165, 167–8.
CHARLES III (of SPAIN), 80.
CHARLES V, 5, 8, 15, 69, 87, 88.
CHARTRES, 3, 175, 216.
CHASTEL (J.), 34.
CHAULIEU (G. de), 230.
CHIAPA, 87-8.
CHILE, 90.
CHINA, 55, 61–2, 63–5, 79–81, 90, 92–5.
Christianization, 175–202.
CIBO (Duchess C.), 35.
CISNEROS (Ximenes de), 2, 86.
Cistercians, 40, 104.
CLAMANGES (N. de), 154, 159.
Class attitudes, 118–21.
CLEMENT VII, 4, 5, 136.
CLEMENT VIII, 61, 101.
CLEMENT IX, 110.
CLEMENT XI, 105.
CLEMENT XII, 210.
CLEMENT XIV, 34, 208.
CLERMONT; MONTFERRAND (d'Auvergne), 33, 105, 142.
CLIMENT (J.), 125.
Cluny, 209.
COAHUILA, 70.
COCHIN (Kerala), 61.
COCHIN CHINA, 65–6.

COLBERT (André, Bishop of Auxerre), 27, 33.
COLBERT (James, Archbishop of ROUEN), 27, 197.
COLBERT (Joachim, Bishop of MONTPELLIER), 27.
COLOGNE, 11, 32, 176, 207.
COLONNA (Vittoria), 35.
COLUMBIA, 78, 85.
COMMINGES, 142.
Communion, 107–8, 133, 197–9, 216–20.
Company of Jesus see *Jesuits*.
COMTE (A.), 129.
Concubinage, 154–6.
Condé, 28.
CONDREN (C. de), 49.
Conformism, 214–24.
Confraternities, 150, 220–24.
Confucius, Confucianism, 92–3.
CONGO, 61, 76–7.
CONSTANCE, 5.
CONSTANTINOPLE, 77.
CONTARINI (N.), 7, 11, 125.
Contraception, 221–4.
COPERNICUS, (N.), 126.
Copts, 78.
CORAM (T.), 221.
Corneille (P.), 28.
CORNET (N.), 103.
CORTEZ (F.), 69.
COTON (P.), 34, 40.
Councils:
– of Basle, 5.
– of Constance, 5.
– of Lateran, 5, 7, 214.
– of Pisa, 4, 5.
– of Trent, xi, 1, 4, 6, 7, 8, 9, 11, 13, 14, 15, 20, 23, 24, 25, 26, 27, 28, 30, 31, 32, 40, 43, 60, 84, 100, 107, 142, 154, 158, 181, 214.
COUTANCES, 149, 193.
COYER (Abbé), 223.
CRANGANOR, 62.
CRASHAW (R.), 52.
CREMA (B. da), 3.
CREMONA, 33, 39.
CREMONINI (C.), 204.
CRETE, 77.
CRULAI, 224.
Crusades, 132.
CUBA, 69, 86.
CUMANA, 86.
CUSA (Nicholas of), see *NICHOLAS OF CUSA*.
CUZCO, 71, 82.
CYRANO DE BERGERAC, 203–4.
CYPRUS, 77.

D

DAHOMEY, 90.
DALMATIA, 136, 157.
DAMASCUS, 78.
DARIEN, 69.
Daughters of Charity, 37, 38, 54, 59.
Dechristianization, 203–31.
DELAMARE (N.), 215.
DELLA CASA (G.), 56.
DENIS THE CARTHUSIAN, 42.
DENMARK, 171.
DESCARTES (R.), 120, 126, 192.
DESHOULIÈRES (Mme), 204.
Diaries, 137–42.
DIDEROT (D.), 204.
DIJON, 45, 206.
DILLINGEN, 33.
Discalced Carmelites see Carmelites.
DOL-DE-BRETAGNE, 144.
DOMENICHI, 7, 8–9.
Dominicans, 3, 40, 49, 56, 63, 69, 70, 77, 82, 86–9.
DONADIEU (B. de), 142.
DOUAI, 101, 170.
DOUBS, 170.
DUBOIS (A.), 137–140.
DUCIS (J.-F.), 220.
DUGUET (J.-J.), 114, 123.
DU LUTH, 76.
DU PERRON (J. DAVY), 40.
DURKHEIM (E.), 129.
DUVERGIER DE HAURANNE, 99, 101, 103, 107–9, 113, 115, 121–2.

E

ECKART (J.), 47.
Education, 175, 227–31.
EMILIA, 179.
ENCISO, 85.
ENGLAND, xi, xvii, 7, 32, 125, 136, 160.
Episcopalism, 109–10.
ERASMUS, 2, 41, 115.
ERTHAL (J. d'), 209.
ESCOBAR (Fr.), 108.
ETHIOPIA, 77.
Eudists, 164, 192.
Evangelization, 89–95.
EVREUX, 18.
Exorcism, 168–70.

F

Feasts, 133–4.
Febronianism, 207.
FEBRONIUS, 207.
FELDKIRCH, 36.
FELINE (Fr.), 224.
FÉNÉLON (Fr. de SALIGNAC DE LA MOTTE), 54, 106, 112, 129.
FERDINAND I (Emperor), 25.
FERDINAND OF ARAGON, 5.
FERDINAND VI (of Spain), 80.
FERRIER (St. Vincent), 160.
FINISTÈRE, 146, 168.
FLANDERS, 132, 151, 159, 195.
FLÉCHIER (E.), 54.
FLEURY (A.-H.), 113, 118.
FLORENCE, 77.
FLOREZ (E.), 125.
FLORIDA, 71.
Folklore, 161–6.
FONSECA (P. da), 101.
FOU-KIEN, 93.
FRANCE, xi, xvii, 6, 24, 25, 26, 28, 34, 35, 41, 74, 84, 108, 111, 130 et seq., 143, 160, 179, 214, 225.
Franciscans, 35, 40, 63, 69, 70, 72, 75, 82, 126.
FRANCIS I, 6.
FRANCIS OF ASSISI (St.), 45, 52.
FRANCIS DE SALES (St.), 37, 40, 41, 48, 142.
FRANCIS XAVIER (St.), 55, 61, 90.
FRASCATI, 27.
FREDERICK II, 203–5.
Freemasonry, 208–11.
FREJUS, 149.
Frères des Ecoles Chrètiennes, see Brothers of the Christian Schools.
FRIULI, 162, 167.
Fronde, 28, 38, 116, 119, 144.

G

GALILEO, 126, 228.
GALLEN (von), 206.
Gallicans, Gallicanism, 25, 26, 110–3, 125, 137, 198, 209.
GASCONY, 211.
GASSENDI (P.), 203–4.
GAULT (J.-B.), 142.
GENEVA, 126, 169, 223.
GENOA, 3.